PERGAMON INTERNATIONAL LIBRARY
of Science, Technology, Engineering and Social Studies

*The 1000-volume original paperback library in aid of education,
industrial training and the enjoyment of leisure*

Publisher: Robert Maxwell, M.C.

# TEACHING SOCIAL SKILLS TO CHILDREN

## (PGPS-89)

# Pergamon Titles of Related Interest

**Apter/Goldstein** YOUTH VIOLENCE: Programs and Prospects
**Morris/Blatt** SPECIAL EDUCATION: Research and Trends
**Plas** SYSTEMIC PSYCHOLOGY IN THE SCHOOLS
**Wielkiewicz** BEHAVIOR MANAGEMENT IN THE SCHOOLS:
Principles and Procedures

# Related Journals
**(Free sample copies available upon request.)**

CHILD ABUSE AND NEGLECT
CHILDREN AND YOUTH SERVICES REVIEW
JOURNAL OF CHILD PSYCHOLOGY AND PSYCHIATRY
JOURNAL OF SCHOOL PSYCHOLOGY

**PERGAMON GENERAL PSYCHOLOGY SERIES**
EDITORS
Arnold P. Goldstein, Syracuse University
Leonard Krasner, SUNY at Stony Brook

# TEACHING SOCIAL SKILLS TO CHILDREN

## Innovative Approaches, Second Edition

Edited by
**GWENDOLYN CARTLEDGE**
Cleveland State University

**JOANNE FELLOWS MILBURN**
Starr Commonwealth/The Hannah Neil Center
for Children

**PERGAMON PRESS**
New York • Oxford • Beijing • Frankfurt
São Paulo • Sydney • Tokyo • Toronto

Pergamon Press Offices:

| | |
|---|---|
| **U.S.A.** | Pergamon Press, Maxwell House, Fairview Park, Elmsford, New York 10523, U.S.A. |
| **U.K.** | Pergamon Press, Headington Hill Hall, Oxford OX3 0BW, England |
| **PEOPLE'S REPUBLIC OF CHINA** | Pergamon Press, Qianmen Hotel, Beijing, People's Republic of China |
| **FEDERAL REPUBLIC OF GERMANY** | Pergamon Press, Hammerweg 6, D-6242 Kronberg-Taunus, Federal Republic of Germany |
| **BRAZIL** | Pergamon Editora, Rua Eça de Queiros, 346, CEP 04011, São Paulo, Brazil |
| **AUSTRALIA** | Pergamon Press (Aust.) Pty., P.O. Box 544, Potts Point, NSW 2011, Australia |
| **JAPAN** | Pergamon Press, 8th Floor, Matsuoka Central Building, 1-7-1 Nishishinjuku, Shinjuku, Tokyo 160, Japan |
| **CANADA** | Pergamon Press Canada, Suite 104, 150 Consumers Road, Willowdale, Ontario M2J 1P9, Canada |

**Copyright © 1986 Pergamon Books, Inc.**

First printing 1986

Library of Congress Cataloging in Publication Data
Teaching social skills to children.

    (Pergamon general psychology series; 89)
    Includes bibliographies and indexes.
    1. Social skills in children--Study and teaching.
I. Cartledge, Gwendolyn, 1943-   . II. Milburn,
JoAnne Fellows, 1925-   . III. Series. [DNLM:
1. Social Behavior--in infancy & childhood. 2. Social-
ization. 3. Teaching--methods. WS 105.5.S6 T253]
HQ783.T43   1986    303.3′2′07    86-2402
ISBN 0-08-031591-7
ISBN 0-08-031590-9 (pbk.)

*Printed in the United States of America*

In memory of our parents,
Samuel and Estelle
Lloyd and Alma

# Contents

# Foreword

In writing the Foreword to the first edition of this book, I identified three major conditions within our society that have made it necessary to teach social skills and concepts in schools. These were and still are relevant:

First, our basic *social* institutions (home, church, and school) are undergoing great changes.

Second, our mobile population contributes to changes in socialization.

Third, the increasing emphasis on *individuality* (do your own thing) encourages all of us to be less responsive to the needs of others.

For most newborns, mothers are the first to relate to them as they begin the socializing process. Others within the family also are influencers. But the American family has been in a state of flux since World War II. With a highly mobile population, working mothers, single parents, and reconstituted families, the family unit as a stable and predictable social institution is now problematic.

As a result, basic perceptions and attitudes of the young are more divergent and less predictable, creating a need for educational options. Some American parents are opting for non-public schools as one way to address this need. Current figures suggest that almost 15% of school-aged children now attend private and church-related schools. Although the range of differences, on certain dimensions, will be reduced by those schools with restrictive admissions, the larger society in which these youngsters are nurtured is essentially the same as for those students who are in public schools. But private school placement will not make an appreciable difference to most students because of the social forces that shape them.

Organized religion is radically changing both in the quality and quantity of influence and range of beliefs. Although religion still exerts considerable influence, its direct impact is on the wane. We no longer can expect the large proportion of school-aged youngsters to be active members of an organized religion, influenced by a prescribed set of values and ethics. A recent (1984) survey found that 60% of Americans reject the dictates of organized religion and are drawing upon their own spiritual feelings to define their faith.

Schools are the third of three traditional institutions used for socializing the young. Now, as never before in American history, all youngsters are

influenced by schools as they move through elementary and secondary programs.

School personnel have always been involved in subtle exchanges between
the various socializing forces in helping to achieve societal goals. But now
they must address the widest range of individual differences known in history. It is ironic that in an era of cultural homogeneity, students' social perceptions are more diverse than ever. Rapid communications, popular culture,
and easy travel have made the world more immediate and accessible. At the
same time the high rate of literacy, affluence, and personal freedom have
combined to provide a wider range of experiences and attitudes.

This combination of a smaller world and diversity creates an educational
challenge of enormous magnitude. Students' perceptions and experiences are
increasingly diverse as they enter school systems and so too are societal
expectations.

Consider, for example, the experiential backgrounds of children as a result
of the popular culture. Many children enter school having spent more time
hearing and relating to mediated unreal images than to real live people.
These experiences have significant implications for school curricula and for
the behavior of those who work in the schools.

Not only do children relate to automated voices, they can now have unreal
experiences. For example, Digital has a supercomputer that is used in making
scenes for movies. This computer simulates reality. Each point of a three-
dimensional object is coded into the computer. The computer then creates
a 3-D model that can be turned, stretched, colored, and shifted. To viewers,
these special effects seem real. If the film shows someone falling off a cliff,
viewers can now feel that sensation.

While schools continue to emphasize cognitive processes, students' learning outside classrooms involve all of their senses. And, while school personnel continue using information-laden tasks in trying to teach societal values,
the moviemakers have a $12 million computer to immerse students in expe-
riences that are often at odds with those same values that schools are
expected to teach.

Expectations change as the popular culture becomes more pervasive.
Social expectations have direct impact on schooling. For example, in the
United States 18-year-olds are permitted to vote. And in Great Britain some
political groups are now advocating for the 16-year-old vote. Yet, intelligent
well-informed adults with accurate historical perspectives find it impossible
to vote in an enlightened way. Issues for voters to consider in our nuclear
age are overwhelming even for that mythical person—the intelligent, well-
informed adult with a historical perspective.

Popular media, particularly TV, are the single most powerful socializers
in our present-day society. Of the three traditional socializing institutions,
only one, religion, has been able to exploit TV successfully. More specifi-

cally, the fundamentalist wing of organized religion is successfully using TV as a medium to socialize. Why have schools, families, and the mainstream religions been so unsuccessful in using TV?

Surely it is a question that needs further research. My suspicions are that TV, as a medium, influences through emotional messages, not through factual ones. That is why talk shows are the most enduring and successful programs. It is not the factual content that influences. The personal, social, and emotional ones are most appealing. *How* the people appear, or *how* they behave are best remembered.

Television is the most ubiquitous of all popular media. Few homes are without it. TV idols, those icons of the popular culture, are known to every child and adult. In 1981, Nielsen found the average viewing time for teenagers was 23 hours a week, almost 26 hours for 6- to 7-year-olds, and 29 hours for 2- to 5-year-olds. Adult men and women, the parents, averaged 29 and 34 hours a week, respectively.

Socializing forces that are internal to schools are well-known to most educators. In general, these are: curricula, school personnel, and students. But external forces shape these.

External forces include the popular culture, families, organized religion, and society's expectations. In most instances the pressures between schools and families are reciprocal. Collaborations between families and schools are natural and can cause change in both directions. The subtle messages sent by both interact. Parents have expectations for schools. In turn, schools expect students to enter with certain competencies and to maintain themselves in the system by possessing reasonable behaviors. When they don't perform, negative consequences occur; students may repeat courses or grades, they may receive low grades, they may leave school before completion.

Contrast the exchanges between schools and homes with collaboration between the popular culture and schools. Here the trade-offs are almost nonexistent. Popular culture influences schooling significantly with little flowing the other way. In other words, popular culture drives or *pushes* the schools without any counter force.

Until this imbalance changes, popular culture will continue to be a serious threat to schooling. With the emergence of television, schooling has become increasingly less valued by the overall culture. And schooling has almost no influence in shaping television. Because that medium directly influences people in powerful ways it overshadows schooling. For example, retail business and schools are interdependent. They must collaborate. But not TV. Schools draw from TV, but television has no need to be responsive to schooling. In fact, in some respects the relationship is adversarial; schools and television compete for the same audiences, for their time and for their attention.

Much of TV's content is at cross-purposes to the school's. Television deals in emotions, entertainment, instant gratification, and conspicuous consumption. Schools focus on cognitive processes, work, and delayed satisfactions. But because of its slickness and the finances that are invested, the messages conveyed through TV are eminently more powerful than those conveyed by schools.

But schools are not totally defenseless against the inroads of television. School personnel have not yet learned how to develop reciprocal relationships and ultimately influence TV as they have with some other aspects of the popular culture. This is new territory for those who work in schools. And some important questions remain: *How are freedom of expression and other rights to be exercised in a society which must increasingly depend upon group efforts? How will we be governed without group standards? Can we have our individual freedoms and a strong society too? Can we educate the young for such a society?*

In this time of rapid change, educational needs are greater than ever, people must exercise increasingly finer judgments about more complex situations. We know that information alone seldom changes behavior and attitudes. Rather, the society shapes our responses; powerful incentives encourage us to choose, and the choices may not always be good for individuals or for this society.

Alone, no book can address these complex issues, for most include both political and educational considerations. The editors of this text clearly are aware of this complexity. There are selections that help in recognizing the need to change our beliefs about how social behavior is acquired, how to identify those behaviors to be taught, and how to go about teaching them. This book should serve as a valuable resource to those practitioners who want to add social skills teaching to their repertoires. By doing so they will help today's children to become better citizens in an increasingly complex world.

*Thomas M. Stephens*
Professor and Chairman
Department of Human Services Education
The Ohio State University
Columbus, Ohio
July 1985

# Acknowledgements

We would like to thank the many people who helped us with various aspects of this book. Some of those who should receive special thanks include: Carol Friedman and Jane Kane, along with other members of the support staff in the Specialized Instructions Department. Appreciation is also extended to Thomas Frew, department chairperson, for his administrative support and personal encouragement.

Publishers and authors who gave us permission to reproduce copyrighted material included:

Arnold, A. (1972). *A World Book of Children's Games*. New York: Harper & Row. Copyright 1972 by Arnold Arnold. Reprinted by permission of Harper & Row.

Fagen, S., Long, N., & Stevens, D. (1975). *Teaching Children Self-Control*. Columbus, OH: Charles E. Merrill.

Gambrill, E.D. (1977). *Behavior Modification*. San Francisco: Jossey-Bass, pps. 498, 499.

Goldstein, A. P., Spratkin, R. P., Gershaw, N. J., & Klein, P. (1979). *Skill-Streaming the Adolescent*. Champaign, IL: Research Press.

Harrison, M. (1977). *For the Fun of It: Selected Cooperative Games for Children and Adults*, pp. 10, 11, 15, 16 as an appendix to *A Manual on Non-Violence and Children*, compiled and edited by Stephanie Judson. Philadelphia: Friends Peace Committee. (1515 Cherry Street)

Orlick, T. (1978). *The Cooperative Spirit and Games Book: Challenge Without Competition*. New York: Pantheon Books.

Prutzman, P., Burger, M.L., Bodenhamer, G., & Stern, L. (1978). *The Friendly Classroom for a Small Planet: A Handbook on Creative Approaches to Living and Problem Solving for Children*. Wayne, NJ: Avery Publishing Group, Inc. Reprinted by permission of the publisher.

Quay, H.C. (1966). Patterns of aggression, withdrawal and immaturity. In H.C. Quay & J.S. Werry (Eds.), *Psychopathological Disorders of Childhood*. New York: John Wiley & Sons.

Spivack, G., & Shure, M. (1978). *Social Adjustment of Young Children: A Cognitive Approach to Solving Real-Life Problems*. San Francisco: Jossey-Bass, pp. 144, 194, 195, 198.

Stephens, T. (1978). *Social Skills in the Classroom*. Columbus, OH: Cedars Press, Inc. Reprinted with permission. All rights reserved.

Streibel, B. (1977). *Conflict Resolution in Children's Literature*. Madison, WI: Center for Conflict Resolution.

Wood, M. (1975). *Developmental Therapy*. Baltimore: University Park Press.

We would also like to thank our families and friends for all the less tangible but equally appreciated kinds of help and support.

# PART 1

# STEPS IN TEACHING
# SOCIAL SKILLS

# Introduction to Part 1

This book is a revision of one originally published in 1980. We have updated the original material and include new sections to enhance its practical application by people who are charged with the socialization of children and youth, both normal and handicapped. The intended audience continues to be teachers in regular and special education classrooms and clinicians who work with children in schools, residential, or outpatient settings. Parents who wish to improve their ability to teach social skills to their children may also find the book useful. In addition, it is intended as a text to be used in programs for training teachers and clinicians in fields such as social work, counseling, and psychology.

The book is concerned with social behaviors, broadly considered as skills to be taught, and the emphasis is placed on building prosocial, adaptive, new behaviors rather than on eliminating problem behaviors or developing motivational systems to increase the performance of behaviors already in the child's repertoire. One major advantage of a social skills approach to treating children with problems is that it is essentially a positive approach, which assumes that children can be taught the skills necessary to behave in different, more acceptable ways. There is a rapidly growing body of research in the application of social skills training with children that supports the validity of this assumption (see, for example, review articles by Cartledge & Milburn, 1978; Combs & Slaby, 1977; Conger & Keane, 1981; Eisler & Frederiksen, 1980; Foster & Ritchey, 1979; Michelson & Wood, 1980; Rinn & Markle, 1979; and Van Hasselt, Hersen, Bellack, & Whitehill, 1979.)*

The authors were encouraged to develop this book through a series of personal experiences with children, teachers, and clinicians in several schools and treatment settings. We have become convinced that social behaviors can and should be specifically taught as part of a school curriculum or remedial therapy program, and that the skills for such teaching should be in the repertoires of all teachers and clinicians. Although parents may less often feel the need to provide systematic teaching in the home, some knowledge of how

---

*References for chapters 1 through 5 appear at the end of Part 1, after chapter 5.

social skills are taught, both purposefully and inadvertently, can add immeasurably to their effectiveness. In addition, parents have an important role in the maintenance and generalization of social skills taught to children in other settings and should be knowledgeable about social skills training carried out by teachers and clinicians.

In clinical settings, a case may be made for teaching social skills to children for the prevention of later psychological disorders. There is evidence that many adults suffering from psychiatric illnesses—particularly anxiety states, reactive depressions, and personality disorders—are also characterized by social inadequacy (Trower, Bryant, & Argyle, 1978). Some longitudinal research (Kagan & Moss, 1962) indicates that childhood deficiencies in social interaction are carried into adulthood.

Much of the data supporting the need for teaching social skills comes from studies of the relationship between social behaviors and school achievement (Cartledge & Milburn, 1978). It has been suggested that the teaching of social skills goes on in the classroom all the time as a "hidden curriculum," even when the teacher does not deliberately engage in social skills instruction. The teacher, like the parent, is a powerful and influential person in the child's life and, as such, serves as a model for social behaviors. In addition, the teacher shapes the child's social behaviors, intentionally or not, through the process of reinforcement. Studies of teacher attitudes and behavior suggest that social behaviors on the part of the student are an important determinant of how the teacher interacts with him. Students with positive social behaviors (for example, those who seek out the teacher, initiate contacts about work assignments, answer or try to answer questions, smile at the teacher, and are attentive during lessons) generally receive more positive teacher attention and have a higher rate of academic success. A series of studies by Cobb and his colleagues (Cobb & Hops, 1973; Hops & Cobb, 1973, 1974; Walker & Hops, 1976) have identified specific social "survival skills" that predict achievement from one academic area to another and have demonstrated that training in these survival skills could bring about an increase in academic achievement.

There is some controversy in research circles about whether the most efficient target for classroom behavior change efforts may be academic responses rather than social behaviors since, for some populations, improvement in academic achievement appears to result in improved social skills, as well as the reverse. Something of a reciprocal relationship appears to exist between improved curriculum, reinforcement of academic responses, and the development of relevant social behaviors. Social behaviors and academic behaviors are so highly correlated that it is difficult to reinforce academic responses without simultaneously reinforcing the social behaviors that make the academic responses possible; for example, attention to the required stimuli, complying with teacher directions, responding under circumstances specified by the teacher. Focusing specifically on social behaviors for direct instruction seems particularly relevant for children with very low levels of the social behaviors determined to be essential to academic success.

Another target group for instruction in social skills are those children with poor peer relationships. The importance of the peer group for the development of social skills is well documented, the quality of children's relationships with peers being predictive of school problems and later psychopathology (Rubin & Ross, 1982). Again, there is a kind of reciprocal relationship between social skills and peer relationships. Children with better interpersonal skills have more opportunities to engage in the activities with peers that, in turn, enhance the learning of social behaviors.

An underlying model serves as a framework for this book. The model exists in a number of versions variously called *prescriptive teaching, diagnostic teaching,* or *directive teaching* (Stephens, 1977). Essentially, the elements are (a) define in specific behaviorally stated terms the behavior to be taught; (b) assess the level of competence possessed by the learner in order to determine his or her initial level of performance; (c) teach the behaviors defined through assessment as lacking in the learner's repertoire; (d) evaluate or reassess for results of teaching; and (e) provide opportunities for practice and generalization, or transfer of behaviors to new situations. In teaching social skills, all these steps need to be present to some degree. The chapter headings, therefore, correspond to these steps: chapter 1 on selection of skills, chapter 2 on assessment and evaluation, chapter 3 on teaching procedures, and chapter 4 on maintenance and transfer. Because of the close relationship between assessment and evaluation, the book combines the two processes, which often involve the same materials or procedures, in chapter 2.

An additional chapter has been added to assist the readers in applying the model in their classrooms or clinics. Ideas for enhancing the effectiveness of instruction in social skills are presented in chapter 5, as well as an example of how the instructional model might be applied to a specific social skill. It is our thesis that, essentially, any practitioner who understands pedagogical principles can write his or her own social skills curriculum. Social skills can then be taught not only in a planned, systematic way but also by seizing the "teachable moment" to instruct children in social skills when events in the child's life reveal a need for such teaching.

In addition to the organizing model, another assumption guided the construction of the book; that is, that social skills contain cognitive and affective as well as overt behavioral aspects. Such cognitive dimensions as negative expectations, the presence of self-defeating thoughts, deficits in social perception, and discrimination and such affective dimensions as anxiety and fear of failure may interfere with performance of appropriate social skills. An attempt is made to include approaches to social skills teaching involving cognitive and affective dimensions of social skills, as well as their behavioral aspects. The contributors to Part II of the book have expertise in teaching social skills to populations reflecting different ages or handicapping conditions, as well as in presenting a variety of unique approaches to social skills instruction.

Although, throughout the book, the authors use such evaluative terms as *appropriate, desirable, proper, positive*, and so forth, when speaking of a social behavior, it should be understood that the social and cultural context of a behavior ultimately defines those terms, as further discussed in chapter 1. It was our intent to emphasize approaches that have empirical foundations or have been demonstrated to be effective with children and youth in bringing about improved social functioning. The material presented in this volume does not constitute a comprehensive review of current literature on social skills for children, but represents, instead, a set of ideas for practice that can be applied by those working therapeutically with children.

# 1
# Selecting Social Skills

What are *social skills*? A number of reviewers and researchers have offered definitions, which range from the narrow and specific to the very broad and general. In an early definition, Libet and Lewinsohn (1973) defined *social skill* as "the complex ability both to emit behaviors that are positively or negatively reinforced, and not to emit behaviors that are punished or extinguished by others" (p. 304). Another frequently quoted definition is that of Combs and Slaby (1977); that is, "the ability to interact with others in a given social context in specific ways that are socially acceptable or valued and at the same time personally beneficial, mutually beneficial, or beneficial primarily to others" (p. 162).

In general, social skills are seen as socially acceptable learned behaviors that enable the person to interact with others in ways that elicit positive responses and assist in avoiding negative responses from them. Morgan (1980) points out that not only do social skills involve the ability to initiate and maintain positive interactions with other people, but they also include "the ability to achieve the objectives that a person has for interacting with others. . . . The more frequent, or the greater the extent to which a person achieves his objectives in interacting with others, the more skilled we would judge him to be" (p. 104). According to the situation-specific concept of social skills presented by Hersen and Bellack (1977), the effectiveness of behavior in social interactions depends on the context and parameters of the situation. Along with behavior skill is the individual's ability to perceive the situation and be aware when a particular set of behaviors will result in positive outcomes.

Trower (1980) breaks social skills into two dimensions: skill components and skill processes. Skill components are single elements, such as looks or nods, or sequences of behavior used in social interactions, such as greetings or partings. Social processes refer to the "individual's ability to generate skilled behavior according to rules and goals and in response to social feedback" (p. 328). This distinction suggests the individual's need to monitor situations and vary behavior in response to feedback from other persons. Eisler and Frederiksen (1980) similarly describe social skills as having both observable aspects and nonobservable cognitive elements. The latter include "expectations, thoughts and decisions about what should be said or done during the next interaction," and abilities such as "the accurate perception of the other person's wishes or intentions, or insight into which response will be the most likely to influence his or her partner's opinion" (p. 9).

The term *social competence* has often been considered synonymous and used interchangeably with social skill. Hops (1983) made clear the distinction between these two concepts: "Competence is a summary term which reflects social judgment about the general quality of an individual's performance in a given situation. The concept of social skills from a behavioral perspective is based on the assumption that specific identifiable skills form the basis for socially competent behavior" (p. 4).

Social skills discussed in this volume will be focused, for the most part, on those behaviors that involve interaction between the child and his peers or adults, where the primary intent is the achievement of the child's or adult's goals through positive interactions. As may be seen in Part II, however, with handicapped people, some simple nonsocial behaviors may need to be taught as prerequisites to subsequent learning of social skills.

## FACTORS IN SOCIAL SKILL SELECTION

In determining what social skills should be taught to children, it is possible to apply both a general set of norms defined by various experts as behaviors necessary for competence as a child in our culture and specific criteria for what behaviors are needed by an individual child to be regarded as competent. Social skill instruction in many ways is similar to teaching academic behaviors. Tyler (1949), in a discussion of curriculum development, suggests that instructional objectives should emerge from the three sources of *the learner, contemporary society*, and *subject specialists* or *experts*. These three dimensions appear to be relevant for the selections of social skills. Such characteristics as the child's age, developmental level, specific skill deficits, and social and cultural milieu, and the findings of researchers and practitioners in the field of social skills instruction must all be taken into account.

### Developmental Theories

Looking at learner characteristics as a way of identifying social skills to be taught, one relevant set of criteria is that suggested by developmental theories. It may be debated whether behavior always develops according to the stages outlined by various theorists, whether some behaviors can be more easily taught and maintained at one stage than at another, and which behaviors need to be taught or simply result inevitably from maturation. At the same time, the stage theories do provide broad indices for social development and assist in the task of determining the sequence in which social behaviors are taught. The developmental theories to be briefly outlined include those of Freud, Erikson, and Piaget, along with Kohlberg's model for moral development.

Freud, through psychoanalytic theory, provides a five-stage developmental system based on psycho-sexual constructs. Stressing biological functions (oral, first year; anal, 1–3 years; phallic or oedipal, 3–5 years; latency, 5–12 years; genital, 12 years to adult), each stage reflects common human experiences that produce conflicts to be resolved. The social implications are that, according to this model, positive attributes or behaviors are acquired by children who successfully progress through each crisis stage. The reverse is the case for those unable to resolve the respective conflicts. For example, early social behaviors are centered around the mother or other principal caretaker with a gradual widening of relationships to others in the home and outside. Central to Freudian theory is the concept of necessary conflict resolution through which the child learns to share relationships and handle feelings of jealousy and anger, theoretically through identification with the same-sex parent (a process that might be said to involve the social skill of imitation or modeling). During "latency," the period when peers and school interests increase in importance, one criterion for successful development would be an increased emphasis on peer relations as opposed to child–adult interactions.

In an extension of Freud's psychoanalytic model, Erikson (1963) presents a similar developmental system of socialization extending from infancy through adulthood, with a set of conflicts to be mastered at each stage, primarily through the development of social behaviors. Erikson suggests that the appropriately socialized child successfully moves through a series of eight stages that begin with trust in others and culminate in adulthood with a realistic, socially approved sense of himself. In Erikson's frame of reference, early social behaviors that develop through the relationship with parents and early caretakers involve the infant's ability to take, to give, and to get others to care for his needs. Also important is the young child's ability to accept adult demands for regulation in various bodily functions as well as in his movement around his environment. Social responses developed with early caretakers become expressed in widening circles with siblings, peers, and other adults; and behaviors involving independence and initiative take on increasing value. In any process of socialization, early social behaviors are taught by parents and caretakers through their responses and their examples. A social skills curriculum for the older child can only attempt to recapitulate early stages of development as they are reflected in the classroom or therapeutic setting. An example of a program involving the application of developmental concepts in a socialization curriculum is that of Wood (1975).

Whereas the preceding developmental theories stressed psychological factors contributing to eventual socialization, Piaget (Inhelder & Piaget, 1964) presents a theory that focuses on cognitive development. Most relevant to the contents of this book is the Piagetian developmental sequence for moral development. In this system, Piaget analyzes children's play behavior relative to rules and games and specifies four stages: (a) motor development, (b) egocentric, (c) mutual cooperation, and (d) development of moral principles. During the first stage of motor development, the child's play is largely motor and individualistic in nature. By the time the child nears the second (i.e., egocentric) stage, occurring approximately between the ages of 2 and 5, the child has begun to apply rules to daily activities. This use of rules is not based on moral judgment but results from the external control of adults and older children, whose standards the child views at this point as absolute and correct. As the child moves into the third stage, mutual cooperation, the belief in the absolute nature of external rules is modified, and the child begins to establish rules according to the particular social circumstances. At this stage, however, the interests of others are an important consideration in rule formulation. At approximately 11 or 12 years of age, the child enters the last stage with the recognition of moral principles in the establishment of social order. During this period, the child begins to recognize the functional importance of rules, the importance of the rights of others, and the importance of rules in the social order; that is, as a mechanism for protecting individual rights. Although this model presents moral development in stages, these stages are not considered to be mutually exclusive, for elements of each exist at all levels; for example, aspects of cooperation and motor development occur during the egocentric stage. The difference, according to Piaget, is in the degree to which specific behavior patterns are found in the respective stages.

Kohlberg (1969) builds on these ideas with a six-stage developmental theory suggesting that morality evolves from primarily egotistical considerations (Stages 1 and 2) to interest in maintaining order and stability (Stages 3 and 4) to the highest levels (Stages 5 and 6), where the individual adheres to inner principles, defining his behavior according to conscience and convictions rather than simply by laws and regulations. Within Kohlberg's model, children with delinquent behaviors are operating at the lower egotistical levels, where the emphasis is on personal gain and the avoidance of punishment. Using this framework, direct instruction, gradually moving through the developmental stages, would be recommended in order to improve social behaviors. An application of this model in social skill instruction is discussed by Bash and Camp in chapter 6.

If one accepts these hierarchies related to moral development as presented by Piaget and Kohlberg, the implications for selection of social skills would be, for example, that behaviors such as sharing and cooperative play could most easily be taught after the age of 2, and acceptance of authority through following directions and understanding consequences can be taught much earlier than behaviors involving independent decision-making. Also implied is that social skills involving understanding of another's point of view could most easily be taught at a later stage and that principles based on one's inner beliefs probably are best established after the child has accepted the importance of order and regulation.

The social skills field has been largely dominated by researchers and clinicians with a behavior analysis or behavior therapy orientation, although the child development field has had a long-standing interest in children's social competence. There is currently an increasing trend toward viewing social skills within a developmental context. Gelfand and Hartmann (1979) pointed out that children of different developmental levels reason differently and that "although children's behavior can be manipulated through altering reinforcement contingencies, their *beliefs* about the causes of their own and other's behavior are often inaccurate and vary with their level of development" (p. 6). Similarly, Harris and Ferrari (1983) suggested that those working to change children's behaviors should be aware that children's understanding and interpretation of events differ from adults. They further stress the need for normative guidelines in developing social behaviors. Normative information not only suggests what kind of social skills are developmentally relevant to teach but also helps in evaluating the effects of social skills training through comparisons with socially competent children.

Developmental considerations have relevance not only for selection of social skills but also for the teaching approaches to be used. An early step in devising social skill instruction is to view the child according to developmental standards and identify the progression needed for desired performance. In order to respond to social skills training, the child may need to learn first to attend to and identify relevant stimuli. Every set of social skills has prerequisites. Brooks-Gunn and Luciano (1985) point out, for example, that until the young child acquires a concept of self, reciprocal relationships are not possible, and that complex social behaviors and social emotions, such as empathy, require that the child has "a concept of self and is capable of taking the role of another or being influenced by someone 'Like me'." Obviously, social skills requiring the use of language can more easily be taught to older children, who employ verbalization in social actions more often than do younger children (Selman, Schorin, Stone, & Phelps, 1983).

## Social Criteria in Skill Selection

In selecting skills for a particular child or group of children, a number of social criteria need to be considered in addition to their developmental levels. There is much variety of opinion in different parts of society, among groups of professionals, even within families, and certainly over time, about how children should act. For example, rather than being "seen and not heard" as in days of yore, children are now being taught assertiveness, measured in terms of loudness of speech, eye contact, duration of speech, and ability to make requests (Bornstein, Bellack, & Hersen, 1977). The cultural context of social behaviors is an important consideration for the selection of social skills to teach a given child. There are numerous examples of cultural differences: people from different cultures stand at different distances from one another; children in some cultural groups are taught not to look directly at others; children in some families or subcultures are taught to hit back rather than engage in some alternative to aggression. Clearly, the teacher or therapist who is concerned with helping the child to be more effective in interpersonal relationships must consider the adult and peer behavior norms of the child's wider environment. The views of the child himself and those in his peer group about what social behaviors are most desirable need to be considered, and these change with age. The child's opinions are particularly important for providing motivation to engage in social skills learning tasks.

The opinions of peers are a relevant source of information about what are essential social skills. Peer relationships are among the most important in a child's life and contribute to the child's social learning. Social skills play a large part in a child's acceptance by peers. Withdrawn or aggressive children tend to be shunned by peers, with the result that they lose opportunities to learn from social experiences (Combs & Slaby, 1977). Similarly, Hartup (1970) suggests a reciprocal relationship between peer acceptance and sociability, "in that sociability may lead to acceptance, but acceptance undoubtedly inspires greater sociability."

Sociometric studies have provided clues to what children consider desirable characteristics in their peers. In a study by Dygdon, Conger, Conger, Wallanda, and Keane (1980), children were asked to describe other children whom they identified as those they liked, disliked, and whom they felt were ignored by their classmates. The major responses for liked children had to do with altruism and participation in play activities. Other frequent reasons included "entertainingness," vocabulary, quantity of speech, motor prowess, and academic efficiency. Similar responses were obtained by Cartledge, Frew, and Zaharias (1985) in a study of the social skill deficits of learning disabled students as perceived by their nonhandicapped peers. These results parallel the correlates of peer acceptance and rejection in a number of studies identified in a review by Hartup (1970), which include friendliness, sociability and outgoingness, frequency of dispensing social reinforcers, social participation, kindness, being helpful, being "good company" or the "life of the party."

Adults may have quite different views of the social skills needed by children, and these may vary according to the situation. In the classroom, for example, teachers value social behaviors that facilitate their task of teaching academic skills. In one study (Milburn, 1974), a group of teachers rated as more important the skills concerned with order, cooperative behavior, accepting consequences, following rules and directions, avoiding conflict, and basic self-help behavior. They valued relatively less the skills that involved initiating contact with others, greeting and conversation skills, being assertive in interpersonal relationships, and performing for others. Critics of the use of behavior modification techniques have pointed out that these procedures are being used too often to develop quiet, controlled, docile, conforming behaviors, the "model" child (Winnett & Winkler, 1972, p. 501)

> who stays glued to his seat and desk all day, continually looks at his teacher or his text/workbook, does not talk to or in fact look at other children, does not talk unless asked to by the teacher, hopefully does not laugh or sing (at the wrong time), and assuredly passes silently in the halls.

This criticism notwithstanding, a number of studies have identified specific classroom "survival skills," which are highly correlated with academic success. These include attending, volunteering answers, complying with teacher requests, following teacher directions, and remaining on task (Cobb & Hops, 1973).

Some bases for selecting social skills are implied in Wolf's (1978) discussion of social validity as a criterion for determining what are socially significant problems for behavior change efforts. Social validity, according to Wolf, can best be established by consumers or representatives of the relevant community according to such criteria as whether the behaviors have social significance in relation to goals desired by society, whether the procedures used to bring about behavior change are acceptable, and whether the effects or results of behavior change are satisfactory to the relevant consumers. In applying the concept of social validity to children's social skills, Gresham (1984) suggests that socially important outcomes of social skill training for children might include "acceptance in the peer group, acceptance by significant adults . . . , school adjustment, mental health functioning, and lack of contact with the juvenile court system" (p. 8). It seems apparent that in selecting social skills to teach to children, the desired outcomes will be an important factor in determining the instructional focus, because the emphasis might be different if the goal were, for example, increased peer acceptance as opposed to classroom success or improved home relationships.

Most often, the need for social skills training for an individual child is identified because of an excess of some behavior considered to be undesirable, where the problem is seen to exist because the child does not have the related acceptable behaviors in his repertoire. The selection of what more desirable behaviors should be taught to replace the problematic ones depends, as suggested above, on many factors, often including subjective assessment on the part of the concerned adult. There are techniques to teach children almost anything that is within their comprehension and capabilities. For that reason, in selecting social skills for children, it seems particularly important to choose those behaviors that will have value to them. The Relevance of Behavior Rule of Allyon and Azrin (1968) states "Teach only those behaviors that will continue to be reinforced after training." In the selection of social skills, application of this rule would help to assure that the behaviors required have some intrinsic value to the child, will benefit the child, and are valued by others in the child's environment who will reward their occurrence.

As is pointed out in chapter 4, the extent to which social skills are generalized and maintained depends to a great extent on environmental responses that keep the behaviors going. Selecting and teaching social skills that are meaningful to the consumers, or audiences (i.e., the child, his peers, parents, and significant others in his environment) should assist considerably in the maintenance of the skills over time.

## INVENTORIES OF SOCIAL SKILLS

In the absence of clear data about what are the most essential skills to teach to children, the practitioner can turn to a number of taxonomies or inventories of social skills, which can assist in narrowing down the vast field of social behaviors to be taught. Because of the many variables involved in determining the selection of social behaviors, it may be difficult to find a social skills inventory that meets all the needs of the individual child or specific group, and it may be necessary to add more behaviors or delete some that are not relevant to the child or the social situation. Inventories provide a useful place to start, however, and can aid in the assessment of social skills deficits. Samples of social skills inventories will be presented later, including one by Wood (1975) for the young, emotionally disturbed child, and ones by Stephens (1978) and Walker et al. (1983) for the elementary school age child. These inventories are all generated specifically for use in schools and serve as the basis for teaching curricula. There is currently a lack of social skills inventories with behaviors more broadly oriented toward the home or residential setting and the community.

The teaching model developed by Wood (1975) for young, handicapped children incorporates many of the principles of the previously mentioned developmental theorists. It attempts to provide a functional system to be used in teaching the emotionally disturbed child. The model presents specific behavior goals according to five stages of development, each of which includes the four "curriculum" area: behavior, communication, socialization, and (pre) academics. The behavior goals are further broken down into specific objectives. For example, the Stage II socialization goal (participating successfully in activities with others) includes the following skills (Wood, 1975, p. 278)

1. to *participate spontaneously* in specific parallel activities with another child using similar materials but not interacting.
2. to *wait* without physical intervention by teachers. (Verbal support or touch may be used.)

3. to initiate appropriate minimal movement toward another child within the classroom routine. (Child, through gesture and action, begins minimal appropriate social interaction with another child.)
4. to participate in a verbally directed sharing activity. (Child passes materials or gives toy to another.)
   Examples:
   a. Child passes cookies within the classroom structure.
   b. Child gives toy to another. (Verbal cues may be used.)
   c. Child can use same paint, water, or box of crayons that another child is using.
5. to *participate* in cooperative activities or projects with another child during play time, indoor or outdoor. (Child is involved actively with another child; verbal support or touch may be used.)
6. to *participate* in cooperative activities or projects with another child during organized class activities. (Child is involved actively with others; verbal support or touch may be used.)

A similar skill listing is provided for each goal presented in the developmental therapy curriculum, essentially analyzing each goal into specific responses that composed the behavior class. Another feature underscoring the utility of the Wood inventory is that the objectives are listed as observable behaviors, and conditions for performance are specified.

Whereas the Wood inventory was developed primarily for young children with "serious emotional and behavioral disorders" in special settings, Stephens (1978) published a social skills curriculum for the classroom that encompasses a greater age range and is not restricted to special populations. Using a task analysis model, the behaviors are grouped into 4 major categories (environmental, interpersonal, self-related, and task-related behaviors), which are further analyzed into 30 subcategories and 136 specific skills (Stephens, 1978, pp. 34–38). Subcategory headings include

- SELF-RELATED BEHAVIORS

  Accepting consequences
  Ethical behavior
  Expressing feelings
  Positive attitude toward self
  Responsible behavior
  Self care

- ENVIRONMENTAL BEHAVIORS

  Care for the environment
  Dealing with emergencies
  Lunchroom behavior
  Movement around environment

- TASK-RELATED BEHAVIORS

  Asking and answering questions
  Attending behavior
  Classroom discussion
  Completing tasks
  Following directions
  Group activities
  Independent work
  On-task behavior
  Performing before others
  Quality of work

- INTERPERSONAL BEHAVIORS

  Accepting authority
  Coping with conflict
  Gaining attention
  Greeting others
  Helping others
  Making conversation
  Organized play
  Positive attitude toward others
  Playing informally
  Property: own and others

Specific responses have been identified for each subcategory. A sample category, subcategory and skill listing (p. 121) follows:

- Major Category:   INTERPERSONAL BEHAVIORS
- Subcategory:   Coping with Conflict
- Skills:   To respond to teasing or name calling by ignoring, changing the subject, or using some other constructive means.

     To respond to physical assault by leaving the situation, calling for help, or using some other constructive means.

     To walk away from peer when angry to avoid hitting.

     To refuse the request of another politely.

     To express anger with nonaggressive words rather than physical action or aggressive words.

     To handle constructively criticism or punishment perceived as undeserved.

For a complete skill listing the reader is referred to the Social Skills List.

The listing of social skills developed by Walker et al. also forms the basis for a curriculum. The target population is composed of mildly to moderately handicapped children in the elementary school grades. Their skill listings include (Walker et al., 1983, pp. 121–122)

- *Area I:*   Classroom Skills
  Listening to the teacher (sit quietly and look at. . .)
  When the teacher asks you to do something (you should do it)
  Doing your best work (follow directions and write neatly)
  Following classroom rules
- *Area II:*   Basic Interaction Skills
  Eye contact
  Using the right voice
  Starting (finding someone to talk to)
  Listening (look at the person and pay attention)
  Answering (saying something after someone talks to you)
  Making sense (talking about the same things)
  Taking turns talking
  Asking questions
  Continuing to talk (keeping the talking going)
- *Area III:*   Getting Along Skills
  Using polite words (saying nice things at the right time)
  Sharing
  Following rules (everyone plays the game the same way)
  Assisting others (doing nice things for others when they need help)
  Touching the right way

- *Area IV:*        Making Friends
  - Good grooming (wash hands and face, brush teeth, clean clothes)
  - Smiling
  - Complimenting
  - Friendship-making (starting, taking turns talking, inviting)
- *Area V:*        Coping Skills
  - When someone says no (find another way to play)
  - When you express anger
  - When someone teases
  - When someone tries to hurt you
  - When someone asks you to do something you can't do
  - When things don't go right

The Stephens and Walker et al. skill listings were both developed through similar social validation processes, in which teachers rated the importance of specified social behaviors for classroom success (Milburn, 1974; Walker et al., 1983). A number of other skills listings have been developed for the elementary grades: for example, Rinn and Markle (1979); Jackson, Jackson, and Monroe (1983); Michelson, Sugai, Wood, and Kazdin (1983).

Based on an analysis of correlates of peer acceptance in elementary school (Hartup, 1970), LaGreca and associates (LaGreca & Mesibov, 1979, LaGreca & Santogrossi, 1980) have identified nine areas for social skill instruction that contribute to positive peer relations. They also analyzed these into skill components. The nine areas include

- Smiling/laughing
- Greeting others
- Joining ongoing activities
- Extending invitations
- Conversational skills
- Sharing and cooperation
- Verbal complementing
- Physical appearance/grooming

An inventory of social competence skills developed by Turnbull, Strickland, and Brantley (1978) identifies skills according to primary, intermediate, junior high, and senior high school levels. An example of an inventory generated by Goldstein, Sprafkin, Gershaw, and Klein for use with adolescents in either a classroom or clinical setting is presented in chapter 10. This group of skills has aggressive adolescents as a target population but is applicable to younger children as well. These skills form the basis for the structured learning curriculum that Goldstein and his colleagues describe in chapter 10 and that has also been adapted for use with younger children (McGinnis & Goldstein, 1984). Each skill is analyzed into a set of behavioral steps that can be translated into specific teaching objectives.

There is considerable similarity among all these inventories, even taking into consideration the differing intended populations. The inventories and lists of skills just described encompass a broad range of social skills that to varying degrees include behaviors related to affective and cognitive processes. Some additional lists of behaviors that are specific to cognitive or affective dimensions of social skills are described next.

## SELECTING COGNITIVE AND AFFECTIVE BEHAVIORS

Affective and cognitive processes are increasingly being recognized as important determinants of social functioning and, therefore, necessary elements in the development and use of social skills. That emotions and cognitive processes are closely related is well established, although as Lewis and Michalson (1983) point out, there are several theoretical positions regarding the nature of this relationship. In some views, the expression of emotion is the consequence of cognitive processes; in others, emotional responses are seen as independent events not based on cognitive antecedents. In the view of Lewis and Michalson (pp. 92–93)

> . . . simple linear models of the relationship between cognition and emotion are inadequate. The relationships between these domains is quite complex, is continuous, and is more finely tuned than is usually depicted by traditional models. In conceptualizing the relationship between emotion and cognition, neither process should be described as causing the other. Rather, the best model is of two processes continually and progressively chasing each other, weaving their separate strands of behavior into a single composition not unlike that of a musical fugue.

Training in social skills related to cognitions and affect concerns internal processes rather than observable discrete social behaviors, and most training programs dealing with these two dimensions include both cognitive and affective elements. Children most often identified as needing such training are characterized as lacking self-control, being impulsive and aggressive, possessing negative self-evaluations, and having poor peer relationships.

### Social Skills Related to Affect

Although emotions or feelings are private events, difficult to measure except through their overt behavioral expressions, the emotions and their manifestations have a role in social skills training. Izard (1977) has defined certain emotions (i.e., interest–excitement, joy, surprise, distress–anguish, anger–rage, disgust–revulsion, contempt–scorn, fear–terror, shame–shyness–humiliation, and guilt) as "fundamental emotions," which in combination form other emotional states (anxiety, depression, love, hostility, and hate). Some of the undesirable behavioral manifestations of emotional states, for example, expressions of anger, indicate a need for social skills training to teach alternate behaviors. Similarly, fear, anxiety, and resulting shyness can interfere with learning and performing social behaviors. Social skills training dealing with emotions can have several interrelated aspects. At the most basic level, it has to begin with recognizing and labeling the expression of emotions in others. The ultimate goal involves learning appropriate or acceptable ways to express a variety of feelings under varying conditions.

The affective dimension of empathy has received considerable attention in recent social skills literature. Empathy, the ability to experience the emotions of others, is considered important if children are to master such interpersonal skills as making and maintaining friendships and resolving conflicts with others. Lewis and Michalson (1983) describe empathy as first requiring the development of a concept of self, in order for children to see themselves in the place of another and thus experience the feelings of another. They suggest also that another aspect of empathy is the child's knowledge of social rules and expectations about what feelings are appropriate in specific situations. Feshbach, Feshbach, Fauvre, and Ballard-Campbell (1983, p. 3) identified the following as essential components of empathy:

1. Recognition and discrimination of feeling | The ability to use relevant information to label and identify emotions
2. Perspective and role taking | The ability to understand that other individuals may see and interpret situations differently; the ability to assume and experience another's viewpoint.
3. Emotional responsiveness | The ability to experience and be aware of one's own emotions.

A fairly extensive literature of suggested teaching approaches to affective education has been developed over the past several decades. One of the conceptual foundations is the taxonomy developed by Krathwohl, Bloom, and Masia (1956), which presents a hierarchy of affective–cognitive behaviors. According to their sequence, the child's affective development follows a pattern in which he first becomes aware of his surroundings, then learns to comply with the existing rules and regulations in his environment, and finally moves through the process of developing a personal value system. One's behavior and value system are considered to be inseparable, in that beliefs are reflected by behavior. Therefore, the instructional goal is to help the child acquire values that foster humane, positive attitudes toward others, anticipating that the child's social behaviors will develop accordingly. The Krathwohl et al. taxonomy provides teaching objectives and items for evaluating outcomes. Another well-known approach to affective education has been the human development program (Bessell & Palomares, 1970), which makes use of the "magic circle" technique to help children (a) understand the similarities and differences between themselves and others, (b) identify and use their own abilities, and (c) understand their role in interpersonal relationships.

A number of recent programs have been developed for teaching specific skills related to affective behavior. Among them are the Developing Understanding of Self and Others (DUSO) program (Dinkmeyer, 1973), Toward Affective Development (TAD) (Dupont, Gardner, & Brody, 1974), and Project AWARE (Elardo & Cooper, 1977). These curricula, and others designed to teach children about feelings, present a number of common themes:

1. The child's sense of himself or herself, self-identity, and the development of self-esteem, which encompasses

   - The ability to see oneself objectively, realistically
   - The ability to identify one's individual characteristics
   - The ability to identify one's positive attributes, assets, strengths
   - The ability to identify and accept one's negative attributes, limitations, imperfections
   - The ability to accept and deal constructively with negative experiences, such as failure and rejection
   - The ability to maintain a consistent positive self-concept in the presence of varying external feedback

2. The child's awareness and expression of his or her own feelings, which involves

   - The ability to recognize his or her feelings associated with different life events
   - The ability to use words to label and describe to others both positive and negative feelings
   - The ability to use appropriate nonverbal as well as verbal means of expressing emotions
   - The ability to understand the function of emotional expression in his or her life, including the relationship between his or her feelings and interpersonal events

3. The child's awareness of the feelings of others, including

   - The ability to infer others' feelings from their verbal communication; for example, tone of voice, words, timing
   - The ability to infer others' feelings from their nonverbal behavior; for example, facial expressions, posture, gestures
   - The ability to infer others' feelings from knowledge of social expectations about which emotions are appropriate to specific situations
   - The ability to be sensitive to the feelings of those who are different from himself or herself

4. The child's awareness of complexities of emotional expression, for example

- The ability to recognize when emotions in himself and others are mixed
- The ability to recognize that feelings can vary over time and among situations

Helping the child to find constructive ways to express feelings in interpersonal situations is complex because it involves not only the child's ability to identify his own feelings but the development of the ability to exercise control and selectivity over his responses. This latter task involves a three-way interaction between emotion, cognition, and motor activity.

## Social Skills Related to Cognition

Training in ways to change cognitions assists in control over emotions and behaviors. Many of the curricula mentioned previously also present ways to teach cognitively oriented skills. Some of the cognitive skills identified as important aspects of social skills training include those involved in social perception, problem solving, self-instructions, cognitive restructuring, and self-evaluation.

*Social Perception*
Social perception is considered to be the person's ability to perceive the parameters of a situation and vary behavior according to feedback from others. An important prerequisite to social skill, it involves both cognitive and affective elements. In addition to the affective skills of identifying and labeling feelings, an important skill is that of role-taking, or empathy, the cognitive and affective ability to take the perspective of another person. Another prerequisite involves a skill mentioned earlier; that is, the ability to make inferences about others' feelings and thoughts from nonverbal cues, such as tone of voice, gestures, and facial expression, as well as from verbal content. Although developmental theories suggest that young children are primarily egocentric and cannot differentiate their own perceptions from those of others, a number of studies with positive outcomes are identified in a review by Urbain and Kendall (1980), demonstrating that children—and in some cases very young children—can through systematic training increase their understanding of others' thoughts, feelings, and perceptions.

*Problem Solving*
A large body of research data and a number of specific teaching programs have been developed around methods of teaching children to solve problems

in interpersonal relations. Goldstein, Carr, Davidson, and Wehr (1981) stress the importance of problem-solving ability to good psychological adjustment and points out that persons too frequently resort to unacceptable ways of solving problems through aggressive behavior. Children, for example, with a repertoire of prosocial ways of achieving goals and solving problems in dealing with others are less likely to act out in dysfunctional ways. Urbain and Kendall (1980) describe problem-solving training as emphasizing adaptive thinking processes. As such, their program differs from one with a psychodynamic orientation, which would stress release of feelings and resolution of internal conflicts. It differs also from training in observable social skills. Training in problem solving presents a process for finding answers rather than a specific set of behaviors or solutions.

A widely used definition of the problem-solving process developed by D'Zurilla and Goldfried (1971) includes these steps:

1. General orientation—the ability to recognize that a problem exists and that a solution can be found;
2. Problem definition and formulation—identifying the various issues involved in the situation:
3. Generation of alternatives—similar to "brainstorming," in which as many solutions as possible are considered;
4. Decision-making—in which a course of action is chosen, based on an assessment of its likelihood to resolve the identified problem; and
5. Verification—implementing the decision and evaluating the extent to which the problem has been resolved, possibly returning to more problem solving if the solution was not effective.

The work of Spivack, Platt, and Shure (Spivack & Shure, 1974; Spivack, Platt, & Shure, 1976; Shure & Spivack, 1978) has made a major contribution to the area of teaching problem-solving skills to children. Oriented first to preschool children, their Interpersonal Cognitive Problem-Solving Program (ICPS) begins with teaching of language and conceptual skills, which are assumed to be prerequisite to the child's ability to go through a problem solving process. These include, for example, knowing the words for expressing alternatives (or, not, and), words for describing emotions (happy, sad, mad), words for alternative solutions (maybe, might, if–then), and words for consequential thinking (why, because). The specific skills addressed in ICPS training, as outlined by Goldstein et al. (1981, pp. 226–228), include

1. Alternative solution thinking, ability to generate different solutions;
2. Consequential thinking, ability to predict the possible outcomes of various courses of action;
3. Causal thinking, ability to see cause and effect relationships;
4. Interpersonal sensitivity, awareness that interpersonal problems exist;

5. Means-end thinking, identification of the steps necessary to achieve a goal; and
6. Perspective taking, recognition of differences in motives and viewpoints, similar to empathy or role taking.

Variations of problem-solving training have been developed by others into programs for use with different age levels. The Rochester Social Problem-Solving (SPS) Program (Weissberg, Gesten, Liebenstein, Doherty-Schmid, & Hutton, 1980), for example, similarly involves teaching children to identify feelings, think of alternative solutions, and anticipate consequences of behavior.

## Self-Instruction

Self-instruction and related skills having to do with self-control constitute another cognitive area relevant to building social skills. Most self-instruction programs are built on an adaptation of a model developed by Vygotsky (1962) and Luria (1961). As described by Meichenbaum (1977, pp. 18–19):

> Luria proposed three stages by which the initiation and inhibition of voluntary motor behaviors come under verbal control. . . . During the first stage, the speech of others, usually adults, controls and directs a child's behavior. In the second stage the child's own overt speech becomes an effective regulator of his behavior. Finally, the child's covert, or inner, speech assumes a self-governing role.

Various studies with children have demonstrated that young children talk out loud to themselves when performing a task and that as children grow older the private speech becomes internalized, "goes underground." The assumption is that much behavior is guided by internalized self-statements, and that the child's behavior can be changed by alterations in his or her self-statements.

Self-instruction with children generally involves teaching children a series of problem solving steps similar to those outlined previously, along with self-controlling verbal statements. The self-instruction statements include, for example (Meichenbaum, 1977, p. 32),

1. problem definition ("What is it I have to do?");
2. focusing attention and response guidance ("carefully . . . draw the line down");
3. self-reinforcement ("Good, I'm doing fine"); and
4. self-evaluation coping skills and error-correcting options ("That's okay . . . Even if I make an error I can go on slowly").

The Think Aloud program (Camp, 1977; Camp, Blom, Herbert, & van Doorninck, 1977; Camp, Zimet, van Doorninck, & Dahlem, 1977) makes use of Meichenbaum's procedures. This program is outlined in chapter 6. Another curriculum for teaching self-control through verbal self instruction

(VSI), also built on the Meichenbaum model, was developed by Kendall (1981). Self-instruction statements include (Kendall & Braswell, 1985, p. 120)

- Problem definition:     "Let's see, what am I supposed to do?"
- Problem approach:       "I have to look at all the possibilities."
- Focusing of attention:  "I better concentrate and focus in, and think only of what I'm doing right now."
- Choosing an answer:     "I think it's this one. . ."
- Self-reinforcement:     "Hey, not bad. I really did a good job."

    or

- Coping statement:       "Oh, I made a mistake. Next time I'll try and go slower and concentrate more and maybe I'll get the right answer."

Kagan and Kogan (1970) distinguish between the differing cognitive processes of reflective and impulsive children. Both may be motivated to appear competent, with doubts about their ability. In the case of some impulsive children, anxiety about competence may result in too rapid, nonreflective responses, whereas in the case of reflective children similar anxiety may result in overly cautious responses. They also identify impulsive children with little or no anxiety over their performance. Cognitive self-control techniques are considered to be most appropriate for impulsive children, who need to learn to "stop and think." These techniques may be less appropriate for anxious, inhibited, reflective children, who might profit more from some cognitive restructuring approaches.

### Cognitive Restructuring

A further aspect of cognitive training related to self-instruction is the alteration of dysfunctional self-statements. A major example of this approach is the Rational Emotive Therapy (RET) model of Albert Ellis (1962). Ellis proposes that maladaptive behavior results from irrational belief systems based on a set of imperatives about what one should or must do or must have happen. Cognition, emotion, and behavior are interrelated; irrational beliefs are responsible for disturbing emotions, which then result in dysfunctional behavior. An RET program developed for children by Knaus (1974) presents the following areas for learning: (a) helping children learn about feelings, (b) challenging irrational beliefs, helping children recognize their irrational belief systems; (c) challenging feelings of inferiority, helping children learn to evaluate themselves and others in positive terms; (d) helping children become realistic about issues related to perfectionism, and (e) teaching children to think in terms of what they would like to have happen rather than irrational "*must* and *should* happen."

A related cognitive area, which is receiving increasing attention, is that of the child's attributions. Kendall and Braswell (1985) distinguish between expectancy and attribution, the former preceding an event or situation and the latter following the event. Attribution is the attempt to explain the event or account for its cause. These authors point out the importance of attributions for generalization of improvement and also for motivation to learn self-control. The child who attributes his failures in interpersonal relationships to causes outside himself, for example, will be less motivated to engage in training to improve his interactions with others. Glenwick and Jason (1984) see the restructuring of attributional style as one of the desired outcomes of cognitive self-control training, suggesting that children who can learn to see themselves as causal agents can enhance their self-esteem and sense of self-efficacy (i.e., the child's expectation of being successful).

*Other Self-Control Procedures*

Another set of cognitive self-control procedures, which have proven useful in changing behavior and show promise for maintaining behavior over time, are those of self-monitoring, self-evaluation, and self-reinforcement. Self-monitoring is the ability to observe and report one's own behavior. Studies have demonstrated that teaching children skills in self-monitoring is more effective for changing behavior if children are trained to evaluate their own performance in a way that corresponds with others' objective evaluations (Bolstad & Johnson, 1972; Santogrossi, O'Leary, Romanczyk, & Kaufman, 1973; Wood & Flynn, 1978). At the same time, another body of data exists to suggest that the act of self-recording alone, regardless of accuracy, can significantly change behavior (Nelson & Hayes, 1981). With children, the difficulty of the task and the type of child involved may be factors; self-evaluation is most useful for children already motivated to improve their behavior (O'Leary & Dubey, 1979).

Self-evaluation refers to the comparison between self-observed behavior and the criteria or performance standards one has set for the behavior. Such standards can either be acquired through direct training (making the standards explicit to the child) or through modeling influences (the child observing how other people evaluate the behavior). The kinds of criteria established for evaluation clearly affect whether the criteria can realistically be met and the evaluation can be positive. Many children seldom make positive self-evaluations, possibly because they set excessively high standards for their own performance. Research on the effect of goal setting on behavior suggests that training children to set realistic performance goals might help to increase motivation and, hence, performance (Sagotsky, Patterson, & Lepper, 1978).

Self-reinforcement is the process of rewarding oneself for the performance of specific behaviors according to some criterion. An explanation for the effect of self-evaluation on behavior change is that the process of attending to one's own behavior and comparing it to a criterion triggers self-reinforcing or self-punishing thoughts, which may in turn serve to increase or decrease the behavior (Nelson & Hayes, 1981). Skill in self-reinforcement involves the child's ability to monitor his behavior, identify positive aspects, and deliver a reward; for example, a positive statement, which could be expressed either overtly or covertly.

Effective self-reinforcement, according to Jones, Nelson, and Kazdin (1977), depends on prior training with external reinforcement, which provides information regarding desirable behavior, the setting of reasonable goals, self-monitoring, and the availability of some external monitoring and external contingencies to encourage self-reinforcement. The importance of self-monitoring, self-evaluation, and self-reinforcement in the maintaining of social skills over time is discussed in chapter 4.

## INDIVIDUALIZING SKILL SELECTION

In the process of selecting and developing specific social skills for instruction to meet individual needs, two sets of procedures are particularly useful: formulating behavioral objectives stated in positive terms, and analyzing broadly stated social behaviors into subcomponents. As mentioned earlier, the need for social skills training often is identified because of a problem or deficit. Social skills training involves helping children discard some behaviors and substitute more acceptable ones. Many of the problem behaviors displayed by children have opposite or incompatible desirable behaviors that could be taught or increased in frequency. For example,

| *Problems* | *Social Skills* |
|---|---|
| 1. The child calls others by uncomplimentary names. | 1. The child makes positive remarks to others. |
| 2. The child frequently interrupts the conversation of others. | 2. The child waits for pauses in the conversation before speaking. |
| 3. The child makes negative statements about his or her ability. | 3. The child identifies something he or she does well. |
| 4. The child cheats when playing games with peers. | 4. The child plays games according to rules. |
| 5. The child throws tantrums when teased by peers. | 5. The child responds to teasing by ignoring or some other appropriate responses. |
| 6. The child laughs at or ignores individuals in need of help. | 6. The child assists individuals in need of help. |

As previously indicated, the social goals adults have for children are generally conceptualized in global terms; for example, to play cooperatively or to assume responsibility. Breaking down such goals into their subcomponents assists the process of defining behavior to be taught. Although there are several models for analyzing a task, the essential steps involve (a) specifying the desired behavior, (b) identifying the subskills of the composite behavior, (c) stating the subskills in terms of observable behaviors, (d) listing the subskills according to sequence of instruction, (e) identifying and implementing appropriate instructional strategies, and (f) evaluating the results.

Moyer and Dardig (1978) present several practical approaches to task analysis. A method developed by Mager (1972) that is especially applicable to social or affective behaviors is summarized by Moyer and Dardig (p. 18) as follows:

1. Write the goal on paper.
2. List the observable behaviors a person would exhibit to show that he or she has attained the goal.
3. Review the list, discarding those behaviors that should not be included and identifying those in need of clarification.
4. Describe what is intended for each goal on the list by determining how frequently or how well the behavior must be performed.
5. Test the statements for adequacy and completeness by determining whether the behaviors in the final list represent comprehensive attainment of the goal.

For a practical application of these guidelines, consider the situation of primary school aged children who tend to be overly aggressive and disagreeable at play. Stated in positive terms, the social goal would be to develop cooperative play behaviors. An example of a systematic performance analysis of this composite behavior would be

1. When presented with an informal play period, the child will approach a peer and suggest a cooperative play activity. (Example: "Let's use these blocks to build a big house.")
2. When engaged in a joint play activity with a peer, the child will suggest respective responsibilities, working toward a common goal. (Example: "I will make this wall and you can make the other one.")
3. While engaged in a joint activity with a peer, the child will participate according to the established rules or procedures. (Example: If it has been previously established how the structure should be built, the child will adhere to this decision unless the matter is fairly renegotiated with all parties.)
4. While engaged in a joint play activity with another peer, the child will assist the other child, if necessary. (Example: "Here is another block for your wall.")

5. While engaged in a joint play activity with a peer, the child will make positive comments to his or her partner. (Example: "I like the big wall you
   built.")
6. Following a joint play activity, the child will work with peer to put away
   play materials.

In analyzing social behaviors, certain factors become obvious. First, social
behaviors do not readily lend themselves to sequential listing. For example,
the subskills in the preceding analysis have been ranked more for temporal
considerations than their importance as prerequisites to subsequent skills. Second, the extent and exact form of the analysis are relative to the specific child.
For example, in the above listing, assumptions were made regarding the
child's oral language skills. Youngsters experiencing difficulties in spontaneous oral language may need instruction in prerequisite language skills, such
as extending an invitation to a peer or making positive statements, before they
can be expected to make these statements during play. Finally, by specifying the exact responses and conditions, the performance and evaluation processes are facilitated. The task analysis process enables both the child and the
evaluator to know what is expected and when the responses are to occur,
essential aspects of social skill instruction.

## SUMMARY

Before social skill instruction can take place, it is necessary to determine
what skills are important for children to learn. A number of considerations
enter into the identification of social skills, among them the child's developmental level, which may facilitate or retard learning and retaining of skills,
the cultural and situational context and the views of those who make up the
child's environment, and the likelihood that given social skills will be valued
and reinforced by others, once they are learned.

Selection of social skills for instruction can be based on inventories of social
behavior, many of which accompany social skills curricula. Most of these
combine behavioral, affective, and cognitive dimensions of skills to be taught.
Skill selection can also be based on an assessment of individual deficits in
social skills. The therapist or teacher can turn the child's problem behaviors
into opportunities for social skill instruction through the development of positively stated objectives, further analyzed into specific components through
a task analysis process.

# 2
# Assessment and Evaluation of Social Skills

Assessment can take many forms, from fleeting observational impressions to systematic recording and the use of standardized instruments. Recently, a number of books and articles have been devoted to the subject of social skills assessment; for example, Eisler, 1976; Foster and Ritchey, 1979; Gresham, 1981; Hersen and Bellack, 1977; Hops and Greenwood, 1981; Michelson, Foster, and Ritchey, 1981; Michelson and Wood, 1980.

Why should a social skills teaching program involve assessment: Social skills can certainly be taught without the sometimes difficult and time-consuming task of prior assessment to determine the extent to which a skill is in the child's repertoire. For researchers, assessment is a necessity, in order to create a basis for measuring the effects of social skills teaching on behavior change. For teachers and clinicians, the most effective interventions also involve assessment, because they, too, must be concerned with the results of their efforts. Assessment helps determine whether the goal should be teaching a new behavior or, instead, arranging the environment so as to encourage the performance of a behavior the child has in his repertoire but does not display.

Mager and Pipe (1970) have a paradigm that is useful to consider in looking at the question of assessment for social skill instruction. They suggest that problem behavior (in this case, lack of social skill in some area) may exist because the desired behavior is not known or has not been taught, because the reinforcing conditions are not sufficient to encourage the behavior, or because there is reinforcement for the undesirable problem behavior. A social skill may, thus, be missing because the child lacks information or ability to perform the behavior, because the environment does not provide sufficient encouragement for the behavior even though he may know how to do it, or because there is a payoff for not carrying out the desired social behavior. Beyond this, another related reason for not engaging in a desirable social skill may be the existence of unpleasant feelings such as fear or anxiety associated with the behavior performance, which are avoided by avoiding the behavior. For example, a child may fail to assert himself constructively in a conflict with another child because he does not know how to go about saying or doing appropriately assertive things, because he does not perceive any benefits from saying or doing something he knows how to do, or because, by withdrawing in a nonassertive way, he is able to avoid the anxiety he may experience by taking risks in conflict situations. It could be argued that most behaviors defined as social skills have some goal associated with them, and a child may be faced with having to choose from among several competing goals. In attempting, through assessment, to determine which of these possible alternatives is operating (i.e., whether the problem is one of skill deficit or motivation), the teacher or clinician can determine the most appropriate intervention.

In the assessment of social skills, there are many problems that interfere with obtaining valid and reliable measures. One of these is that many behaviors are situation specific; a child may display a behavior in one situation but not in another. Such a discrepancy may exist because the conditions that encourage the behavior are different or are perceived by the child to be different in differing situations. In this context, the question of whether one is assessing knowledge of a social skill or ability to perform the behavior becomes an issue. As Bandura (1977b) pointed out, because people learn many behaviors by observing others, a child may have some cognitive understanding of what would be desirable social behaviors but may not be able to translate the behaviors into actions. It becomes necessary, therefore, to assess both the child's knowledge of a behavior and whether he can perform it under appropriate circumstances. Because motivational factors in the form of reinforcing conditions in the environment may also have some effect on the child's performance of a social behavior, it would seem that the most accurate assessment of performance would take place under highly reinforcing circumstances. Hence, the teacher or practitioner also needs to know what contingencies of reinforcement are operating in order to structure assessment situations in a way to make them highly positive.

A further problem in the assessment of social skills is that of reliability among different persons. There are many sources of data about a child's social behavior, including a variety of adults, peers, and the child himself. Various studies have determined that there is often little agreement between researchers and parents, between parents and teachers, and between adults and children in their ratings of subjects on social behavior. Children's self-perceptions about their social behavior do not correlate highly with others' perceptions, but the child's view is still an important piece of assessment information, particularly in relation to motivation for change and response to social skills teaching.

In addition to problems with validity and reliability related to situational aspects of social skill performance, as was pointed out in the preceding chapter, there are wide variations among persons and groups about what is regarded as acceptable social behavior on the part of children. Such lack of agreement creates problems in establishing criteria for determining when a behavior should be taught or defining criteria for mastery of a newly taught behavior. Developmental levels must also be taken into consideration in establishing criteria. A high school student might be considered to have good greeting skills if he can (a) establish eye contact, (b) smile, (c) say "hello," (d) provide his name, (e) ask for or say the other person's name, and (f) extend his hand and shake hands. A preschool child might be considered to have adequate greeting skills with only the first three or four behaviors.

In discussing criteria, it could be argued that it is sufficient for the teacher or clinician to determine only whether the behavior occurs at all in the desired situations. If the behavior does not occur or occurs very infrequently in a given siguation, then teaching the behavior in that context seems indicated. If the behavior occurs with low frequency and with poor quality, teaching the behavior may also be indicated, in order to increase the child's ease with the behavior. For example, a child who is only able to greet an adult with stammering and lack of eye contact may need practice in greeting skills based on the quality of the responses, even though he demonstrates that he knows what to say.

Of the assessment methods that will be outlined, some involve questionnaires or rating scales of various kinds that can be completed by those knowledgeable about the child: the teacher, parent, other children, or the child himself. Other methods involve observing the child's actual performance of various behaviors, either in the natural environment or in a situation set up to be analogous to the natural environment. Still other procedures involve ways to test the child's knowledge of social responses, apart from whether or not he can actually perform the behaviors in social situations. Assessment procedures selected by the practitioner depend on several factors; for example, (a) the nature of the behavior being assessed, (b) whether one is assessing an individual child or a group of children, (c) what other resources, in terms of observers and equipment, are available, (d) the availability of informants knowledgeable about the child, and (e) the developmental level of the child and his ability to read and to provide self-reports.

Because there are problems of validity and reliability with most social skill assessment approaches, the accuracy of assessment results is enhanced by the use of multiple methods rather than a single method, more than one setting, and input from more than one person. In addition to multiple methods of assessment, as pointed out by Ollendick and Hersen (1984), there needs to be assessment of "multiple targets of change," that is, overt behaviors, affective states, and thoughts or cognitions, because all contribute to social competence and learning social skills. In the material that follows, social behavior assessment approaches to be employed by adults knowledgeable about the child, primarily teachers and parents, are outlined first. These are followed by peer assessment techniques, those based on self-reports, and finally approaches to be used for assessment of cognitive and affective behaviors.

## ASSESSMENT BY ADULTS

Methods most commonly used by knowledgeable adults in assessing a child's observable social behaviors include a variety of scales, inventories, and observation techniques. The observations can be made in the natural environment or in situations structured to produce the behaviors of interest. In the next section some of the most commonly used standardized instruments are described, followed by inventories associated primarily with social skills curriculum materials, and individually tailored rating scales designed for specific situations.

### Behavior Checklists and Rating Scales

A first step in the formal assessment process may be the employment of rating measures or checklists, wherein individuals closely associated with the child—such as parents, teachers, or mental health workers—indicate the presence, absence, or extent of certain behaviors in the child's repertoire. In format, checklists tend to be binary (i.e., involve one of two responses indicating whether the behavior does or does not exist) and rating scales provide more choices along a continuum indicating the extent of the behavior. As an initial procedure, checklists or ratings are generally considered to be a method of screening for identification rather than indepth comprehensive assessment of social competence. Rating instruments may be classified according to either the person providing the behavior evaluation or the nature of the reporting form, as well as by content and subject of the rating. Behavior checklists or rating scales can be published versions (usually backed up with data related to validity and reliability) or instruments devised by the practitioner to meet a specific need. Social skills inventories designed for teaching programs can also be used as checklists for assessment.

As adults closely associated with children, teachers are often called on for behavior ratings, and there is evidence that teacher ratings compare favorably with other kinds of assessment of social behavior (Bolstad & Johnson, 1972; Greenwood, Walker, & Hops, 1977; Greenwood, Walker, Todd, & Hops, 1979). Some research indicates that there is wide individual variation among teachers on accuracy of ratings, and Reardon, Herson, Bellack, and

Foley (1979) suggest that accurate reports from teachers depend on the extent of opportunities to observe the relevant behavior. An advantage of teacher ratings, as pointed out by Beck (1986), is that teachers observe children in a standardized environment, which enables them to make comparisons among children of the same developmental level.

Parents are the other group of adults most often called on to provide assessment data. There are also problems with reliability of parent reports; parent reports typically do not correlate highly with other measures. Parents may not have experience with various types of deviant behavior and may either overreact to or underreport deviant child behaviors (Beck, 1986). Humphreys and Ciminero (1979) suggest, however, that parent reports should be included and compared with other assessment data because parent perceptions and attitudes may be part of the problem requiring remediation.

Behavior checklists and rating scales have certain advantages. They are easy to administer and easy to analyze, making it possible to use copies of the same instrument to obtain responses from several different informants on the same child. For example, one child could be rated by his parents, his teacher, his school counselor, and so forth. A comparison of the multiple responses would aid in identifying the most salient behaviors to address and some understanding of how the child functions in various settings. To be most useful, rating scales should have items that are clearly enough defined to have the same meaning for all raters, should be descriptive rather than inferential, should be relatively simple and quick to complete, should have established reliability and validity, and should take age and sex differences into account (Rie & Friedman, 1978).

*Standardized Instruments*

Behavior checklists and rating scales, both published and unpublished, exist in large numbers. Walls, Werner, Bacon, and Zane (1977) discovered over 200 and published a review of 166 of these. Their list left out a number of familiar instruments. Many checklists and rating scales have been subjected to research to determine their reliability and validity. Some of those most often used in social skills assessment are described here.

The Quay–Peterson Behavior Problem Checklist (Quay & Peterson, 1975), a 55-item rating scale for children and adolescents, emerged from the identification of problem behaviors among normal public school children (grades K-8) and special populations (institutionalized juvenile delinquents, children in classes for the emotionally disturbed, and children seen in child guidance clinics). An analysis of these behaviors resulted in four major factors: The first factor, *conduct disorder*, is characterized by restlessness, attention-seeking, and disruptiveness. *Personality problem*, the second factor, refers to behaviors such as self-consciousness and feelings of inferiority. The third factor, *inadequacy-immaturity*, includes preoccupational and attentional deficits; behaviors such as gang membership and school truancy make up the fourth factor, *socialized delinquency*. Although the authors state that the items refer to easily observable behavior, the items tend to refer more to classes of behavior such as impertinence, irritability, and irresponsibility than to specific responses. The original Quay–Peterson checklist has undergone extensive empirical validation, and it has recently been revised (Quay–Peterson, 1983). Its value appears to reside primarily in its usefulness for classifying children according to the four categories of social/emotional disturbance rather than the identification of specific behavior deficits.

An instrument that provides for the rating of more specific behaviors is the Walker Problem Behavior Identification Checklist (WPBIC) (Walker, 1970). Standardized on fourth, fifth, and sixth grade children, this checklist is designed to identify children with behavior problems severe enough to classify them as emotionally disturbed. The checklist contains 50 items that have been factored into five scales of disturbed behavior: (a) acting-out, (b) withdrawal, (c) distractibility, (d) disturbed peer relations, and (e) immaturity. One feature of this scale is that it discriminates between boys and girls, allowing for more "problem" behaviors among boys because this is "typical" in the general population. A girl who receives a score of 12 or higher could be considered maladjusted, whereas a boy would need a score of 22 for the same classification, suggesting an interesting distinction that may change as sex roles become redefined in our culture. In terms of social skill instruction, the WPBIC provides a pupil profile according to the five scales, enabling the examiner to identify problem areas that could receive further attention for both assessment and instruction.

The Child Behavior Checklist (CBCL) (Achenbach & Edelbrock, 1983) contains 118 items and is designed for children 4–16 years of age. Data are to be provided by parents or parent surrogates. There are three social competence scales: (a) *activities*, the amount and quality of the child's involvement in jobs and chores, in sports, hobbies, and games; (b) *social*, the quantity and quality of the child's social activities with others, and (c) the *school scale*, for school-age children only, assessing the quality of school performance and any related problems. Accompanying forms include the 113-item Teacher's Report Form and the 97-item Direct Observation Form. The CBCL has been subjected to considerable empirical investigation and found to have high test–retest reliability and high agreement between parents. There are also considerable normative data available. The CBCL has the limitation that the scales and many of the items are global rather than specific, but it does focus on social competence. When combined with the related teacher forms, it provides an opportunity to compare more than one kind of assessment and compare ratings of both parents and teachers.

A recently developed rating scale, the Matson Evaluation of Social Skills for Youth (MESSY) (Matson, Rotatori, & Helsel, 1983), is specifically designed for assessing social behavior. It uses items fitting the definition of social skills selected from standardized instruments, such as those described previously. The scale was developed through research with children ages 4–18. Teachers are to rate 64 items on a five-point scale as to how often the child demonstrates the behavior. There is also a self-report version. Sample items include

- Becomes angry easily.
- Gripes or complains often.
- Brags about self.
- Slaps or hits when angry.
- Helps a friend who is hurt.
- Is a sore loser.
- Smiles at people he or she knows.
- Asks questions when talking with others.
- Explains things more than needs to.
- Talks a lot about problems or worries.
- Thinks that winning is everything.

The MESSY is a relatively new scale that has promise for the assessment of social skills because its focus is specific to social behavior. With some exceptions that call for considerable inference on the part of the adult rater (e.g., "Feels angry or jealous when someone else does well...Is afraid to speak to people...Thinks good things are going to happen."), the items describe observable behavior.

There are numerous other commonly used measures for assessing overt behaviors. Some of these include the Devereux Behavior Rating scales (Spivack & Swift, 1967); the Pittsburgh Adjustment Survey Scales (Ross, Lacey, & Parton, 1965); The Missouri Children's Behavior Checklist (Sines, Parker, Sines, & Owen, 1969), designed for parents; the Louisville Behavior Checklist (Miller, 1967), also designed for parents; and the School Behavior Checklist (Miller, 1972). Some behavior scales are designed for special populations; for example, the AAMD Adaptive Behavior Scale (Lambert, Windmiller, Cole, & Figueroa, 1974), which is intended specifically for persons with mental retardation, and the Conners Teacher Rating Scale (CTRS), and Conners Parent Rating Scale (CPRS) (Conners, 1970), designed to measure hyperactivity and evaluate the effects of drug therapy.

*Instruction–Evaluation Inventories*

A number of social skills curricula have checklists or inventories that can be useful either for pre- or postevaluation of the application of the curriculum or as independent assessment instruments. One example is the Social Behavior Assessment (SBA) (Stephens, 1980), a 136-item inventory corresponding to skills to be taught in the social skills in the classroom curriculum (Stephens, 1978). It is designed to be completed by an informed teacher or classroom observer. Scores denote areas in which instruction is needed. The items were developed through a social validation process (Milburn, 1974), and there is good evidence for reliability and validity (Stephens, 1981; Gresham & Elliott, 1984). (See Appendix C, Social Skills List, for the specific skills on which the SBA is based.)

Similar instruments include the PEERS Program Social Interaction Rating Scale (SIRS) (Hops et al., 1978) developed for withdrawn children; the RECESS program (Walker et al., 1978), which is a rating scale related to a curriculum for aggressive children; and the ACCEPTS Placement Test (Walker et al., 1983), involving 28 items corresponding to the ACCEPTS social skills curriculum. The rating received by the child on each item suggests whether the child should receive instruction in that skill. Another example is the skill checklist developed for use with Goldstein's structured learning curriculum (McGinnis & Goldstein, 1984).

*Informal Scales and Inventories*

In assessing social skills, one is often concerned only with particular aspects of the child's interpersonal skills, such as the ability to participate in a group project with a peer, engage in a conversation with an adult, demonstrate an ability to make friends, or show appropriate affect in various situations. Here, the examiner is concerned with identifying the specific responses that constitute that general behavior or attitude and with determining the presence of that response in the child's behavioral repertoire, rather than describing the child along the entire range of interpersonal social skills. For such purposes, the most practical checklists are probably those developed by the practitioner.

Mager (1972) provides a model for developing observable objectives for nonobservable goals. For example, perhaps the concern is for the child to demonstrate a more "positive attitude" toward his peers. Once the goal is stated, the next step is to determine the specific behaviors children exhibit that are indicative of positive peer attitudes. Responses may include smiling at peers, giving compliments, participating in games with peers, making positive statements about peers, and helping peers when asked. After progressing through various steps of refinement, a list of observable behaviors is produced that can be used as a checklist for the designated behavioral goals. Thus, for the goal of positive attitudes, a specific behavioral listing may include responses such as those listed above as well as additional ones specific to the child and setting. For example, an examiner-constructed behavior checklist might state:

**Directions:**
For each of the listed behaviors, rate the child according to the following scale.

| | CHILD DEMONSTRATES: | | | |
| --- | --- | --- | --- | --- |
| NO SKILL 1 | LITTLE SKILL 2 | ADEQUATE SKILL 3 | GOOD SKILL 4 | CONSIDERABLE SKILL 5 |

*Politeness*

| | | | | |
| --- | --- | --- | --- | --- |
| 1. Makes eye contact | 1 | 2 | 3 | 4 | 5 |
| 2. Smiles | 1 | 2 | 3 | 4 | 5 |
| 3. Says thank you | 1 | 2 | 3 | 4 | 5 |
| 4. Says please | 1 | 2 | 3 | 4 | 5 |
| 5. Offers to assist others | 1 | 2 | 3 | 4 | 5 |
| 6. Makes appropriate apologies | 1 | 2 | 3 | 4 | 5 |
| 7. Addresses others appropriately | 1 | 2 | 3 | 4 | 5 |
| 8. Makes positive comments to others | 1 | 2 | 3 | 4 | 5 |

*Cooperation*

| | | | | |
| --- | --- | --- | --- | --- |
| 1. Follows group rules | 1 | 2 | 3 | 4 | 5 |
| 2. Complies with reasonable requests | 1 | 2 | 3 | 4 | 5 |
| 3. Takes turns | 1 | 2 | 3 | 4 | 5 |
| 4. Shares appropriately | 1 | 2 | 3 | 4 | 5 |
| 5. Participates in group activities | 1 | 2 | 3 | 4 | 5 |

This scale shows behavior categories analyzed into more specific responses on which the child is to be rated. With informally constructed scales, the examiner would concentrate on the behaviors that are of concern for a particular child or setting; for example, assessment in a residential setting might include more interpersonal, as opposed to task-related, behaviors, while the opposite would be more appropriate at a school. Finch, Deardorff, and Montgomery (1974) suggest that individually tailored behavior rating scales, such as the one just described, may be used for assessing and recording behavior change in settings where the staff has insufficient time to obtain ongoing observational data. They propose individualized rating scales made from descriptions of the subject's behavior gathered from knowledgeable people, clinical notes, the individual's self-descriptions, and direct observation. An individualized scale is consistent with criterion-referenced procedures, in that the assessment focuses on the child's ability to perform the particular skill rather than comparing the child to his peers, as with the previously described standardized scales.

Behavior checklists are quick, easy-to-administer screening devices for children and adults. Although they may be useful in documenting global impressions, they have limitations for social skills assessment. Checklists and rating scales are subject to bias on the part of respondents, as well as to errors related to respondents' ability to remember accurately. Checklists are useful as pre- and posttest measures if items are highly specific. Despite various shortcomings, behavior checklists can be of value as an initial procedure in assessing social skills and deficits, particularly in combination with other assessment measures.

## Observation of Performance

The most obvious (but not necessarily the easiest) way to assess the performance of social behaviors is to observe the child and see what he or she does. Behavioral observation, according to Wildman and Erickson (1977) is often regarded as the "ultimate validity criterion" against which other forms of assessment are measured. Because of the differences in behavior in different situations, it may be necessary to gather observational data from persons who see the child in different contexts. The following discussion includes procedures for assessing behaviors in the natural environment and in contrived situations, which include the interview and analogue measures.

### Assessing in the Natural Environment

Observing the child in everyday surroundings produces a wealth of information of varying degrees of relevance. In order to capture and process all the data available through observation, a number of different methods have been devised. One approach to documentation of observation is a written description, in the form of diaries or narratives, sometimes called *continuous recording*. Bijou, Peterson, and Ault (1968) suggest a four-column format for this kind of recording, which involves documenting the time, antecedent events, child responses, and consequent events. Recording events in a temporal sequence makes it possible not only to describe specific behaviors but also to form hypotheses about the relationships between a behavior and its antecedents and its consequences. Such hypotheses, in relation to social skills, are particularly useful in determining the conditions that facilitate the expression of desirable social behaviors.

Narrative recording is used to describe any behaviors that occur, without focusing on particular behavior. Methods for systematic recording of specific behaviors include (a) event recording by means of tally marks, wrist counters, and other counting devices; (b) duration recording; (c) time sampling techniques involving time intervals; and (d) the use of coding or rating systems related to the observed behavior.

Assessing social skills, particularly as alternatives to some identified problem behaviors, usually involves dealing with nonexistent or low-frequency behaviors. Mann (1976) suggests that event recording—that is, the recording of each occurrence of each event (behavior)—is a preferred process with infrequent behaviors. It is probably the simplest method, requiring only a means of recording and a set of discrete behaviors that can be reliably identified by the observer. The kinds of social skills that might be documented using event recording could include, for example, asking or answering questions, greeting skills, raising hand in class, or saying "please" and "thank you".

Cooper (1981) details a set of devices and procedures for event recording that include (a) a counter, such as a golf counter, worn on the wrist, (b) a hand-tally digital counter, such as the grocery store counter, (c) a "wrist tally board," which is a notepad worn on the wrist or clothing of the observer or the child, and (d) objects such as buttons or paper clips that can be transferred from one place to another (pockets, for example), when the event occurs; a simple clipboard, paper, and pencil could also be used. Eisler (1976) suggests that for the most reliable recording, the observer should limit the number of behaviors recorded to no more than two at a time.

Duration recording, or recording how long the behavior occurs, is more appropriate for social behaviors that occur for an extended period and that have a clearly defined beginning and end. Cooper (1981) also suggests duration recording for behaviors that occur at high rate, such as rocking, running, tapping objects. Duration recording is useful when the teaching goal is to lengthen or shorten the period of time. For example, one might wish to lengthen the amount of time the child spends in constructive play or in conversation with peers or shorten the amount of time the child delays before complying with an adult request. A watch or wall clock with a second hand or, ideally, a stop watch are generally used for duration recording, along with a means of noting the numbers obtained. Cooper (1981) suggests that duration recording may be used in two ways: as a simple time duration (e.g., 5 minutes); or as a percentage of some specified time period, obtained by dividing the total time into the recorded time duration.

A time sampling or interval recording process involves recording the occurrence or nonoccurrence of a behavior during or at the end of a specified time interval. It is used when it is not practical to observe for extended periods of time, for high-rate behaviors, or behaviors that do not have a clear-cut beginning or end. Interval recording, to be accurate, requires considerable training of observers and practice, and it requires the observer's undivided attention. It gives an estimate of frequency or duration of behavior across time intervals.

Many methods of observational recording are complex and, thus, more appropriate to a research setting, where more resources are available. One such method, often used in research related to social behavior, involves the application of codes or checklists for recording, which helps to enhance agreement among observers as well as condense the vast amount of observational data in any social situation. Foster and Ritchey (1979) point out that observational code categories referring to specific behaviors help to minimize the need for inference. They point further that "reliability of observational data is largely under experimenter rather than subject control and can be enhanced with code refinements and good observer training (p. 630)." At the same time, codes tend to omit data related to situational factors (Michelson, Foster, & Ritchey, 1981). The use of codes requires clear objective definitions of behavior and observers trained to use the code. There are few, if any, commonly used codes for recording social skills. Michelson et al. (1983) suggest that existing observation codes vary considerably in the behaviors observed and complexity of observation systems because of factors such as "situational specificity and the idiosyncratic characteristics of social behavior" (p. 17). These authors have developed a social skills observation checklist, and Michelson and DiLorenzo (1981) have developed a peer interaction observation code for assessing children's behavior in semistructured settings. The use of more than one observer to establish reliability related to interobserver agreement is considered essential in gathering accurate data. Individual perceptions can be biased by expectations and prejudices, and observers can vary in their speed and efficiency in recording.

Considerable concern is expressed in empirical circles about the reactive effect of observation, or the possibility that the fact of observation will serve to change the observed behavior. To lessen reactive effects, observation should be as unobtrusive as possible. Kent and Foster (1977), in reviewing studies on reactivity of observation procedures, conclude that, although the presence of an observer may sometimes affect the observed behavior, such findings are not always present, and not all behaviors are affected by observers. Some data suggest that when reactivity is present, such effects usually occur at the beginning of observation but weaken over time. For social skills assessment, where the goal is to determine skills and deficits for teaching purposes, observation effects could be considered an asset if they serve to strengthen the incentives operating in the assessment situation and, thus, motivate the child to display his most positive behaviors.

For more detailed information regarding observation techniques, the following resources might be consulted: Barton and Ascione, 1984; Cooper, 1981; Gelfand and Hartman, 1984; Kent and Foster, 1977; and Wildman and Erickson, 1977.

### Permanent Products

Cooper (1974) defines permanent products as tangible evidence of behavior that can be measured after the behavior occurs. Although permanent products may have more applicability in academic assessment, there are approaches to social skill assessment through observation that involve a product. Because behavior goes by quickly and accurate observations are difficult, an increasingly practical means of assessing behaviors in the natural environment involves the use of video- and audiotapes to capture the behavior and make it accessible for later evaluation. Such devices are particularly useful for the researcher, where reliability of assessment is a concern. In a social skills program to increase appropriate dinnertime conversation, for example, tape recordings were made at home during the dinner hour and analyzed according to conversational categories, making possible both assessment and ongoing evaluation (Jewett & Clark, 1976). Audio- and videotapes are also valuable where the behaviors of more than one child are being assessed at a time. For the teacher and therapist, video- or audiotape recording can be a useful tool in assessing the child's social skill deficits, in enabling the child to assess his or her own skill deficits, and in demonstrating improvements by comparing tapes before and after training.

Permanent products play a role where behaviors to be assessed in the natural environment cannot be directly observed but must be inferred from observable results; for example, assessing the degree of a child's compliance with a request to clean his room. Other social skills may involve the production of a product; for example, the ability to write a thank you note or take a phone message, or the tangible results of a group project designed to assess ability to work cooperatively in a group and share materials.

### Setting Up "Contrived" Situations

Because it is sometimes inefficient to wait for a behavior to occur in the natural environment in order to collect observational data, Stephens (1978) suggests arranging the natural environment in such a way as to require or facilitate the behavior, then watching for its occurrence. An example of such a contrived assessment situation would be that for the skill "to share toys and equipment in a play situation" (p. 293):

> During a free-play or recess period, have the target student play with some available toys or equipment alone for a short time. Then send another student over to play with the same toys or equipment. Observe whether the first (target) student willingly allows the second to play with the toys, and if he plays together with the second student. Or, establish a small group activity, such as drawing pictures with one set of magic markers or pens given to target student for all to share. Observe target student for sharing behavior.

One might observe how a child handles winning or losing by setting up a competitive game, or one might establish a task-oriented group in order to assess, for example, the child's ability to follow rules related to the task, ask permission to use another's property, stay on task, share materials, work cooperatively, ask for and give help, use "please" and "thank you."

A systematic and structured approach to the contrived naturalistic scene is that used in research by Wood, Michelson, and Flynn (1978), as described in Michelson et al., 1983, and Beck, Forehand, Neeper, and Baskin (1982) in which trained confederates are used. This strategy has been described by Michelson et al. (1983) as a "candid camera" method. In the Beck et al. study, skill at entering a group is assessed by directing a child to join two peers who are playing a game. The peers have been instructed in responses that vary, depending on the approach behaviors exhibited by the subject. The Wood et al. measure, the children's behavioral scenario (CBS), is a contrived interview to be conducted by an adult. It involves both questions to elicit assertive or nonassertive responses and arrangement of the physical environment in ways which invite assertive or nonassertive behaviors. The contrived aspects of the environment, for example, include inviting the child to sit down in the only available chair, which is covered by an attache case, or asking the child to write something, offering him or her a pencil with a broken point.

This assessment approach is easy and efficient, its main disadvantage being an ethical one. Michelson et al. (1983) suggest that because this kind of assessment involves deception, it is important that children be debriefed afterward, that parental approval be obtained, and that there be no harmful aspects to the experience.

### The Interview as an Assessment Situation

The clinical interview is a common form of assessment, which can yield useful initial information about a child's social skills. The interview as a method for assessing social skills has not received a great deal of empirical attention, but as Gresham and Elliott (1984) point out, children are often referred for social skills instruction after data have been gathered through interviews with parents or teachers. Interviews with adult sources can provide important information related to the child's social skill deficits and the conditions under which various social behaviors are exhibited or are lacking. Similarly, interviews with parents and teachers can add to the social validity of assessment data in revealing what social behaviors in the child they are likely to approve of and reinforce. Such interviews can be most productive and the data gathered most accurate if questions are somewhat standardized and oriented toward gathering specific information. One outline, such as the following adapted by Burke and DeMers (1979, p. 56) from Kanfer and Saslow (1965, 1969), could be adapted to gathering information about a child's social behaviors:

1. *Initial analysis of the problem situation.* A preliminary formulation of client behaviors into problematic (i.e., behavioral excesses and deficits) and nonproblematic behaviors (i.e., client strengths and assets).
2. *Clarification of the problem situation.* A more intensive analysis of the problem behaviors in terms of who defines them as problems (e.g., client, parent, teacher, etc.), under what conditions these behaviors occur, and what consequences result if the behavior is changed or remains unchanged.
3. *Motivational analysis.* Identification of specific incentives and inhibitors of behavior which have successfully influenced this client in the past.
4. *Developmental analysis of client and problem behavior.* A case-history type review of significant biological and/or social factors which may have led to current functioning.

5. *Analysis of client's self-control abilities.* Exploration of degree to which the client can control his unacceptable behavior when motivated to do so.
6. *Analysis of social relationships.* Exploration of significant others in the client's life and the interactions and influences exerted between the client and the significant others.
7. *Analysis of the social-cultural-physical environment.* Exploration of how expectations, values, and physical surroundings may be influencing the client's behavior.

An interview with a child might be considered one kind of contrived situation that can provide observational data on a variety of social behaviors as well as self-report information. Interviews with children old enough to be verbal provide self-report content related to how the child regards his own social behavior and perceives his own strengths and deficits in dealing with others. Perhaps just as important, it can serve as an opportunity to observe the social skills that are manifested in the interview situation. These can include, for example,

- The child's ability to sit quietly, pay attention to the adult, maintain eye contact, listen.
- The child's ability to communicate about his behaviors and feelings, ability to describe situations and his role in them, his ability to put thoughts into words, his vocabulary, his voice quality and articulation, the length of his answers, the relevance of his replies, his ability to initiate as well as respond.
- The nature of affect displayed by the child, whether he is comfortable in a one-to-one situation with an adult, his greeting skills.

A small group interview reveals a different set of behaviors for observation, especially those related to peer interactions:

- The nature of the child's interaction with peers, whether he initiates or follows, whether he is easily influenced into group misbehavior, how he participates in a group task.
- The nature of the child's verbal behavior with peers, whether he initiates and carries on conversations, makes relevant comments, listens to others, is positive with peers.

In addition to observational information, it is possible to assess the child's knowledge of appropriate social behaviors by structuring the content of the interview around questions related to social behaviors. Eisler (1976) provided a list of interpersonal behavior situations that might be explored in an interview with adult clients about their history of interpersonal response patterns. Adapted to children, the list could include

1. The ability to express opinions contrary to those of peers, parents, teachers;

2. The ability to ask favors of someone;
3. The ability to initiate conversations with peers and adults;
4. The ability to refuse unreasonable requests from friends and strangers;
5. The ability to invite a peer to play;
6. The ability to compliment someone;
7. The ability to receive compliments;
8. The ability to ask for help in solving problems;
9. The ability to resist pressure from peers to behave in an unacceptable way.

   In the treatment of an adult, the interview is probably the primary source of information about the client. When dealing with children, the interview may present special problems. Responding to another person in a one-to-one interview situation involves a complex set of communication skills, which the child may not yet possess. Children are considerably less likely than adults to be able to engage in self-monitoring of feelings and responses and to be able to report about them to someone else. In addition, children seldom present themselves to a teacher or therapist expressing concern about their own problems or behavior deficits. A discussion oriented toward identifying their difficulties can potentially engender resistance and avoidance. To counter such responses, Goldman, L'Engle Stein, and Guerry (1983) stress the need for the interviewer to keep the child comfortable through an attitude of acceptance and the use of techniques to relax the atmosphere, such as lessening demands, allowing the child to move around, or taking a break for snacks. It is often useful to have food and play materials, such as clay and crayons, available to help make the interview situation less formal.

   Evans and Nelson (1977) have suggested that, because of the child's limited behavioral repertoire, the skill of the interviewer in communicating with children is particularly important. In interviewing children, the typical approach of asking questions is often inhibiting and counterproductive (Dillon, 1979). As alternatives to direct questions in an interview, he proposes the use of declarative statements, phrases, deliberate silences, nods, etc. Open-ended questions rather than those requiring a yes or no answer are generally recommended. Karoly (1981) suggests eliciting the child's participation through relating vague or exaggerated details of an episode of misbehavior, to encourage the child to present his view of the situation. Goldman et al. (1983) suggest that accuracy of "facts" stated by the child is less important than is understanding the child's point of view. They suggest that the interviewer summarize the child's statements and make sure the child agrees that they have been understood.

   To the extent that the child can recognize and talk about his or her interpersonal problems and conflicts, the interview can potentially help provide a rationale for social skills instruction and thus enhance the child's motivation. The interview has been criticized as a source of reliable social skills assessment data (Atkeson & Forehand, 1981; Rinn & Markle, 1979), with the suggestion that it can be combined with other assessment procedures. At the same time, it is perhaps one of the most easily available and convenient places to start gathering assessment information.

*Analogue Measures*

Because many social behaviors are difficult to structure and observe in a natural situation, an approach that has been used for many years to provide access to more complex or infrequent social behavior is the analogue, in particular a simulation or role play representing an interpersonal encounter. As an assessment technique, role playing has the advantages of permitting the practitioner to study the environmental conditions under which the response occurs as well as the response itself (Goldfried & D'Zurilla, 1969) and arrange a variety of conditions so that many responses can be assessed and studied. In addition, according to McFall (1977), analogue measures, such as role playing, enable the researcher to control extraneous variables, avoid the possibility of the harmful consequences, which could occur in similar real life situations, and offer the practical advantages of efficiency and economy.

Role playing is a dramatic process that involves several components (Corsini, 1966, p. 9):

1. *It is a close representation of real life behavior.* Although staged, every effort is made to reconstruct the natural conditions as closely as possible. The situations enacted are ones which the participant has either previously encountered or will very likely experience in the near future.
2. *It involves the individual holistically.* That is, the participant is required to respond totally to the situation. In role playing the participant must think or employ cognitions, he must respond emotionally or use feeling, and he must act or use drama.
3. *It presents observers with a picture of how the patient operates in real life situations.* This aspect provides assessment information so that the observer can determine skill competence under various social conditions.
4. *Because it is dramatic, it focuses attention on the problem.*
5. *It permits the individual to see himself while in action in a neutral situation.* Roleplaying provides a mechanism whereby the individual may analyze his own behavior and recognize how certain actions can trigger various responses (sometimes negative ones) from others.

Goldfried and D'Zurilla (1969) defined standards that have been used in the development of role play assessment instruments. These are (a) *situational analysis*, an environmental survey to identify the most meaningful, problematic situations that an individual typically encounters; (b) *response enumeration*, possible alternative responses to various problem situations; (c) *response evaluation*, which responses are most effective in receiving favorable reactions in the natural environment; (d) *development of measure-*

*ment format*, the mode of responses to be used by the child in order to assess competence in various social situations; that is, role playing, written responses, naturalistic observations, etc., and (e) *evaluation of the measure*, whether the assessment procedures adhere to recognized psychometric principles; that is, are valid, reliable, computed according to sound scoring procedures, and standardized so that they provide for performance comparisons across populations. Situation analysis and response enumeration are particularly important in role play assessment, because assessment research demonstrates that the quality of role playing increases when the person being assessed can relate to or identify with the assessment situation.

An example of role play tests using the Goldfried and D'Zurilla model mentioned above is that of Edelson and associates (Edelson & Cole-Kelly, 1978; Edelson & Rose, 1978). The authors identified problem conditions common to children and incorporated them into role play assessment scenes covering interpersonal skill in various situations. Another test that follows the Goldfried and D'Zurilla model is the Problem Inventory for Adolescent Girls (PIAG), in which extensive interviews were held with adults and adolescents to identify problem situations and responses (Gaffney & McFall, 1981).

*Role Play Assessment Instruments.* Common aspects of role play instruments for children include

- *Practice situation.* Prior to the actual testing situation, scenes are used to determine if the child understands what is expected. They can also be used as a mechanism for warming up to the role playing situation.
- *Standard script.* In order to ensure uniformity of testing conditions, scripts are developed and delivered by a narrator.
- *Prompts.* Following each scene presented by the narrator, a prompt is given to which the child is expected to respond. For example, a scene is described by the narrator in which the child is being teased, then the prompter actually delivers the taunting statement to which the child is to respond. Prompters who are within the child's peer group can provide an additional element of realism to the situation.
- *Videotaping and rating.* Videotaping the role played scene makes it possible to review and evaluate.

One of the most extensively researched role play instruments for children is the Behavioral Assertiveness Test for Children (BAT-C), which was developed by Bornstein et al. (1977) and has since been refined and modified; for example, in the Behavioral Assertiveness Test for Boys (BAT-B) (Reardon et al., 1979) and the Children's Interpersonal Behavior Test (CIBT) (Van Hasselt, Hersen, & Bellack, 1981). Focusing on assertive behaviors in school, examples from the original nine-scene instrument include (Bornstein et al., 1977, p. 186)

Female Model

> *Narrator*: "You're part of a small group in a science class. Your group is trying to come up with an idea for a project to present to the class. You start to give your idea when Amy begins to tell hers also."
>
> *Prompt*: "Hey, listen to my idea."
>
> *Narrator*: "Imagine you need to use a pair of scissors for a science project. Betty is using them, but promises to let you have them next. But when Betty is done she gives them to Ellen."
>
> *Prompt*: "Here's the scissors, Ellen."
>
> *Narrator*: "Pretend you loaned your pencil to Joannie. She comes over to give it back to you and says that she broke the point."
>
> *Prompt*: "I broke the point."

Michelson et al. (1983) have also developed a role play test (the Social Skills Role Play Test) for children, which corresponds to their Social Skills Observation Checklist and assesses several social skill areas.

In order to increase the similarity to the natural environment, role playing assessments may be provided through audio- or videotapes. Under these conditions, the individual must respond to various situations as presented on the tapes. Every effort is made to make the scenes realistic, employing theatrics, such as background sound effects, actors, and confederates who are as similar as possible to the type of person being described in the scene. For example, if the assessment situation consists of one child responding to another on the playground, noises would be included in the background and a child (confederate) would be used to record the comments to which the child being assessed would respond. Responses made by the child being assessed may be either oral or physical; it is assumed that the closer the approximations are to reality, the more natural will be the child's responses. A third alternative is paper-and-pencil responses in the form of multiple-choice questionnaires, where the child must indicate which of the listed behaviors he or she would perform under the conditions presented. Although somewhat more difficult for children, another type of paper-and-pencil response has an open-ended format, requiring the child to generate his or her own natural reaction to the taped situation.

Audio- and videotape assessment measures are considered to have special advantages in that (a) they more closely approximate real-life conditions, (b) it is possible to structure audiotapes to assess characteristics specific to a particular child, (c) they may be administered without an examiner present, (d) one may employ nonverbal as well as verbal communications with videotapes (Nay, 1977), and (e) they also make it possible to present identical stimuli in assessing more than one child. The most obvious disadvantages of using videotapes as an assessment tool are equipment costs and the time involved in staging scenes in order to obtain the desired effects. Furthermore, responding to the taped situations requires only single responses and does not allow for ongoing interaction. In live role playing the interaction may be continued beyond the initial response, resulting in a more thorough and, possibly more accurate, assessment of how the child would respond under such conditions.

Audio- and videotape assessment conditions are very similar to those in the previously described role playing; that is, the child is instructed how to respond, a narrative describing the situation is provided, a confederate actor makes a comment to which the individual being assessed must respond, and the response is made according to some predetermined mode. Despite the increased interest in audiovisual methods in social skill assessment, very few examples are found in the research literature, and these have been devised primarily to assess social competence in college students or adult mental patients rather than children. Examples of such measures are found in Arkowitz, Lichtenstein, McGovern, and Hines (1975) and Goldstein et al. (1973).

The use of role play tests for assessment of social skills has generated considerable debate. McFall (1977, p. 153) points out some of the limitations of analogue measures like role play tests:

> Analogue methods . . . invariably require certain compromises with reality. While they may help generate interpretable solutions to simplified experimental problems, their solutions may or may not have relevance for the "real life" problems that initially prompted the research. Reasoning by analogy necessarily involves making abstractions about certain ways in which two things seem to be similar, while ignoring all of the other ways in which they may be different. It is assumed that the abstracted similarities somehow capture the essence of the phenomenon being studied, and that little of essence is left among the overlooked differences. Whether the solutions generated by analogue methods actually have relevance, or external validity, is a function of the particular analogies chosen . . .

The validity of role play tests in predicting actual social behavior in real-life situations has been further questioned (Bellack, Hersen, & Lamparski, 1979; Bellack, Hersen, & Turner, 1978, 1979). Some of the particular limitations of these tests for children have been addressed by Van Hasselt et al. (1981) and Matson et al. (1983), who found little relationship between role play performance and other measures of social skills.

Bellack, Hersen, and Turner (1979) suggest that one factor limiting external validity of role play tests for children is children's lack of role taking ability or ability to respond in a role play situation as if it were an actual situation. They point out also the anxiety-arousing aspect of role playing, which could influence behavior "above and beyond the context of the simulated interaction (p. 677)". They hypothesize, additionally, that role play tests requiring more extended interactions than do those typically requiring only one response might enable the subject to respond in a more characteristic way.

Like all other social skill assessment approaches, role play tests have both advantages and limitations and are best used along with other measures.

## ASSESSMENT BY PEERS
### Sociometric Procedures

Along with parents and teachers, peers provide another important source of data about social behavior. Evaluations by peers are typically obtained through sociometric techniques. These procedures, designed to study group dynamics and relative social status, have been used in a variety of social situations. For children, they have been applied largely in the classroom, where the intent was initially to identify compatible groupings in order to facilitate learning. More recently, however, sociometric measures have been recognized as an effective tool for identifying and predicting social maladjustment in children and adolescents.

Sociometrics may be used to supplement other social skills assessment techniques in order to identify children with social skills deficits. Because researchers have established a relationship between childhood peer rejection and later-life social maladjustment, such as juvenile delinquency or emotional disturbance (Roff, Sells, & Golden, 1972), an apparent related use of sociometric assessment is for prediction. However, Foster, Bell-Dolan, and Berler (in press) point out that few of the studies demonstrating this relationship were based on sociometric measures, therefore, the predictive validity of sociometrics is yet to be established. Sociometric methods differ in format and are classified according to the way they are implemented; that is, nominations, paired comparisons, and roster-ratings (Hops & Lewin, 1984; Hymel, 1983).

*Nominations*
Nominations are the most commonly used and simplest form of sociometric assessment. Individual children are required to nominate their peers according to the degree of acceptance or nonacceptance. Positive measures and responses (e.g., "who do you like the most?") are generally preferred, but it has been determined that negative responses (e.g., "who do you like the least?") are also necessary, in order to distinguish between those who are disliked and those simply ignored. It has been shown that children who are not identified when using positive measures may not necessarily be rejected but rather overlooked during the selection process. In using peer nominations, the child typically is directed to identify three children he likes the most and then three children he does not like or likes least.

Obtaining valid peer nominations is a major consideration with sociometric assessments, especially with young children. Moore and Updegraff (1964)

developed a sociometric procedure for use with nursery school children ranging in age from 3 to 5 years. Individual interviews were conducted, wherein
the responding child was presented with a board containing individual pictures of each child in the group. The examiner assisted the child in identifying each picture, then the child was asked to find someone he especially
liked. After four choices were made, the child was directed to identify someone he didn't like very much for four more choices. Following this step, the
examiner pointed to the pictures of children not selected and asked the
responding child if he liked or disliked that child. Responses were scored
according to positives, negatives, and order of choice, with weights being
assigned to the respective choices. For example, a child selected first as being
liked received $+8$ points, while the first disliked child selected received $-8$.
Similarly, the second liked received $+6$ and second disliked $-6$, with the
remaining two points being 4 and 3. Positives and negatives selected as a
result of the examiner's pointing to them received $+1$ and $-1$ point. Com-
putation of the assigned points yielded composite sociometric scores for each
child, with well-liked children receiving the highest scores. In addition to
votes based on affect, peer choices can be made according to specific activities such as play and academic tasks. For example, children taking Miller's
(1977) Sociometric Preference Test might be given a list of classmates and
directed to "Choose five persons you would most like to work with" (p. 20).
The five choices are to be designated by ordinal numbers as illustrated.

| | |
|---|---|
| Mark A. | 3rd |
| Peter B. | |
| John B. | 4th |
| Mary C. | |
| etc. | |

As social competence data obtained from peers have gained in popularity,
there has been a corresponding increase in the sophistication of assessment
procedures and peer status categories as well. Initially, researchers focused
on targeting the socially isolated child, later moving into differentiating
within this group the rejected and neglected child (Gottman, 1977). Subsequently, Coie, Dodge, and Coppotelli (1982) conceptualized a five-category
peer status paradigm consisting of popular, rejected, neglected, controversial, and average children. Popular children are those who receive many
most-liked votes and few least-liked; rejected children receive many least-
liked and few most-liked votes; neglected children receive a few of both

most-liked and least-liked votes; controversial children receive many of both most-liked and least-liked votes; and average chldren are a referent group that falls midway between the other four extremes. Within this model, Coie et al. present the polar opposites of popular-rejected children and neglected-controversial children. Whereas neglected children, for example, received few acceptance or rejection nominations, controversial children received many of both. Although the controversial category is a point of contention (Newcomb & Bukowski, 1983), Coie (Coie & Dodge, 1983; Coie et al., 1982) asserts that controversial children are a distinct, high-risk group that should be considered in sociometric assessments. Controversial children are described as having leadership characteristics but are also disruptive, a profile consistent with juvenile delinquents.

A major limitation of sociometric procedures is that knowing a child's level of acceptance or rejection does not specify the personal attributes or shortcomings that contribute to the social status (Connolly, 1983; Foster & Ritchey, 1979; Hymel, 1983). Therefore, more structured peer assessments such as Who Are They (Bowman, DeHaan, Kough, & Liddle, 1956) and Class Play (Bower, 1960) are recommended. The Who Are They test requires each child to identify a classmate who he feels is best described by various statements designed to measure leadership, aggression, withdrawn behavior, and friendship. Sample items include: "Who are the good leaders?" and "Who are the boys and girls who make good plans?" Coie et al. (1982) adapted the Bower Class Play Test into 24 behavioral questions such as, "This person starts fights. He or she says mean things to other kids and pushes them and hits them" (p. 559). For each item the children in this study were to nominate three children they felt characteristically exhibited this type of behavior. These data yielded behavior correlates of cooperativeness, support, and physical attractiveness for accepted children, while the correlates for the rejected group were disruptiveness and aggression. Corroborating data are provided in other studies with upper elementary children (DiLorenzo & Foster, 1984) and preschool children (Quay & Jarrett, 1984). Similarly, Carlson, Lahey, and Neeper (1983) conducted a structured interview and found rejected children to be associated with antisocial behavior. Although positive behaviors tend to be associated with peer acceptance and negative behaviors with rejection, this relationship is not clear-cut. Foster, Delawyer, and Guevremont (in press), for example, found that while positive behaviors exceeded negative behaviors, grade-school children reported "friends" to perform a significant number of negative behaviors. In a study of the behavioral correlates of peer acceptance among non-LD elementary aged children toward an LD-labeled child, Cartledge et al. (1985) found that even though the positive behaviors of being kind and saying nice things were more commonly attributed to the LD child, that child was less likely to be selected for friendship and social interaction. Milich and Landau (1984) advise that aggressive children probably should be divided into subgroups of aggressive and aggressive–withdrawn. They found aggressive boys to be rejected but many of them were viewed positively, as well. On the other hand, aggressive–withdrawn boys, those with low peer interaction rates, had significantly higher rejection rates and were considered of greater risk for later adjustment problems.

An instrument designed for the sociometric evaluation of secondary students is the Adjustment Scales for Sociometric Evaluation of Secondary-School Students (ASSESS) (Prinz, Swan, Liebert, Weintraub, & Neale, 1978). ASSESS consists of five scales, each of which is analyzed into several observable behaviors considered to be indicative of this category. The scales and representative behaviors are (p. 497):

1. Aggression–Disruptiveness; e.g., "Are rude to teachers."
2. Withdrawal; e.g., "Are sort of ignored."
3. Anxiety; e.g., "Are nervous when called upon to answer in class."
4. Social Competence; e.g., "Can work well in a group."
5. Academic Difficulty; e.g., "Do poorly in school."

Students are expected to put an X beneath the names of peers they feel are characterized by these various descriptions. The authors report the instrument to be a reliable and valid peer assessment for adolescents.

*Paired Comparisons*

One concern with sociometric assessments through nominations is that children, particularly young children, will name peers impulsively or fail to nominate a peer due to not remembering that child's name. Paired comparison sociometric assessment is designed to circumvent these limitations. With this procedure, the names or pictures of only two peers are presented at a time, and the responding child is directed to indicate either a positive or negative nomination for one of the pair. Each child in the group is paired with every other child in the group, thus avoiding the possibility that a classmate might be overlooked and ensuring the stability of any particular nomination. Sociometric scores are derived according to the number of positive or negative choices each child receives from his or her peers. This procedure yields a large number of data points that contribute to the greater reliability of the paired-comparison measure (Hops & Lewin, 1984; Hymel, 1983).

An obvious disadvantage of paired-comparison assessments is the time needed for its administration. Vaughn and Langlois (1983) employed a complete paired-comparisons procedure with 40 preschool children. The individually administered assessments necessitated two to three 15-minute sessions. Total time estimates for this group assessment range from 20 to 30 hours. This is compared to the one 5-minute individual session required for an assessment using nominations (Hymel, 1983), which would have a total time estimate of $3\frac{1}{4}$ hours for the same population. A reliable and less time-consuming subsample approach developed by Cohen and Van Tassel (1978) still is considered to involve more time than nominations (Hymel, 1983).

*Roster and Rating*

A method used more with school aged children is the roster and rating sociometric questionnaire. The roster is an alternative to the more common fill-in instrument, where the child is expected to write in names of peers.

The roster-rating instrument provides children with a listing of classmates and a rating scale for indicating peer attitudes. The Spontaneous Choice Test (Miller, 1977), for example, specifies ratings according to a 3-point scale labeled "like," "dislike," and "indifferent." Opposite each name the child is expected to place a check based on which term most accurately conveys his/her feelings toward the child being rated. Upon encountering Mary J.'s name, for example, her best friend probably would check the column under like as shown below (adapted from Miller, 1977, p. 20):

|         | LIKE | DISLIKE | INDIFFERENT |
|---------|------|---------|-------------|
| Mary J. | ✔    |         |             |
| Others  |      |         |             |

The more popular format is the alphabetized roster with a 5- or 7-point scale following each name of each child in the group. The respondent is expected to rate each member listed on the scale according to how much he likes or dislikes the named child. Each child's score is the average of all of his ratings. This method is considered to have certain advantages in that it allows for ratings by all group members and, by providing ratings on a continuum, it avoids some of the unpleasant ethical aspects of negative ratings (Hymel & Asher, 1977). An example of a 5-point rating scale follows.

**Directions:**
How do you feel about your classmates? Circle the number that best tells how you feel about each classmate.

|          | I LIKE THIS PERSON A LOT. | I LIKE THIS PERSON. | DON'T KNOW VERY WELL. | DON'T CARE FOR THIS PERSON. | DON'T LIKE THIS PERSON AT ALL. |
|----------|------|------|------|------|------|
| John R.  | 5 | 4 | 3 | 2 | 1 |
| Roy P.   | 5 | 4 | 3 | 2 | 1 |
| Linda W. | 5 | 4 | 3 | 2 | 1 |
| Others   | 5 | 4 | 3 | 2 | 1 |

Ratings also tend to indicate general likeability of a peer, not whether that peer is chosen for friendship (Connolly, 1983; Schofield & Whitley, 1983). For example, in studying the effects of race on peer preferences in a desegregated setting, Scofield and Whitley found stronger racial preferences with peer nominations than with roster-rating measures. A meta-analysis conducted by Schofield and Whitley (1983) of previous research in this area corroborated their findings, supporting their contention that "peer nominations reveal friendships, whereas the roster-and-rating technique assesses interpersonal acceptance, a much less intimate form of relationship" (p. 243). Hymel (1983) points out that although rating scale scores are more highly related to social competence, they are less useful in identifying rejected children and determining social impact.

Sociometric techniques can be administered in various ways and appear to be useful in providing valuable information about children's social development. There are, however, several considerations or cautions to be noted for their implementation. For very young children, sociometric evaluations should be obtained through individual interviews, making certain the child understands the directions and responds properly. Similar procedures may be necessary for somewhat older children with special needs. By third grade, the child is probably able to make sociometric ratings through paper and pencil tasks. Another consideration important for school aged children is the preference for same sex and same race peers. For that reason, choices may be based largely on these variables rather than social interaction factors, and these variables need to be taken into account when analyzing the results. Foster et al. (in press) suggest that group designation may change depending on whether ratings are conducted according to same sex or include both sexes. They speculate that, by changing the gender of the raters, a rejected group in one study could become a neglected group in another study. Similarly, physical appearance plays a major role in peer assessments, particularly for girls, and thus may unfairly distort the social competence evaluations of individual subjects. With preschool children, Vaughn and Langlois (1983) also found physical attractiveness to correlate with social status, particularly for girls. Using pictures as part of a sociometric assessment may result in peer judgments of social competence being unduly biased by physical appearance.

In order to account for the tendency of children to base ratings of a peer on a recent negative experience, it is recommended that the sociometric procedure be administered two or more times over a period of weeks in order to obtain accurate results. Although positive nominations are generally the more preferred and reliable, negative nominations are necessary in order to discriminate accurately between rejected and overlooked children. One alternative to a "dislike" or "least-liked" statement is of the use of 5- or 7-point scales where children are required to rate on a continuum. Such alternatives may not be necessary, however, because empirical investigations do not support the notion of deleterious effects resulting from negative peer nominations (Hayvren & Hymel, 1984). Rating scales appear to be better indices of tolerance or likeability and, thus, may be a more appropriate peer measure of social skill but not of social impact. Ratings also seem to have greater reliability than those instruments that require children to write in or nominate the names of peers.

A final issue pertains to the biasing effect of parental consent. Foster et al. (in press) point out that consent is more likely to be obtained from parents with professional/managerial occupations whose children tend to fall within the average or above intelligence range. This phenomenon limits the opportunity for adequate study of the full range of peer interactions and potentially excludes children evidencing significant social skill deficits.

## SELF-ASSESSMENT

Another approach to social skills assessment is to involve the child in assessing his own social competence through the use of various scales, checklists, and self-monitoring techniques. Although one may question the child's ability to perceive accurately his own social behavior or his effect on others, these reports may provide valuable assessment data. The child's responses may be used to compare discrepancies between his self-perceptions and assessments of him made by others, to identify critical areas for instruction based on the child' misperceptions of his own behavior, and to determine changes in self-assessment pre- and posttreatment. Self-reports are observable behaviors in themselves.

There are numerous problems with self-reports. Gresham and Elliott (1984) stress that "children's self-report measures have not been found useful in predicting peer acceptance, peer popularity, teacher ratings of social skills, role play performance, or social behavior in naturalistic settings" (p. 297) and therefore should not be used for selection or outcome measures. Michelson et al. (1981) point out further that difficulties in reading and comprehension and developmental factors along with "misreading, misinterpretation, cheating, indifference, and external environmental factors" can all contribute to inaccurate self-assessment on the part of children. At the same time, the child's perception of himself is an important factor related to motivation for learning social behaviors and the lasting effects of social skills training.

The section that follows presents several means of obtaining self-report data related to social behavior, measures of self-esteem and perceived social competence, and procedures for self-monitoring social behavior.

## Self-Assessment of Social Behaviors

One kind of self-report measure that has been designed to assess overt social behaviors is the assertiveness scale. The Children's Assertive Behavior Scale (CABS) (Michelson et al., 1983) is a 27-item pencil-and-paper, multiple-choice instrument designed for elementary school age children. It measures specific responses to brief situations reflecting behavior categories such as empathy, conversation making, requests, and compliments. The authors report extensive data for this instrument indicating positive reliability and validity (Michelson & Wood, 1982). For each item, the child is required to choose one of five possible choices, indicating how he would respond in that situation if the "someone" in the situation was (a) another youth, or (b) an adult. The range of choices include very passive, passive, assertive, aggressive, and very aggressive. The authors have also developed a second instrument with the same items to be rated by the teacher. A sample item of the self-report instrument, with the responses labeled on an aggressive-passive continuum, might ask (Michelson et al., 1983, p. 222):

1. Someone says to you, "I think you are a very nice person."
   You would usually:
   a. Say "No, I'm not that nice." (very passive)
   b. Say, "Yes, I think I am the best!" (very aggressive)
   c. Say, "Thank you." (assertive)
   d. Say nothing and blush. (passive)
   e. Say, "Thanks, I am really great." (aggressive)

The Matson Evaluation of Social Skills for Youth (MESSY) (Matson et al., 1983), referred to earlier in the section on assessment by adults, is a self-report instrument that is broader in scope than the previous measure, focusing on a range of social behaviors and also feelings and cognitions. Instead of multiple choice, it requires children to rate themselves on a 5-point scale. The items are similar to those on the teacher scale it accompanies, but translated into the first person, that is, "I become angry easily." ... "I gripe or complain often."

## Self-Esteem Measures

Self-report scales dealing with self-concept or self-esteem attempt to measure the child's sense of him- or herself in terms of feelings of self-worth, acceptance, success, and competence in various areas. Such measures may be useful in assessing the effects of social skills training on children's views of themselves.

One such instrument, which has been widely used, is the Self-Esteem Inventory developed by Coopersmith (1967). The inventory contains 59 items, and for each one, the child is required to check whether that statement is like or unlike him. For example (p. 265),

|                                            | LIKE ME | UNLIKE ME |
|--------------------------------------------|---------|-----------|
| 1. I spend a lot of time daydreaming.      | ——      | ——        |
| 2. I'm pretty sure of myself.              | ——      | ——        |
| 3. I often wish I were someone else.       | ——      | ——        |
| 4. I'm easy to like.                       | ——      | ——        |

The Coopersmith instrument yields a total score that is interpreted as an index of self-esteem.

Another well-known self-regard instrument is the 80-item Piers–Harris Self Concept Scale (*The Way I Feel About Myself*) (Piers, 1984). This scale is also a unidimensional measure of children's self-concept, which can be used with a wide variety of ages from primary through secondary level and including special children. There are extensive data establishing reliability and validity. Children answer yes or no to such statements as "My parents expect too much of me...I am often mean to other people...I have a good figure...I am a good person."

A more recently developed instrument, The Perceived Competence Scale for Children (Harter, 1982), makes an attempt to measure the child's sense of personal competence across several domains rather than as a unitary concept. There are subscales for cognitive, social, and physical competence, and an independent subscale for general self worth. The 28-item scale can be used for elementary and junior high students. The question format is different from other self-worth measures in that it makes possible a broader range of responses and, thus, according to the author, reduces the tendency to give socially desirable responses. The example is from the general self-worth category (Harter, 1978, p. 2):

| Some kids feel good about the way they act. | BUT | Other kids wish they acted differently. |
|---------------------------------------------|-----|-----------------------------------------|
| Really true for me       Sort of true for me |     | Sort of true for me       Really true for me |
| ☐                        ☐                   |     | ☐                         ☐                |

Since one subscale specifically measures the child's perceptions of his or her social competence with peers, this instrument has particular relevance for social skill assessment. Harter reports a fairly high correlation between sociometric ratings and social subscale scores.

Other self-esteem measures are oriented more to older youth, for example the Self-Esteem Scale by Rosenberg (1965) and the Tennessee Self-Concept Scale (Fitts, 1965). Additional instruments are being developed to measure "self-efficacy" (Bandura, 1977a); that is, perceived social competence, for example, The Children's Self-Efficacy for Peer Interaction Scale (CSPI) (Wheeler & Ladd, 1982), which measures the child's view of his or her ability to use verbal persuasion in peer settings, and the Social Skills Self-Efficacy Scale (SSES) (Keane & Tryon, 1984), which is a more global measure of the child's perceived self-competence.

The validity of self-report measures of competence in relation to actual competence is open to question. Harter (1982) suggests, however, that low correlations between the child's perceived competence and indices of competence, such as teacher ratings and achievement tests, are not necessarily indicative of poor validity of the competence measure. She suggests that such findings "have implications for program-evaluation efforts, suggesting that a goal should be to foster a *realistic* sense of competence rather than enhancement per se. That is, reduction in the magnitude of discrepancy scores may be as critical as outcome variables as a mean increase in the competence score" (p. 96).

## Self-Monitoring

Self-monitoring, or having the child observe and record his own social behavior, is included as an assessment technique even though it has a number of limitations. Self-recording has been identified as reactive, since the child knows the target behavior and the purpose of the recording, and the self-recording can, thus, result in behavior change. Shapiro (1984) makes the point that it is difficult to differentiate between the use of self-monitoring as an assessment strategy and self-monitoring as intervention. In a number of studies, for example, self-recording alone has been successfully employed as an intervention to bring about positive behavior. Another major problem with self-monitoring is that of reliability. Self-recording can be monitored by others if the behavior is observable, and checking by others improves accuracy. If the child is recording private events, such as thoughts and feelings, however, reliability becomes more problematic.

Self-reporting is a skill that needs to be taught before it becomes a useful means of assessment. In teaching self-monitoring, it is necessary first to make sure the child can identify the presence of the target behavior when emitted, then provide the child with a means of recording the behavior. Any of the observation techniques included earlier could be used by the child with some instruction; for example, using a counter, a tally sheet, or a time piece to record frequency or duration of a specific behavior. A child trying to develop the skill of ignoring another child who teases him could, for example, record on a wrist counter his attempts at ignoring. Edelson and Rose (1978) used self-report procedures in which children developed a weekly diary of problem situations. One important aspect of self-monitoring instruction would be to teach the child to identify the situational events preceding and following the target behaviors. Mahoney (1977, p. 252) suggests the following sequence:

1. Give explicit definitions and examples of target events and explain their possible relevance to the problem(s) at hand;
2. Give explicit self-monitoring instructions (i.e., how to self-record);
3. Illustrate (model) self-monitoring with a sample form;
4. Ask the client to repeat the target definitions and self-monitoring instructions; and
5. Test their understanding by having them monitor several trial instances described by you.

For children, it seems particularly important for the behavior to be simple and easily defined and for only one behavior to be selected at a time. As discussed earlier, self-reports have questionable reliability as assessment tools and are most useful when combined with data from other sources. The skill of self-monitoring, however, may be useful in enhancing social functioning as well as in assisting in the generalization of social skills over time. Self-monitoring is discussed further in chapters 3 and 4.

## ASSESSMENT OF AFFECTIVE AND COGNITIVE BEHAVIORS

The point has been made earlier that thoughts and feelings are relevant to the instruction of social skills, because how children feel and think in social situations affects their social behavior, and because socialization involves learning culturally defined acceptable public ways to express these inner events. Because cognitions and affect are difficult to measure directly, assessment usually begins with verbal self-reports, even though these are difficult to validate independently. Self-reporting of inner events is a complex set of behaviors involving the ability to recognize and label one's own thoughts and feelings and report on them verbally to someone else. Programs to teach such behavior should be part of a social skills training program and may have to be carried out before self-reporting can be useful as an assessment technique. Roberts and Nelson (1984) point out the need to assess inner events in the context of developmental levels, since children improve on self-reporting skills as they grow older.

### Assessing Affect

Assessing affect has an advantage over assessing cognitions per se, in that there are physiological manifestations of feelings that can be more directly measured. Because physiological arousal accompanies such negative emotions as fear, anxiety, apprehension, and anger, bodily changes often take place that can be observed. Technological means such as measures of skin response and cardiac activity have been used in research studies with adults to measure physiological aspects of fear and anxiety. Practical considerations, however, make it unlikely that these will become popular assessment procedures with children in schools or clinical settings.

## Self-Reports of Affective Behavior

A number of scales and checklists have been developed for self-reporting affective states such as fear, anxiety, and depression. The same caveats exist for these self-report instruments as for others mentioned previously.

A scale developed for the self-reporting of anxiety by children is the Children's Manifest Anxiety Scale (CMAS) (Casteneda, McCandless, & Palermo, 1956). The CMAS has been revised by Reynolds and Richmond (1978) and renamed What I Think and Feel. Children respond to the 37 items by circling yes or no to statements such as "I worry about what is going to happen... I have bad dreams... I worry about what other people think about me." The General Anxiety Scale for Children and the related Test Anxiety Scale for Children, both by Sarason, Davidson, Lighthall, Waite, and Ruebush (1960) are similar in format. Another approach to the assessment of anxiety is the State–Trait Anxiety Inventory for Children (STAIC) and State–Trait Anxiety Inventory (STAI) for adolescents and adults (Spielberger, 1973). These scales involve two separate parts, one to measure "state" anxiety, feelings at a particular moment in time, and the other to measure "trait" anxiety by indicating the frequency of anxious behaviors.

In assessing anxiety and fear in adults, one common approach is the Fear Survey Schedule, in which the individual indicates on a scale the degree of his fear of listed objects or events. Many variations of the fear survey technique have been developed for use with different groups (Hersen, 1973). These scales have differing degrees of reliability and ability to predict adult behavior in potentially fear–inducing situations. A Fear Survey Schedule for Children developed by Scherer and Nakamura (1968) calls for children to rate their degree of fear related to such items as "Being in a crowd... The sight of blood... Strange-looking people."

Another approach to self-reporting of fear is Wolpe's (1958) Subjective Units of Discomfort Scale (SUDS), adapted by Walk (1956) with the concept of Fear Thermometer, on which children rate their responses in stressful situations on a scale from 0 to 100. A highly stressful situation has a SUDS rating of 100, while a low stress situation is closer to 0. The child is taught to recognize the difference in his feelings and physiological reactions along the SUDS continuum 0–100 in specific situations.

For assessing depression in children ages 7–17, the Children's Depression Inventory (CDI) (Kovacs, 1981) has been developed as a modification of the Beck Depression Inventory. The child rates statements reflecting depressive symptoms on a 3-point scale as to degree of applicability. The items are intended to reflect the child's feelings during the past week related to such symptoms of depression as insomnia, withdrawal, sadness, shame, pessimism; that is, "I have trouble sleeping every night... Things bother me all the time... I feel like crying every day." Another self-report instrument is the Children's Depression Scale (Lang & Tisher, 1978; Tisher & Lang, 1983), which contains similar depressive statements and includes positive statements as well. This instrument yields both a depressive score and a positive score, along with scores on a range of subscales representing different areas of depression.

## Affective Assessment by Adults and Peers

Although most measures of affect are self-reports, the behavioral manifestations of feelings lend themselves to assessment by others as well. For example, in the assessment of anxiety, the Test Anxiety Scale for Children (Sarason et al., 1960) has a teacher rating scale as well as the self-report scale. The Louisville Fear Survey for Children (Miller, Barrett, Hampe, & Noble, 1974) was developed to be used by either a parent, another adult, or the child as rater to indicate the intensity of fear generated by various stimuli. The Children's Depression Scale has an accompanying adult form intended for use by parents, teachers, etc., which makes it possible to compare the child and adult responses. An additional approach to assessment of depression is the Peer Nomination Inventory for Depression (Lefkowitz & Tesiny, 1980). According to the authors, this instrument correlates well with teacher and self-ratings. A sociometric measure, it is read aloud to a group of children who are instructed to draw a line through names on a class roster of classmates who can be described by questions such as "Who often plays alone? . . . Who thinks they are bad? . . . Who doesn't try again when they lose?" Along with 13 items describing depression, six additional items describe happiness and popularity.

Observation of facial expression and various "body language" manifestations of inner states is a frequent means of gathering data on affect in children. Many behaviors have been interpreted to be outward signs of inner reactions. Some of these include the condition of body stiffness or relaxation; the tensing of muscles of neck and shoulders; flushing; trembling hands or hand wringing; chewing fingers; nail biting; thumb sucking; stroking, twisting, or pulling out hair; biting or licking lips; frequent throat clearing; frequent trips to the bathroom or many drinks of water; heavy breathing, signs of anguish such as tears, wailing, moaning, or sobbing; signs of happiness such as smiling and laughing; speech indicators such as stammering, inability to speak out loud, hesitation in speech, voice tremors, talking to oneself; or physical symptoms such as headaches, stomachaches, or vomiting. A very stressed child may regress and wet or soil his pants. The hyperactive child may attempt to reduce feelings of anxiety through continual verbal and bodily activity. Conversely, a child in a state of panic can be immobilized and mute. And, of course, the child's face can present a variety of clues from which inferences about thoughts and feelings can be made. In reviewing studies predicting altruism and empathy from facial expression and gestures, Goldstein and Michaels (1985) conclude that use of facial expressions is a promising approach, stating that "trained raters can make reliable discriminations of emotions from children's...facial behavior." Glennon and Weisz (1978) devised a 30-item scale, the Preschool Observation Scale of Anxiety (POSA) using observable behavioral indicators such as those just outlined to assess anxiety in preschool children. In a study in which children were observed in a testing situation, they report high correlation of POSA scores with three independent measures of anxiety completed by parents and teachers. They also report sensitivity to situational variation in stressors, in that anxiety scores were significantly lower in a second session designed to be less anxiety-producing. Making use of overt manifestations such as those described above to assess inner events can have utility as a basis for hypotheses to be tested in other ways.

## Assessing Cognitive Behaviors

In the process of assessing cognitive factors relating to social skills, the goals are to determine whether the child has cognitive understanding of the behaviors being taught, whether he is engaging in faulty cognitions that interfere with desirable social behavior, or whether he is lacking in problem-solving strategies that would facilitate desired social interactions and overall competence. Although it can be argued that a child may show behaviors under assessment conditions that he may not translate into actual behavior in the natural environment, this information is valuable for instructional purposes. As indicated previously, teaching approaches should differ considerably for the child who knows what a desirable social response would be but for various reasons fails to perform, as opposed to the child who is inappropriate because he doesn't know what to do.

Measures for assessing the child's knowledge of desirable social responses generally use the analogue format described earlier. The further the assessment conditions are removed from real-life events, the greater the likelihood that one is assessing cognitions rather than the actual responses the child would make within the described situation. Paper-and-pencil analogues (more than other analogue categories) may be important primarily for gathering information about the extent to which the child is able to specify rather than perform the correct social response (Nay, 1977). In this assessment approach, a social situation is presented, typically in writing, to which the child must give the appropriate social response in open-ended or multiple-choice form. An example of the multiple-choice form is Wood and Michelson's Children's Assertive Behavior Scale (1978), presented earlier under self-report scales. A multiple-choice instrument designed to assess problem-solving skills is the Purdue Elementary Problem-Solving Inventory (PEPSI) (Feldhusen, Houtz, & Ringenbach, 1972), in which children select among alternative solutions to problem situations presented by means of cartoon slides. Open-ended instruments require the child to tell what should be done or how he would act under the conditions presented. Examples of the open-ended method are the Spivack and Shure (1974) measures described later in this section. Related to analogue approaches are social knowledge measures, which ask students what they would do in hypothetical social situations presented in pictures or videotapes (LaGreca & Santogrossi, 1980).

Another aspect of assessment of cognitive processes is that of assessment of faulty cognitions, for example, maladaptive self-statements, assumptions, and beliefs, perfectionistic thinking, and inaccurate attributions, where the child fails to accept responsibility for his behavior but attributes his actions to external factors (Meichenbaum, 1977). The basic task in assessing a child's cognitions is to get the child to identify his faulty self-statements, especially those that occur while he is engaged in some maladaptive behavior. Several techniques have been identified by Meichenbaum (1976) for assessing a child's cognitions. One of these involves videotaping the child during assessment on some behavioral measure, such as the previously described role play test. The tape is replayed, and the child is asked to share the thoughts he experienced during the enactment. Cognitions are probed, particularly in scenes where social skill deficits are observed. Attention is then given to other similar situations in an effort to determine to what extent this particular pattern is indicative of the child's general thought processes.

In a related procedure, imagery is used in an interview situation rather than with overt behavioral enactment of the problem situation. The child is asked to imagine a problem scene, to close his eyes and "run a movie through his head," describing his thoughts while mentally reliving the situation. For example, the child experiencing difficulty in approaching a peer for social interaction, or talking in class, or taking a test, would visualize himself in these situations and share the things he would say to himself while so engaged. The objective is to determine if the child is emitting self-statements that are self-defeating or counterproductive to the desired behavior.

There are few well-developed and tested means for assessing attributions and thinking styles related to self-efficacy in children. Bugental, Whalen, and Henker (1977) looked at attributions related to internal/external locus of control by means of a structured interview, in which children were asked to explain their school success and failure. Kendall and Braswell (1985) suggest that self-efficacy could be assessed by asking children prior to a testing session on a problem-solving task how confident they are that they will complete the task, then comparing the responses to actual task performance. Two self-efficacy scales are mentioned in the preceding section on self-assessment.

A third aspect of cognitive assessment is to determine the child's ability to engage in constructive problem solving. Spivack and Shure (1974) developed several instruments for measuring the cognitive problem-solving skills of young children. The Preschool Interpersonal Problem Solving Test (PIPS) assesses the child's ability to think of alternative solutions; the What Happens Next Game (WHNG) measures consequential thinking; and the Means-Ends Problem Solving Test (MEPS) investigates the child's ability to conceptualize means toward a goal.

The PIPS test has two parts, one presenting conflict situations with a peer; the second, with mother. In the first part, the child is given seven basic stories involving one child playing with a toy that is wanted by a second child. The child being assessed is required to tell what the child in the story who wants the toy might do to resolve the situation; for example (Spivack & Shure, 1974, p. 194):

> "Here's (child A) and here's (child B). A is playing with this truck and he has been playing with it for a long time. Now B wants a chance to play with the truck but A keeps on playing with it. Who's been playing with the truck for a long time? You can point. That's right, A. (Point to A.) Who wants to play with it? That's right, B. What can B do so he can have a chance to play with the truck?" (If there is no new relevant response: "What can B say . . . ?").

Following the completion of this section, the child is given five additional stories, where the child in the story does something to anger his mother; for example, "A broke his mother's favorite flowerpot and he is afraid his mother will be mad at him. What can A do or say so his mother will not be mad?" (p. 195). Again, the child is expected to give solutions to these problems. The child is probed to give as many different solutions as possible. Each alternative is counted as one point, yielding a total PIPS score for both parts of the test.

The second test, the What Happens Next Game, is designed to determine whether the child is able to anticipate consequences to certain behaviors. It is described as a game because the examiner begins telling a story, and the child is required to complete it. The child is given five stories of peer conflicts with toys and five stories involving the child doing something without adult permission. Examples of both types include (Spivack & Shure, 1974, p. 198):

> 1. "A had a truck and he was playing with it. B wanted to play with that truck. So B grabbed—you know, snatched—that truck. Tell me what happens next."
> 2. "Here's A and this is Mrs. Smith. A saw Mrs. Smith's little poodle dog on her porch and took it for a walk. But A did not ask Mrs. Smith if he could take it. What happened next in the story?"

In testing, the focus is on whether the child is actually able to specify realistic consequences to various events and, if so, the number of different consequences identified.

The Means–Ends Problem Solving Test involves the child in attempting to fill in the middle part of a problem situation where the child is presented with the beginning and ending; for example (Spivack et al., 1976, p. 65):

> Al (Joyce) has moved into the neighborhood. He (she) didn't know anyone and felt very lonely.
> The story ends with Al (Joyce) having many good friends and feeling at home in the neighborhood. What happens in between Al's (Joyce's) moving in and feeling lonely, and when he (she) ends up with many good friends?

The child's response is scored in terms of "means" (i.e., inputs that lead to problem solution), "obstacles" (i.e., additional problems the child adds to the script that interfere with a solution), and "time" (i.e., using time as a means to solve the problem). The Children's MEPS is designed for elementary school children and is given orally in order to maintain attention and minimize problems related to inability to read.

A modification of the Spivack and Shure PIPS has been devised by Rubin, Daniels-Beirness, and Bream (1984), which provides for both qualitative and quantitative assessment of problem-solving skills. It asks children to describe what story characters would do to resolve problem situations. The number of relevant alternatives presented are tallied and in addition the experimenter probes for further responses. Answers are also coded according to type of problem-solving strategy presented; that is, "prosocial; agonistic; authority-intervention; bribe; trade or finagle; or manipulative affect."

In discussing the assessment of cognitions, Roberts and Nelson (1984) suggest the need to teach and reinforce correspondence between verbal reports of inner events and observable motor behavior. If assessment is to be used for evaluation of the effects of treatment on the cognitive domain, they stress the need for behavioral measures such as observation along with rating scales and checklists. Krasnor and Rubin (1981) similarly point to limitations of approaches such as the Spivack and Shure measures described earlier; for example, the possible lack of personal relevance for the child, the relatively narrow content areas, the predominately verbal nature of the responses, weak psychometric strength, and lack of direct relationship to actual strategies used by children. They suggest instead that episodes of actual problem-solving behavior in real or simulated situations be content analyzed along several dimensions, making it possible to determine the child's actual effectiveness in problem solving and draw inferences related to cognitive processes. The areas of assessment are (Krasnor, 1982, p. 114):

> (a) the child's sensitivity to social task variables; (b) the quantity and quality of the child's repertoire of social strategies which can be employed to solve social problems; (c) the degree to which the child "matches" a strategy to a specific situation, reflected both in the effectiveness of the strategy in achieving the goal and in the social acceptability of the strategy; and (d) the child's sequencing of SPS attempts after failure.

## Assessing Social Perception

As mentioned in chapter 1, the skills that make up accurate social perception or social sensitivity are becoming increasingly recognized as important components of interpersonal competence. Social perception is a complex process, involving a number of different cognitive and affective subskills, among them the ability to identify and label the feelings of others, role taking (i.e., the ability to take the cognitive or affective perspective of another), and social inference (the ability to draw causal inferences from social situations). Well-established means of assessing different aspects of social perception are not abundant, and those that exist relate primarily to cognitive and affective role taking ability (that is, the ability to think about what another is thinking and the ability to infer how another is feeling), along with empathy (the ability to share the feelings of others).

The ability to take the role of the other is frequently assessed through the presentation of scenarios, such as those originally developed by Flavell, Botkin, Fry, Wright, and Jarvis (1968) and modified by Chandler (1973), in which the child knows more about a story than someone else and is asked to tell the story from the point of view of the less-informed person. In Chandler's process, to assess affective and cognitive role taking, a story is portrayed in a cartoon sequence with a new character introduced midway in the sequence, a "bystander" who is unaware of preceding events. The child is asked to explain events from the perspective of the new unenlightened character, leaving out the facts that he knows. For example, in a series entitled "Fear," a child is shown breaking a window, running home, the neighbor with the broken window knocking on the boy's door, and the father observing the boy crouching in fear as he hears the knock on the door. The unenlightened character in this sequence is the father. The student is asked to describe what he thinks the father is thinking as he observes his son's response to the knock on the door. The respondent is considered to be able to take the role of this character accurately if he ascribes to the father a recognition of the emotional reaction in his son but does not attribute it to the antecedent events described in the preceding pictures. If the respondent gave a response such as "he probably thinks he broke a window," he would be reacting according to his own perspective rather than that of the uninformed character.

Feffer and Gourevitch (1960) developed a cognitive Role-Taking Task using background scenes and cut-out figures from the MAPS test (Shneidman, 1952). The child is to tell a story about the scene and then retell the story from the point of view of each of three characters. The authors identify three different stages in role taking that can be assessed through this task: (a) a simple refocus in which the child changes the story when retelling it from the point of view of different characters, but does not show coordination between perspectives; (b) consistent elaboration, showing sequential coordination between perspectives; and (c) change of perspective, in which the child can view all perspectives simultaneously.

A cognitive role-taking assessment procedure developed by Selman and Byrne (1974) involves a filmstrip, in which an open-ended dilemma is presented. One of the dilemmas involves, for example, Holly, a child who likes to climb trees, but after a fall promises her father not to climb trees again. Later a friend's kitten is caught in a tree. Holly, as the only one who can climb trees well enough to rescue the kitten, is caught in a dilemma. Subjects are asked to retell the story to demonstrate that they remembered it and are then asked a series of standard questions to assess role-taking level. These levels include egocentric role taking, in which the child cannot distinguish between a personal interpretation and what he/she considers the correct perspective; subjective role taking, in which he/she realizes that people may interpret the same data differently; self-reflective role taking, in which the child recognizes that people may think or feel differently because of different values or purposes; and mutual role taking, in which the child can take an objective third-person perspective of others' points of view.

Empathy and affective role taking are often confused. In reviewing definitions of empathy, Goldstein and Michaels (1985) conclude that empathy combines several meanings; that is, (a) taking the role of another, seeing the world as the other sees it, and experiencing the feelings of the other; (b) being able to read nonverbal communication and interpret the feelings expressed; and (c) conveying a feeling of caring or sincere effort to understand and help. Feshback (1982) also describes a similar three-component model of empathy. A study by Feshback and Roe (1968) formed the basis for much of the research on assessment of empathy. The assessment technique, the Feshback & Roe Affective Situation Test for Empathy (FASTE), involves a series of slides showing real children in one of four affective situations: happiness, sadness, fear, and anger. Themes used for each of the four affects were

1. Happiness: birthday party, winning a television contest;
2. Sadness: a lost dog
3. Fear: child lost, frightening dog;
4. Anger: the toy snatcher, false accusation.

A narrative accompanied each. There were identical sequences with both male and female figures. After viewing a slide sequence children were asked to state how they felt, with the answers used as an index of empathy. Empathic responsiveness was defined as the degree to which the child's reported emotional state matched that of the story character. By asking "How does the child on the screen feel?" the FASTE was also used in this study as a measure of social comprehension. Feshback and Roe found that degree of empathy could not be accounted for solely by degree of comprehension of others' feelings.

Some disadvantages of this approach have been pointed out (Eisenberg-Berg & Lennon, 1980): the stories might be too brief to evoke vicarious emotional responding; emotions like fear and anger may be too complex for very young children to understand; asking for verbal responses might be inappropriate for very young children; and having unfamiliar persons as experimenters might create anxiety in subjects. Their variation used four longer stories, accompanied by three illustrations each, which assessed only sadness and happiness. Empathy was assessed both verbally and nonverbally, in that after children were asked to describe how they felt, they were asked to point to pictures with children's facial expressions registering happiness, sadness, anger, and no emotion, and asked: "point to the picture that tells me how this story made you feel."

Several more recent measures of empathy have been devised by Feshback (1982) to attempt to assess different dimensions of empathy. These include the Affective Matching Measure, the Emotional Responsiveness Measure, and the Feshback and Powell Audiovisual Test for Empathy. In the Affective Matching Measure, children are presented with black and white drawings of children in situations that evoke different emotions. Affective facial cues of the main character have been deleted. Subjects are asked to pick out from a sheet displaying five faces, with expressions of happiness, pride, anger, sadness, and fear, the one that matches how the character in the picture feels. In the Emotional Responsiveness Measure, children are presented with five taped vignettes of $1\frac{1}{2}$ minutes, which are designed to evoke either pride, happiness, anger, fear, or sadness. After each tape, the child is asked to rate on a nine-point scale the degree to which he feels the indicated emotion.

The Audiovisual Test for Empathy involves a series of 2-minute videotapes of stories with children experiencing the same five different emotions. A child can be tested individually, shown the videotapes, and asked how much he or she feels — a little, some, or very much. In groups, children are given response sheets listing eight emotions, asked to circle the emotion that describes that feeling, and indicate on a ten-point scale how much they feel. An empathy score is based on the degree to which emotional responses correspond to the affect conveyed by the child in the videotape. All the above measures were developed with third- and fourth-grade children and based on self-reports of situations in their lives that evoked various emotions. All the measures had versions for both boys and girls and attempted to control for both sex and racial bias.

Another recent approach to assessment of empathy is the Index of Empathy for Children and Adolescents (Bryant, 1982), a paper-and-pencil adaptation of an adult measure of emotional empathy (Mehrabian & Epstein, 1972). Children were asked to respond yes or no to 22 statements, such as "It makes me sad to see a girl who can't find anyone to play with... I get upset when I see a girl being hurt... Even when I don't know why someone is laughing, I laugh too." The author demonstrates satisfactory reliability and preliminary construct validity and suggests that this is a convenient and practical measure for studying the expression of empathy in children. She cautions, however, that this is not a direct measure of empathy, but rather requires the child to think about and report on his or her own empathic responses.

Two approaches to assessing another aspect of social perception, social inference, include the measurement developed by Barrett and Yarrow (1977) and the Test of Social Inference (Edmonson, de Jung, Leland, & Leach, 1974). In the Barrett and Yarrow process, the child is shown five videotapes of social interaction that involve a child or young adult. In each sequence, an affective experience is followed by an abrupt change in behavior. For example, one sequence shows a child working successfully on a manual task, his parents are heard arguing angrily, and the child is then shown having difficulty with the task. Subjects are tested for retention of events, asked to explain why the character behaved as he had, and scored on the basis of their ability to explain the final events by using information from the earlier events. The Test of Social Inference (Edmondson et al., 1974), developed primarily for an adult handicapped population, can also be used with nonretarded children, ages 7–13. It is a test of social situation comprehension involving 31 pictured situations, which are to be interpreted. It can be used with both readers and nonreaders. The Test of Social Inference is designed to assess the individual's ability to interpret cues regarding others' intentions and attitudes and make inferences about what may happen within a social situation.

Very few of the instruments designed to measure aspects of social perception have been subjected to extensive validity and reliability studies. Enright and Lapsley (1980), in a review of role taking instruments, concluded that only the cognitive role taking measures of Chandler and Selman possess sufficient validity to be used in educational programs and no affective role taking measures to date meet that criterion. Morrison and Bellack (1981) stress the need for more instruments to assess social perception skills, in particular ones that can account for the variability of social perception across situations and that can assess some of the several possible reasons for social perception deficits: for example, failure to listen or attention to irrelevant cues, failure to look, failure to integrate what is seen and heard, and lack of understanding of what is seen and heard.

## SUMMARY

Assessment prior to the teaching of social skills helps determine which social behaviors are missing from the child's repertoire and thus need to be taught and which behaviors need only to be increased through altering motivational conditions. Assessment assists also in determining the effectiveness of teaching and clinical interventions.

Adults, such as parents and teachers, are the major source of information about children's social behavior. Rating scales and inventories are frequently used to gather data for screening purposes from adults because such measures are easy to administer and lend themselves to comparisons among raters. Such instruments include standardized behavior checklists and rating scales, inventories associated with social skills curricula, and informal scales and inventories designed for specific settings or situations.

Observation and recording of the child's performance of social skills in various aspects of the natural environment provide the most specific and relevant information. Observational data can be gathered in a variety of spontaneous situations, or events can be structured to elicit the behavior being assessed. An interview can serve as one such contrived situation that lends itself to the observation of a number of interpersonal behaviors as well as yielding information about the child's perceptions of his situation. Other data can be gathered in the natural environment through permanent products, especially the use of video- and audiotapes.

Simulations of events in the environment through role playing provide another source of observational data, particularly for behaviors that would be difficult to observe in the child's everyday situations. Assessment through role playing can be carried out using spontaneous enactments of problem situations or through more standardized means using prepared scripts that prompt responses. Role playing scenarios can be delivered by live players or through audio- or videotaped presentations. Role play approaches to social skills evaluation have a number of limitations related to validity in predicting social behavior in actual situations.

A number of sociometric procedures have been devised that make it possible to gather data from peers about children's degree of acceptance and social behavior deficits as seen by peers. The most commonly used procedures are nominations, in which children nominate peers according to degree of acceptance or nonacceptance; paired comparisons, in which children make choices between pairs of peers; and roster-ratings, in which children are presented with rosters of the entire group to rate. Like other social skills assessment procedures, sociometric techniques cannot be relied on as a sole measure of social behavior.

Another source of information about social behavior is the child himself. Approaches to self-assessment include self-report measures, in the form of paper-and-pencil checklists or rating scales assessing social behavior, and self-esteem and self-monitoring procedures, in which the child observes and records his own social behavior. Self-monitoring is limited as an assessment technique by reactive effects along with the amount of skill needed to observe, measure, and report on one's own behavior. These approaches are most useful when combined with data from other sources.

Along with determining the behaviors the child emits in various social situations, it is also important to identify the child's emotions and cognitions that may interfere with or facilitate social competence. The child's ability to perceive and interpret various aspects of social situations is another significant aspect of social skill. Because of outward manifestations of emotion, affect can be observed and, thus, measured more easily than cognitions or social perception. There are a number of scales and checklists for both self-reporting and assessment by others of emotional states such as fear, anxiety, and depression. Assessment related to cognition includes paper-and-pencil and open-ended measures of social skills knowledge and problem-solving techniques. Aspects of social perception such as role taking ability, empathy, and social inference are assessed primarily through the presentation of scenarios followed by questions to determine the extent of the child's understanding or involvement.

Although there are an increasing number of approaches to the assessment of social skills, each one has limitations. It becomes important not to rely on a single method of assessment but rather to make use of multiple methods and more than one informant, to make assessments if possible in more than one setting, and to measure not only observable social skills but cognitive and affective dimensions as well.

# 3
# The Teaching Process

When the social skills to be taught have been identified, and it has been determined through assessment whether the child can perform those behaviors, the practitioner is ready to teach the skills that are lacking or not a comfortable part of the child's repertoire of social behaviors. Learning takes place primarily through observation, imitation, and feedback from the environment; children learn social skills in much the same way they learn academic concepts. The steps in instruction can be seen as involving first the presentation of a stimulus; second, the eliciting of a response to the stimulus; and third, providing feedback about the correctness of the response, followed by further refinement of responses and practice in correct responses. In social skills instruction, the first step can be a demonstration, a verbal description, a picture or diagram, or any of many other stimuli describing the behavior. The desired response from the child is his attempt to reproduce the stimuli through imitation. The feedback provided for the response can take a variety of forms, but needs essentially to convey information about whether and how the response should be repeated or changed. Opportunities are then needed for further imitation, further feedback, and practice.

This chapter deals with the instructional process and outlines the salient features of social skills teaching. Many of these have been described in research literature with empirically demonstrated positive results. Procedures for teaching observable social behaviors almost always involve some aspect of social modeling or learning by imitation. Social modeling is also important for the teaching of adaptive ways of thinking and feeling in social situations, particularly where the internal events can be reflected in some overt behavior. Relaxation procedures are included here as a social skill because they can be translated into coping methods to be used in stressful interpersonal situations, as can be various cognitive coping strategies. A number of other elements, considered to be necessary for effective social skill instruction will be discussed in chapter 5.

## SOCIAL LEARNING — MODELING AND ROLE PLAYING

Social learning theory provides the framework for the procedures most commonly employed in social skills training. The process of producing a model of social behavior that enables another to learn by observation and imitation is a sequence labeled *social modeling*. An individual observes another person's behavior and then imitates that behavior by behaving similarly under similar circumstances. Social modeling is considered to be the method whereby most social behaviors are learned, especially during the developing years when children learn to imitate the behaviors of significant others in their lives, such as parents, teachers, and peers. For example, young children playing with dolls will be observed to care for and speak to their dolls in a manner similar to the way their parents treat them or a sibling. In later years, these same children may note aspects of their behavior that reflect that of their parents even though, in many cases, there is a conscious desire not to emulate their parents' child-rearing practices. On a broader scale, the presentation of models through the mass media (i.e., television, films) has extensively affected our life-styles so that it influences the products we consume and the entertainment we pursue. Whether through the mass media or direct observation, there is evidence that models also influence the degree to which we engage in aggressive, passive, or assertive behaviors (Bandura, 1973).

The power of social modeling in modifying behaviors and in developing new ones has been thoroughly documented under laboratory conditions. Investigators have used these procedures to help children acquire such behaviors as increased social interaction for isolated children (O'Connor, 1973), an increased tendency to give to charity and to help others (Rosenhan & White, 1967), and improved conversation skills involving asking for and giving information (Zimmerman & Pike, 1972). Social modeling also has been used extensively to develop assertive behaviors (McFall & Lillesand, 1971) and has shown to be effective in eliminating or reducing such maladaptive behaviors in children as aggression (Chittenden, 1942). In addition to facilitating the development of novel responses, it has been argued that there is greater likelihood that new behaviors acquired through modeling will be maintained following treatment compared to those developed through operant techniques only (Combs & Slaby, 1977). According to Bandura (1977b), observational learning depends on the learner's ability to attend to and understand the models' responses, the learner's ability to code and retain these responses for future use, and the presence of incentive conditions, motivating the learner to perform the observed behavior. Therefore, skill training using this model typically consists of (a) *instructions*, which include a social skill rationale, the identification of specific skill components, and information on skill performance, encompassing both verbal directions and social modeling; (b) *skill performance*, involving learner reproductions of the target skill, trainer feedback, and trainer reinforcement; and (c) *practice*, emphasizing production of the behavior at future times and under a variety of conditions.

## Giving Instructions

*Providing a Rationale*

At the initial stage of instruction the learner needs to be given a purpose, or rationale, for the skill, particularly if the target behavior is not one typically valued by the learner or the significant others in his environment. One goal in establishing the social skill purpose is to provide the learner with information about the usefulness and inherent advantages of the social skill rather than simply presenting the skill as something one is expected to do. Skill-deficient children often persist in their maladaptive responses because they fail to connect their behavior with aversive consequences or they are unable to identify and perform alternative behaviors that would produce more desired results. Therefore, at this point, the instruction needs to be geared toward helping the learner recognize the value of the behavior based on the potential consequences and benefits. Stories and films might be used for this purpose. Through a story, for example, a child might be made aware of the facilitating effects of cooperation over competition in making friends. Instructional procedures designed to increase awareness of behavioral consequences and the value of socially appropriate behaviors are the basis of the Spivack and Shure (1974) problem-solving model discussed later in this chapter.

*Identifying Skill Components*

Rather than simple responses, individual social skills are actually complex processes, frequently consisting of a chain of behaviors. The child needs to be able to identify the specific subskills that make up the comprehensive social skill. For example, what responses are required in greeting someone, in making a friend, or in being assertive? In the first case, the child would be expected at least to make eye contact, say "hello," give his name, and perhaps smile. Skills such as making friends and good sportsmanship are even more complex, but still lend themselves to analysis. The components of approach behavior for the purpose of friendship-making have been identified as greeting, asking the other child for some information such as "Where are you from?" inviting the other child to do something with him, and telling the child something like "I like to play ball" (Gottman, Gonso, & Rasmussen, 1975). One method for helping the child determine skill components is to involve the learners in the process of behavior analysis. For example, for the skill of making friends, a story or role play could be presented that depicts children successfully making friends, followed by a discussion to identify the specific responses that helped the fictional characters to make friends. As the behaviors are generated, they are listed and sequenced in order of occurrence such as,

1. Say, "Hi, how are you? My name is _____. What's yours?"
2. Ask something like, "Where are you from?" or "What are you doing?"
3. Invite him or her to do something, "I want to play checkers. Would you like to play with me?"

In using this approach the trainer would use the children's own words as much as possible and take into consideration the developmental levels and cultural differences of the children. For example, older youths (particularly boys) might include a handshake in this sequence, the configuration of which might differ from one cultural group to another. It might also be necessary to establish whether each child understands the nature of each behavior listed and the child's ability to reproduce it in a natural rather than mechanical fashion. One approach might be to ask children to demonstrate their suggested responses; for example, "George, what else might you ask a new child? Would you show us how you would ask that?"

Instructions need to be tailored to the child's intellectual, chronological, and social skill development level. Very young or low-functioning children, for example, may have difficulty identifying, analyzing, or providing a rationale for the desired social skill. Similarly, young children may need assistance in determining what the specific responses are and how they should be made. For low-functioning children, certain overt actions such as shaking hands and making eye contact may have to be prompted physically, as well.

Children with limited behavioral controls probably would benefit most from brief, direct introductions, such as those provided in a social skill curriculum by Jackson et al. (1983, p. 7), exemplified in their sequence:

*Teacher 1*: Today we are going to talk about introducing yourself to someone you don't know and introducing two people who don't know each other. To introduce yourself, you
_____ Use a pleasant face and voice.
_____ Look at the person.
_____ Tell the person your name.
_____ Ask for the person's name.
To introduce two people who don't know each other, you
_____ Use a pleasant face and voice.
_____ Look at each other.
_____ Tell each person the other's name.

On the other hand, older, more sophisticated learners would enjoy and respond to more extended discussions. Michelson et al. (1983), for example, suggest initiating social skill instruction with brief "lectures" interspersed with discussion questions. The lecture and questions are intended to help the learner understand the nature of the social skill, the rationale for performing it, and the specific responses that comprise the social behavior.

*Presenting a Model*

At this stage of the instructional process the learner needs to be presented examples of how the composite behavior is performed. One strategy is to demonstrate the behavior through a model. Important factors to be considered in presenting a model include

1. Model characteristics;
2. Attention to the model;
3. Recognition of specific responses made by the model;
4. The mode of presentation.

It has been established that characteristics of the model can either facilitate or inhibit the tendency of the observer to copy the modeled behavior. Modeling is enhanced when the observer perceives the model as important, successful, and someone with whom he can identify. It should be noted, however, that models representing exceptionally high standards or unfamiliar life-styles and models with low prestige or perceived incompetence may prove to be ineffective.

Obviously, for modeling situations to be most effective, the observer must be attentive. Attention may to some extent be a function of the model's characteristics and the reinforcing properties of the presentation. "Setting the stage" by establishing the importance of the particular social behavior and providing reinforcers or contingencies for paying attention can also increase attention. Related to attention is the ability to recognize and understand the exact responses produced by the model. Observation without understanding would result in inadequate or partial imitation, at best. Therefore, it is suggested that after the skill has been modeled, the observer be assisted in identifying and sequencing the exact responses exhibited by the model. Marlatt and Perry (1975) suggest the use of videotapes with a narrator's comments dubbed over the action, in order to draw the child's attention to the most salient aspects of the observed behavior.

In addition to these factors, the learning process can be facilitated by the way in which the modeling is presented. Goldstein, Sprafkin, and Gershaw (1976, p. 6) provide guidelines for "modeling display," suggesting that the behaviors be presented

    a. in a clear and detailed manner,
    b. in the order from least to most difficult behaviors,
    c. with enough repetition to make overlearning likely,
    d. with as little irrelevant (not to be learned) detail as possible, and
    e. with several different models, rather than a single model.

Another variable to be considered in presenting models is the importance of negative examples. Ladd and Mize (1983) point out that negative models may be instructional in making more explicit the parameters of the desired behavior, thus limiting the possibility of overgeneralization. To illustrate, they give the following example (p. 141):

> after witnessing a variety of approach behaviors, children may have inferred a strategy such as "to play, I have to go up to other children" but overgeneralized it to include aggressive as well as prosocial initiations.

In devising an instructional program, along with multiple models the social skills trainer should consider the various sources for models. Adults may serve as effective models for young children, as may puppets and story characters. For adolescents, however, adults in their immediate environment may have less influence over their behavior than peers, rock stars, or movie idols. Several ways of presenting models in social skills instruction are outlined, including the use of puppets, taped models, models through books, and live models.

*Puppets.* Although generally considered most appropriate for the younger child, puppets can serve as effective models for the older child or adolescent as well. The determining factor with puppets, as with other forms of models, is relevance or the extent to which the child can identify the characters depicted. For example, one effective social skills instruction program with junior high school youngsters used puppets in the role of the school cheerleaders, athletes, and other individuals commonly found in a junior high school. In addition to being attractive and possibly increasing attention to the learning situation, puppets can be used to depict social situations of immediate concern in a way that is less threatening and, in some cases, less embarrassing than if live models were used. Puppets provide an element of objectivity so that the child unwilling to deal directly with his own actions may be willing to view, discuss, and eventually role play the same behaviors with puppets.

Puppets may also take the form of fictional characters such as Winnie-the-Pooh or television favorites such as Sesame Street characters. In addition to commercially available puppets, children may be assisted in making their own puppets. Personally made puppets can contribute to model identification and attractiveness. Handmade puppets may range from rather elaborate productions made of fabric cut from patterns, papier mache, or clay, to very simple models made of socks, paper bags, boxes, tin cans, construction paper with drawn features, or figures cut out and pasted on tongue depressors.

A program that makes extensive use of puppetry is the Developing Understanding of Self and Others (DUSO) Program published by American Guidance Service. For each lesson, a variety of instructional strategies are used including problem stories, discussions with puppets, live role playing, and role playing with puppets. In this program, puppets are used to present the problem, to model desired behaviors, and to role play possible alternative responses. For example, in one lesson dealing with verbal aggression, the initial activities with the two main puppet characters help children to understand the importance of avoiding making unpleasant comments to others, while the role playing with a puppet focuses on helping children to identify appropriate ways of expressing positive and negative feelings.

As the child develops more skill and becomes more comfortable in dramatic activities, it is to be hoped that he will prefer to engage in live role playing, discarding symbols and props, such as puppets. Responses practiced under live role playing conditions should be easier to transfer to everyday situations.

*Taped Models.* Models may also be presented through media, such as films, television, radio, audio- and videotapes, magazines, and newspapers. Although references can be made to positive role models found in the mass media, these sources lend themselves less easily to formal social learning instructions because of the difficulty in controlling content and ensuring that the most desirable material will be viewed or read. Greater control can be exercised with specific video- and audiotapes designed for social skill instruction. The efficacy of film-mediated models in producing new social responses has been thoroughly documented (Bandura, 1969). The typical method of presentation is to show a model demonstrating a skill, for example, encountering and effectively resolving a conflict situation. One such modeling videotape described by Goodwin and Mahoney (1975) involves controlling aggression while being provoked. The tape shows the model coping with verbal aggression from peers by engaging in various self-statement such as, "I will not get angry," "I will not fight." The self-statements were dubbed onto the tape to illustrate the model's thought processes. While viewing the tapes, the coping mechanisms used by the models (i.e., cognitive self-statements) were highlighted so that the observers were aware of the exact behaviors (in this case cognitions) that helped the model to cope successfully with the situation.

Although audiotapes have not been used as extensively for social modeling, they are particularly useful for modeling skills in verbal communication and demonstrating affect. For example, audiotapes may be used to model the delivery of assertive statements with appropriate tonal quality and emotion. Modeling instructions that have been taped allow for additional presentations so that, where necessary, the behavior may be reviewed repeatedly until learned.

*Models Through Books.* Along with tapes and films, books may serve as another source of symbolic modeling for children and adolescents. Stories that have been realistically written with believable and significant characters can be used to teach a child how to respond to various social situations. For example, the story *Ira Sleeps Over*, written for younger children by Bernard Waber, describes how a young boy handles a problem after listening to the misadvice of his sister, suggesting that one should follow his own best judgment and not worry about others laughing at him.

Stories and books may be particularly powerful social learning tools, for they present models with an additional dimension and in greater depth. As Eisley and Merrill (1984, p. 4) point out:

> Stories have a somewhat unique advantage over even actual observation of individuals behaving virtuously or unvirtuously. Stories are able to report the *inner* thoughts, beliefs, desires, and motivations of the actors. Stories have another advantage for educators. Although many contexts naturally occur in which human virtues are manifest, pedagogically and ethically they are not as susceptible to classroom demonstration and manipulation as are concrete and defined concepts. Therefore, the most practical tools left to an instructor for teaching human virtue concepts are stories and certain kinds of dramatization.

In one study (Cartledge, 1984), brief stories were used to introduce the social skill strategies taught to elementary school children. When reviewing appropriate responses for previously taught skills, the children were observed to make frequent references to story characters and situations, indicating that these stories not only provided social skill rationales and models, but facilitated the subsequent recall and execution of the desired behaviors as well. A resource for identifying stories dealing with children's problems is the *Book Finder* published by American Guidance Service. The reader is also referred to the materials list in the Appendix of this book. The following criteria are suggested by Cianciolo (1965) for selection of books for "bibliotherapy." The selections should

1. Focus on a particular need;
2. Be written on the child's level;
3. Center on the problem;
4. Have realistic approaches;
5. Have lifelike characters; and
6. Accurately depict groups the characters represent.

*Live Models.* Live models are another option for modeling presentations. Live modeling is staged in a manner similar to that of taped presentations. In contrast to tapes, however, live procedures provide for greater flexibility so that alternative responses may be demonstrated. For example, in the social skill situation involving responses to verbal aggression, there are several viable options available to the child; for example, engaging in certain cognitions in order to maintain control, leaving the scene, reporting the situations to an adult authority figure, and so forth. A role play situation could be structured with the practitioner and the child or the child with other children acting out the various alternatives. Following each enactment a discussion would ensue to determine factors, such as what response occurred (e.g., walking away), whether it was effective (e.g., did it stop the taunting), how the actor(s) felt, and what other responses one might use in this situation. Inappropriate responses might also be displayed in order to demonstrate relative effects. Thus, with live modeling, children could observe several alternatives and assess the consequences to these behaviors. For example, depending on the social situation, reporting to an adult may result in more taunting, suggesting that other responses should be considered. The learning experience may be enhanced by permitting children to reverse roles; for example, being the taunter and the one taunted. The obvious disadvantage of using live models is that the trainer cannot be certain that the behavior will be displayed accurately, and it is more difficult to reproduce the scene for later viewing (Eisler & Frederickson, 1980).

Peers may serve as highly effective models in social skill instruction and can assist in individualizing social skill lessons. The existing research shows that peer imitation begins in infancy, that reinforcement contingencies may facilitate peer modeling, and that peers have been used successfully in social skills development among both very young and older children (Rubin, 1982). The facilitating effects of peers in social skill training can be seen in a study conducted by Bierman and Furman (1984), where children were taught conversational social skills. Children instructed under conditions with competent peers were found to experience greater peer acceptance and enhanced self-perceptions compared with subjects receiving individual instruction without peer involvement.

Children functioning on low levels who are unable to benefit from traditional social modeling or role playing techniques may profit from individual instruction where they are assisted by peers in copying and reproducing the desired social responses. Ascher and Phillips (1975) describe such a procedure, labeled *guided behavior rehearsal*, where trained peer guides, competent in the particular social area, used modeling and behavior rehearsal to help adult clients gain greater social competence. The guide was responsible for accompanying the client to various social situations in order to model appropriate behaviors, for conducting training sessions where specific responses were rehearsed, and for providing feedback and reinforcement for approximations to desired responses. In one case, these procedures were successful in teaching a neurologically impaired young man exactly how to initiate and engage in conversation, with the result that his social skills were improved and he was enabled to sustain relationships.

Similar procedures have been successfully used with children (Csapo, 1972). A socially skilled child is assigned to a peer with social deficits to assist in areas such as playing with peers, resisting aggression, and engaging in conversations. The peer model is trained in modeling techniques for the target behaviors to be developed and in techniques for prompting and reinforcing the incompetent child. Children selected to serve as models should be respected by the other child, should be skilled in the social behaviors to be developed, and should be similar in background; for example, age, sex, and socioeconomic status.

Ensuring that the observer attends to and understands the most important aspect of the modeling situation is a major consideration related to presenting the model. Such understanding may be encouraged by discussing the modeling display afterward, helping the child to identify what happened and the events that should be given the most attention. In videotaped presentations, trainers frequently use narration, where the narrator points out the most salient features as the scene develops. Furman (1980) points out that this is important for young children in order to facilitate understanding and recall and for older children in order to minimize their tendency to overlook that which appears irrelevant but is actually germane.

Coaching is another method for instructing the child on how the behavior should be performed. In contrast to modeling, coaching relies largely on verbal directions given in a training sequence over a series of training sessions. Oden and Asher (1977) used coaching procedures to facilitate skills for making friends in children. These procedures are described in detail in chapter 8 of this book. Although to varying degrees, both modeling and coaching employ verbal instructions, demonstrations, enactments, and feedback. These similarities may account for the finding that modeling plus coaching in one teaching sequence does not contribute an additive effect to social skill acquisition; that is, the performance of subjects receiving both modeling and coaching was not greater than subjects receiving only modeling or coaching (Gresham & Nagle, 1980; McFall & Twentyman, 1973).

## Skill Performance

### Guided Rehearsal

Observed behavior will not necessarily be learned unless some mechanism is put into operation whereby the behavior display is remembered and subsequently reproduced. Trying out the modeled behaviors under supervised conditions will help the child produce them successfully in real-life situations. Behavior rehearsal (Rose, 1972) represents a form of structured role playing that enables the child to act out and practice the new behaviors. Bandura (1977b) suggested that practice may be conducted through covert responding, verbal responding, and motoric reproduction.

*Covert Responding.* Covert responding essentially refers to cognitive images about a particular event. It has been established that imagery can be used effectively to develop both academic and social behavior. Behaviors coded through imagery can be retrieved later for appropriate responding. When engaged in social skill instruction, the use of imagery or covert responses can be prompted by helping the learner to reproduce in his mind or imagine the behavior that had previously been modeled. For example, the child has just been exposed to a modeling session designed to teach appropriate responses to verbal aggression. The child may then be directed to imagine the scene and possible responses, for example: "You are walking home from school and two pupils from your class are following you. They begin to tease you because you struck out during the baseball game and your team lost. Imagine what you will do next."

Imagined resolutions to this scene may include such responses as

1. An assertive statement such as, "I know I struck out but everyone does sometimes, and I won't feel bad because I did this time."
2. An emphatic statement such as. "I know you are upset because we lost the game and I am too, but I tried my best."
3. Physical avoidance, e.g., leaving the scene by taking another route home or going into a public building such as a store or library.

Obviously, the responses employed would depend partly on the circumstances and the particular students. For example, in one situation, verbally assertive statements may serve to extinguish undesirable behavior; in another situation they may provoke more aggression. Children may generate undesirable responses from, for example, a verbally aggressive statement like, "Maybe I'm not such a good baseball player, but I'm the best speller in this class." Through imagining consequences, children may be helped to recognize that although the immediate results may be rewarding, the long term effects of counter-aggression may be aversive. Rather than identifying one pat solution for each conflict situation, the aim is to help children recognize that a variety of alternatives may exist, and that the ones used should be those most likely to resolve rather than exacerbate the situation. The imagery procedure may include

1. Child closes eyes while scene is depicted by practitioner.
2. Child is directed to imagine performing the designated response.
3. Child is directed to imagine reactions to his response.
4. Practitioner directs child through some scene with alternative responses.
5. Child and practitioner identify the most natural and appropriate responses that the child would employ under similar circumstances in the future.

Covert responses could be used as a desensitizing device for the shy or inhibited child. After a period of imagining various personal enactments, the youngster may become more relaxed and willing to participate in overt rehearsals. Another advantage identified by Eisler and Frederikson (1980) is that covert rehearsal can be employed more easily under a variety of circumstances. The youngster could be directed to imagine his appropriate responses immediately before some anxiety-producing event. As the child approaches a verbally aggressive peer, for example, he may covertly practice assertive, empathic, or avoidance behaviors as possible solutions to this problem situation. An obvious shortcoming of covert responding, particularly for young children, is that it cannot be observed and, thus, there are limited possibilities for corrective feedback and performance evaluation. For this reason, covert rehearsal probably should be employed in addition to, not instead of, overt behavior rehearsal. Before engaging the child in imagery, it may be advisable to use relaxation techniques in order to reduce any anxiety associated with conflict situations. Relaxation will be discussed later in this chapter.

*Verbal Responding.* An extension of the steps used for covert responding or imagery is verbal responding. Retention and appropriate performance can be enhanced by having the child talk through the desired responses, elaborating on the previous imagery sequence. At each step, the child describes the scene again in his own words, restating the alternatives and verbalizing possible consequences to proposed resolutions.

*Motor Responding.* Although the two previous response types may be used independently, they also may be viewed as preparation for making motor responses. Here the child is required to act out (typically in a role playing format) the responses that he has observed, that he has visualized through imagery, and that he has verbalized. Role play essentially consists of four basic parts:

1. Setting the stage: describing the scene, selecting participants, and assigning and describing participant roles.
2. Enactment: participants interact with each other, dramatizing respective roles.
3. Discussion/evaluation: performances are evaluated by participants and observers, and alternative responses identified.
4. Reenactment: scene is played again, incorporating suggestions from step 3; different participants may be identified.

As previously discussed, the practitioner may choose live enactments or symbolic representations, such as puppets.

In addition to providing for the practice of desired behaviors, responding through role playing has other advantages. It allows for switching roles so that the participants can view both sides of the situation. This is especially important for the child who tends to exhibit behaviors that are annoying to others. For example, the child who frequently engages in teasing may be the object of the taunting in the role play. Another advantage is the opportunity to observe consequences of specific responses. The child who chooses to counter aggression with more aggression or with extreme passivity, for example, may realize that he has simply negatively escalated rather than resolved the situation. By observing the consequences, children may begin to recognize the importance of alternative behaviors. A third advantage of enactment through role playing is that it facilitates memory. New behaviors are more effectively learned and maintained if the memory of practice incorporates a motor component such as overt role playing.

*Feedback*

As with all learning, feedback is critical to social skill development, since by receiving information about his performance the child is able to make the necessary corrections to improve his skills. Feedback may take a variety of forms: for example, (a) verbal feedback, where the child receives corrective instructions or praise; (b) reinforcement, where correct responses earn tangible reinforcers; and (c) self-evaluation, where a system is devised to enable the child to evaluate himself. As just indicated, the typical role play situation incorporates a discussion/evaluation phase for the purposes of either indicating better ways to perform the behavior or suggesting other ways to respond, such as, "Smile when you shake hands, George" or "Another way to make friends with Marie is to ask her to play a game with you." For behaviors performed correctly, the trainer should compliment the child, being careful to praise specific responses; for example, "You really did a good job of following the rules when you played checkers, George." Van Houten (1980) points out the facilitating effects of feedback when given immediately, frequently, and publicly to the group as well as individually. The last condition refers to the importance of informing the group of how well they are doing in order to promote and foster a group spirit that contributes to social skill development.

Video- and audiotapes are valuable self-evaluation tools and may be especially effective for the adolescent who has difficulty accepting feedback from other sources. The simulated social interactions are taped and afterward the participants evaluate their performance according to specified criteria. The effects may be somewhat dramatic in cases where the youngster is completely unaware of how he presents himself or the effect he has on others; e.g., the child who tends to scowl or yell may recognize how negative these behaviors are by observing them on tape. Teaching children how to monitor and evaluate their own behavior involves assisting them in understanding what are the goals of various social interactions and how to determine whether a particular encounter was successful. Self-evaluation is another aspect of the role play discussion/evaluation phase. This may be provided by guiding the child through a sequence of questions. For example, using the previous scene of verbal aggression

- What did you want to happen?
- Did they stop teasing you?
- What else did you do?
- Were you pleased with the way you got them to stop? (Or why do you think they didn't stop?)
- If you were being teased again, would you do the same thing?
- What would you try to do better? Why?
- How do you feel about yourself in this situation?
- How do you think the boys feel?
- Do you want to remain angry at these boys?
- What will you do the next time you meet these boys?

Ladd (1981) helped third-grade students to evaluate themselves by conducting self-evaluation sessions. Following the behavior rehearsal of the target skill with a peer, the researcher met with the individual child and "reviewed observed skill performance, elicited children's perceptions of peer's responses, discussed reasons for undesirable outcomes, and encouraged children to adjust their performance accordingly" (p. 174). Kendall (1981) suggests training the child to use a self-evaluation chart with adult monitoring of the evaluations over a period of time to assess how closely the child's evaluations match those of the trainer.

*Reinforcement.* Feedback may also be provided through reinforcement systems. Contingencies frequently are attached to social behaviors so that correct performance results in desired reinforcers. If the social skills instructor determines that feedback through verbal reinforcement is insufficient to motivate the child or children to increase desirable social responses in social modeling or role playing, tangible or token reinforcement systems may be established. It may be necessary to differentiate between reinforcers given for participation regardless of the quality of the responses and those that provide positive feedback for the desired responses. As a suggested set of procedures,

1. Define clearly what behaviors will be rewarded. For example, in role playing to teach assertive behavior, reinforcers can be given for such target behaviors as looking at the person you are speaking to, speaking in an appropriate tone of voice, smiling at the person you are relating to, making verbal responses without hesitating, and making positive or relevant verbal statements.
2. Provide reinforcers in a form appropriate to the child, e.g.,
   a. edibles, such as cereal or candy for a very young or low-functioning child,
   b. poker chips or other tangible kind of token,
   c. points on a chart or on the chalkboard.

3. Deliver reinforcers either
   a. during the activity immediately following the target behavior, along with verbal feedback, e.g., "good eye contact, John," or "that was a good reply," provided the giving of verbal feedback is not disruptive of the activity;
   b. or in an individual or group evaluation session after the activity, i.e., "In that last role play, how many points should we give John for eye contact?"

In the last situation, the discussion around awarding of points can serve as corrective verbal feedback. For this purpose, the most ideal arrangement would be the availability of videotapes to review, discuss, and use as the basis for awarding points. Whether tokens or points need to be exchanged for backup reinforcers in the form of privileges, activities, or tangible items will have to be determined by the trainer, based on an assessment of existing motivation levels. It is important to remember to reinforce liberally for steps in the right direction, since initial attempts at learning social skills are likely to be awkward and far from perfect.

An example of the use of tokens in social training is an adaptation used by Rotheram (1978) of a technique suggested by Flowers (1975). Rotheram's program makes use of different colored tokens to convey different kinds of feedback in assertiveness training with children and adolescents. Passive behavior is indicated by a blue token, aggressive behavior by a red token, and assertive behavior by a green token. These tokens are held either by student directors or the instructor supercoach and are given out during role playing to identify a behavior as assertive, passive, or aggressive. These tokens are primarily intended for cueing to teach discrimination, but according to Rotheram, the tokens quickly acquire reinforcement power and are an aid in group management. In addition to the red, blue, and green tokens, her procedures include yellow tokens delivered by the instructor for behavior management and to reinforce efforts to learn the new assertive behaviors.

*Practice*

*Practice for Maintenance.* The practice format and the responses required from the learner may vary. As discussed in the previous section, the child is first expected to practice the behavior through some overt and/or cognitive enactment directed by the social skills trainer. These enactments, accompanied by prompting and feedback, are continued until some acceptable level of proficiency is attained. Once this performance standard is reached, practice under less structured and closely supervised conditions might be programmed. For example, children might be organized into small groups in order to engage in social skill games or informal role plays. Independent practice in the form of a worksheet may have particular utility in situations where group size and structure are not conducive to extensive overt enactments under the trainer's supervision. The format for these worksheets may vary widely so that for any particular skill, for example, the child may be asked to

1. Write a brief essay indicating appropriate behaviors to be performed under specified conditions.
2. Complete a cartoon sequence depicting appropriate responses for a problem situation.
3. Complete a crossword puzzle, where the target words refer to appropriate social behavior.
4. Draw a picture depicting appropriate social action.

An example of a worksheet is presented in chapter 5 (Figure 5.1) in the sample teaching strategy. If worksheets are used, care should be taken to vary them, make them enjoyable, and not to use them as busy work. Otherwise, the activities might become aversive and counter the effectiveness of the social skill instruction.

*Practice for Generalization.* Finally, opportunities are provided to practice the behavior in other conditions and with other people. After the child has consistently made appropriate responses to verbally aggressive statements, for example, the trainer may direct the child to practice these behaviors when teased on the playground or at home with his siblings. The child is also directed to report back to the trainer the results of these practice sessions, at which point the child is praised for his successes and receives additional instructions, if necessary. In practicing behaviors in other settings, it is important to determine if the child is able to assess the social situations and make the most appropriate responses. For example, making an assertive remark and leaving the scene may be an appropriate way to respond to verbal aggression from a peer or sibling but not necessarily from a parent or teacher. An additional consideration in such cases may be to make sure the child does not deliberately create negative situations for the purpose of practicing the assigned behaviors. Techniques and procedures for behavior maintenance are discussed in greater detail in the next chapter. The basic steps just outlined — instructions, skill performance, and practice — were presented by Northrop, Wood, and Clark (1979) as a 10-step sequence for "social skill teaching interactions," which they apply both in structured sessions and in spontaneous "incidental teaching" following the occurrence of a problem. The steps are as follows:

1. Positive approach to student — Instructor makes initial contact or opening statement in a nonpunitive manner. May be a greeting or descriptive praise but should not include punishing statements.

2. Description of inappropriate behavior — Instructor describes inappropriate behavior in detail to student.
3. Description of appropriate behavior — Instructor describes desired or appropriate and effective behavior to student.
4. Rationale for the appropriate behavior — Instructor describes consequences, both good and bad, that could be received following appropriate and inappropriate behavior: What's the link to real world (reason for performing behavior), long term payoff.
5. Modeling of desired behavior — Instructor demonstrates the appropriate (and may include the inappropriate) ways to perform the defined social skill.
6. Request for student to practice — Instructor requests the student to practice the desired behaviors in role playing. The instructor should develop the role play scene to include necessary social stimuli; e.g., other peers, adults.
7. Feedback during practice — Instructor provides both positive and negative feedback on student's performance by describing those behaviors that are good, adequate, or need improvement and by offering constructive suggestions for future performance.
8. Requests for additional practice by student — Instructor requests students to attempt role playing again and suggests specific behavior changes and improvement to be included; might use cues.
9. Praise for accomplishments — Instructor delivers praise to student for performance and participation.
10. Give "homework" practice assignment — Instructor requests the student to attempt the trained social skill in another setting, at another time, or with different people. Instructor should reemphasize the desired behaviors and rationales to be utilized by the student.

In this sequence, practice is carried out first through role playing and feedback in the instructional setting, then in the student's natural environment. Further steps could be added: reporting back results of homework and further role playing practice in the training environment to improve on the in vivo practice experience.

## COGNITIVE AND AFFECTIVE METHODS

Another dimension of social skill instruction relates to internal thinking and emotional states. The mediational processes (thinking) that occur between the presentation of environmental events (stimuli) and the individual's reactions to these events (responses) are considered to direct behavior and thus are highly relevant to teaching social skills. Thoughts about a social encounter are greatly determined by how the social situation is perceived.

Therefore, interventions geared toward improving social perceptions need to be considered. Emotions that can be triggered either by internal or external events also influence our social responses. Feelings and thoughts interact and cannot be separated easily. In social skills training the intent is to help the child become aware of his feelings and thoughts and to develop styles of behavior that facilitate social interaction. Presented in the following section are instructional approaches designed to help children become aware of the impact of thoughts and feelings on social behavior and, accordingly, develop ways to produce more adaptive behaviors.

## Social Perception

Social perception refers to one's ability to interpret a social situation accurately. Every human interaction presents a myriad of interpersonal events, such as facial expressions, physical gestures, verbal statements, and tones of voice, all of which are to be taken in, synthesized, and interpreted so that the interpretation adequately reflects the given circumstances. A direct relationship has been suggested between the ability to read social situations and overall social skill (Chandler, 1973; Morrison & Bellack, 1981; Rothenberg, 1970). Social perception has been variously defined, and as Morrison and Bellack (1981) point out, it is a complex process involving many factors. For example, if an individual misreads a social situation, is it due to misunderstanding what is seen or heard, attending to irrelevant stimuli, or failing to attend? McFall (1982) discusses social performance in terms of decoding, decision making, and encoding systems. He proposes that within any social situation the individual must decode or read environmental cues, use a set of decision-making skills, and then act on the environment with motoric responses. Decoding skills, which can be equated with social perception, are described as "the processes by which the incoming sensory information is received, perceived, and interpreted" (p. 24). McFall stresses the importance of social perception, in that deficient decoding will likely result in inadequate social performance. The scientific literature also indicates that social perception is a developmental process (Moyer, 1974), although even very young children are aware of others feelings (Borke, 1971), that it correlates with intelligence (Morrison & Bellack, 1981; Rothenberg, 1970), that children with special needs appear to be less socially perceptive (Rothenberg, 1970; Wong & Wong, 1980), and that social perception skills, such as role taking, can be taught (Chandler, 1973; Morrison & Bellack, 1981).

Until recently little attention has been given to direct and systematic instruction for social perception. For instructional purposes, social perception has tended to be viewed largely as either (a) a communication process where nonverbal and verbal communication are stressed, (b) a psychological process where the role of emotions predominate, or (c) a decentering process where one learns to develop understanding of others and to take the role of the other. A few distinct methods for teaching social perception have been identified that reflect these theoretical positions.

### Communication

Improved communicative competence is one approach to heightening the learner's social understanding. Within this orientation, social perception deficits are considered to be indicative of an inability to accurately interpret and relate the various signals and symbols in the environment. The child who fails to recognize that a certain situation demands reverence or that a particular voice inflection signifies anger or sarcasm will probably respond inappropriately, possibly resulting in negative consequences. Programs attempting to develop social perception through instruction in nonverbal communication tend to emphasize the understanding of what is being communicated through facial expressions, through physical gestures and body movement, through voice cues, and through other physical/environmental cues such as physical proximity and physical appearance (Minskoff, 1980a, 1980b; Wiig & Semel, 1976).

Minskoff (1980a, 1980b) outlines a remedial social perception program focused on nonverbal communication. The curriculum provides for learning in four major skill areas: (a) to help the child comprehend body language, such as facial expressions, gestures, and posture; (b) to help the child understand the significance of spatial elements in social situations, for example, the distance people maintain between them, which may provide valuable information about their personal relationship; (c) to help the child interpret vocalic cues, such as loudness, and paralanguage, such as yawns; and (d) to help the child become aware of artifactual cues, such as cosmetics and clothing, for example, to note the significance of an individual wearing a policeman's uniform and its related authority. For each of these areas Minskoff recommends that children be directed to discriminate, use, and apply these cues in staged social situations. Although suggestions for instruction are given, a packaged curriculum program is not provided. According to Minskoff, such programs would have limited value because "the teaching materials must be tailored to the specific social problems of the students and therefore have to be created by the teachers" (1980a, p. 121).

Nonverbal communication is also stressed by Wiig and Semel for developing social perception in adolescent learning-disabled youngsters. They view social perception as a function of language or the communication process and, thus, social perception problems imply a nonverbal communication disorder. A procedure suggested by Wiig and Semel (1976) for teaching the youngster to perceive the social situation accurately is to identify a film or filmstrip with an obvious dynamic visual sequence. The film is presented in its entirety, followed by a review with the students of the contents "to determine the social and emotional context for further analysis" (p. 312). On a subsequent showing, the film is stopped periodically so that students can predict the actions of the characters. The film is then continued in order to verify or reject the student's predictions. If incorrect, the relevant cues are discussed and the prediction is revised and restated.

In addition to nonverbal communication, social perception training attempts to help the learner develop increased understanding and skill in positive communication. Such skills are useful for evoking positive responses in others as well as enabling one to communicate needs and feelings more clearly. Teaching positive communication skills can begin with having children identify the statements of other people that make them feel happy and warm toward that person, then using those behaviors as the basis for role playing. Such a list might include, for example, greeting someone in a positive way, giving another person a compliment, saying something nice about someone to a third person, or expressing appreciation. Fagen, Long, and Stevens (1975, p. 166) present a series of questions that have the goal of teaching positive communication with others in situations that could otherwise result in negative interactions:

1. If someone did not agree with you, how would you want him to tell you? How could you tell someone that you don't agree with him, in a way that is not mean?
2. If someone did not like what you did, how would you want him to tell you? How could you tell someone that you don't like what he did, in a way that is not mean or hurtful?
3. If someone did not like what you said, how would you want him to tell you? How could you tell someone that you don't like what he said to you, in a way that is not mean?
4. If you were not sharing, how would you want someone to tell you? How could you tell someone that he is not sharing?
5. If you lost a game, what could someone say to make you feel better? What could you say to someone who has lost a game?
6. If you make a mistake, what could someone say to make you feel better? What could you say to someone who has made a mistake?
7. If you got into trouble, what could someone say to make you feel better? What could you say to someone who has gotten into trouble?
8. If someone were angry with you, how would you want him to tell you? What could you say to someone who has made you angry?
9. If you were afraid, what could someone say to make you feel better? What could you say to someone who is afraid?
10. If you were crying, what could someone say to make you feel better? What could you say to someone who is crying?

Wiig (1982) provides a comparable, more structured program, termed *prosocial communication skills* and designed to develop positive communication skills among incompetent children and youth. The prosocial communication skills are divided into four categories: ritualizing, informing, controlling, and feeling. *Ritualizing* refers to communication rituals commonly found in everyday speech, such as greetings, introductions, and responses. *Informing* involves the way one goes about giving, obtaining, and responding to information, such as asking questions ("What is that?") and reacting appropriately to information received ("It is a robot"). *Controlling* pertains to speech acts used to control another's behavior and ways they may be used most effectively. For example, "No, I won't" versus "I would rather not do that." The last category, *feeling*, addresses expressing ("I feel great today") and comprehending attitudes and feelings ("You are worried"). The skills within each of these categories are taught according to a structured learning approach, which includes directions, modeling, and practice, similar to that outlined earlier in this chapter.

### Role Taking

As the child develops and experiences a steady improvement in the ability to identify and understand emotions in others, there is a corresponding decline in egocentrism. Egocentric thought, one's inability to take on the perspective of another, is considered to interfere with social perception and, thus, contribute to maladaptive behaviors. Training in role taking involves teaching participants to assume various roles in interpersonal situations. An informal version of role taking is frequently employed in conflict resolution strategies where participants in the conflict are required to reenact the event but to take the role of the other person. Role playing and social modeling, predominant methods for teaching social skills, have considerable value in teaching social perception through role reversal techniques.

Chandler (1973) describes an intervention procedure used with delinquent youth designed to help them see themselves as others see them and to improve role taking abilities. Under the supervision of trainers, the youths designed dramatic skits that they enacted, videotaped, and reviewed. Although developed and produced by the youths, guidelines for these dramas were that (p. 328):

1. the skits developed by the participants be about persons their own age and depict real-life situations (i.e., not episodes involving TV or movie characters),
2. there be a part for every participant,
3. each skit be rerun until each participant had occupied every role in the plot,
4. that the video recordings be reviewed at the end of each set or tape in an effort to determine ways of improving them.

The findings of this investigation showed that the youths receiving this training made significant improvements over their control group peers both in terms of the role taking posttest and an 18-month follow-up of reported delinquent behaviors.

*Empathy*

Another approach to teaching for social perception is to provide instruction about the dimensions of emotions and how the understanding of emotions can be used to interpret human behavior. Empathy may be viewed as an extension of role taking. Greenspan (1981) terms it *affective role taking* (p. 19). The emphasis here is on affective behavior; that is, the degree to which the observer is able to identify and understand the other's feelings, to take the perspective of the other, and to become emotionally aroused over the circumstances of the other. Empathy generally is defined in terms of one individual's response to the emotions of another. The child who observes a friend experience some misfortune, for example, and experiences sad feelings is demonstrating empathy. However, the response may be based on the extent to which one either recognizes the feelings of the other *or* experiences the same feelings as the other (Strayer, 1980). Although both processes relate to emotions, the former may be more cognitive than affective. Therefore, skill in displaying emotional responsiveness is based on one's ability to recognize and label emotions or feelings in himself and others and to find constructive means for expressing feelings in interpersonal situations. Approaches to teaching about emotions are described in the next section.

## Affective Behavior

Most affective education programs begin with teaching the child to identify and label the emotions of others from various observable indicators; that is, facial expression, body language, voice tone, and verbal content. Teaching the child to "read" emotions from facial expressions is probably the most important place to start. Developmental psychologists have pointed out the significance of facial expressions in early communication between mothers and infants. They consider the human face an important factor in social development, in that the face provides the most immediate and specific information about a person's emotional state. Another part of this task is teaching the child to connect emotions with preceding events in the environment so he understands that emotions do not occur randomly but have antecedents. A further task is acquainting the child with the range of possible human emotions and enabling him to make discriminations about them.

Some initial approaches to teaching children how to identify feelings would involve presenting various emotions in a variety of ways, asking the child to label and enact them. Sample activities may include

1. Present pictures of faces from books or magazines to help the child learn to identify and label emotions. Have the child make up stories about why the people in the pictures are happy, sad, or otherwise.

2. Have the child draw faces reflecting emotions and tell stories explaining
the emotions, provide a scene for the child to relate to, for example,
Draw a face for someone who just had his money stolen.
Draw a face for someone who just won a prize.
Draw a face for someone who is being chased by a bully.
3. Have an adult model facial and bodily gestures and have children identify what emotions are involved.
4. Have children draw cards with names of emotions written on them and
role play emotions for each other or identify in a guessing game. A variation could ask for the child to role play the emotion with facial expressions, body language, or voice tone, and words.
5. Have the children develop a vocabulary of feelings, a "feelings diction-
ary" making lists of synonyms for words describing feelings, using them
to label pictures, for spelling words, or as the basis for game. Pictures
of faces might be displayed on a bulletin board labeled with a list of
descriptive words.

In order to teach the child to be aware of and label his own feelings, initially an adult may need to make inferences about the child's feelings and
provide information to call his attention to the cues the child is giving out:
"You are smiling, Mary. Are you feeling happy?" "You have a frown on
your face, John. Can you tell me what you are feeling? What happened to
make you feel that way?" The adult can also provide a model by identifying and labeling his own feelings, along with providing information to
explain the feelings. Along with learning to identify his own feelings, the
child can learn that others may have different feelings in the same situations.
Some activities for teaching the child to label his own emotions could
include:

1. Have the child draw his own face or role play how he would feel in different situations, for example, "Draw the face that shows how you would
feel
. . . if you fell in the mud with your new clothes on."
. . . if your pet had not come home all day."
. . .if you were opening presents on your birthday."

2. Provide an exercise using sentence completion; for example, "For me,
happiness is _____," accompanied by drawings. Have children compare
notes on their answers in a discussion.

3. For negative emotions use a technique like the "Feeling thermometer"
or the SUDS (Subjective Unit of Disturbance Scale) concept (Wolpe, 1958;
Wolpe & Lazarus, 1966). Using a drawing of a thermometer with a scale
1-100, children may develop a hierarchy of low to high discomfort situations. For example, arriving late at school may create a SUDS of 30; having to present an oral report may be an 80; having to take a failing grade

home may be regarded as 100. By generating discussion, and ranking a series of hypothetical problem situations, a child can learn that not all of his peers would regard a situation with the same degree of emotion. In discussing the rating of problem situations, the physiological indicators of discomfort can also be identified; for example, heart pounding, breath short, hands sweating, blushing; and a discrimination made between when these reactions signal anxiety, anger, or fear and when they may merely indicate excitement. Beyond talking hypothetically about the SUDS level, the SUDS concept can be used to identify feelings in role plays and can be translated into the natural environment by using *SUDS* as a cue word; i.e., "What's your SUDS level?" to create awareness of negative affect and the need to exercise self control of behavior.

4. A somewhat similar approach is the Boiling Point List (Curwin & Curwin, 1974). This exercise is designed to provide awareness for the child of how he acts when angry and what produces the greatest anger. The procedures involve providing a list or having the students generate a list of anger-producing situations and rate each one on a 1-5 scale (pp. 35-37):

(1) I get extremely angry in this situation.
(2) I get mildly angry in this situation.
(3) I get irritated in this situation, but not very angry.
(4) This situation only slightly bothers me.
(5) This situation does not anger me at all.

Sample situations of the Boiling Point List include

(1) when someone tells on you,
(2) when you try out for something and don't get it,
(3) when your friends do something without you,
(4) when you want to play with your friends but you have to go visiting with your family,
(5) when someone borrows something of yours and breaks it,
(6) when you want to do something and no one wants to do it with you,
(7) when you are unjustly accused of something,
(8) when you lose money,
(9) when you do something good and no one notices,
(10) when someone causes you to get in trouble.

Some guidelines suggested by Fagen et al. (1975) are relevant to the task of teaching children to recognize and label their own feelings. For group discussions related to emotions they suggest the following (pp. 66-67):

No individual should be pressured to respond or to divulge his feelings: Teacher or peers might question one another out of interest, but an explicit norm should be established for the "right to privacy" or the "right to pass."

It should be recognized that participation by pupils may be verbal, nonverbal, or vicarious: Students can be learning without saying or doing anything. The right to be silent, to listen, and to observe should be respected at all times.

The watchful member is often learning more about emotions and acceptance of them (including his own) than is the rapid talker.

Practice with more impersonal and less anxiety-laden issues should be provided before taking up any directly personal or high-anxiety issues: For example, feelings about television, the weather, sports, etc., can be introduced before beginning to talk about feelings about parents, teacher, or other students. In this way, students can first learn that differences are acceptable, that retaliation or hurt is not a consequence of honest expression, and that feelings are not right or wrong.

The teacher should continually reiterate that feelings can be pleasant or unpleasant and enjoyable or painful, but he should emphasize that they are never bad or wrong: A clear distinction should be made between a person's right to own any and all feelings and his responsibility to place limits on acting on this feelings.

Feelings are most usefully introduced by focusing on some present event, experience, or issue: Questions introduced by: "How do you feel when . . .?" or "What thoughts or feelings do you have . . .?" or "When do you feel that way?" are preferable to questions in the past tense.

Emotional responsiveness, the ability to identify and share the emotional experiences of others, is based on the individual's understanding of his own emotions. In addition to teachings geared to the child's own feelings such as the ones just given, the child should have the opportunity to learn to respond to the feelings of others. An example of teaching for emotional responsiveness is given by Feshbach et al. (1983) in their curriculum designed to teach the spectrum of empathic behaviors to elementary school aged children. The children are given an excerpt from the book *A Tree Grows in Brooklyn*, informed that it is about children of their ages, then, following the story, are engaged in a discussion about how they feel and the causes of these feelings. A variety of activities are included in this curriculum: problem solving, role playing, and simulations. Feshbach et al. (1983) field tested this curriculum empirically and reported encouraging findings of improved prosocial behaviors among empathy-trained children.

The ultimate goal in learning about the feelings of oneself and others is to help the child to find constructive ways to express feelings in interpersonal situations. This is complex because it involves not only the child's ability to discriminate and respond internally but the development of the ability to exercise control and selectivity over his overt responses as well. This latter task involves a three-way interaction between emotion, cognition, and motor activity. Social skills training aimed at teaching behavioral control of emotion is most effective if it develops awareness in the child of his feelings in a situation, awareness of the cognitive evaluations he is making about the situation and his own feeling state, and a mastery of the range of behaviors to engage in, related to the situation. In helping the child make a distinction between his thoughts and feelings and his behavior, Fagen, Long, and Stevens (1975, p. 178) suggest using the following points as the basis for discussion:

1. All thoughts and feelings are OK and normal to have.
2. Thoughts and feelings can be private property; complete freedom is possible for thoughts and feelings.
3. All actions or behaviors are not OK; some are illegal, harmful to self or others, or against the rules.
4. Behaviors or actions cannot be private property; complete freedom is not possible for behavior.
5. Thoughts and feelings are different from behavior; you can think and feel things without needing to do them or without blaming yourself for having mean or "bad" ideas.

Several of the strategies in the cognitive approaches discussed later in this chapter also are geared toward helping the child to make the connection between thoughts, feelings, and behavior.

Training in communicative processes, empathy, and role taking may be effective in enabling the individual to become more socially perceptive. Because this is a relatively new area, literature on training procedures is limited and even more sparse is the research demonstrating the efficacy of the instructional techniques currently identified. There is a need not only for efficacy studies but also for an investigation of the specific emotions and perceptions as they relate to the developmental process. For example, Moyer (1974), in a study with kindergarten and third-grade children, found that expressions of happiness were the easiest to identify and communicate, with anger second. Fear and sadness were next, being of equal difficulty. Surprise was the most difficult, especially for the kindergarten subjects. Most programs present these emotions in a parallel fashion without allowing for differences in difficulty or the additional time it would take to develop understanding of a particular emotion. Research is also needed to define better the nature of the imperceptive child. For example, some children with social deficits tend to misperceive because they focus on only one part of the social situation; for example, they look only at the face and not the body movements.

Although there is a tendency for social perception and social skill to be equated in the literature, Morrison and Bellack (1981) view social perception as a precursor of social skill. They differentiate between having a "repertoire of response skills" and social perception, which is knowing when and how to make the particular response. In teaching for social perception, one needs to be aware that improvement in reading the social environment does not automatically lead to improved performance without direct social skill instruction. The reverse also appears to be true (Morrison & Bellack, 1981). Empirical support is given to this position through studies which failed to find relationships between social perception assessments and social skill ratings (Cartledge, Stupay, & Kaczala, in press; Hansen, 1983; Maheady, Maitland, & Sainato, 1982). Therefore, the social skills trainer would be well advised to incorporate teaching relative to comprehending environmental cues into instruction focused on the behavioral manifestation of specific social skills.

## Relaxation

Another set of procedures that enhance the child's ability to control thoughts and feelings involves the use of systematic relaxation. Relaxation provides a means of altering negative feeling states and delaying the impulsive expression of negative emotions long enough to think of alternatives. Relaxation training has been widely used by behavior therapists as part of systematic desensitization procedures to assist phobic or anxious adult clients in confronting emotionally charged and fear-producing situations. Relaxation is useful because the physiological state of relaxation is incompatible with fear, anger, and anxiety-provoking cognitions and feelings. Relaxation is incompatible also with aggressive motoric responses. Along with teaching relaxation, a procedure known as *conditioned relaxation training* or *cue-controlled relaxation* involves teaching the person to relax in response to a self-produced cue word such as "relax" or "calm." The ability to become relaxed in anger or anxiety-producing interpersonal situations is a social skill that is being increasingly recognized as having relevance for children as well as adults. Children trained in relaxation possess a tool that can potentially enable them to decrease feelings of anxiety, fear, or anger in stressful social situations and substitute a constructive behavior for a less appropriate impulsive response to the problem situation. Some general steps in teaching relaxation to children follow.

*Teach Prerequisite Skills.* Cautela and Groden (1978) have identified a set of readiness skills that may need to be assessed and taught prior to relaxation training. These involve being able to sit in a chair for 5 seconds, maintaining eye contact for 3 seconds, imitation skills, and following directions.

*Set the Stage.* Relaxation training should take place in a quiet, calm environment. Dim lights, soft music, and the absence of distracting loud noise or visual stimuli will facilitate the atmosphere of relaxation. Children can be taught relaxation either sitting in comfortable chairs or lying on the floor on rugs or mats. Bean bag chairs lend themselves to relaxation. Cautela and Groden start with having the child sit in a chair with his head up and hands in his lap, identifying that as the "relaxing position." It is possible to build in stimulus control aspects by providing a special relaxation chair or thick rug in the home or classroom to which the child can remove himself and practice relaxation as an alternative to engaging in some problematic behavior. The voice tone of the adults is also important in relaxation training. Instructions should be given in a calm and even somewhat monotonous tone.

*Teach the Concept of Relaxation.* The most widely used techniques for teaching relaxation involves variations of those originally introduced by Jacobson (1938), in which relaxation is taught by alternately tensing and releasing various groups of muscles and becoming aware of the sensations of tension and relaxation.

There are differences of opinion about whether tension should be presented to children along with relaxation, especially for hyperactive or highly tense children. In using contrasting tension and relaxation, most writers on the subject suggest a much shorter period of tension for children than for adults, not more than 2–5 seconds. Cautela and Groden suggest an alternative to tensing for children for whom the use of tension may be contraindicated. A statement like "relax your arm" is accompanied by a tactile approach such as stroking the child's arm. Another approach is having the child shake his hands and fingers while keeping his arms at his side. Continued shaking will lead to fatigue in the hands and arms and a feeling of relaxation when the shaking is discontinued. Several other aids can be used to help the child understand the concept of relaxation with or without the use of tension. One of these is modeling by an adult, who can demonstrate tension and relaxation in his arms, for example, and let the child feel the difference. Another is the use of analogy and imagery. Concepts like a wooden soldier, broomstick, or robot can convey stiffness and tension, whereas a rag doll or melted ice cream can be equated with relaxation. Developing the concepts of relaxation through movement exercises is a useful approach with young children, who may easily be able to become limp rag dolls, melt to the floor, float like a feather, or drop like a heavy brick. Kendall and Braswell (1985) suggest the Robot–Rag Doll game, where children are assisted first to tense like robots and then to relax like floppy rag dolls. Having the child imagine happy, restful scenes can also facilitate relaxation, and pictures of clouds, forests, or the sea can serve as aids for imagery. It can be suggested that the child may feel like floating on a cloud, on the lapping waves of a lake, or like walking in space.

*Introduce Relaxation in Muscle Groups.* Relaxation training for adults as developed by Bernstein and Borkovec (1973) takes the client through a sequence related to different muscle groups. In their procedures for children, Cautela and Groden (a) alter the sequence of muscle groups from that typically suggested for adults, (b) recommend various physical manipulations and analogies to help the child to relax, and (c) incorporate breathing exercises into the training. The client is directed to systematically attend to, tense, and relax the various muscle groups of the body. Most relaxation talk includes (a) directions to tense and/or relax particular parts of the body, "First think about the muscles in your forehead. Let every muscle in your forehead relax. Relax, relax, the muscles in your forehead"; (b) directions to experience the feeling of relaxation, usually stated several ways, "See how soft and smooth your forehead feels. You can feel the tension going out of your forehead as you feel more and more relaxed. See how different and nice it feels to be relaxed." In relaxing the arms, for example, the procedure is as follows (Cautela & Groden, 1978, p. 53):

> Demonstrate the position of holding your right arm out straight, making a fist, and tightening your whole arm from your hand to your shoulder. Ask the child to feel the parts that are tight (biceps, forearm, back of arm, elbow, above and below wrist and fingers). Ask the child to tighten his arm as you teach him to feel the tightness with his other hand. Use synonyms such as stiff or wooden-like. Next, tell him to gradually relax his arm back to the relaxing position. Repeat with the other arm. The child should gradually learn to tighten and relax his arm to the cue "Tighten your arm." It may be helpful to stroke his arm while it is in the relaxing position. Ask him to think of how those muscles feel as they begin to feel loose. Looseness can be tested by the "limp procedure." Lift his hand up and let it drop in his lap like a limp rag doll.
>
> Criteria: Child can, upon request, tighten and relax each arm. The muscles should look tight and feel tight to the touch.
>
> Problem: Often it is difficult for some children to make a fist and hold their arm out straight. This can be shaped by first holding your left arm under the child's elbow for support while having him push against your hand in an open palm fashion. Another way to shape a tight fist is to ask the child to tighten his outstretched hand around your index finger with his palm down.

Similar procedures are followed with other muscle groups. During training, the child is taught to take a deep breath, hold it, and let go slowly while saying the word "relax" to himself. The process is repeated five times. The breathing exercise is particularly important for cue-controlled relaxation. The ability to produce a physiologically relaxed state upon exhaling and repeating a cue word, such as "relax," is the principal aspect of relaxation training that might be regarded as a social skill when it can be used in troublesome interpersonal situations.

Relaxation instructions ("patter") have been written out and recorded for use in a rote fashion. An area of debate involves the use of taped versus live training procedures. Taped procedures save time and can have considerable utility for the researcher who needs to have a standardized process. For the teacher or clinician working with children, the use of relaxation tapes can be a way to encourage the inexperienced person to get started without the need to become thoroughly familiar with relaxation patter. Most research indicates, however, that tapes are less effective than live presentations for teaching relaxation. They proceed at a set pace and thus do not allow for assessment feedback about how the child is responding before moving to the next set of instructions.

*Practice.* Most relaxation programs suggest practice once or twice a day until skill at relaxing is achieved. Once the procedures are learned, relaxation tapes or records can be useful for inducing relaxation in practice sessions or in the absence of the original trainer. A number of programs have incorporated relaxation as a self-control procedure along with other behavior change techniques. One of these is the Turtle program (Schneider & Robin, 1975). The Turtle technique involves a combination of coping behaviors that include (a) teaching the child to withdraw into an imaginary shell by pulling his arms and head in close to his body and closing his eyes when he feels threatened in a problem situation. "You can hide in your shell whenever you get that feeling inside you that tells you are angry. When you are in your shell, you can have a moment to rest and figure out what to do about it"; (b) teaching the child to relax his muscles while "doing turtle"; and (c) using problem-solving techniques in which the child thinks through alternative courses of action for dealing with the problem and their various consequences. Children are also taught to discriminate when it is better to "do turtle" or to "stick their neck out" in a more assertive manner. This program illustrates a multielement approach to teaching self-control alternatives to impulsive striking out through the use of cues (i.e., "stop," "do turtle") along with relaxation to lessen negative emotions and provide a delay in response, thus allowing the child time to consider the other courses of action he had learned.

Jackson et al. (1983) have incorporated relaxation scripts into their social skill instruction program. The relaxation scripts accompany each social skill to be taught and are structured so that the individual relaxation exercise progresses from teacher to pupil direction and control. In this program relaxation training is intended to facilitate social interaction, since the child is taught to employ breaching techniques and positive self-statements under stressful social situations.

## Cognitive Approaches

Cognitive approaches to social skill instruction focus on helping the child acquire thought patterns considered to be functional for social competence. Although various models exist (Wilson, 1978), they may be grouped according to two primary intentions: to alter the statements the child makes to himself; or to develop cognitive problem-solving skills. The common element present in all models is the theoretical position that cognitions play a major role in directing behavior and, thus, the child's maladaptive behavior may be indicative of inadequate thinking styles.

### Altering Belief Systems

One theoretical framework for altering belief systems stems from the Rational Emotive Therapy (RET) model developed by Albert Ellis (1962). The basic premise is that maladaptive behaviors largely result from irrational belief systems that influence what we say to ourselves and, thereby, control our behavior. Ellis (1977) takes the position that inappropriate behavior is less a function of a particular event than of what one says to himself about the event. The child who receives a failing mark, for example, may exhibit more maladaptive behavior if he tells himself that he is worthless and dumb or that it is terrible and catastrophic to fail. The objective of rational models is to help the individual identify the events leading to specific behaviors, to analyze irrational belief systems considered to be controlling these reactions, and to replace these systems with rational ones that are more likely to lead to adaptive behavior. In examining irrational belief systems, Ellis (1977) suggests looking for the things one tells himself he should or must do or must have happen. Examples of these beliefs as listed by Gambrill (1977, pp. 498, 499) include:

1. The idea that it is a dire necessity for an adult human being to be loved or approved by virtually every significant other person in his community.
2. The idea that one should be thoroughly competent, adequate, and achieving in all possible respects, if one is to consider oneself worthwhile.
3. The idea that certain people are bad, wicked, or villainous and that they should be severely blamed and punished for their villainy;
4. The idea that it is awful and catastrophic when things are not the way one would very much like them to be;
5. The idea that human unhappiness is externally caused and that people have little or no ability to control their sorrows and disturbances.
6. The idea that if something is or may be dangerous or fearsome, one should be terribly concerned about it and should keep dwelling on the possibility of its occurring;
7. The idea that it is easier to avoid than to face certain life difficulties and self-responsibilities;
8. The idea that one should be dependent on others and needs someone stronger than oneself on whom to rely;
9. The idea that one's past history is an all-important determinant of one's present behavior, and that because something once strongly affected one's life, it should indefinitely have a similar effect;
10. The idea that one should become quite upset over other people's problems and disturbances; and
11. The idea that there is invariably a right, precise, and perfect solution to human problems, and that it is catastrophic if this correct solution is not found.

The principles of RET have been adapted into a therapeutic program for children (Bernard & Joyce, 1984). Initially, the focus is on increasing the child's awareness of his own maladaptive behavior. Intervention at this stage is geared toward helping the child to recognize the variety of possible reactions to any one situation, some more adaptive than others, and helping the child to become more receptive to his own behavior change. These understandings are then followed by the ABCs of RET. That is, (a) understanding the variety and range of emotions, (b) understanding that our thoughts about people and events, not the people and events themselves, produce specific feelings, and (c) understanding the difference between rational and irrational thoughts. After the child has acquired these basic RET concepts, various techniques are used to help the child employ more rational beliefs. For example, one procedure involves helping the child to substitute rational self-statements for the previous unsuccessful ones. Among other techniques are disputation and practical problem solving, where children are taught to (a) challenge and restate irrational thoughts and (b) perform new adaptive behaviors that force them to discard previously held self-defeating thoughts. The final stages of RET include practice and homework exercises, where children are directed to apply the newly acquired thoughts and behaviors under real-life conditions.

Knaus (1974) has incorporated RET procedures into an instructional program for children called *rational–emotive education* (REE). Designed to be used by the classroom teacher, the objective of REE is to help the child to develop rational belief systems that foster more positive feelings and, thus, lead to more adaptive behaviors. The program contains five major learning areas that include

1. Feelings — Helping children become aware of feelings, their origins and various modes of expression.
2. Challenging Irrational Beliefs — Helping children to recognize irrational belief systems, their effects and how to develop cognitive styles that would enable the children to challenge these irrational thought patterns on their own.
3. Challenging Feelings of Inferiority — Helping children recognize the complex nature of individuals, that each person has positive aspects as well as negative ones, and that children should not view themselves or others in terms of a single attribute, whether good or bad.
4. Learning, Mistake-Making and Imperfection — Helping children to understand the nature of the learning process, differences of opinion, and mistakes in order to develop a more realistic approach toward learning and to avoid the pitfalls of perfectionism.
5. Demanding, Catastrophizing, and Challenging — Teaching children to challenge irrational *must* and *should* systems, which lead to "catastrophizing" and "awfulizing" and to replace them with more reasonable attitudes of *desire* and *prefer*. That is, the child will learn to think in terms of the things he would like to happen rather than the things that he demands happen.

Also included are teaching activities for seven special topics: (a) responsibility (roles and rules); (b) perspective (viewing a situation from more than one perspective); (c) stereotyping; (d) teasing and name-calling; (e) bullies, victims, bystanders; (f) guided protest (the child as a consumer); and (g) friendship. An example of the classroom application is the approach suggested by Knaus to help children understand that feelings come from thoughts. In the Happening–Thought–Feeling–Reaction diagram, an event is written out on the board in diagram form. Using name calling as the problem event, the diagram would be, for example,

| HAPPENING | + | THOUGHT | = | FEELING | REACTION |
|---|---|---|---|---|---|
| Arthur calls James' mother a name | | It's terrible to have my mother called a name.... I can't stand it....I have to get him for that.... | | Strong anger (out of control) | James hits Arthur, fight results |

In order to demonstrate how different thoughts could lead to different feelings and actions, the same diagram can then be developed with alternative thoughts, feelings, and reactions generated by the children,

| HAPPENING | + | THOUGHT | = | FEELING | REACTION |
|---|---|---|---|---|---|
| Arthur calls James' mother a name | | He doesn't even know my mother....He wants me to get angry....I don't have to do what he wants.... | | Mild anger or annoyance | James ignores Arthur, and walks away |

According to the author, the program is geared to children from fourth to eighth grades but can be adapted for younger or older youngsters. It is intended to be presented several times weekly for approximately a 9-month period.

### Altering Self-Statements

Although RET utilizes self-statements, Bernard and Joyce (1984) distinguish RET from other cognitive approaches in that the aim of RET is to change one's philosophy or basic belief system, whereas other cognitive methods are focused more on cognitive behaviors, such as altering self-speech or employing verbal mediation. For example, stress-inoculation training (Meichenbaum, 1977) places more emphasis on (a) developing specific thinking skills or verbal mediators, and (b) applying these skills under stressful conditions. Meichenbaum describes stress-inoculation training as a three-step process, wherein the individual is helped to conceptualize the problem, to develop cognitive coping skills, and to apply the skills under stressful conditions. In the first step, the child is aided in understanding the antecedent events and the cognitive and physiological aspects of the problem (what events provoked the emotional event), the physical responses that accompanied the emotions (increased heartbeat, sweating, etc.), and the self-statements that directed the emotional overt behaviors (such as flight in fear or fighting in anger). The techniques used to develop these understandings include engaging the child in a discussion, inquiring how he felt under these conditions, and encouraging the use of imagery. With imagery, the child is directed to relive a recent event and to "run a movie through his mind." For example, if the problem situation involves excessive anger and extreme reactions, the child might be asked to reconstruct his most recent tantrum, from which it would be determined that (a) he gets angry whenever he makes an incorrect response to his academic work; (b) he feels hot and starts to breathe hard; (c) he feels that he is a dummy and no good when he gets something wrong; and (d) he starts to cry, to yell, to destroy his papers, and to throw things.

After the situation has been analyzed and the child realizes the events that precipitated his behavior, he is then trained to practice certain coping self-statements. Meichenbaum (1977, p. 155) presents a four-phase model with ample self-statements to be employed for rehearsing coping cognitions that consists of (a) preparing for a stressor — recognizing the nature of the situation ("What is it you have to do?" or "You can develop a plan to deal with it"); (b) confronting and handling a stressor — using statements to increase courage and self-confidence ("Just 'psych' yourself up — you can meet this challenge" or "One step at a time; you can handle the situation"); (c) coping with feeling overwhelmed — recognizing that reactions to the situation will occur and trying to keep these feelings under control ("You should expect your fear to rise" or "Don't try to eliminate fear totally; just keep it manageable"); and (d) reinforcing self-statements — assessing one's performance and making complimentary self-statements ("It worked; you did it" or "You can be pleased with the progress you're making").

A similar sequence for anger based on this model has been devised by Novaco (1975). Adapting Novaco's categories to children, self-statements for the example of the child overreacting to corrective feedback might include

- Preparing for provocation
    If the teacher marks something wrong I can handle it.
    I know what to do if I get upset.
    Making a mistake is not so bad.
- Impact on confrontation
    Keep calm.
    Think about the ones you got correct.
    It's silly to get angry about one problem.
    The teacher is really right to show me what I did wrong.
    Being corrected helps me learn.
- Coping with arousal
    I'm beginning to breathe hard; I should relax.
    Stop and think about all the good work you did today.
    Try to keep cool.
- Reflection on provocation
    (when conflict is unresolved)
    It partly worked.

I can do better next time.
This is hard to do but I'll keep trying.
(when conflict is resolved or coping is successful)
I did a good job that time, I even smiled at the teacher.
I can be a good student. The teacher likes for me to keep calm when I make a mistake.

In teaching a child to apply coping skills under various stressful conditions, several techniques are used to facilitate skill application. Relaxation exercises are employed to reduce the child's emotional reactions and to aid in producing coping self-statements. Through imagery, the child is instructed to place himself in a stressful situation, for example, "Imagine that you are in class and you just finished taking a spelling test. You are saying things to yourself that will help you prepare for the teacher correcting your paper, such as, 'I can handle it if I have made a mistake; I will not get angry.' You remind yourself that even though you got two wrong you did get eight correct. The teacher tells you that you did a better job on this spelling test. You say, 'thank you,' and congratulate yourself for controlling yourself."

*Note*: The child may also be taken through a less successful resolution such as "You tell yourself to keep cool but you feel hot and shaky inside. Then you notice tears running down your face and you put your head on your desk to continue crying. A few minutes later the teacher tells you that you did better on this test. You thank her and tell yourself that even though you weren't completely controlled at least you didn't have a tantrum or throw books. You will do better next time." Role playing may also be used, providing for a more explicit demonstration of behaviors and, thus, greater opportunity for feedback and self-evaluation.

Controlling impulsive or aggressive behaviors is the focus of another form of verbal mediation. Referred to as *self-instructional training* (SIT) (Meichenbaum, 1977), the goals are (a) to get the child to interrupt himself before performing some inappropriate behavior, and (b) to train the child to guide his behavior through "internal dialogue." To effect the first goal, instructional techniques include cueing the child that a problem situation exists and that he must stop and think out how he will proceed. Labeled *thought stopping* and initially used with adults, this procedure was devised to help the individual discontinue nonproductive or self-defeating thought processes. For example, the individual who tends to engage in excessive self-denigrating thoughts might say "stop" out loud or to himself to terminate the thoughts, and then direct his thinking along a more productive path. In adapting thought stopping for children, environmental or physiological stimuli are identified that can be used as signals for the child to stop and employ prescribed thinking skills. For example, Palkes, Stewart, and Kahana (1968), in a program to train hyperactive boys to perform paper-and-pencil tasks, used large cue cards that included statements such as, "Before I start any of the tasks I am going to do, I am going to say: STOP!"

After interrupting himself, the child is expected to use internal mediators or to talk to himself in order to guide himself through the problem situation. Training for such "thought structuring" is exemplified by a sequence developed by Meichenbaum and Goodman (1971) where the intent is to show a child how to think through a difficult task (Meichenbaum, 1977, p. 32):

1. An adult model performed a task while talking to himself out loud (cognitive modeling);
2. The child performed the same task under the direction of the model's instructions (overt, external guidance);
3. The child performed the task while instructing himself aloud (overt self-guidance);
4. The child whispered the instructions to himself as he went through the task (faded, overt self-guidance); and finally
5. The child performed the task while guiding his performance via private speech (covert self-instruction).

An example of the modeling situation might be (Meichenbaum & Goodman, 1971, p. 117):

Okay, what is it I have to do? You want me to copy the picture with the different lines. I have to go slow and be careful. Okay, draw the line down, down good; then to the right, that's it; now down some more and to the left. Good, I'm doing fine so far. Remember go slow. Now back up again. No, I was supposed to go down. That's okay. Just erase the line carefully.... Good. Even if I make an error I can go on slowly and carefully, Okay, I have to go down now. Finished. I did it.

In this example, impulsive second-grade children were being trained to use self-talk in order to monitor their behavior and respond more accurately. The problem situation was performance on various paper and pencil cognitive tasks such as the Porteus Maze tests. As noted from the model, such training is designed to move the child gradually from copying the verbalization of the model, to independently making these statements out loud, to finally internalizing them in the form of thoughts. The ultimate goal is that, through repeated presentations, the child will be trained to use this thought pattern automatically when confronted with problem situations. Kendall (Kendall & Braswell, 1985; Kendall & Morison, 1984) points out that this is a "coping" model as opposed to the "mastery" model, typically provided in behavioral modeling. Under the "coping" condition the observer is privileged not only to know the model's self-statements, which illustrate the model's internal stresses resulting from the task, but also how the model is able to use self-speech to overcome emotional barriers and to eventually experience success. With the absence of overt cognitive processes in behavioral modeling the observer is not informed of the model's self-statements that aid in coping and skill performance. Under these conditions, the observer may mistakenly attribute the model's greater competence to innate skill rather than personal effort and, thus, rule out the possibility of imitating the model's behavior. Kendall cites empirical evidence demonstrating the superior effects achieved through cognitive modeling compared to behavioral modeling. Training in cognitive modeling is recommended to progress systematically from relatively innocuous cognitive tasks such as games and puzzles to more emotionally laden interpersonal problem solving (Kendall & Braswell, 1985). An important factor in this example is the provision for failure. The trainer purposely encounters failure and demonstrates coping self-statements. This sequence is exemplified in the Think Aloud Program used by Camp (1977) initially to control aggressive behaviors in young boys and detailed in chapter 6 of this book.

## Problem Solving

Children, as well as adults, are constantly confronted with conflict situations that, depending on how approached, may either be resolved with little difficulty or could be exacerbated. It appears that one critical factor is problem solving ability, since good problem solvers tend to evidence better social adjustment than those with limited skills in this area (Richard & Dodge, 1982; Spivack & Shure, 1974). D'Zurilla and Goldfried (1971) provide a problem-solving method for adults consisting of (a) general orientation; (b) problem definition and formation; (c) generation of alternatives; (d) decision making; and (e) solution verification. A variation of this model, involving determining the problem, alternative responses, the appropriate solution, and evaluation, can be employed in developing decision-making skills in children.

*Problem Definition and Formulation.* Before an individual can pursue the solution to a problem, he must be able to recognize that a problem exists (Meichenbaum, 1975). Helping a child to recognize a problem may be approached in various ways, for example, identifying and compiling problem situations encountered by a particular child or by children of a younger age group or by having older children list their own problematic situations. The situations are discussed with the child in order to help him understand the nature of the problem and the related environmental and emotional factors. The goal is to help the child to develop a thinking style to use to define problems independently. A series of questions may be used to help the child recognize aspects of the problem; for example, (a) identifying feelings of being upset, (b) identifying when upset feelings started, (c) determining what happened to make him upset, and (d) determining what he wants to have happen instead of what did happen. For example,

*Trainer*: You look upset, Ray.
 (*Child indicates he's not upset.*)
*Trainer*: Is that why you're not participating with your group in the listening center?
 (*Child indicates he doesn't enjoy the listening center.*)
*Trainer*: But you enjoyed those stories yesterday and today we're playing your favorite story.
 (*Child indicates that he is disappointed because he was to act as leader and show the book while listening but another child was doing it.*)
*Trainer*: OK, so the problem is that you want to be leader, isn't it?
 (*Child agrees.*)
*Trainer*: You really want to listen to the story, don't you?
 (*Child agrees.*)

Once the child clearly understands what his problem is, he can begin to consider solutions.

*Determining Alternatives.* In this step, the child is assisted in generating various alternative responses and the possible consequences to these solutions. For data collection, the child would list as many alternatives as possible, including those that might be undesirable. Alternatives for the example just presented might include

- Taking the book from the other child;
- Asking the other child to let him be leader;
- Telling the teacher she had promised him to be leader today;
- Crying;
- Saying nothing and not participating with the group; or
- Saying nothing and participating with the group.

In a formal teaching situation, the list of responses may be depicted through simple stick pictures and displayed on a bulletin board or written on the chalkboard to help children remember the alternatives and their corresponding consequences (Spivack & Shure, 1974). Data analysis occurs when youngsters are required to review their suggested responses in terms of possible consequences; for example, "If you told the teacher she promised to let you be leader today, what do you think will happen?" The consequences also may be listed in a manner similar to that for the alternatives.

The *Consequences Game* (McPhail, 1975) is an example of an instructional approach designed to train adolescents to predict consequences. The set includes 71 cards, with humorous drawings that depict various environmental and social situations, such as, "Someone ignores a call for help, because she thinks that the person calling may be drunk or fooling around," or "Someone always believes what people tell him." The youth is then engaged in a discussion or similar activity to determine the effects this behavior would have on others, why he should avoid this act, and what to do instead.

*Determining Solutions.* This decision-making step involves matching the listed alternatives and consequences. Following the Spivack and Shure suggestions, the pictured behaviors could be coordinated so that the child sees that response X could possibly lead to consequence Y. For older children, words may be substituted for pictures. Also, at this point, behaviors may be ordered so that children list the alternatives from most preferred to least preferred. Another consideration is the need to identify the exact way to carry out the most desirable alternative (Goldfried & Goldfried, 1975). Once the child has determined the most desirable way to resolve the situation, he should be assisted in trying it out. The behaviors may first be practiced through role playing. Behavior rehearsal is especially important if the actual problem situation is anxiety provoking and if the desired response consists of complex behaviors unfamiliar to the child. Depending on the nature of the problem and suggested solutions, the application sequence may entail

* Modeling of the suggested response — The trainer demonstrates how the responses should be made.
* Behavior rehearsal — The child acts out the desired behavior in a manner similar to that demonstrated by the trainer. Under role play conditions, a variety of responses may be considered and tried out in order to assess the relative effects.
* Application in real-life conditions — The child tries the solution in the real situation. The trainer aids the child in assessing the results and in determining alternatives, if necessary. The child is encouraged to use problem-solving strategies in his daily living.

*Evaluation.* The evaluation is conducted with the child, in order to determine the effectiveness of the applied strategy. As with problem identification, the child may need guidance in deciding whether he accomplished what he wanted. If desired goals have not been met, the child is then helped to find other or additional ways to approach the situation.

The effective use of problem-solving strategies is partly based on the child's abilities: to understand the nature of the problem, to identify alternative responses, to think through various responses and their consequences, and to evaluate the alternatives in terms of desired ends. However, before embarking upon problem-solving instruction, incorporating the above steps, it should be noted that this model demands certain prerequisite abilities that the learner, especially young children and children with special needs, may not have. Problem solving requires that the learner possess basic language skills, reasoning skills (ability to understand relationships, to identify realistic alternatives, and to anticipate consequences), ability to engage in sustained attention, and sufficient memory skills to retain learning. In constructing a problem-solving training program for preschool, inner city children, Spivack and Shure (1974) developed instructional activities for systematic teaching of preproblem-solving skills, consisting of the following abilities and concepts:

1. Language — Basic language skills involving the understanding and use of words such as *and, or, is, same, different.*
2. Emotions — Labeling emotions, identifying emotions in others, and learning to cope with various feelings.
3. Situation Analysis — Recognizing that any situation consists of several factors that must be considered before acting.
4. Preferences — Understanding that people have preferences and that these differ among individuals.
5. Causal Relationships — Understanding the relationship among events and the effect one may have on another's behavior.
6. Fairness — Considering the rights of others.

Using a game format, the authors provide for extensive instruction in the preliminary skills before directly engaging the child in problem-solving strategies. The remainder of the script focuses on skills directly related to problem solving; that is, identifying alternative solutions, anticipating consequences of specific acts, and matching the consequences to their respective solutions. During the training, the teacher conducts several sessions designed to help the child identify as many alternatives as possible to a problem situation. For example, "Robert is riding on the bicycle but Georgie wants to ride also. What can he do?" The teacher assists the children in listing solutions, such as

• asking Robert to let him ride;
• asking the teacher;
• grabbing the bicycle from Robert; or
• giving Robert something to let him ride the bicycle.

The next set of sessions deals with identifying consequences for certain events. An act is presented, such as Georgie pushing Robert off the bike, and the children are guided in thinking out "what might happen next?" A list of consequences might include

• Robert may cry;
• Robert may hit Georgie;
• Robert may tell the teacher; or
• Robert may get hurt.

The two previous skills are combined in the final series of lessons: a problem is presented, the child is prompted to think of a solution for the problem and immediately to identify the possible consequence to these actions. Values are not attached to the solutions suggested by the child, but it is hoped that the child will think through the various alternatives and choose the best course on his own. The authors stress that the program is not designed to teach children *what* to think but *how* to think in problem situations.

For slightly older children, second to fourth grades, Weissberg et al. (1980) developed a similar problem-solving curriculum. An important feature of the instruction is to encourage children to persist and to think of other solutions when the previously chosen alternative is unsuccessful. During the role play enactments, the teacher often takes the role of the spoiler, ensuring that the suggested behavior will fail. The teacher then prompts pupils to generate and try another solution. An example from one of the strategies follows (Weissberg et al., 1980, pp. 100–101):

*George*:   We're upset because Pete took our ball and there's nothing else to play with.

*Karen*:   Our goal is to get the ball back.

*George*:   (*to Karen*) What do you think we should do?

*Karen*:   We could (*Propose a solution and its consequence*)

*George*:   We could (*Propose another solution and its consequence*)

*Karen*:   Let's try (*The best solution from the previous activity*)

When George and Karen try their solution to get the ball back, Peter (played by the teacher) SHOULD REFUSE TO GIVE IT. Then interrupt the role play and review what took place:

Class, George and Karen stated their problem and goal. They even thought of some solutions and their consequences. (*Solution X*) seemed like a good solution but it didn't work. They didn't reach their goal of getting the ball back.

How did George and Karen feel when their solution didn't work? (*Disappointed, discouraged, sad, tired, mad, let down. Have a brief discussion of the fact that this is natural and that the person may be tempted to give up.*)

Class, what do you think George and Karen should do next? (*The answer you want here is: Try again!*)

That's right. It's important for good problem solvers to try again!

Consistent with the Spivack and Shure program, the goal of the Weissberg et al. curriculum is to help children learn to solve problems independently in socially appropriate ways. The authors suggest that with modifications for developmental considerations, this curriculum could be adapted for older children and special populations.

Problem-solving procedures have been used extensively to train and assess groups of children and youth. The research literature, however, although generally showing improved performance in problem-solving cognitive skills resulting from training, reports equivocal effects of problem-solving training on social behavior and adjustment. Weissberg et al. (1981), for example, found that problem-solving training positively affected the social adjustment of suburban but not urban third grade students. Although there are reports of positive effects of problem-solving training on social behavior (Elardo & Caldwell, 1979; Spivack & Shure, 1974), some of the more recent investigations have failed to obtain similar relationships (Kendall & Fischler, 1984; Olexa & Forman, 1984). These mixed findings call into question some basic assumptions about problem solving; that is, (a) their mediational properties, (b) the psychometric properties of the assessment instruments, and (c) the appropriateness of this training for differing groups.

The observation that socially maladjusted subjects performed less well on measures of problem-solving cognitive skills logically led to the assumption that problem-solving training would contribute to more adaptive behaviors. The failure consistently and conclusively to find the problem-solving behavioral link has caused researchers to search for other influences. Kendall and Fischler (1984), for example, found some evidence of IQ as a contributing factor to the problem-solving, behavioral adjustment equation. Another confounding influence may relate to the psychometrics of the instruments used to measure both problem-solving skills and adaptive behavior. It may be that these measures are neither sufficiently sensitive or valid to adequately assess treatment gains.

A final and critical consideration is the appropriateness of this training for special populations, such as urban and learning disabled children. Although Spivack and Shure (1974) report favorable results with urban preschool children, they identified language difficulties as a potential interference. For successful implementation Spivack and Shure found it necessary to develop vocabulary, word meaning, and language concepts, such as the understanding of conditional If..., then... statements. Beyond language, however, some researchers (Olexa & Forman, 1984; Weissberg et al., 1981) point out difficulties with urban populations due to the tendency for these children to generate more aggressive behavior alternatives as part of the training procedures geared toward identifying a variety of alternative solutions. Under these conditions, problem solving was considered to be counterproductive in that aggressive, maladaptive pupil behaviors seemed to increase in proportion to training. This phenomenon appears to provide support for the position taken by Hopper and Kirshchenbaum (1979), that the quality of alternatives probably should be emphasized over quantity. It may be necessary, under such conditions, for trainers to exercise more control so that aggressive, antisocial alternatives are minimized and prosocial solutions are maximized. If, indeed, these aggressive alternatives are causing negative behaviors to escalate, then the reverse also should be true.

Hazel, Schumaker, Sherman, and Sheldon-Wildgen (1982) assessed the relative effects of social skill and problem-solving training on LD (learning disabled), nonLD, and court-adjudicated adolescents. They found that, while the LD group acquired the social skills to a level comparable with the other two groups, the LD group failed to demonstrate similar progress in problem solving that was commensurate with the nonLD and court-adjudicated peers. These findings with urban and LD populations indicate the need for differential application of social problem-solving training in order to address the specific needs and differences of the respective groups. These concerns notwithstanding, social problem solving continues to be a promising strategy for increasing social competence. There is an obvious need for a refinement of procedures in order to adequately assess the effects of interpersonal problem-solving training and to implement the training procedures more discriminantly.

In employing cognitive and affective methods for social skill training, certain considerations and cautions appear warranted: (a) Training should be presented in a relaxed rather than rigid manner, establishing rapport and individualizing the curriculum according to the child's developmental and skill levels. For very young children, play may be used as the point of initiating self-instructional training. For example, the trainer might talk his way through a skill game and assist the child to perform in a similar manner. In another example, for older children who may be less inclined to reveal their own self-statements or to verbalize outwardly, the trainer may use tapes' or scenarios of others in problem situations and have the child suggest what the fictional character might be thinking. For the child who has difficulty talking out loud during training, the trainer may monitor self-statements by periodically interrupting the child and asking what he is saying to himself. (b) Due to the heavy reliance on language and cognitive abilities, the child with language, cognitive, and attentional deficits may require extensive, systematic instructions before cognitive mediation procedures can be taught. Attention must be given to prerequisite skills, as identified in the discussion on problem-solving strategies. After acquiring the basic skills, the child can be involved as a "collaborator" in determining the training procedures to be used. Through questioning, the trainer may get the child to identify, on his own, an effective self-training strategy rather than imposing one on him. The child's own language should be used when possible. There is good evidence that this instruction needs to be tailored to meet the unique needs and idiosyncracies of specific populations. (c) One major pitfall encountered in training children in self-talk is that the statements may become mechanical, in which case they are not controlling the maladaptive behavior. To counter this occurrence, it is suggested that training should be conducted so as to impress upon children that they are only to say what they mean. A serious learning climate should be established, possibly placing reinforcing contingencies on behaviors indicative of sincerity and appropriate self-statements. (d) Training can be enhanced by including modeling and behavioral rehearsal, relaxation, and imagery techniques. It appears that the opportunity to practice modeled cognitions is a critical factor and may determine the effectiveness of the training. Kendall and Morison (1984) stress the importance of integrating cognitive and behavioral methods, stating, "The judicious utilization of cognitive and behavioral methods will maximize treatment efficacy" (pp. 279–280). (e) A final consideration is the quantity of instruction. The various kinds of procedures outlined here are designed to be presented over an extended period of time, ideally on a daily basis. The trainer using cognitive approaches should be committed to regular instruction over a period of weeks. During the following training, monitoring should take place to make certain the child's self-talk and overt actions are congruent and that the child appears to continue using internal mediators to direct appropriate responses.

## SUMMARY

Teaching social skills involves many of the same procedures as teaching academic concepts; that is, the exposure of the child to a model for imitation, eliciting an imitative response, providing feedback about the correctness of the response, and structuring opportunities for practice. One method for teaching complex social behaviors is through the imitation of a model or social modeling. The social modeling process requires that the learner recognize the value of the behavior to be learned and is able to identify the specific responses that make up that behavior, that the behavior be modeled in a way that is attractive and understandable to the learner, that the learner be provided with opportunities to practice the behavior using various response modes, and that the learner receive feedback on his performance from others as well as through self-evaluative procedures. A behavior may be demonstrated, but if the child is unable to conceptualize the responses involved or does not recognize the importance of the behavior, social modeling is unlikely to occur. The trainer should also expect that initial efforts to produce novel behaviors may be awkward and unnatural, with a need for continued practice and feedback.

Thoughts and feelings are also relevant to social skills training. Various approaches have been developed for teaching social perception skills, along with affective and cognitive behavior. The focus of social perception training can involve both verbal and nonverbal communication; it can include training in cognitive role taking; and it can emphasize training in empathy, often viewed as an extention of role taking.

Approaches to teaching social skills related to emotions involve the child recognizing and labeling his own feelings and those of others, along with learning socially desirable ways to express his emotions. Activities for teaching about feelings also involve helping the child recognize the differences in his emotional responses and those of others in similar situations and develop some understanding about the role of his thinking processes in generating his feeling states. In teaching the child to express emotions in constructive ways, a problem-solving approach can be applied in which the child identifies and role plays problem situations, alternative responses, and outcomes, along with examining alternative thoughts and feelings that could be associated with the problem. Training the child in relaxation can offer another means of controlling negative emotions, because a relaxed state leads to a lessening of tension, anxiety, and anger. Learning to respond to relaxation cues with a state of relaxation may allow the child time to initiate constructive alternatives to impulsive emotional behavior.

The use of cognitions in teaching social skills focuses on efforts to structure thinking styles that are functional for directing social behaviors. One area of emphasis is the elimination of irrational, self-defeating, or faulty thought patterns, replacing them with more rational or productive ones. A second focus is the development of structured thought patterns to be used under certain conditions or for specific behaviors; that is, Meichenbaum's stress inoculation training and self-instructional training. Problem-solving procedures geared toward modifying the child's cognitions help the child to analyze social situations accurately and make decisions based on the possible alternatives and consequences. Although cognitive models vary, they share a common reliance on language, some prerequisite skills on the part of the learner, and intensive instruction over an extended period of time.

The models described in this chapter are not mutually exclusive. As a matter of fact, most efforts toward social skill instruction employ elements of each of these approaches and there is good evidence that the most efficacious approaches incorporate behavioral, cognitive, and affective methods.

# 4
# Generalization and Maintenance of Social Skills

Once social skills have been selected, assessed, and successfully taught, the remaining task is to make sure the child can exhibit the skills when and where it is desirable to use them. The social behaviors need to be generalized from the instructional setting to other settings where they would be appropriate and from interactions with one set of people to others. They also need to be maintained over time. Stokes and Baer (1977), in their review of literature related to behavior generalization, point out that generalization does not automatically occur but needs to be planned and programmed as part of the training process. Some techniques that will be described as effective for generalization include (a) varying the aspects of training, (b) training mediators, and (c) changing the contingencies of reinforcement.

## ASPECTS OF TRAINING

The ways in which social behaviors are taught appear to influence whether the new behaviors will occur in settings beyond the training site and whether they will occur with persons other than the trainer. Two specific considerations within the training process involve varying the settings for training and varying trainers.

### Training in Different Settings

A frequent occurrence in behavior change programs is that newly acquired behaviors are maintained only within the setting where the child is instructed and do not naturally transfer to other settings. Wahler (1969), for example, found that behaviors taught at home did not generalize to school until the procedures implemented at home also were instituted in school. Similarly, Berler, Gross, and Drabman (1982) failed to achieve transfer of social skills developed in clinical settings into the regular classroom. The child who learns social skills in the classroom may not express them elsewhere unless specific steps are taken to develop such transfer. Ideally, social skill instruction should take place in the setting where the behavior is to occur. If, for example, the target behavior is increased participation in classroom discussions, then instruction in this behavior should take place in the classroom. An example of teaching a skill in multiple settings is provided by Murdock, Garcia, and Hardman (1977), in a study where mentally retarded children were taught to articulate words. Each child was taught by one trainer in a small room, by a second trainer in the corner of a regular classroom, and by a third trainer in a learning center for individualized activities. Not only did the children learn to say the words consistently in these settings, but they also generalized the words to other settings, where training had not been conducted. A significant aspect of this study was that the behaviors did not begin to generalize to other settings until they were taught in at least two settings. Subsequent research also has demonstrated the facilitating effects of instruction in multiple settings on the generalization of verbal responses in language-disordered subjects (Carr & Kologinsky, 1983; Handleman, 1979). In another study using multiple settings, Van Den Pol and his colleagues (1981) conducted training in the classroom and natural environment, in order to effect the acquisition, maintenance, and generalization of restaurant skills by mentally retarded clients.

Although it may not be necessary to provide formal instruction in every setting or condition frequented by the child, procedures such as the following may be used to facilitate the transfer of these behaviors to other conditions:

• Set up role plays where the child demonstrates how he will perform this behavior in other settings. For example, "Let's act out how you will greet a guest who comes to your house."
• Establish reinforcing conditions for expressing the target behavior in other settings. For instance, using the greeting example, specified individuals in other settings may prompt and reward the child for responses such as smiling, making eye contact, and saying "hello" upon an initial encounter.
• Assist the child in developing a personal recordkeeping system or diary, wherein he records performing the target behavior in other settings, with incentives for his performance.

It is not always possible to provide instruction under natural conditions. An alternative approach is that of "equating stimulus conditions" (Walker & Buckley, 1974). The intent with this procedure is to increase the similarity between the training and natural environments. In their study Walker and Buckley altered the special class where the behaviors were developed, so that it more closely resembled the regular class where students were expected to manifest these behaviors. Changes included increasing the workload and using social rather than tangible reinforcers. Eisler and Frederiksen (1980) stress the importance of realistic conditions, suggesting that the training situation include physical surroundings, participants, problems, and encounters representative of the ones the learner is most likely to experience under real-life conditions. An additional discussion of encouraging transfer through the "rule of identical elements" is provided in chapter 10 of this book.

When teaching for transfer, the social skills trainer should structure the procedures to ensure that the child's behavior is controlled by explicit aspects of the training, not incidental factors. For example, in a study with autistic children, Rincover and Koegel (1975) found that behaviors learned in instructional settings failed to transfer to a second setting because the children were responding to incidental stimuli, such as the trainer's hand movements instead of his verbal commands. When these unintentional behaviors were introduced into the second setting, the children responded as they had under treatment conditions. An important consideration with this study is that, although the desired responses were produced, they were not under the control of the intended stimulus, the verbal command "touch your chin." These findings emphasize the importance of analyzing the social skill instruction situation in order to ensure that the child's behavior is being triggered by the appropriate social stimuli. A child, for example, may learn to make assertive responses only in the presence of a supportive peer group, or a child may depend on certain nonverbal behaviors such as eye contact from the teacher to signal behaviors such as making appropriate greetings. When removed from these conditions, the child may be less inclined to make assertive responses or appropriate greetings, even though the behaviors may be warranted by the situation. Along the same vein, the child needs to learn responses appropriate to particular settings and different people. While learning to generalize, the child must simultaneously learn to discriminate according to environmental stimulus conditions, and these skills should be explicit in the instructional program. For example, one uses different greetings to authority figures such as teachers, to peers, and to family members, and different greeting behavior in church than on the playground.

In order to introduce a broader range of stimuli, similar to real-life conditions, the instructional setting should vary according to group constellation and size, allowing for different responses and environmental conditions. It appears that the most effective training conditions (i.e., individual or group) are dictated primarily by the behaviors to be learned, the child's skill level, and the conditions under which the child will have to perform the behavior under natural circumstances (Phillips, 1978). For example, the child learning to talk in class should receive instruction in large groups; on the other hand, the reverse may be necessary for the child being taught to engage in conversation with a peer. In the first example, however, it may be necessary to conduct training sessions that gradually move the child from individual to large group settings.

## Training with Different People

Using more than one trainer is suggested in order to avoid the possibility that new behaviors will remain under the control of one trainer and will fail to generalize, as described earlier in the Rincover and Koegel (1975) study. Two trainers might alternate in training sessions, keeping conditions similar but requiring the child to respond to the social situation rather than the trainer. A study by Stokes, Baer, and Jackson (1974) illustrates this point. More than one trainer was used to teach institutionalized mentally retarded children to greet others by waving. The first trainer, using prompting and shaping procedures, taught the child to make the greeting response. A second trainer was used when probes revealed no generalization or only transitory generalization to other staff members. The researchers found that generalization of the greeting response to staff not involved in the training was most effective when the child was taught by more than one trainer.

Other members of the child's environment, such as teachers, parents, and peers, might be trained to instruct, prompt, and reinforce the desired social behaviors. The following guidelines for such instruction are adapted from Gelfand and Hartmann (1975):

1. Generally outline the instructional program.
2. Provide trainees with a written description of the instructional session, and invite them to observe your training.
3. Following observation, discuss procedures in detail.
4. If necessary, provide for additional observations.
5. Rehearse training sessions through role play where trainee provides instruction.
6. Observe trainee's instruction of child in social skills.
7. Provide corrective feedback either during or following session.
8. Provide tape recordings of your training sessions for the trainee to listen to and practice.

Walker and Buckley (1974) trained teachers in order to effect behavior generalization from a special class to the regular classroom. They found instructions in behavior modification procedures to be less effective than precise written descriptions, discussion of the procedures, and periodic classroom visits to provide direct assistance. For example, in a maintenance strategy the teacher was given detailed information on the child's academic materials, reinforcement system, and exactly how the reinforcement program for academic and social behaviors should be implemented. Similarly, Wiig and Bray (1983) coordinated teacher and parent instruction of prosocial communication skills in young children by providing a "home activity sheet" that corresponded with each social communication skill taught in the classroom. The sheet included instructions to the parents and a series of home based activities designed to reinforce the target social communication skill.

Along with significant adults in the child's life, the peer group can be used to provide social skill training and maintenance. Stokes and Baer (1977) emphasize the advantages of training peers to help maintain behaviors in that peers are generally found in both training and generalization settings. Children exercise considerable control over each other, and in many cases it becomes critical to enlist their involvement in the social skills instruction. Consider, for example, the child whose peers reward verbal and physical aggression, behaviors that may be incompatible with the social skills being taught.

Group contingencies are one method of encouraging peer support of desirable behavior. Walker and Buckley (1974) employed "peer programming procedures," where the target child, upon making the desired responses, was able to earn a specified number of points to be exchanged for a reward for the entire class. The objective was to make it profitable for the peer group or other members of the child's environment to support and reward appropriate rather than inappropriate behaviors. This was a group-oriented contingency, the type described by Greenwood and Hops (1981) as a "dependent" system. In their research review, Greenwood and Hops determined the most effective group-oriented systems to be "interdependent" systems, in which contingencies are based on the ability of the group as an aggregate to meet some preestablished criterion or goal. Lew and Mesch (1984) used an interdependent group-oriented contingency to help middle-school students improve their academic and social behavior. Less academically and socially competent subjects were assigned to small groups with more competent peers. The combination of performance standards and contingent reinforcement were found to improve social interaction and academic achievement. The effects were observed to be maintained for most subjects, even after contingencies were removed. In employing group-oriented contingency systems, the social skills trainer should attend to the following factors:

- Make sure that reasonably attainable goals are established. Goals that are set too high initially may be frustrating, giving little incentive to try. As progress is made, goals may be raised gradually.
- Make sure that target children (in dependent systems) do not become victims, receiving punishment for inadequate responses as opposed to praise and encouragement for approximations.
- Make sure that the peer group understands what the target behaviors are and exactly how to provide support and encouragement. Peer understanding may be developed through instruction sessions that include role playing the target behaviors and appropriate peer responses.

- Make sure that rewards to be earned are highly desired by the group. Program rewards to be faded gradually once the behaviors appear to have stabilized and become maintained and supported largely by social and other natural reinforcers.

Although peers have been shown to be effective behavior change agents, a review of the research regarding peer effects on maintenance and generalization of social interaction behaviors on the part of withdrawn children reveals that peers interact minimally with these children (Strain, Kerr, & Ragland, 1981). Studies showed that when trained children are returned to natural environments, competent children do not automatically interact with and reinforce their less competent peers. These findings lead Strain et al. to advocate more extensive intervention strategies, such as structuring peer social systems, similar to those described earlier, in order to create peer environments more supportive of trained subjects. Another recommendation for increasing peer support of behavior maintenance and transfer (Strain et al., 1981) was to train skill-deficient children in social skills more consistent with those of their more competent peers. Beirman and Furman (1984) provide supportive evidence for this position. In their study, preadolescent children either (a) were coached individually on conversation skills, (b) were engaged in a group experience, (c) received coaching and the group experience, or (d) received no treatment. Coaching was found to increase and maintain conversation skills. Peer acceptance, however, was found to persist only among subjects trained in the groups with competent peers. Another contributing factor, according to the authors, was the use of a "superordinate goal" as part of the group experience. The children were informed that they were to work together on a group project; that is, "make friendly interaction films for the university" (p. 155). Collaborating on this larger goal was considered to promote positive peer attitudes, which were enhanced by the improved conversation skills of the skill-deficient subjects. Thus, it appears that peers may be instrumental in behavior maintenance and generalization, if the social skills taught are those that parallel those of the more competent peers, competent children are included in training sessions, and conditions enhancing group cooperation are established.

Multisetting, multiperson instruction can be enhanced by programming practice or homework activities into the training. The "barb" approach, developed by Kaufman and Wagner (1972), to teach adolescents positive ways to respond to anger-producing stimuli, is an example of providing practice in other settings and with other persons. The principal stimulus for response is the "barb," a remark intended to evoke a negative emotional reaction. Adolescents are taught to respond with eye contact, a pleasant facial expression, a moderate tone of voice, and verbal responses that help avoid problems and possibly obtain positive consequences. Techniques for teaching these alternatives to temper tantrums or aggressive responses to barbs include building rapport, modeling, role playing, cueing, cue fading, and intermittent reinforcement. After the initial training, the techniques include a planned program for generalization, involving barbs delivered by a variety of persons in different places with token reinforcement for desired responses. The program for one youth was as follows (Kaufman & Wagner, 1972, p. 87):

1 & 2. Exploration, role playing, expectations, rapport building with several barbs delivered during private sessions: 1 week
3. Training, cueing, immediate reinforcement; one barb per day, coordinator only, cue before barb, one token per behavioral requirement: 1 week
4. Cue fading; three staff members delivering barbs: 2 weeks
5. Stimulus generalization; all but three unit staff delivering barbs, temper control required during evening activity: 2 weeks
6. Additional requirement and generalization; facial expression requirement, all unit staff delivering barbs: 2 weeks
7. Fixed ratio reinforcement; all staff plus teachers delivering, all requirements to be met to earn tokens: 3 weeks
8. Further generalization; three barbs per day, seven tokens per barb, staff, students, administrators delivering barbs: 1 week
9. Further fixed ratio; three barbs per day, must pass all to earn tokens: 3 weeks
10. Rotating barb; five barbs per day, random barb earns tokens: 3 weeks
11. "Intermittent" reinforcement, random programming: 14 weeks

This program demonstrates a number of generalization principles. It moves from practice with anticipated barbs delivered by one therapist in one setting to random barbs delivered by a gradually increasing number of adults and then peers in other settings. Barbs are initially preceded by cues, then the cues are gradually eliminated. The schedule of reinforcement is changed from continuous immediate reinforcement, to a fixed schedule, and then to an intermittent schedule, the last being closest to the kind of recognition provided in the natural environment. Shaping is also recommended by Eisler and Frederiksen (1980), who advise the use of "graded" homework assignments with the difficulty of the assignment gradually increasing until the desired level of social skill performance is reached.

Along with trainers and settings, Gelfand and Hartmann (1984) also note the importance of varying training examples. Real-life events rarely occur exactly as presented under treatment conditions. Therefore, children need the opportunity to respond to a variety of examples in order to avoid rigid, situation-specific behavior.

## Training Mediators

A promising approach to programming for generalization is that of developing cognitive mediators to assist the child in generalizing and maintaining appropriate behaviors in settings, times, and conditions beyond those explicitly involved in training. According to Bandura (1977b), response patterns can be represented in memory and retained in symbolic form primarily through imagery and verbalization. There are data indicating that behavior learned through observation is acquired and retained more effectively with mental and verbal rehearsal in addition to behavioral rehearsal. Although a number of questions have been raised (Franks & Wilson, 1978) related to the utility of cognitive strategies for generalization, Meichenbaum (1977), Stokes and Baer (1977), and others see the development of mediators as having considerable potential, particularly when they are deliberately programmed as strategies for generalization.

*Language as a Mediator*

Because most cognitive processes are verbal rather than visual, language is the mediator most often involved in training for generalization. Stokes and Baer (1977) point out that language serves as a common stimulus "to be carried from any training setting to any generalization setting that the child may ever enter" (p. 361). A simple method for using language as a mediator is having the child state what he did or might do while engaging in a social behavior. For example, the child learning to exhibit appropriate behavior after winning a game might verbally list his responses as

1. After my partner congratulates me, I will say, "Thank you" and smile.
2. I will compliment him for playing a good game.
3. Then, I will ask him if he wants to play another game.
4. If he says "yes," I will let him go first.

The use of language as a mediator was demonstrated in a study conducted by Risley and Hart (1968) with preschool children. Food rewards were provided to the children for accurate reports of their use of play materials. The authors viewed the self-reports as having a generalizing effect on the children's play, because behaviors for the subsequent day were altered to correspond with the previous verbal descriptions, suggesting that "saying" could be considered to control "doing."

Another example of language as a mediator is provided by Clark, Caldwell, and Christian (1979) in a study using self-reports to generalize conversation skills to other settings. Children who had been taught conversation skills in the classroom were directed to practice these skills during lunch period. Following lunch, the students indicated on a questionnaire whether they had made certain responses; for example, "Did I ask a classmate about his or her mom, dad, brother, or sister?" The accuracy of these reports was ascertained through a videotape monitoring system that taped the children during lunch. Rewards were given for making the desired statements and truthfully reporting them. According to the authors, the combination of accurate self-reports and delayed reinforcement was effective in maintaining conversational skills. In another study, Barton and Ascione (1979) found that sharing behavior among young children persisted and generalized only when children were taught to use language to accompany their sharing.

Self-instruction and problem-solving cognitive approaches are also potentially useful for behavior generalization. Because these procedures employ language to develop problem-solving strategies, it is reasoned that the skills developed will be more lasting and more easily transferred to a variety of situations and behaviors. In a review of self-instruction research with children, Kendall (1978) concludes that treatment that stresses "metacognitive development" (i.e., awareness of one's thinking processes) is most likely to lead to generalization. Meichenbaum (1977) presents evidence of the efficacy of self-instruction for behavior generalization and durability, when the training required overt rather than covert self-instructions and the training was conducted over more extensive periods of time. A variation of self-instruction is the stress inoculation model (described earlier in chapter 3), which Meichenbaum presents as a procedure explicitly developed for generalization training. More recent research in this area, however, suggests that these procedures are probably most effective when presented under conditions of participant modeling and gradual exposure to the anxiety producing event (Prins, 1984; Sheslow, Bondy, & Nelson, 1983).

Support for the facilitative effects of problem-solving procedures in producing behavior maintenance and transfer is provided by Richards and Perri (1978). Using college students concerned about academic underachievement, the authors compared a treatment program that involved fading instructions in study skills and self-control procedures to a second program that used the D'Zurilla and Goldfried problem-solving model (see chapter 3). A 3-week evaluation revealed that maintenance of desired behaviors, as evidenced by exam scores and grade point averages, was greater for the problem-solving group than the fading group. Considering the brief time period for the follow-up evaluation, the relative sophistication of the subjects used in the study, and the cognitive nature of the behaviors being taught, the authors caution against loosely generalizing these results to other populations and behaviors. Lochman, Burch, Curry, and Lamprom (1984) also successfully used problem-solving procedures to reduce the disruptive, aggressive behaviors in preadolescent boys. They observed behavior generalization to the home and maintenance over time. In chapter 6 of this book, Bash and Camp provide anecdotal evidence of behavior generalization resulting from a combination of self-instruction and problem-solving methods. One other cognitive activity related to generalization of social skills, that of self-evaluation, is discussed elsewhere in this chapter as well as in chapter 2.

*Imagery as a Mediator*

Visual imagery is another mediator that may be incorporated into the child's social training program, usually in combination with language. Bandura (1977b) points out that visual imagery is particularly important when verbal skills are lacking. A common technique for the development of imagery is to provide visual stimuli in the form of drawings, photographs, films, etc., and ask the child to close his eyes and imagine himself in the pictured situation. DeMille (1967, p. 37), in a book of children's imagination games that provide practice in visualization, suggests the following means of facilitating visual imagery:

> When you ask the child to imagine something going on in the yard at his school, he may say, "It's too far away. I can't see it." This problem can be handled step by step.
> An easy visualization is to look at the room in which the game is being played, then close the eyes and see a mental image of it. If the child can do that, then ask him to remember or imagine how the next room looks. Then another familiar room that is farther away—perhaps your garage, or a neighbor's or a relative's living room. After that, more and more distant places can be visualized, until the school yard—or the North Pole—is within easy reach. Do not be concerned about the vividness of the images. The child only has to say that he imagines or remembers how a place looks. The brightness, completeness, or constancy of the mental image is unimportant.

Some procedures for developing imagery related to the teaching of social skills through covert rehearsal techniques are outlined in chapter 3. The use of imagery for generalization of social skills would involve asking the child to imagine himself engaging in the target behavior under the familiar training situation, then introducing variations to be imagined; for example, other persons, places, and future times. Evidence of the long-term effects of imagery can be seen in a study conducted by Harris and Johnson (1983). College students were trained to use imagery to reduce test anxiety. The procedures involved first imagining scenes of situations where the subjects had previously performed well and then transferring that confidence to the anxiety-provoking academic condition. Imagery training not only resulted in a reduction of reported test anxiety but improvements in grade point averages as well. Grade averages deteriorated for a waiting control group. These data were analyzed and reported for the term following training, attesting to the durability of the imagery treatment. Although conducted with college students, these findings are relevant to children in that imagery research has shown that "children respond to imagery instructions in a manner similar to that of adults" (Hermecz & Melamed, 1984, p. 167).

*Expectations as Mediators*

A further cognitive mediational variable related to generalization is that of expectations. Bandura (1977a) speaks of "efficacy expectations" as "the conviction that one can successfully execute the behavior required to produce the outcomes" (p. 103). Although not involving children, Nicki, Remington, and MacDonald (1984) used self-efficacy as a treatment condition to reduce cigarette smoking. Subjects in the self-efficacy groups initially were to identify and adhere to situations where they were confident they would not smoke. Gradually, training proceeded to conditions where they were less confident of not smoking. During follow-up, these subjects were more successful in abstaining from cigarette smoking than were the nicotine fading and control groups. Bandura (1977a) suggests that efficacy expectations are generated through (a) "performance accomplishments" — awareness of one's actual successful performance; (b) "vicarious experience" — awareness of other's successful performance; (c) "verbal persuasion" — suggestions and exhortations from others or from oneself; and (d) reducing "emotional arousal" — the ability to apply various means of controlling emotions in stressful situations. Applying these dimensions to the generalization of social skills, the teacher or clinician can enhance the child's expectations of future success by training in actual skills, providing examples of successful models, suggesting through discussion and other verbal means how the learning of social behaviors will be helpful in the future, and engaging the child in various kinds of learning (e.g., relaxation) to develop feelings of competence in stressful interpersonal situations. Related to this can also be the establishment through role play, discussion, imagery, etc., of expectations about the kinds of situations in which the social skills will be appropriate in the future.

An example of "verbal persuasion" can be seen in a study conducted by Katz and Vinceguerra (1980). While attempting to change reinforcement schedules, the researchers found that task-related behaviors were best maintained when the subject received statements stressing the subject's ability and personal competence. The subject was more likely to stay on task when told "You're doing such a good job, I don't think you need as many tokens today," as opposed to, "I can't give you as many tokens today because I ran out," or when not given any reason for the absence of tokens.

Related to self-efficacy is the concept of attributions, which refers to the reasons an individual gives for various personal experiences. Failing a major exam, for example, may be attributed to external events such as bad luck or teacher dislike or to internal events like lack of competence. Children who internalize, attributing behavior change to personal efforts, are more amenable to social skill intervention and behavior generalization than those who externalize (Glenwick & Jason, 1984; Kendall & Braswell, 1985). Glenwick and Jason (1984) point out that a greater sense of self-control can be developed in children through strategies that create a gradual movement from external contingencies toward self-management procedures.

## CONTINGENCIES OF REINFORCEMENT

The maintenance of social behaviors, once they have been taught, is also referred to as *resistance to extinction, durability,* or *generalization over time.* The principal factor supporting maintenance of social skills over time is reinforcement and the contingencies of reinforcement operating in the settings where the social skills would be expressed. The learning of social skills is facilitated by reinforcement and feedback. For generalization to occur, the nature of reinforcement needs to be changed, and there are a number of ways in which this can take place. The sources of reinforcement can be changed, particularly from external to intrinsic sources of reward; the ways in which reinforcement is given can be changed; and the kinds of rewards provided can be changed.

## Changing the Timing of Reinforcement

In the process of teaching new social behaviors, reinforcement needs to be provided immediately on a continuous basis for correct responses. Once behaviors are learned, behavior will occur most readily over time if the timing or schedule for reinforcement is "thinned" to occasional reinforcement, provided on an intermittent and unpredictable basis. Stokes and Baer (1977) suggest introducing noncontingent reinforcement, even "random or haphazard" delivery of reinforcement to assist in generalization, with the goal of establishing conditions in which the subject "cannot discriminate in which settings a response will be reinforced or not reinforced" (p. 358). Fowler and Baer (1981) report a study conducted with preschool children to assess the effects of delayed reinforcement on behavior generalization. The subjects in this study were instructed to perform various social behaviors, such as making statements of praise or sharing with peers. Although rewards were provided only for responses made during one period of the school day (contingent), the investigators found that these behaviors were more likely to generalize to other (noncontingent) times if rewards and feedback were delayed until the end of school day, approximately $1\frac{1}{2}$ to $2\frac{1}{2}$ hours later. The authors attributed the generalization effect primarily to the fact that the children were unable to discriminate between the contingent and noncontingent conditions. That is, the subjects felt they had to make the targeted responses "all day" in order to receive the desired reward. The use of delayed reinforcement as mentioned above, in addition to assisting in the generalization of behavior across settings and people and the transfer of sources of reinforcement from one set of persons to others, also assists in thinning reinforcement schedules. Related to thinning schedules is the fading technique used by Greenwood et al. (1977), which involved the gradual removal of aspects of the behavioral program; that is, recording, classroom rules, and chart of progress from an elementary school classroom. The resulting maintenance of appropriate behavior in the classroom was superior to that in classrooms where the program was terminated without a maintenance strategy.

Rhode, Morgan, and Young (1983) provide another example in which reinforcement thinning and self-evaluation procedures were used to program behavior from a special education resource room to regular classroom. In the resource room, students were taught to evaluate themselves and self-administer points, initially every 15 minutes. This schedule was gradually thinned to self-evaluation every 30 minutes. At this point, the procedures were transferred to the regular classroom, where self-evaluation proceeded systematically so that students provided themselves with points only every 2 days, then no points, then only verbal self-evaluation, and ultimately no overt, but possibly private self-evaluations.

Use of contingency contracts (Dardig & Heward, 1980; DeRisi & Butz, 1975; Homme, Csanyi, Gonzales, & Rechs, 1969; Kanfer, 1975) can be an aid to generalization and maintenance of social skills, because contracts provide a means by which rewards can be delayed and the source of reinforcement changed from one person to another. Further, the existence of a contract can serve as a reminder for children to engage in the target behaviors beyond the training setting. The contract can be made between the child and the trainer with rewards provided in the training setting for target behaviors to be carried out in another setting. It could also be established between the parent and child with the trainer serving as negotiator for the target behaviors to be performed in the home. The contract can be verbal or written, formal or informal, but a written contract, signed and witnessed, may be taken more seriously by all participants. A contingency contract related to social skills should have the following components: (a) The social behavior clearly defined so all concerned can agree whether it has occurred; (b) the performance criteria for the behavior; that is, how much of the behavior has to occur to earn the payoff and under what circumstances it should occur; (c) the reward to be provided when criteria are met and who provides the reward; and (d) a means of determining whether the reward has been earned. Homme et al. (1969) provide some criteria for a successful contingency contract. The contract reward should be immediate at first; initial contracts should reward small steps; the contract should be fair; the terms of the contract should be clear; the contract should be honest (i.e., carried out immediately according to the specified terms); and the contract should be positive.

Stephens (1978, p. 377) provides the following example of a social skills contingency contract.

Teaching Strategy

*Skill*: The student makes positive statements when asked about himself.

*Contingency Management*
1. Present the task to the student in specific terms. When someone asks you to tell about yourself or about your work, think of some good things to say.
2. Define a consequence valued by the student which will be given following demonstration of the desired positive verbalization about himself.
3. State the contingency. If student says positive things when asked about himself, he will receive the agreed-upon desirable consequences.

4. Listen for the behavior to occur naturally, and reinforce it when it occurs according to established contingency. Or, set up a situation in which the behavior can occur. Give the student an activity at which he does well. Ask the student questions about himself and his work. If he responds to questions about himself or his work with positive statements, he will receive the established reward.

5. Example: Todd is a bright, well-behaved student in Mr. Downs' class. In spite of Todd's assets, Mr. Downs suspects that he has a poor "self-concept," because Todd, when asked about his work, usually makes some negative response such as "It's no good," or "I could have done better." He is critical not only of himself but of others as well, and he is quick to find fault with what other students do. Mr. Downs feels that possibly some of Todd's negative statements are perpetuated by the reactions they get when he "runs down" himself or his work. For example, somebody always responds by saying something like, "Oh no, Todd, it's *good*." Mr. Downs sets up a conference with Todd and discusses with him his observations – that Todd has many good qualities and accomplishments, but that he continually looks for negative things to say about himself and others. He describes to Todd and rehearses with him some positive statements he would like him to make instead. He helps Todd understand the difference between "bragging" and being realistically proud of one's accomplishments and acknowledging them when asked. Mr. Downs sets up a contract with Todd. For every positive statement Todd can make about himself or someone else when he is asked, Mr. Downs will give Todd two trading stamps. He will provide a bonus of five stamps if Todd can come and point out to him something good he or someone else has done which Mr. Downs is unaware of. Mr. Downs puts Todd in charge of a bulletin board labeled "Blowing Our Horn," on which are put positive observations about members of the class, which Todd and the others supply.

A further advantage of the contingency contract is the potential for involving the child in setting his own rewards and criteria for reinforcement, thus moving the social behaviors closer to maintenance by self reinforcement.

## Changing the Nature of Reinforcement

Kinds of external reinforcement vary from social reinforcement (i.e., praise, smiles, positive attention, positive physical contact), to various forms of tangible reinforcers (such as food, toys, etc.), to generalized conditioned reinforcers (such as tokens or points that can stand for a wide variety of reinforcing events). The work of Premack (1959) established that almost any high-rate, presumably more preferred, activity can serve as a reinforcer for a low-rate, presumably less preferred, activity. Because reinforcement is defined by its positive effect on behavior, effective reinforcers cannot always be predicted in advance. In chapter 2, it was suggested that reinforcers as well as social skills be assessed to determine what kinds of rewards will encourage the child to engage in social skills training or perform the social behavior he has learned. The child who can progress from a need for immediate edible rewards, to a token exchange system, to behavior maintained by social rewards is considered to have become more highly socialized. If social skills instruction begins initially with tangible reinforcers, maintenance over time will be enhanced if the trainer moves toward the use of social reinforcement, because praise, smiles, and attention are potentially available in almost all settings. If social rewards do not initially serve as reinforcers, they can take on reinforcing value if they are paired with whatever is actually reinforcing to the child. Gelfand and Hartmann (1975, 1984) suggest exaggerating the praise and smiles at first so the child will attend to them, then gradually eliminating the artificial reinforcement, maintaining the behaviors with occasional praise or some other natural contingency. A variety of social and backup reinforcers are also recommended in order to sustain interest and motivation and to simulate real-life situations.

### Changing the Source of Reinforcement

Rewards for social behaviors come primarily from persons in the external world or from intrinsic sources related to the satisfaction inherent in behaving in approved ways. If social skills to be taught are selected with attention to some of the criteria outlined in chapter 1, especially the "relevance of behavior" rule, persons in the natural environment will respond in ways that keep the behaviors going. Social skills are, by most definitions, behaviors that will be reinforced by others. Such skills as positive approaches to others, conversation skills, problem-solving skills, and ability to express emotion constructively are all behaviors to which others will generally respond positively. As Phillips (1978) points out, "social skills . . . imply reciprocity, interaction, and mutual reinforcement" (p. 8). Stokes and Baer (1977) speak of "behavioral traps," that is, entry responses that expose the child to a community of natural reinforcers. For example, teaching an isolated child the skills to make friends will open up many new opportunities for positive experiences.

Although many social skills may, by their nature, evoke maintaining responses from the external environment, some planning and programming for generalization and maintenance through altered reinforcement may be necessary. It may be necessary at first, for example, to program a change in source of reinforcement from the teacher or therapist to persons in the child's larger environment. Enlisting the support of parents, peers, and other relevant people in the child's life is particularly necessary for transfer of the social behaviors taught in the school or clinic to the wider environment. As Baer (1981) points out, the success of such programs is seriously jeopardized if the significant others in the child's life are not in agreement with the child's changed behavior. In transferring reinforcement to the home or another setting, the social skills trainer will need to assess the parents' or others' ability to provide positive feedback. It may be sufficient to inform the parents or others that, for example, "Our social skill of the week is paying compliments. Please respond positively when John says something nice to you, even if he is not very smooth about it," or "John will bring home a feedback slip. Please mark a point on it whenever he makes a positive comment to someone." A program to transfer the source of reinforcement can involve reinforcement provided initially in the training setting based on behavior emitted there, reinforcement continued in the training setting given on a delayed basis from data provided by the home, then reinforcement transferred to the home, based on behaviors expressed in the home. A program using such a transfer of reinforcement was carried out by Jewett and Clark (1976): conversational skills were taught in preschool then practiced at home during the evening meal. Audiotapes were made of the mealtime conversation and scored the next day, with a snack provided at school as a reinforcer for children who had used the trained comments at home during the previous evening meal. Ultimately, the entire program was transferred to the home.

Many parents may easily be able to provide praise and other reinforcers, possibly initiating contingency contracts to maintain social behaviors. For parents without the skills to provide contingent reinforcement, numerous parent training programs and materials are available (for example, Allvord, 1973; Becker, 1971; Cooper & Edge, 1978; Goldstein, Keller, & Erne, 1985; Krumboltz & Krumboltz, 1972; Miller, 1975; Patterson, 1977; Patterson & Gullion, 1976; Smith & Smith, 1976), and it may be necessary for the practitioner to build parent training into the social skills training program. Along with parents, peers and siblings are potent sources of reinforcement. The use of peers to promote generalization is discussed in a previous section of this chapter, as well as in chapter 10.

An additional means of transferring the source of reinforcement from the therapist or teacher to others in the natural environment is to provide the child himself with skills to elicit reinforcement, referred to by Stokes and Baer as "teaching the subject a means of recruiting a natural community of reinforcement to maintain . . . generalization" (1977, p. 354). Related to the ability to self-reinforce (discussed below) and also to use verbal mediators, the child needs to be able to recognize when he has done something praiseworthy and learn how to call others' attention to it in a way that encourages positive responses. Seymour and Stokes (1976) report a study in which adolescent girls in an institutional setting were trained through discussion and role playing how to "cue" staff to provide praise for their work improvement. In using this approach, there might be merit in developing cohorts in the environment who are willing to reward the child's positive remarks about himself, since this behavior has some risks of being misused or misunderstood by others.

A procedure that combines several elements (i.e., practice in other settings, teaching the child to elicit reinforcement, and transferring reinforcement to others) involves giving the child a card or feedback slip to carry after he has learned a skill. As he moves through the school or other environments, he is instructed to watch for opportunities to practice the target skill, then present the card to an available adult to mark confirmation that he performed the behavior satisfactorily. This technique is useful in a setting where the relevant adults can be informed in advance that, for example, children in Miss Jones' class are practicing giving compliments, will be carrying feedback slips, and that it would be helpful for the adult to mark the card and provide social reinforcement for a good attempt at a compliment. Later, the teacher or therapist can ask the child to describe verbally each of the compliments he paid, and he can be reinforced again for the report.

## Developing Self-Management Skills

Perhaps the most effective source for reinforcement is the child himself. Self-management appears to be one of the more promising means by which behaviors can be maintained over time. Bandura (1977b) regards the ability to regulate one's own behavior by self-produced consequences as the highest level of development in the developmental hierarchy of incentives and refers to self-reward as a "generalizable skill in self-regulation that can be used continually" (p. 144). The ability to self-regulate can be regarded as a social skill that has the following component parts: (a) adopting standards by which performance is to be evaluated; (b) monitoring one's own behavior; (c) evaluating one's performance according to the standards set; and (d) providing self-reinforcement, based on the degree to which the behavior meets performance standards.

Standards for self-management are developed either through criteria that are taught or through observation of the standards set by others. Polsgrove (1979) summarizes the following conclusions from the review of literature by Masters and Mokros (1974, p. 123) on children's self-reinforcement processes:

1. Children may more readily adopt externally imposed than modeled standards for self-reward;
2. Children tend to select the self-reinforcement standards of more lenient social models;
3. When a model's imposed standards conflict with his modeled standards for self-reinforcement, children tend to adopt the more lenient standards;
4. In general, children more readily adopt the self-reinforcement standards of competent, powerful models but not necessarily those of nurturant models;
5. Children tend to imitate self-regulatory behavior of models whose performances are closer to their competence levels rather than those who show superior performances;
6. A model's praise may increase a child's imitation of self-controlling behavior.

Whether performance standards should be determined by the children or imposed externally is an issue that has not been clearly established. Felixbrod and O'Leary (1973), for example, found self-determined and externally imposed standards to be equally effective. In a more recent study, however, Dickerson and Creedon (1981) found that children who establish their own performance standards showed significantly greater academic improvement than others whose standards were set by the teacher. Another finding was that the children in the self-selection group tended to set relatively stringent standards, which the authors speculated contributed to their superior performance. In a related study, Jones and Evans (1980) also found that subjects under self-determined, stringent conditions performed better than children in lenient or control groups. In both the Dickerson and Creedon and Jones and Evans studies, children in the higher performing groups were prompted to set performance standards that appeared to be operative for the superior achievements of the self-determined, more stringent standards groups. These findings provide support for the position that self-determined and stringent standards are important to successful self-management among children.

Self-monitoring involves observing and recording one's own behavior according to some established standard. It may be used for assessment (as discussed in chapter 2) and/or behavior change. In order to be effective with children, the procedures need to be kept simple and the directions made very clear. Workman (1982, pp. 46–47) gives the following guidelines for employing self-monitoring procedures in the classroom:

1. Determine exactly what student behavior (target behavior) you want to improve.
2. Design and copy the recording sheet you want to use.
3. Make the recording sheets available to your students.
4. Explain to your students exactly what behavior you want them to record, and tell them how you want them to improve.
5. Have the students begin recording and charting their own behavior.

Individual recording forms such as the one in Figure 4.1 are prepared with the child's name and date and taped to the child's desk to be marked according to specified directions and the criteria established for the target behavior. In making the standards explicit and clear, Workman advises that the behavior be defined and posted such as:

Talking-out means
1. you said something to another student or to the whole class, but
2. you did not raise your hand, and
3. the teacher did not give you permission to speak.

Studies conducted using self-monitoring have shown these procedures to be effective in changing and maintaining desired behaviors (Nelson & Hayes, 1981; Sagotsky et al., 1978). Sagotsky et al. (1978) report self-monitoring procedures alone (without the application of externally administered contingency systems) to be effective in increasing the studying of fifth- and sixth-grade

## SAMPLE MONITORING CARD

**Put an X in a square each time you talk out without permission.**

| MONDAY | | | | | | | | | |
|---|---|---|---|---|---|---|---|---|---|
| TUESDAY | | | | | | | | | |
| WEDNESDAY | | | | | | | | | |
| THURSDAY | | | | | | | | | |
| FRIDAY | | | | | | | | | |

**Figure 4.1.** Self-monitoring card (adapted from Workman, 1982, p. 48)

students. Many of the studies using self-monitoring have employed correspondence training wherein the child is taught to report his own behavior accurately. Robertson, Simon, Pachman, and Drabman (1979), for example, implemented correspondence training by first having teachers rate the children's behavior and give the children this feedback. The children were then directed to rate their own behavior. Their ratings were matched with those of the teacher, with rewards for matching the teacher's ratings, thus increasing the probability that in the future they would make accurate assessments. After children demonstrated skill in rating their own behavior, teacher matchings were no longer required. Rewards were administered based on the children's reports.

Self-evaluation is part of the correspondence training process in that the child has to apply some evaluative criteria before rating his behavior. In the Robertson et al. (1979) study children were to describe their behaviors as either being "good," "okay," or "not good." Wood and Flynn (1978) developed a self-evaluation token system with delinquent youth, in which external reinforcement for room cleanliness was transferred to a self-reinforcement system. Accuracy of self-evaluation was developed by giving two sets of points, one for room cleanliness and the other for the extent to which self-evaluations agreed with those of an independent adult observer. After an 80% level of agreement was reached, the independent observation was discontinued, and accurate self-evaluation was maintained by random spot checks. Bolstad and Johnson (1972) provided disruptive elementary school children with self-observation cards and instructed the students in recording their own behavior. At the end of each session, their data were matched against those of an observer, and fewer points were awarded if the self-observation was inaccurate. Bolstad and Johnson (1972) make a case for the self-monitoring procedures as practical and inexpensive for the classroom teacher because once the child has learned to monitor his own behavior, the self-evaluation process can be maintained with only occasional checks by the teacher.

Self-reinforcement can be viewed as a natural outgrowth of self-evaluation where positive or negative verbalizations result, depending on the degree to which one's self-evaluations meet expected criteria (Nelson & Hayes, 1981). Like reinforcement delivered by external sources, self-reinforcement can take a variety of forms. Self-reward can range from self-administered tokens or points, to self-contracting for tangible items, to internalized rewards by means of positive self-statements. The latter could be considered the ideal and an ultimate goal of social skills training. As mentioned earlier, contingency contracts can be useful vehicles for developing self-reinforcement, since it is possible to increase the child's participation in the contracting procedure by gradual steps. Homme et al. (1969) provide the following stages for that process:

Level 1: Manager-controlled system in which the manager determines the reinforcer and the task and delivers the reward.

Level 2: Transitional step with partial control by student, where student assumes joint control with the manager either over the amount of reinforcement or the amount of task.

Level 3: Second transitional step in which manager and student share equally in determining both the reinforcer and the task.

Level 4: Third transitional step in which the student assumes full control of either the task or reinforcer and shares joint responsibility with the manager for the other.

Level 5: Student controlled contracting, in which the student has assumed full control of determining both the amount of reinforcement and amount of task.

Children may need to be taught through specific procedures how to make positive self-statements. Procedures for altering negative self-statements are outlined in chapter 3. Stephens (1978, p. 374) provides a teaching strategy for the social modeling of the skill, "The student makes positive statements when asked about himself":

Teaching Strategy

Skill: The student makes positive statements when asked about himself.

Social modeling

1. Identify a need for the behavior through a classroom discussion. Use stories, film strips or other aids where available. Bring up such points as the

fact that everyone has good qualities and does some things well, even though no one is perfect. Have the class identify reasons why it's good to know about your own good qualities and recognize the things you do well. Have the class try to distinguish between behavior which could be considered "bragging" or inappropriately building oneself up at the expense of another, and behavior which involves appropriately saying positive things about oneself and what one has done. Generate with the class some positive sentences one might use to describe one's accomplishments. For example, "I like my picture." "That was a good hit I made." "I'm happy that I got 100 in spelling."

2. Identify specific behavior to be modeled. When someone asks you to tell about yourself or about something good you've done, try to think of something positive to say. (Stress that one need not be perfect or do everything perfectly in order to find good things to say about oneself.)

3. Model the behavior of the class. Describe to the class some realistic positive traits you possess and skills you have. For contrast you might insert some negative comments and have students distinguish between the two.

4. Give each student an opportunity to practice. Make up a list of positive statements as prompts. Give each student a copy of the list. Go around the class and have each student find a statement which he could apply to himself and read it in response to a prompting question from the teacher. Go around the class again and have each student think of another statement which is not on the list. Provide prompts wherever necessary. Reward students who make appropriate responses.

5. Maintain through reinforcement the behavior of making positive statements about oneself or one's accomplishments.

Although behavior change may be effected through self-monitoring and self-evaluation procedures, the research clearly demonstrates the greatest efficacy for self-management when reinforcement contingencies are employed (Fantuzzo & Clement, 1981; Gross & Drabman, 1982). Another important contributing factor is subject training. Workman (1982) suggests using modeling and behavior rehearsal to ensure that the child understands exactly how the target behavior is to be performed, as well as how to employ the self-management techniques. Stevenson and Fantuzzo (1984) report using modeling, behavior rehearsal, and correspondence matching for two 2-hour sessions in order to train one subject in a self-control sequence. In addition to self-recording, self-evaluation, and self-reward, the researchers considered other facilitating variables to include (a) the student's booster sessions, (b) the student's voluntary participation, and (c) the student's opportunity to determine goals and reinforcers.

The progression of the child from self-administered tangible rewards to internalized rewards in the form of positive statements and thoughts can be programmed through shaping and fading procedures. Based on some of the limited research in this area, the following steps are suggested for moving the child from self-provided, extrinsic rewards to self-administered, intrinsic rewards for appropriate social behaviors, with the understanding that movement from one part of the process to the next needs to be paced according to the success experienced at any one point:

1. Establish with the child the specific behavior to be rewarded and the criteria for reinforcement. Establish with the child the reward he will provide for himself, beginning with tangible rewards, if necessary, at whatever level is appropriate.
2. Initiate correspondence training, providing practice in self-monitoring with rewards for accuracy.
3. Initiate self-reinforcement, providing verbal reinforcement from the trainer for both the social behaviors and the appropriate delivery of self-reinforcement.
4. Have the child accompany self-reinforcement with a verbal description of what he did to gain the reward. For example, have the child place a star on a chart at the end of a play period for target behaviors such as sharing or taking turns, then describe what he did to earn the star, giving himself an additional star for an accurate description.
5. Ask the child to think silently to himself what he did to earn the reward before he makes the statement.
6. Move to less frequent self-administered, tangible rewards and verbal descriptions, requiring the child to remember for a longer time what he did to earn the reward.
7. Discontinue the use of self-administered, tangible rewards but require verbal reports, reinforced by external praise.
8. Discontinue regular verbal reports but periodically use probes and reminders. "I saw you help Mary when she fell down. Did you congratulate yourself for doing something nice for someone else?"

The self-control procedures just outlined require children to "self-administer a program therapists or teachers would apply if they assumed the role of primary treatment mediators" (Gross & Wojnilower, 1984, p. 511). Those authors question whether behavior under these conditions is definitely being "self-directed." They argue, for example, that teachers generally monitor the application of self-control procedures and, therefore, the contingencies for maintaining a particular behavior are not always clear. That is, children may continue to engage in desired actions because they are still under the control of the standards and contingencies established initially by the teachers, not because these responsibilities have been transferred to the child. Another related caution is the importance of children administering self-reinforcement accurately, which, if rewarded inappropriately, could result in the reinforcement of maladaptive behaviors.

For older children and adolescents, training in behavioral principles has been shown to be a means for enhancing self-control (Brigham, Hopper, Hill, DeArmas, & Newsom, 1985; Gross, Brigham, Hopper, & Bologna, 1980).

Brigham et al. describe a study with middle-school disruptive youths, who were enrolled in an after school class designed to provide an overview of behavioral theory and understanding about specific behavior change techniques. After acquiring this information, the subjects were instructed in the specifics of self-management and directed to employ these procedures in managing their own behavior. For a 3-year observation period, the researchers reported significant reductions in disciplinary actions for the majority of the students. The encouraging results from both the Brigham et al. (1985) and Gross et al. (1980) studies suggest that rudimentary knowledge of behavioral theory and techniques may be a critical component for the development of self-control skills in older children and youth.

Although, theoretically, social skills may be trained and generalized across settings and persons and maintained over time through altered contingencies and self-reinforcement, realistically it may be necessary occasionally to provide more training. Periodic booster sessions are one way of providing for maintenance of behavior change (Hersen, 1979; Stevenson & Fantuzzo, 1984), although Franks and Wilson (1978) caution that booster sessions are most effective if they are timed to occur before a behavior has been allowed to deteriorate. Similarly, a teacher may need to present occasional abbreviated review lessons for previously learned social skills. Baer (1978) suggests that the concept of "savings" is relevant to the issue of generalization. Even though a behavior may be taught once and then require occasional reteaching for new settings or maintenance over time, the fact of the initial instruction will serve to decrease the time and effort required to provide additional teaching.

## SUMMARY

Specific programming needs to be built into social skills instruction to assist in the generalization of the social behaviors to different settings and people and the maintenance of the behaviors over time. For newly learned skills to transfer from one setting to another, it is advisable to structure the training setting to resemble the real-life environment as closely as possible. It is also helpful to use more than one setting during the training and more than one trainer. Involving people from the natural environment (e.g., parents and peers) in the training is particularly helpful for facilitating generalization.

The use of mediators in the form of language, imagery, self-instruction, problem-solving skills, and expectations can be a way to extend training into new environments, because these can be carried into any setting through the child's cognitive activities. Techniques for maintaining behaviors over time generally involve changes in the contingencies of reinforcement surrounding the social behaviors. Changes can be made in the sources of reinforcement from the trainer to someone in the natural environment, and in the timing

of reinforcement from frequent predictable reinforcement to infrequent intermittent rewards. Contingency contracts are a useful way to change both the
source and timing of reinforcement. The kinds of external reinforcement provided can also be changed from tangible rewards to more natural social reinforcement, and efforts can be made to develop the child's ability to monitor,
evaluate, and provide his own internalized rewards for desirable social behavior. Even though behaviors can be programmed to generalize over time, persons, and settings, it may still be necessary to provide occasional reteaching
to make sure that the child will continue to reap the positive benefits gained
from learning social skills.

# 5
# Integrating the Steps: Issues in Application

Along with the procedures outlined in the first four chapters of this book, some additional factors need to be considered for effective social skill instruction. As with all teaching, basic and critical ingredients are the learner's attending behaviors and willingness to engage in the learning task. Therefore, attention needs to be given to the conditions that motivate learning, as determined by skill relevance, performance contingencies, and activity enjoyment. Much of the social skill training reported in the literature has taken place in schools. And most of the social skill curriculum programs have been designed for classroom application, for both remedial and preventive purposes. For that reason, some of the problems associated with social skill instruction in the schools are addressed in this chapter. Finally, a sample social skill strategy is provided, incorporating the social skill teaching steps as detailed in the first part of this book.

## FACILITATING INSTRUCTION

### Increasing Relevance

There is a direct relationship between the value the child attaches to the behavior to be taught and that child's willingness to participate in the learning and eventually to perform the behavior. Therefore, an important first step is to help the child to associate a meaningful and positive value to the social skill to be learned. The trainer might initiate a discussion about the skill in question, establishing its relevance for the child, why it is important, what benefits come from learning this skill, and what disadvantages come from not knowing this behavior. Such a discussion could relate to specific problem situations children are experiencing, possibly disguised or put in a fantasy context.

Another means of increasing relevance is to use techniques appropriate to the age level of the young person, making sure the behaviors selected for development are meaningful to the child. For example, the interest of elementary-age children in forming clubs might lend itself to a "social skills club," which meets under established conditions at some desirable place and time. For adolescents, the use of media such as videotape feedback with opportunities to operate the equipment themselves could enhance interest, as could providing as many opportunities as possible for self-direction in the selection of skills, the development of scenarios for role playing, and evaluating progress.

## Increasing Motivation

Basic to motivation is the teacher or therapist's ability to present himself or herself as a positive stimulus. In other words, the nature of the relationship that exists with the child, or children, will affect the child's involvement. Along with the adult's ability to provide support and encouragement, there are other ways to set the stage or provide the stimulus that will encourage the child to participate. Depending on the type of skills to be taught, the conditions of the setting, and the ages of the children involved, a number of procedures could be used in varying combinations to create motivating conditions.

One procedure might be the use of materials such as stories, filmstrips, films, and other audio-visual media to set the stage. A variety of such materials have been identified for all age groups (Michelson et al., 1983; see also Appendix A of this book). Another method is to tie social skill teaching into bulletin boards for visual presentations through pictures, photographs, cartoons, or student-produced artwork related to the skill. To illustrate, a bulletin board could highlight the Skill of the Week or could present a sports figure or other hero emphasizing the behavior. A picture could be captioned, for example, "O. J. Simpson says, 'Be a good sport'" with specific sportsmanlike behaviors outlined below. (*Peanuts* cartoons are a fertile source for social skills ideas.)

The establishment of expectations that some positive benefits will result from engaging in the task at hand is another possibility for increasing motivation. Such benefits could include both the future payoffs from knowing the behaviors and such immediate benefits as having refreshments or reducing homework assignments. It is important to schedule social skills training at a time when it would not compete with high-interest activities.

The instructor needs to make sure social skills instruction is not set up to imply that participants are deficient in some way, thereby creating a stigma effect. When instruction is presented with humor, play, and in ways to ensure the child's success, extrinsic reinforcement may not be necessary. However, children who are less easily motivated may need a contingency contract where activities, privileges, or tangible reinforcers can be offered in exchange for engaging in social skills training. Badges, ribbons, or certificates can serve as incentives.

A contingency management system may help encourage participation or manage behavior in the group during instruction. It is important that rewards for participating not be confused with feedback for performance, because the criteria for each would be quite different. Teacher praise for participating and making good attempts at learning the social behavior is an essential aspect of encouraging motivation. The following is an example of rewarding performance for learning the skill of making positive comments to others: "To reward children who are learning to make positive statements, give each child a card to carry and give points for every positive comment they are observed to make. Exchange the points at the end of the day or the end of the week for something they value. For example, for every ten points their name could go on a card to be placed in a fish bowl for a drawing."

## Using Social Skills Games

Another means for enhancing social skills activities is through games. Presenting social skills instruction in the form of games can assist the instructor in a number of ways. For one, playing a structured game requires the exercise of various social skills. The game can become a vehicle for teaching such skills as taking turns, sharing materials, being a good winner or loser, teamwork, cooperation, attention to details, following rules, self-control, and various problem-solving skills. For another, games have considerable merit as a way to motivate children to participate, because games imply fun and an element of play rather than work. Using games may be particularly useful where social skills content can evoke anxieties and resistance. As pointed out by Gordon (1972), games simulate real-life situations and provide a means of testing out real-world events. At the same time, games create distance from real life and involve a suspension of the usual forms of evaluation. Games provide an opportunity for the child to learn the consequences of his actions without actually having to suffer them. In a game, mistakes and exposure of ignorance are more tolerated. Games usually encourage laughing and joking, which can be instrumental in relieving anxiety and facilitating involvement.

Games can be classified as paper and pencil, board games, role play games, or hybrid games that involve a combination of the others (Heitzmann, 1974). Some of the common elements for presenting social skills instruction in game format include (a) an aspect of chance, such as drawing a card or spinning a wheel; (b) unknown aspects to be discovered by guessing; (c) dramatic features, elements of surprise or novelty; (d) material presented in ways conveying humor or fun; (e) opportunities for active participation and a variety of kinds of activities or modes of response; (f) well-defined limits and rules; (g) clearly understood goals or objectives to be reached involving the learning of specific concepts or skills; and (h) immediate feedback about the results of one's actions.

Almost any social skills content can be put into game format through very simple means, for example, picking a skill out of a hat to role play, or having teams take turns playing a form of charades in which a specific emotion or coping strategy is pantomimed to be guessed by the other group. A number of manufacturers are now marketing do-it-yourself game kits with blank boards, dice, spinners, markers, and other game equipment (see resource materials list in Appendix A). Game boards are more complex and limit the number of players but, at the same time, provide opportunities for considerable variety. Board games require a defined sequence of activities involving the order of player turns and the sequence of decisions or steps each player must make (Glazier, 1970). In a social skills board game, for example, players can move along the board according to a chance spin or roll of the dice, draw cards requiring the verbal or performance demonstration of a social behavior, and may land in a penalty box with a performance requirement in order to escape.

Foxx and McMorrow (Foxx, McMorrow, & Mennemeier, 1984; Foxx, McMorrow, & Schloss, 1983) used a social skills board game with mentally retarded adults. Specifically, the experimenters adapted the Parker Brothers' *Sorry* game so that the game cards indicating the number of spaces to be moved on the board also included statements intended to elicit responses from the participants regarding various social situations. For example, the authors described one of the social vocational card statements as, "You are working on an assembly task and your supervisor says, 'You're not doing that right.' What should you do?" Game participants were prompted and reinforced for socially appropriate verbalizations. The game, *Stacking the Deck, a Social Skills Game for Retarded Adults*, has been available commercially and is designed to improve general social skills, social vocational skills, and social sexual skills (Foxx et al., 1984). Although targeted for adults, the social situations and cards could easily be modified so that they are appropriate for adolescents and specific to the groups' particular social skill needs. The results of studies with this game demonstrated significant increases in correct responding under simulated conditions, but less convincing findings were obtained within the natural work setting. Games of this sort provide an excellent format for practicing desired behaviors; however, skill trainers also need to program for prompts and rewards in the natural environment in order for behavior transfer to occur.

Role play games require the development of scenarios that are relevant and close to the child's reality, along with identification of roles to be assigned. Flowers (1975) stresses that the behaviors to be taught must be clearly defined.

"The rule is generally that if you don't know what you want the client to be able to do he generally won't do it" (p. 171). An example of a social skills game involving role playing is the commercially marketed *Roll-a-Role Game*. The equipment includes a large red plastic cube and a large blue plastic cube, with roles printed on each side of the cubes (e.g., elderly man, neighbor lady, single girl), a deck of Talk Topics cards, a Where-It-Happens chart, and a 3-minute timer. Two players roll the cubes; the outcome determines their roles as well as the location for the role played conversation. The locations, indicated by numbers on the cubes, include front yard, hospital room, car, stranded in elevator, shopping center, in the park, telephone, airplane, laundromat, waiting room, and porch. A timekeeper draws a Talk Topic card and reads it, allows time for planning, and then sets the timer for 3 minutes, during which the players carry out a role play related to the topic on the card. The cards include such topics as

> RED is very shy and has no close friends. RED asks BLUE why this is true. BLUE wants RED to have friends and tries to build up his or her confidence. RED starts.

> RED brags to BLUE that he or she has found a wallet and intends to keep it. BLUE considers this immoral and tries to persuade RED to turn it in. RED starts.

The cards in the game are not specific to social skills or to children but, again, relevant cards could be made up and substituted. Because role playing is itself a social skill that needs to be learned if it is to be used in other social skill instruction, a game such as this could be useful for developing skill in role playing. A more detailed discussion of role playing procedures was presented earlier.

A game designed by Flowers (1975) to teach a specific social skill is the *Self-Confidence Game*, in which self-confidence is defined as a student raising his hand to answer a question from the teacher in a classroom. Questions are made up by students from classroom material and placed in a question box. Teams of three students each are assigned on a random basis, and others are appointed to be moderator, blackboard scorer, handraising judge, score keepers, and timer. The game process is similar to a College Quiz Bowl format, in that questions are presented to the teams, the first person to raise his hand can attempt to answer, and members of the opposing team can raise their hands and answer a question that has been missed. The game is divided into three phases. In Phase One, those players who answer less than 10% of the questions are identified as the low self-confidence students. In Phase Two, the low self-confidence students are placed on teams together and only compete against each other. In Phase Three, the teams are again assigned on a random basis to determine whether the Phase Two treatment has resulted in increasing the child's handraising in regular competition. Results obtained from studies with the game indicate significant increases in volunteering to answer questions and in correct answers in the game, as well as generalization to the regular classroom, improvement in grades, and increase in other forms of participation.

The game techniques developed by Gardner (1975) for use in psychotherapy with children lend themselves to the teaching of social skills, even though they were not devised for that purpose. *The Talking, Feeling, and Doing Game*, for example, involves a board, dice, playing pieces, cards that ask questions or give directions requiring verbal or motor responses, and reward chips that children receive for responding. The players move on the board according to the throw of the dice and land on squares instructing them to draw cards from one of three piles, related either to motor "doing" tasks, verbal expression of feelings, or more cognitive "talking" tasks. Because of the game's intended use in psychodynamically oriented psychotherapy, most of the cards are oriented toward eliciting feelings and areas of psychic conflict. Some, however, present tasks relevant to social skills, for example: "You're standing in line to buy something, and a child pushes himself in front of you. Show what you would do." Some of the "feeling" cards could lend themselves to teaching the child to label his own feelings and those of others; that is, "What's something you could say that would make a person feel good?" New cards could easily be devised with tasks involving verbal responses to indicate knowledge of a particular social behavior or brief scenarios that could be stimuli for role playing.

In their pupil activities book, *NICE*, Kaplan, Crawford, and Nelson (1977) present several classroom games designed to strengthen such social skills as problem solving, making friends, and positive communication. In a Pickle, for example, is a board game intended to help students think through problematic situations. The board is depicted as a large jar of pickles with each pickle representing one movement space. After moving the number of spaces indicated on a thrown die, the player then selects the problem card containing situations such as, "What would you do if you saw the person next to you cheating on a test?" or "What would you do if you had borrowed your best friend's record and accidentally scratched it?" The player reads the card aloud and all of the players discuss the dilemma for a possible solution. Other examples in this publication are the Friendship Cup Race, where players are directed to perform a sequence of actions to a peer (e.g., "Try to make your friend laugh"), in order to enhance friendships, and NICE-O, a variation of the traditional Bingo game, which uses "nice" words that have been generated by the players.

Another classroom resource is *Games Children Should Play* (Cihak & Heron, 1980). The focus here is on the development of social communication skills, including sending and receiving messages, problem solving, and being assertive. Assertive activities for young children include role plays such as, "Ask someone to play in your game" or "Your teacher and some of the parents gave the class a party. Thank one of them."

The Animal Town Game Company (1984–1985) has been established explicitly for the purpose of promoting social games. Cooperative and non-competitive games are emphasized, but even competitive games stress desired social values. *The Sleeping Grump*, a game for children, ages 5–8, is one example of a game developed by Animal Town. In this game, the Jack-in-the-Beanstalk theme is given a more positive, humanistic treatment in that the Grump starts out as a villian but the kindness and cooperation displayed by the players during the game help to bring out more humane characteristics in the Grump. Additional cooperative games and activities are discussed in chapter 9 of this book.

Some cautions about the use of games need to be presented. Social skills can be introduced or practiced in game format, but the connection between what is done for fun and its application to the real world needs to be made at some point. This could possibly be accomplished by a discussion after the game in which practical applications are identified or by references back to the game when a relevant problem arises. If the intent of the game is to provide practice in a specific skill, it is important to structure the game so each player has an opportunity to make the required response and cannot become a "winner" solely by chance; he can only win on the basis of his performance of the target behavior. The criteria for winning should relate to the concept or skills to be learned. Another caution relates to the need to minimize win-lose situations in social skills games, unless, perhaps, the target social skills are those encountered in competitive games; that is, being able to win or lose with good sportsmanship and being able to cope with failure. If rewards are given during the game, they should ideally be given for participation rather than for winning or losing. Further, the game should be constructed so players are not "out" and then eliminated from the game without an opportunity to be rotated quickly back in to ensure ongoing participation. Because much of the learning that takes place in games results from imitation of others' successful behavior, the composition of the group or the team needs to be structured so weak members are paired with stronger members.

## IMPLEMENTING SOCIAL SKILLS TEACHING IN SCHOOLS

Although the schools are a major socializing institution, social skills do not typically appear as part of the formal instructional curriculum nor does the professional staff naturally or readily assume this responsibility. Thus, the initiation and maintenance of social skill programs in the schools are accompanied by some unique and significant considerations. These concerns are addressed in the following section.

## Administrative Considerations

Social skill programs, particularly in schools, require administrative support in various forms. First, whether or not social skills are to be taught is usually an administrative decision. Ideally, the instruction should be school- or system-wide in order to increase the likelihood that the behaviors taught will be valued and reinforced in the larger environment. Related to this, administrators need to provide curriculum materials and allow for flexibility in scheduling so that social skills can be taught effectively and regularly.

Second, administrators need to be knowledgeable in ways to conduct social skill instruction in order to serve as curriculum leaders. This will, as well, enable them when interacting with students to employ techniques and reinforcers that are consistent with classroom instruction. Administrators also need to serve as models, making a concentrated effort to exhibit the social and problem-solving behaviors desired in their learners.

Finally, rewarding consequences need to occur for social skills instruction and development. Teachers need to be encouraged and reinforced for providing training, and children need to be recognized for appropriate behavior. Administrators are uniquely positioned for this purpose in that in addition to privately administered praise they can provide for school-wide recognition through bulletins, posters, campaigns, and assemblies.

## Trainer Considerations

A critical but rarely articulated issue is the receptivity of teachers to providing formal, direct social skills instruction. Teachers readily acknowledge the importance of social competence to the child's school and eventual adult success; however, they are sometimes reluctant to assume nonacademic teaching duties, insisting instead that social skill instruction should be relegated solely to other social institutions such as the family and church. Although this position is understandable, teachers need to be reminded of the major socializing importance of the school. For some children the school may be the primary resource for developing socially appropriate behaviors. Additionally, teachers need to become aware of the relationship between social skills and academic achievement (Cartledge & Milburn, 1978) and of the ever-present "hidden" curriculum, which may inadvertently result in the learning of undesired social behaviors. An explicit social skills program is one remedy for this.

Although the legitimacy of formal social skill training in the school is frequently questioned, teacher resistance may emanate more realistically from issues such as time involvement, the nature of the intervention, and teacher skill. Witt, Martens, and Elliott (1984), for example, found the amount of time needed to plan and implement behavior management procedures to be the determining factor in teacher acceptance of these strategies. The teachers were less receptive to the interventions that consumed more time than the lower time-consuming interventions. In an earlier study with preservice teachers (Witt & Martens, 1983), along with reduced time factors, the authors also found a preference for positive, (i.e., praise, rewards) over reductive (i.e., time-out, response cost) strategies. There is little doubt that teachers frequently find themselves unduly burdened with extraneous, nontraditional teaching and managerial duties. On the other hand, attention to the social development of their assigned students needs to be recognized as an explicit aspect of their professional responsibility.

Related to teacher receptivity are the issues of teacher skill, training, and motivation. Social skill trainers need to understand the skill-training process thoroughly, independent of commercially prepared materials, before they can be effective in their instruction. Although there are various approaches, the direct instruction model is the one reflected in most social skill teaching. The basic elements of this model are represented in chapters 1–4 of this book, which outline methods for targeting, assessing, developing, and maintaining social behaviors. Although many social skill programs provide training scripts, a thorough understanding of the skills training model will enable the trainer to innovate where necessary and to provide instruction for the unique needs of the learner. Another knowledge base needed by the skill trainer relates to operant technology. For some learners, particularly the handicapped (Walker et al., 1983), social skill acquisition, maintenance, and application are contingent on the trainer's ability to manipulate environmental events so that the learner is motivated to learn and experiences consequences likely to promote continued skill performance. Operant procedures can be employed to facilitate these outcomes.

The structure of teacher training typically consists of an intensive workshop training period prior to the initiation of social skill instruction in the classroom (Cartledge, 1984; Weissberg & Gesten, 1982). During this period teachers are instructed in the principles of social skill training and behavior modification, assessment procedures, curriculum materials, and specific techniques of lesson implementation. Once classroom instruction commences, teachers participate in periodic inservice sessions for continued training and program development. Throughout the implementation of the program, teachers are visited by consultants, who observe and assist with classroom instruction.

Teachers typically are encouraged to volunteer for social development programs, with incentives such as free university credit (Weissberg & Gesten, 1982), personal motivation, or monetary compensation along with an opportunity for university credit (Cartledge, 1984). Although compensations are important for teacher participation, they can present other complications. Teachers largely under the control of external incentives are more likely to participate minimally and to provide marginal classroom instruction. Reppucci and Saunders (1974) describe this as a "second-order" situation, where the behavior trainer is trying to bring about change through a third person; that is, teacher. They point out the difficulty of trying to control the behavior of teachers under these conditions, particularly when the behavior trainer is a consultant without any administrative command.

Even among internally motivated teachers, however, there is the matter of individual skill. Weissberg and Gesten (1982) found improved instruction with experienced teachers, that is, the quality of social skill instruction systematically improved as teachers had the opportunity over the period of two or three years to practice and refine their skills. Social skill training in the schools also demands sufficient competent trainers to consult regularly with teachers who require assistance with teaching procedures. The problems noted here are common to behavioral intervention programs and it is obvious that extra measures need to be taken to ensure that teachers are effective in their instruction. As with the development of any skill, opportunities for extensive practice with adequate feedback are critical for this purpose.

Other school professionals, such as school psychologists and guidance counselors, are uniquely positioned to provide social skill training to children in schools. These professionals have some distinct advantages in that they are not constrained by the limitations of classroom conditions, they can more easily restrict the size of their student groups, and their professional orientation tends to be more closely aligned with the theoretical underpinnings of social skill training. The roles of these professionals, particularly the school psychologist, have been broadened (Cartledge & Milburn, 1983), establishing their potential for preventive social skill training, for intervening with problematic or handicapped students, and for consulting with classroom teachers.

Keeping in mind the previously noted pitfalls relative to behavior generalization and maintenance, it is not recommended that social skill training in the schools become the singular responsibility of ancillary professionals, such as school psychologists and counselors; at the very least, a collaborative effort is in order. The effectiveness of separate social skill training with special personnel will be increased considerably if the peer group of the target subjects is taught similar skills and if teachers and peers can be enlisted to reinforce newly acquired behaviors. What is being suggested, therefore, is that under such conditions the classroom teacher conduct parallel instruction in the classroom, primarily for those not in the special training group, and that the teacher establish reinforcement systems so that newly acquired behaviors are rewarded under natural conditions.

Social skill trainers need to be able to communicate their social development program to the significant others in the child's environment and to enlist their support and involvement. Social validation becomes salient for this issue. Obviously, trainers need to select behaviors that are not only relevant for the learner but also behaviors that others in the learner's environment agree are important and thus are likely to reinforce. There are occasions, however, when behaviors crucial to the child's social development are not valued by others in the natural environment. In these cases, the trainer needs skill to interpret to these persons the critical nature of what is being taught and demonstrate the importance of the social skill for the learner. Many parents and peers, for example, view counteraggression as a requisite survival skill and, therefore, will encourage children to respond to provocation almost exclusively with physical force. Although the immediate results of such actions may be rewarding, the long-term effects are potentially counterproductive, causing aggression to escalate and producing a continuing conflict cycle for the child with his peers and others. Thus, it becomes important that the child's significant others are helped to recognize the value of other nonaggressive options and accordingly reinforce the child for employing these alternatives.

## Instructional Considerations

To be most effective, formal social skill instruction needs to occur regularly and continuously. At least two sessions a week are recommended (Cartledge, 1984; Michelson et al., 1983). The amount of time allocated for each session should be determined by the developmental level of the learners. Cartledge (1984), for example, found primary-aged children performed best in shorter periods, that is, 15–25 minutes, whereas 45–60 minute sessions were appropriate for upper-elementary-age subjects. The duration of the social skill instructional program is another important contributing factor. There is evidence connecting social skill development to the quantity of instruction provided (Edleson & Rose, 1981; Weissberg & Gesten, 1982). Instruction over a period of 5–6 weeks is probably too brief, and longer time periods, of several months to several years, may be needed in order to obtain desired effects.

In school, social skill instruction might be viewed as preventive and developmental in nature so that it becomes a part of the formal curriculum and is taught on an ongoing basis. As students make progress, the instruction moves to other skills, and the curriculum spirals in that more complex and sophisticated skills are taught at higher grade levels. Similar to the academic curriculum, there is a need to provide periodic review or booster sessions for previously taught skills.

Although a formal social skill training program is being advocated, teachers need to be flexible in order to take advantage of events for spontaneous incidental teaching. Teachers can capitalize on a "teachable moment" to provide impromptu social skills instruction at the time the skill deficiency is manifested. For example, "The children are engaged in a basketball game. One child misses a thrown ball and is taunted by another child who calls him 'butter fingers' with other children joining in the name-calling. Social skill instruction can be initiated at this point by stopping the game, discussing with the children the preceding events, enacting a role play of what happened, reversing the roles by using some of the previously taunting pupils as objects of name-calling, then role playing more positive things to say to someone who is experiencing difficulty. During the discussion the teacher would attempt to elicit from the students an understanding and identification of the negative, painful effects of name-calling, of alternative positive statements such as, 'Good try,' or 'Don't feel bad—we all miss sometimes,' and of the facilitative potential of encouraging words. The game could then resume with the teacher watching for and reinforcing students who are providing positive encouragement for each other."

The ways in which children are grouped is another variable to be considered in social skill instruction. Children may be taught social skills in varying group sizes. Small groups of 10 or fewer are generally preferred (McGinnis & Goldstein, 1984). As the group size increases, the instructor needs to be aware of potential interferences such as limited opportunities to respond, pupil inattention, limited opportunities for feedback, and so forth. Therefore, for larger groups adult cotrainers (McGinnis & Goldstein, 1984; Michelson et al., 1983) or peers trained as small group leaders (McGinnis & Goldstein, 1984) are recommended. Another procedure employed by Cartledge (1984) for large groups was to extend the number of sessions alloted to each skill, allowing for guided practice for each student but sufficiently varying the activities to ensure pupil attention. There is some evidence that the most critical aspect of the training may be the behavior practice (Weissberg & Gesten, 1982).

The grouping of children may occur in ways to enhance peer support and reinforcement and provide children with peer models. A single child by himself may be harder to engage in social skills training than, at least, a duo, where two children can provide motivation for each other. Elementary-age children may prefer same sex groups. Social skill instruction will be facilitated if groups contain competent children along with skill-deficient subjects (McGinnis & Goldstein, 1984; Beirman & Furman, 1984). In some settings, it may be necessary to avoid stigma by using the whole class or developing groups based on criteria other than need for social skills training. Some possible problems resulting from group instruction should be noted, as well. It may be more difficult to bring about behavior change in group situations where peers are providing reinforcement for the incompatible, maladaptive responses. Reppucci and Saunders (1974, p. 655) cite research indicating that

Behavior patterns maintained by informal peer contacts in most natural settings are seldom accessible to more than partial modification by the usually less-powerful contingencies available to the behavior modifier or staff mediators.

It is important that social skill trainers have realistic expectations regarding the possible outcomes of such training. First of all, trainers need to be perceptive about the child's potential capacity and rate of growth. As with cognitive skills, children vary in ability and speed of learning. Therefore, instructional standards need to be established individually, focused on helping each learner reach his fullest potential rather than according to some idealized, inappropriate goal. Second, according to Michelson et al. (1983), other extraneous factors such as home, medical, or emotional problems may limit the effects of training. But, if nothing else, this instruction may impress upon the child the need to make some changes at a later time. They also point out that social skill training is not a panacea for all childhood disorders. It may be necessary to use social skill training in conjunction with more intensive professional intervention.

## Parental Considerations

As noted previously factors related to the home and parents can either facilitate or interfere with social skills instruction. To the extent possible parents need to become an integral part of the social skill instructional program. They need to be informed of the relevance of social skill development to their child's immediate and future success. The behaviors to be learned need to be identified, giving parents the opportunity to discuss or negotiate any behaviors that are inconsistent with their value systems. Parents then need to be appraised of the procedures used to teach social skills and instructed in ways to reinforce and evaluate these behaviors at home. In their social skill curriculum, Jackson et al. (1983) provide Home Notes for each social skill to be taught. These sheets detail the social skill, behavioral components, and the quality of the child's responses. On the bottom portion of this sheet, the parent is to evaluate the child on the same behaviors at home and then return the sheet to the trainers. Exercises of this nature may provide a means for achieving the participation and cooperation of initially reluctant or resistant parents.

## Evaluation Considerations

Evaluation procedures are a major problem in social skill instruction in natural settings, particularly as they pertain to efficiency, validity, and available resources. The most easily administered pupil assessments are paper-and-pencil measures, such as multiple choice self-report instruments (e.g., Children's Assertive Behavior Scale, CABS, Michelson et al., 1983) or sociometric ratings. Despite the ease with which they can be administered, scoring is time-consuming and, most important, they are not necessarily congruent with pupil behavior under real-life conditions. Sociometric rating measures are more valid than self-report assessments, but the analysis may be highly complicated and the results provide little, if any, information on individual behavior change.

An evaluation of changes in behavior adjustment can be obtained through behavior checklists or adult ratings, however, these must be completed by blind observers. This eliminates the possibility of using teachers who have provided the social skill training. Limited resources or available school staff usually mitigate against employing uninformed observers over an extended period of time. Other means of evaluation such as recording the number of infractions for target pupils, before and after training, are desirable but probably not a realistic expectation, even for a committed school staff.

The problems discussed earlier under teacher motivation and skill are magnified when considering their impact on program evaluation. If effects are minimal, are these due to invalid procedures or to the limitations on the part of the teachers either in their willingness or ability to teach? The Weissberg and Gesten (1982) finding that pupil improvement corresponds with refinement of teacher skill underscores the validity of this question. Cartledge (1984) also observed higher ratings among pupils assigned to the teachers showing the most skill and evidence of teaching ability. In order to evaluate social skill instruction in the schools effectively, one must use valid procedures such as direct observations, which require extensive resources for observers and data analysis.

## APPLYING A SOCIAL SKILLS TEACHING MODEL

The instructional methods for social skill development as presented in the first four chapters of this book are consistent with the "prescriptive" or "directive" teaching model (Stephens, 1978). Essentially, the elements are (a) define in specific, behaviorally stated terms the behavior to be taught; (b) assess the learner's competence in order to determine his initial level of performance; (c) teach the behaviors that assessment shows are lacking in the learner's repertoire; (d) evaluate or reassess for results of teaching; and (e) provide opportunities and activities for maintenance and generalization or transfer of the behaviors to new situations. These steps and procedures can be adapted to almost any social behavior that can be defined in terms of observable actions, enabling practitioners to develop their own social skills curriculum (Milburn & Cartledge, 1979). The example that follows translates a problem situation into a social skills teaching strategy.

### Application of the Model

*Problem*

Many undesirable behaviors in children continue to occur and even increase because other children pay attention to them. These behaviors could be decreased and sometimes extinguished entirely by teaching children to ignore these behaviors in their peers.

*Step 1. Define the Behavior to be Taught.* Teaching objective: When the child encounters teasing or annoying behavior from another child, he will ignore it.

*Step 2. Assess the Behavior.* Observe and identify the children who are most easily distracted or who react most to annoying behavior from others. Observe what happens as a consequence of their reactions and determine: (a) Do these children know what "ignoring" means and how to do it? (b) Are there incentives to encourage them to ignore the other child or are they, perhaps, receiving some satisfaction themselves from the results of their reactions? (c) Are there cognitive and affective aspects of the problem situation that might need to be changed? For instance, is the teasing or annoying behavior interpreted by the child as a reason for anger and aggressive retaliation?

*Step 3. Plan and Implement Teaching Activities.* These include:
1. Motivate pupil interest by providing a rationale for the desired social behavior through a discussion, film, story, etc. An activity such as the following story could be used.
"Buffy came into school crying again. Buffy often came into school crying, but this morning was worse. Her face was dirty, her clothes were torn, and her books and papers were all messed up. Patricia, one of the nicest and cleverest students in the school, came to Buffy, put her arms around her, and asked her what was the matter.

'They are always bothering me,' wailed Buffy. 'They're always picking on me!'

'Who?' asked Patricia. 'Come with me, Buffy, and tell me what happened.'

Buffy went with Patricia and told her the whole story. She told Patricia that every morning on the bus some of the other boys and girls would call her names. When they did that, Buffy would cry and yell at them and call them names back. Then the other boys and girls would laugh at Buffy and call her more names. This morning Buffy became so angry she started to hit some of the boys and girls. They fought her back and that's how she got her clothes and papers torn and dirtied.

'Well, Buffy,' said Patricia, 'I'm sorry these terrible things happened to you, but I think you need to learn how to handle these boys and girls.'

'I can't fight all of them,' cried Buffy. 'I tried today, and you see what happened.'

'I'm not talking about fighting,' replied Patricia, 'I'm talking about my secret weapon — *ignoring*. After school today, I will teach you how.'

Every day after school, Patricia helped Buffy to practice ignoring. Before long Buffy was coming to school happy like the other students because the boys and girls on the school bus had stopped teasing her."

2. Engage students in a group discussion. Talk about what *ignoring* means, how to do it, and when to do it. Have the students give you examples of behaviors that would be good to ignore, as well as times when a behavior should not be ignored. Discuss other alternative reactions, the advantages and disadvantages of each, and possible outcomes of different ways of behaving. Have students relate the discussion to actual incidents in the classroom or on the playground. Your discussion can be set up at a structured social skills lesson time or can take place in an impromptu fashion after a problem has occurred. The problem situation can become the scenario for role playing.

3. Draw out of the discussion an operational definition in terms that children can understand. For example, *ignoring* means "Walk away," "Turn your head away," "Don't answer." Write these behaviors on the chalkboard.

4. Identify cognitive behaviors. The Happening–Thought–Feeling–Reaction Diagram (Knaus, 1974), discussed earlier in chapter 3, would be useful to help children understand how different thoughts can help one to ignore by controlling feelings. Assist students in identifying constructive self-statements that could be used under such conditions: "I am not going to get in trouble"; "He's just trying to make me cry, I won't let him." List self-statements on chalkboard as specific behaviors to use when ignoring. Help students to practice them.

5. Set up a role playing situation, in which the teacher and a student or two students demonstrate ignoring, using actual or hypothetical situations. For a more dramatic impact, demonstrate both appropriate and inappropriate responses. Give students an opportunity to tell you whether or not ignoring has occurred. Divide the students into pairs and give them problem situations in which to role play ignoring. ("Ignore someone who is poking you"; "Ignore someone who is making faces at you"; "Ignore someone who is calling you a name.") Have the students reverse roles and take turns being ignorer and ignoree. Bring the group together to demonstrate to each other and evaluate each other's ability to ignore.

6. Praise students who are giving good demonstrations and provide corrective feedback for those who are having difficulty. It may be necessary to repeat the discussion and role play practice on more than one occasion.

7. Provide a model yourself by showing that many inappropriate student behaviors can be eliminated by ignoring.

8. Additional pupil practice can be provided through worksheets such as that in Figure 5.1. For each of the situations depicted, students are to identify constructive self-statements and behavioral responses.

*Step 4. Evaluate.* Observe the children's behavior in problem situations to determine whether their reactions to teasing are decreasing, whether they appear to be turning away and ignoring teasing remarks and annoying behav-

**Figure 5.1.** Worksheet

ior. Because ignoring is sometimes difficult to observe or interpret and teasing may be subtle and hard to detect, systematic evaluation would probably involve counting specific problem behaviors that could decrease as a result of ignoring; that is, talk outs, fights, on /off task behavior. If the problem behavior is decreasing, you will need to build in adequate reinforcers to maintain positive responses. If the behavior is not changing, more assessment of the antecedents and results of the problem behavior may be necessary, along with more training sessions.

*Step 5. Program for Maintenance and Transfer.* This program consists of the following:

1. Provide rewards to keep positive behaviors going. Praise the children when they appear to be ignoring teasing. In order not to call attention to the child being ignored, you may need to deliver the praise subtly or at a later time, with a comment such as, "Marvin, I'm proud of how well you are trying to ignore George when he kicks the back of your chair" or "Louise, I like the way you kept on working and ignored Larry's singing behind you."

Public postings might be used as a means of reminding and rewarding students for this behavior. One example might be the use of "teasing tags," which are happy faces cut out of construction paper with room for a child's name. Children observed, by either the teacher or another child, constructively handling teasing will have their names written on a teasing tag. The tag is hung on the bulletin board with a praise statement such as, Social Skill Super Stars.

2. Set up a contingency contract. A contract could be individual to the child; for example, "If you ignore John's humming and tapping during reading period, you may help me bring in the film projector." A contract can also be a group contract, for example: "If the class can ignore anyone who is talking out and acting silly from now until recess, we will have 5 minutes longer for recess."

3. Teach children to monitor their own behavior. A child trying to develop the social skill of ignoring could, for example, record his attempts at ignoring on a tally sheet or a wrist counter. Although self-monitoring may be questionable as a source of reliable data, it can have a motivational effect that can keep a new social skill going.

4. Set up role plays and discussions to show the children how they can benefit from using ignoring in problem situations with their classmates or siblings at home and in the neighborhood. Make sure the children understand the circumstances when ignoring is appropriate. For the most successful transfer, let the parents know what you are doing and encourage them to reinforce the child's efforts to ignore in problem situations.

5. Make homework assignments, such as the one given in Figure 5.2, where students are to record conflict situations and the behaviors they employed to resolve the problem. These assignments can serve as reminders to children to practice these behaviors at other times and under various conditions. They need to be adapted, however, to the students' skill and developmental levels. Therefore, in some cases only simple oral reporting of recent actions may be

Now that you have learned how to ignore teasing, you are ready to practice these behaviors at home as well as at school. Think about this for the next 3 days. Then, in the space below, tell about one time that you did a good job of ignoring teasing.

1. What was the problem behavior that you wanted to ignore?

_____

_____

_____

2. How did you ignore it?

_____

_____

_____

3. What did you say to yourself to help you ignore the behavior?

_____

_____

_____

4. What did the other person do?

_____

_____

_____

5. Did this solve the problem?

_____

_____

_____

6. How did you feel afterward?

_____

_____

_____

**Figure 5.2.** Homework for Ignoring Teasing/Negative Behavior

required, while for highly able students essay assignments of considerable detail may be appropriate.

## SUMMARY

Successful social skill instruction is dependent upon a variety of factors including the needs and interests of the learner, the attitudes and skills of the trainer, and the teaching conditions. Learner interest and participation can be stimulated by making social skill instruction meaningful, reinforcing, or fun. Activities that are developmentally appropriate and that help the youngster understand why it is important to learn a particular social behavior contribute to skill relevance and pupil motivation.

Techniques that either increase the reinforcing properties of the instructional activities or reward attending behavior provide additional means for promoting pupil interest and involvement. Learning can be facilitated by the attractive, creative presentation of social skill teaching lessons, and when necessary, more powerful incentives in the form of rewards should be employed to sustain attention and enhance performance.

The use of games as an instructional tool is particularly useful for providing motivation and introducing social skills teaching in a nonthreatening context. Social skills games can involve the use of a game board as well as simple procedures devised by the teacher or therapist. Other games use role playing or simulation of realistic situations. Social skills games should deemphasize competition and provide sufficient opportunities for participation and practice in the skills to be learned.

Although social skill instruction can be conducted successfully in the schools, there are some potentially mitigating factors pertaining to teacher training and skill, administrative support, evaluation, and parental participation, all of which need to be addressed. Schools are uniquely structured to create an environment wherein social skills can be taught and systematically reinforced by its immediate members (i.e., peers, teachers, administrators, ancillary staff, etc.), thereby contributing to the durability of learned behaviors. Recognizing their powerful role, the aid and participation of parents need to be solicited as well, further solidifying the child's newly acquired skills. Schools can be instrumental in preventing as well as providing remedies for mild to moderate social skill problems. Teacher training and support are critical ingredients to effective social skill instruction. Another important factor is the ease with which the strategies can be administered, avoiding procedures that overly tax teachers in time and skill. Whether or not the social skill instruction is effective needs to be determined by adequate evaluation. School settings, however, present special evaluation problems and therefore require that additional measures be taken to ensure efficient and valid procedures.

By using some of the same processes by which children naturally learn social behaviors, a social skills curriculum can be developed to fit the behavioral needs of children. With procedures such as social modeling or role playing and verbal mediation, accompanied by reinforcement techniques, social skill trainers can build new behaviors and increase the frequency of desirable social behaviors in children.

# References (Chapters 1-5)

Achenbach, T. M., & Edelbrock, C. (1983). *Manual for the Child Behavior Checklist and Revised Child Behavior Profile*. Vermont: Queen City Printers.

Allvord, J. R. (1973). *Home token economy: An incentives program for children and their parents*. Champaign, IL: Research Press.

Allyon, T., & Azrin, N. (1968). *The token economy*. New York: Appleton-Century-Crofts.

Arkowitz, H., Lichtenstein, E., McGovern, K., & Hines, P. (1975). The behavioral assessment of social competence in males. *Behavior Therapy, 6*, 3-13.

Ascher, L. M., & Phillips, D. (1975). Guided behavior rehearsal. *Journal of Behavior Therapy and Experimental Psychiatry, 6*, 215-218.

Asher, S. R., Singleton, L. C., Tinsley, B. R., & Hymel, S. A. (1979). A reliable sociometric measure for preschool children. *Developmental Psychology, 15*, 443-444.

Atkeson, B. M., & Forehand, R. (1981). Conduct disorders. In E. J. Mash & L. G. Terdal (Eds.), *Behavioral assessment of childhood disorders*. New York: The Guilford Press.

Baer, D. M. (1978, September). Remarks as discussant, Symposium on Research and Technological Consideration of Generalization and Maintenance Variables. *American Psychological Association Convention*, Montreal.

Baer, D. (1981). *How to plan for generalization*. Lawrence, KS: H & H Enterprises.

Bandura, A. (1969). *Principles of behavior modification*. New York: Holt, Rinehart & Winston.

Bandura, A. (1973). *Aggression: A social learning analysis*. Englewood Cliffs, NJ: Prentice-Hall.

Bandura, A. (1977a). Self-efficacy: Toward a unifying theory of behavioral change. *Psychological Review, 84*, 191-215.

Bandura, A. (1977b). *Social learning theory*. Englewood Cliffs, NJ: Prentice-Hall.

Barrett, D. E., & Yarrow, M. R. (1977). Prosocial behavior, social inferential ability, and assertiveness in children. *Child Development, 48*, 475-481.

Barton, E. J., & Ascione, F. R. (1979). Sharing in preschool children: Facilitation, stimulus generalization, and maintenance. *Journal of Applied Behavior Analysis, 12*, 417-430.

Barton, E. J., & Ascione, F. R. (1984). Direct observation. In T. H. Ollendick & M. Hersen (Eds.), *Child behavior assessment*. Elmsford, NY: Pergamon Press.

Beck, A. (1970). Cognitive therapy: Nature and relation to behavior therapy. *Behavior Therapy, 1*, 184-200.

Beck, A. (1976). *Cognitive therapy and emotional disorders*. New York: International Universities Press.

Beck, S., Forehand, R., Neeper, R., & Baskin, C. H. (1982). A comparison of two analogue strategies for assessing children's social skills. *Journal of Consulting and Clinical Psychology, 50*, 596-597.

Beck, S. (1986). Methods of assessment II: Questionnaires and checklists. In C. L. Frame & J. L. Matson (Eds.), *Handbook of assessment in childhood pathology: Applied issues in differential diagnosis and treatment evaluation.* New York: Plenum Press.

Becker, W. C. (1971). *Parents are teachers.* Champaign, IL: Research Press.

Bellack, A., Hersen, M., & Lamparski, D. (1979). Role-play tests for assessing social skills. Are they valid? Are they useful? *Journal of Consulting and Clinical Psychology, 47*, 335–342.

Bellack, A., Hersen, M., & Turner, S. (1978). Role-play tests for assessing social skills: Are they valid? *Behavior Therapy, 9*, 448–461.

Bellack, A., Hersen, M., & Turner, S. (1979). Relationship of roleplaying and knowledge of appropriate behavior to assertion in the natural environment. *Journal of Consulting and Clinical Psychology, 47*, 670–678.

Berler, E. S., Gross, A. M., & Drabman, R. S. (1982). Social skills training with children: Proceed with caution. *Journal of Applied Behavior Analysis, 15*, 41–53.

Bernard, M. E., & Joyce, M. R. (1984). *Rational-emotive therapy with children and adolescents.* New York: John Wiley and Sons.

Bernstein, D. A. & Borkovec, T. D. (1973). *Progressive relaxation training.* Champaign, IL: Research Press.

Bessell, H. & Palomares, U. (1970). *Methods in human development, theory manual and curriculum activity guide.* San Diego, CA: Human Development Training Institute.

Bierman, K. L., & Furman, W. (1984). The effects of social skills and peer involvement on the social adjustment of preadolescents. *Child Development, 55*, 151–163.

Bijou, S. W., Peterson, R. F., & Ault, M. H. (1968). A method to integrate descriptive and experimental field studies at the level of data and empirical concepts. *Journal of Applied Behavior Analysis, 1*, 175–191.

Bolstad, O. D., & Johnson, S. M. (1972). Self-regulation in the modification of disruptive classroom behavior. *Journal of Applied Behavior Analysis, 5*, 443–454.

Borke, H. (1971). Interpersonal perception of young children. Egocentrism or empathy? *Developmental Psychology, 5*, 263–269.

Bornstein, M. R., Bellack, A. S., & Hersen, M. (1977). Social-skills training for unassertive children: A multiple-baseline analysis. *Journal of Applied Behavior Analysis, 10*, 183–195.

Bower, E. M. (1960). *Early identification of emotionally handicapped children in school.* Springfield, IL: Charles C Thomas.

Bowman, P. H., DeHaan, R. F., Kough, J. K. & Liddle, G. P. (1956). *Mobilizing community resources for youth.* Chicago: University of Chicago Press.

Brigham, T. A., Hopper, C., Hill, B., DeArmas, A., & Newsom, P. (1985). A self-management program for disruptive adolescents in the school: A clinical replication analysis. *Behavior Therapy, 16*, 99–115.

Brooks-Gunn, J., & Luciano, L. (1985). Social competence in young handicapped children: A developmental perspective. In M. Sigman (Ed.), *Children with emotional disorders and developmental disabilities: Assessment and treatment.* Orlando, FL: Grune & Stratton.

Bryant, B. K. (1982). An index of empathy for children and adolescents. *Child Development, 53*, 413–425.

Bugental, D. B., Whalen, C. K., & Henker, B. (1977). Causal attributions of hyperactive children and motivational assumptions of two behavioral-change approaches: Evidence for an interactionist position. *Child Development, 48*, 874–884.

Burke, J. P., & DeMers, S. T. (1979). A paradigm for evaluating assessment interviewing techniques. *Psychology in the Schools, 16*, 51–60.

Camp, B. (1977). Verbal mediation in young aggressive boys. *Journal of Abnormal Psychology, 86,* 145-153.

Camp, B. (1978, October). *Cognitive-behavior therapy with children.* Symposium, Second National Conference on Cognitive Therapy Research, New York.

Camp, B. W., & Bash, M. A. S. (1981). *Think aloud: Increasing social and cognitive skills—A problem-solving program for children (primary level).* Champaign, IL: Research Press.

Camp, B. W., Blom, G. E., Herbert, F., & van Doorninck, W. J. (1977). "Think aloud": A program for developing self-control in young aggressive boys. *Journal of Abnormal Child Psychology, 5,* 157-169.

Camp, B. W., Zimet, S. G., van Doorninck, W. J., & Dahlem, N. W. (1977). Verbal abilities in young aggressive boys. *Journal of Educational Psychology, 69,* 129-135.

Carlson, C. L., Lahey, B. B., & Neeper, R. (1983). Peer assessment of the social behavior of accepted, rejected, and neglected children. *Journal of Abnormal Child Psychology, 12,* 187-198.

Carr, E. G., & Kologinsky, E. (1983). Acquisition of sign language by autistic children II: Spontaneity and generalization effects. *Journal of Applied Behavior Analysis, 16,* 297-314.

Cartledge, G. (1984). *Formal social skills instruction in the schools: Report.* Unpublished manuscript.

Cartledge, G., Frew, T. W., & Zaharias, J. (1985). Social skill needs of mainstreamed students: Peer and teacher perceptions. *Learning Disability Quarterly, 8,* 132-140.

Cartledge, G., & Milburn, J. F. (1978). The case for teaching social skills in the classroom. *Review of Educational Research, 1,* 133-156.

Cartledge, G., & Milburn, J. F. (1983). The how-to of effective social skills training. *Directive Teacher, 3,* 12.

Cartledge, G., Stupay, D., & Kaczala, C. (in press). Relationship between social skills and social perception in L.D. and nonhandicapped elementary-aged children. *Learning Disability Quarterly.*

Castaneda, A., McCandless, B. R., & Palermo, D. F. (1956). The children's form of the Manifest Anxiety Scale. *Child Development, 27,* 317-326.

Cautela, J. R., & Groden, J. (1978). *Relaxation—A comprehensive manual for adults, children, and children with special needs.* Champaign, IL: Research Press.

Chandler, M. (1973). Egocentrism and antisocial behavior: The assessment and training of social perspective-taking skills. *Developmental Psychology, 9,* 326-332.

Chittenden, G. E. (1942). An experimental study in measuring and modifying assertive behavior in young children. *Monographs of the Society for Research in Child Development, 7*(1, Serial No. 31).

Cianciolo, P. J. (1965). Children's literature can affect coping behavior. *Personnel and Guidance Journal, 43,* 897-903.

Cihak, M. K., & Heron, B. J. (1980). *Games children should play.* Glenview, IL: Scott, Foresman and Company.

Clark, H. B., Caldwell, C. P., & Christian, W. P. (1979). Classroom training of conversational skills and remote programming for the practice of these skills in another setting. *Child Behavior Therapy, 1,* 139-160.

Cobb, J. A., & Hops, H. (1973). Effects of academic survival skill training on low achieving first graders. *The Journal of Educational Research, 67,* 108-113.

Cohen, A. S., & Van Tassel, E. (1978). A comparison of partial and complete paired comparisons in sociometric measurement of preschool groups. *Applied Psychological Measurement, 2,* 31-40.

Coie, J. D., & Dodge, K. A. (1983). Continuities and change in children's social status: A five-year longitudinal study. *Merrill-Palmer Quarterly, 29*, 261–282.

Coie, J. D., Dodge, K. A., & Coppotelli, H. (1982). Dimensions and types of social status: A cross-age perspective. *Developmental Psychology, 18*, 557–570.

Combs, M. L., & Slaby, D. A. (1977). Social skills training with children. In B. B. Lahey & A. E. Kazdin (Eds.), *Advances in clinical child psychology, 1.* New York: Plenum Press.

Cone, J. D., & Hawkins, R. H. (1977). *Behavioral assessment.* New York: Brunner/Mazel, Inc.

Conger, J. C., & Keane, S. P. (1981). Social skills intervention in the treatment of isolated or withdrawn children. *Psychological Bulletin, 90*, 478–493.

Conners, C. K. (1970). Symptom patterns in hyperkenetic, neurotic, and normal children. *Child Development, 41*, 667–682.

Connolly, J. A. (1983). A review of sociometric procedures in the assessment of social competencies in children. *Applied Research in Mental Retardation, 4*, 315–327.

Cooper, J. O. (1974). *Measurement and analysis of behavioral techniques.* Columbus, OH: Charles E. Merrill.

Cooper, J. O. (1981). *Measurement and analysis of behavioral techniques* (2nd ed.). Columbus, OH: Charles E. Merrill.

Cooper, J. O., & Edge, D. (1978). *Parenting strategies and educational methods.* Columbus, OH: Charles E. Merrill.

Coopersmith, S. (1967). *The antecedents of self-esteem.* San Francisco: Freeman.

Corsini, R. J. (1966). *Roleplaying in psychotherapy: A manual.* Chicago: Aldine.

Csapo, M. (1972). Peer models reverse the "one bad apple spoils the barrel" theory. *Teaching Exceptional Children, 4*, 20–24.

Curwin, R. L., & Curwin, G. (1974). *Developing individual values in the classroom.* Palo Alto, CA: Education Today Company, Inc.

Dardig, J. C., & Heward, W. L. (1980). *Sign here: A contracting book for children and their parents.* Columbus, OH: Charles E. Merrill.

Deluty, R. H. (1979). Children's action tendency scale: A self-report measure of aggressiveness, assertiveness, and submissiveness in children. *Journal of Consulting and Clinical Psychology, 47*, 1061–1071.

DeMille, R. (1967). *Put your mother on the ceiling.* New York: Walker.

DeRisi, W. J., & Butz, G. (1975). *Writing behavioral contracts: A case simulation practice manual.* Champaign, IL: Research Press.

Dickerson, E. A., & Creedon, C. F. (1981). Self-selection of standards by children: The relative effectiveness of pupil-selected and teacher-selected standards of performance. *Journal of Applied Behavior Analysis, 14*, 425–433.

Dillon, J. T. (1979). Defects of questioning as an interview technique. *Psychology in the Schools, 16*, 575–580.

DiLorenzo, T. M., & Foster, S. L. (1984). A functional assessment of children's ratings of interaction patterns. *Behavioral Assessment, 6*, 291–302.

Dinkmeyer, D. (1973). *Developing understanding of self and others* (DUSO Program). Circle Pines, MN: American Guidance Service, Inc.

Dupont, H., Gardner, O., & Brody, D. (1974). *Toward affective development.* Circle Pines, MN: American Guidance Service.

Dygdon, J., Conger, A. J., Conger, J. C., Wallanda, J. L., & Keane, S. P. (1980, September). *Behavioral correlates of social competence and dysfunction in early childhood.* Paper presented at American Psychological Association, Montreal, Canada.

D'Zurilla, T. J., & Goldfried, M. R. (1971). Problem solving and behavior modification. *Journal of Abnormal Psychology, 78*, 107–126.

Edleson, J. L. (1978). *A behavioral roleplay test for assessing children's social skills: Testing booklet.* Unpublished manual, University of Wisconsin – Madison.

Edleson, J. L., & Cole-Kelly, K. (1978). *A behavioral roleplay test for assessing children's social skills: Scoring manual.* Unpublished manual, University of Wisconsin – Madison.

Edleson, J. L., & Rose, S. D. (1978). *A behavioral roleplay test for assessing children's social skills.* Paper presented at the annual convention of the Association for the Advancement of Behavior Therapy, Chicago.

Edleson, J. L., & Rose, S. D. (1981). Investigations into the efficacy of short-term group social skills training for socially isolated children. *Child Behavior Therapy, 3,* 1–16.

Edmonson, B., de Jung, J., Leland, H., & Leach, E. M. (1974). *The test of social inference.* Freeport, NY: Educational Activities, Inc.

Eisenberg-Berg, N., & Lennon, R. (1980). Altruism and the assessment of empathy in the preschool years. *Child Development, 51,* 552–557.

Eisler, R. M. (1976). Behavioral assessment of social skills. In M. Hersen & A. A. Bellack (Eds.), *Behavioral assessment: A practical handbook.* Elmsford, NY: Pergamon Press.

Eisler, R. M., & Frederiksen, L. W. (1980). *Perfecting social skills.* New York: Plenum Press.

Eisley, M. E., & Merrill, P. F. (1984, April). *Effects of context vs. substance in stories portraying moral behavior.* Paper presented at the annual meeting of the American Research Association, New Orleans.

Elardo, P. T., & Cooper, M. (1977). *AWARE – Activities for social development.* Menlo Park, CA: Addison-Wesley (Innovative Publishing Division).

Elardo, P. T., & Caldwell, B. M. (1979). The effects of an experimental social development program on children in the middle childhood period. *Psychology in the Schools, 16,* 93–100.

Ellis, A. (1962). *Reason and emotion in psychotherapy.* New York: Lyle Stuart Press.

Ellis, A. (1977). The basic clinical theory of rational-emotive therapy. In A. Ellis & R. Grieger (Eds.), *Handbook of rational-emotive therapy.* New York: Springer.

Enright, R. D., & Lapsley, D. K. (1980). Social role-taking: A review of the constructs, measures, and measurement properties: *Review of Educational Research, 50,* 647–675.

Erikson, E. (1963). *Childhood and society.* New York: Norton.

Evans, I., & Nelson, R. (1977). Assessment of child behavior problems. In A. R. Ciminero, K. S. Calhoun, & H. E. Adams (Eds.), *Handbook of behavioral assessment.* New York: Wiley.

Fagen, S. A., Long, J. J., & Stevens, D. J. (1975). *Teaching children self-control.* Columbus, OH: Charles E. Merrill.

Fantuzzo, J. W., & Clement, P. W. (1981). Generalization of the effects of teacher and self-administered token reinforcers to nontreated students. *Journal of Applied Behavior Analysis, 14,* 435–447.

Feffer, M., & Gourevitch, V. (1960). Cognitive aspects of role-taking in children. *Journal of Personality, 29,* 384–396.

Feldhusen, J., Houtz, J., & Ringenbach, S. (1972). The Purdue Elementary Problem-Solving Inventory. *Psychological Reports, 31,* 891–901.

Felixbrod, J. J., & O'Leary, K. D. (1973). Effects of reinforcement on children's academic behavior as a function of self-determined and externally imposed contingencies. *Journal of Applied Behavior Analysis, 6,* 241–250.

Feshbach, N. D. (1982). Sex differences in empathy and social behavior in children.

In N. Eisenberg-Berg (Ed.), *The development of prosocial behavior*. New York: Academic Press.

Feshbach, N. D., Feshbach, S., Fauvre, M., & Ballard-Campbell, M. (1983). *Learning to care*. Glenview, IL: Scott, Foresman and Company.

Feshbach, N. D., & Roe, K. (1968). Empathy in six- and seven-year olds. *Child Development, 39*, 133–145.

Finch, A. J., Jr., Deardorff, P. A., & Montgomery, L. E. (1974). Individually tailored behavioral rating scales: A possible alternative. *Journal of Abnormal Child Psychology, 2*, 209–216.

Fitts, W. H. (1965). *Manual for the Tennessee self-concept scale*. Los Angeles: Western Psychological Services.

Flapan, D. (1968). *Children's understanding of social interaction*. New York: Columbia University Press.

Flavell, J., Botkin, P., Fry, C., Wright, J., & Jarvis, P. (1968). *The development of note taking and communication skills in children*. New York: Wiley.

Flowers, J. V. (1975). Simulation and role playing methods. In F. H. Kanfer & A. P. Goldstein (Eds.), *Helping people change*. Elmsford, NY: Pergamon Press.

Foster, S. L., Bell-Dolan, D., & Berler, E. S. (in press). Methodological issues in the use of sociometrics for selecting children for social skills research and training. In R. J. Prinz (Ed.), *Advances in behavioral assessment of children and famillies* (Vol. 2). Greenwich, CT: JAI Press.

Foster, S. L., Delawyer, D. D., & Guevremont, D. C. (in press). A critical incidents analysis of liked and disliked peer behaviors and their situational parameters in childhood and adolescence. *Behavioral Assessment*.

Foster, S. L., & Ritchey, W. L. (1979). Issues in assessment of social competence in children. *Journal of Applied Behavior Analysis, 12*, 625–638.

Foster, S. L., & Ritchey, W. L. (1985). Behavioral correlates of sociometric status of fourth-, fifth-, and sixth-grade children in two classroom situations. *Behavioral Assessment, 7*, 79–93.

Fowler, S. A., & Baer, D. H. (1981). "Do I have to be good all day?" The timing of delayed reinforcement as a factor in generalization. *Journal of Applied Behavior Analysis, 14*, 13–24.

Foxx, R. M., & McMorrow, M. J. (1984). *Stacking the deck, a social skills game for retarded adults*. Champaign, IL: Research Press.

Foxx, R. M., McMorrow, M. J., & Mennemeier, M. (1984). Teaching social/vocational skills to retarded adults with a modified table game: An analysis of generalization. *Journal of Applied Behavior Analysis, 17*, 343–352.

Foxx, R. M., McMorrow, M. J., & Schloss, C. W. (1983). Stacking the deck: Teaching social skills to retarded adults with a modified table game. *Journal of Applied Behavior Analysis, 16*, 157–170.

Franks, C. M., & Wilson T. (1978). *Annual review of behavior therapy: Theory and practice* (Vol. 6). New York: Brunner/Mazel.

Furman, W. (1980). Promoting social development: Developmental implications for treatment. In B. B. Lahey & A. E. Kazdin (Eds.), *Advances in clinical child psychology*. New York: Plenum Press.

Furman, W., & Beirman, K. L. (1983). Developmental changes in young children's conceptions of friendship. *Child Development, 54*, 549–556.

Gaffney, L. R. & McFall, R. M. (1981). A comparison of social skills in delinquent and nondelinquent adolescent girls using a behavioral role-playing inventory. *Journal of Consulting and Clinical Psychology, 49*, 959–967.

Gambrill, E. D. (1977). *Behavior modification*. San Francisco: Jossey-Bass.

Gardner, R. A. (1975). *Psychotherapeutic approaches to the resistant child*. New York: Jason Aronson, Inc.

Gelfand, D. M., & Hartmann, D. P. (1975). *Child behavior analysis and therapy*. Elmsford, NY: Pergamon Press, Inc.

Gelfand, D. M. & Hartmann, D. P. (1979, September). *Behavior analysis and developmental psychology. What we can learn from one another*. Paper presented at the American Psychological Association convention, New York.

Gelfand, D. M., & Hartmann, D. P. (1984). *Child behavior analysis and therapy* (2nd ed.). New York: Pergamon Press.

Glazier, R. (1970). *How to design educational games*. Cambridge, MA: Abt Associates.

Glennon, B., & Weisz, J. R. (1978). An observational approach to the assessment of anxiety in young children. *Journal of Counseling and Clinical Psychology, 46,* 1246–1257.

Glenwick, D. S., & Jason, L. A. (1984). Locus of intervention in child cognitive behavior therapy. In A. W. Meyers & W. E. Craighead (Eds.), *Cognitive behavior therapy with children*. New York: Plenum Press.

Goldfried, M., & D'Zurilla, T. (1969). A behavioral–analytic model for assessing competence. In C. D. Spielberger (Ed.), *Current topics in clinical and community psychology* (Vol. 1). New York: Academic Press.

Goldfried, M. R., & Goldfried, A. P. (1975). Cognitive change methods. In F. H. Kanfer & A. P. Goldstein (Eds.), *Helping people change*. Elmsford, NY: Pergamon Press.

Goldman, J., L'Engle Stein, C., & Guerry, S. (1983). *Psychological methods of child assessment*. New York: Brunner/Mazel, Inc.

Goldstein, A. P., Carr, E. G., Davidson, W. S., & Wehr, P. (1981). *In response to aggression*. Elmsford, NY: Pergamon Press.

Goldstein, A. P., Keller, H., & Erne, D. (1985). *Changing the abusive parent: Teaching self-control, parenting and interpersonal skills*. Champaign, IL: Research Press.

Goldstein, A. P., Martens, J., Hubben, J., van Belle, H., Schaaf, W., Wiersma, H., & Goldhard, A. (1973). The use of modeling to increase independent behavior. *Behavior Research and Therapy, 11,* 31–42.

Goldstein, A. P., & Michaels, G. Y. (1985). *Empathy*. Hillsdale, NJ: Lawrence Erlbaum Associates, Inc.

Goldstein, A. P., Sherman, M., Gershaw, N. J., Sprafkin, R., & Glick, B. (1978). Training aggressive adolescents in prosocial behavior. *Journal of Youth and Adolescence, 7,* 73–92.

Goldstein, A. P., Sprafkin, R. P., & Gershaw, N. J. (1976). *Skill training for community living: Applying structured learning therapy*. Elmsford, NY: Pergamon Press.

Goodwin, S. E., & Mahoney, M. J. (1975). Modification of aggression through modeling: An experimental probe. *Journal of Behavior Therapy and Experimental Psychiatry, 6,* 200–202.

Gordon, A. K. (1972). *Games for growth*. Chicago: Science Research Associates.

Gottman, J. (1977). Toward a definition of social isolation in children. *Child Development, 48,* 513–517.

Gottman, J., Gonso, J., & Rasmussen, B. (1975). Social interaction, social competence and friendship in children. *Child Development, 46,* 709–718.

Greenspan, S. (1981). Social competence and handicapped individuals: Practical implications of a proposed model. In B. K. Keogh (Ed.), *Advances in special education: Socialization influences on exceptionality.* Greenwich, CT: JAI Press.

Greenwood, C. R., & Hops, H. (1981). Group-oriented contingencies and peer behavior change. In P. S. Strain (Ed.), *The utilization of classroom peers as behavior change agents.* New York: Plenum Press.

Greenwood, C. R., Walker, H. M., & Hops, H. (1977). Some issues in social interaction/withdrawal assessment. *Exceptional Children, 43,* 490–499.

Greenwood, C. R., Walker, H. M., Todd, N. M., & Hops, H. (1979). Selecting a cost effective screening device for the assessment of preschool social withdrawal. *Journal of Applied Behavioral Analysis, 12,* 639–652.

Gresham, F. M. (1981). Assessment of children's social skills. *Journal of School Psychology, 19,* 120–133.

Gresham, F. M. (1984, August). *Social skills: Social validation of assessment and treatment methods.* Paper presented at the annual meeting of the American Psychological Association, Toronto.

Gresham, F. M., & Elliott, S. N. (1984). Assessment and classification of children's social skills: A review of methods and issues. *School Psychology Review, 13,* 292–301.

Gresham, F. M., & Nagle, R. J. (1980). Social skills training with children: Responsiveness to modeling and coaching as a function of peer orientation. *Journal of Consulting and Clinical Psychology, 48,* 718–729.

Gross, A., Brigham, T. A., Hopper, C., & Bologna, N. (1980). Self-management and social skills training: A study with predelinquent and delinquent youths. *Criminal Justice and Behavior, 7,* 161–184.

Gross, A. M., & Drabman, R. S. (1982). Teaching self-recording, self-evaluation, and self-reward to nonclinic children and adolescents. In P. Karoly & F. H. Kanfer (Eds.), *Self-management and behavior change.* New York: Pergamon Press.

Gross, A. M., & Wojnilower, D. A. (1984). Self-directed behavior change in children: Is it self-directed? *Behavior Therapy, 15,* 501–514.

Handleman, J. S. (1979). Generalization by autistic-type children of verbal responses across settings. *Journal of Applied Behavior Analysis, 12,* 273–282.

Hansen, M. (1983). *A re-examination of the relationship between cognitive role taking and social competence in children.* Paper presented at American Psychological Association, Anaheim, California.

Harris, G. M., & Johnson, S. B. (1983). Coping imagery and relaxation instructions in a covert modeling treatment for test anxiety. *Behavior Therapy, 14,* 144–157.

Harris, S. L., & Ferrari, M. (1983). Developmental factors in child behavior therapy. *Behavior Therapy, 14,* 54–72.

Harter, S. (1978). The perceived competence scale for children: A new measure. Unpublished manuscript.

Harter, S. (1982). The perceived competence scale for children. *Child Development, 53,* 87–97.

Hartup, W. W. (1970). Peer interaction and social organization. In P. H. Mussen (Ed.), *Carmichael's manual of child psychology* (vol. 2). New York: Wiley.

Hayvren, M., & Hymel, S. (1984). Ethical issues in sociometric testing: Impact of sociometric measures on interaction behavior. *Developmental Psychology, 20,* 849–884.

Hazel, J. S., Schumaker, J. B., Sherman, J. A., & Sheldon-Wildgen, J. (1982). Group training for social skills: A program for court-adjudicated, probationary youths. *Criminal Justice and Behavior, 9,* 35–53.

Heitzmann, W. R. (1974). *Educational games and simulations.* Washington, DC: National Education Association.

Hermecz, D. A., & Melamed, B. G. (1984). The assessment of emotional imagery training in fearful children. *Behavior Therapy, 15,* 156–172.

Hersen, M. (1973). Self assessment of fear. *Behavior Therapy, 4,* 241–257.

Hersen, M. (1979). Limitations and problems in the clinical application of behavioral techniques is psychiatric settings. *Behavior Therapy, 10,* 65–80.

Hersen, M., & Barlow, D. H. (1976). *Single case experimental designs: Strategies for studying behavior change.* Elmsford, NY: Pergamon Press.

Hersen, M., & Bellack, A. S. (1977). Assessment of social skills. In A. R. Ciminero, K. S. Calhoun, & H. D. Adams (Eds.), *Handbook for behavior assessment.* New York: Wiley.

Homme, L., Csanyi, A. P., Gonzales, M. A., & Rechs, J. R. (1969). *How to use contingency contracting in the classroom.* Champaign, IL: Research Press.

Hopper, R. B. & Kirschenbaum, D. S. (1979). *Social problem-solving skills and social competence in preadolescent children.* Paper presented at the meeting of the American Psychology Association, New York City, September.

Hops, H. (1983). Children's social competence and skill: Current research practices and future directions. *Behavior Therapy, 14,* 3–18.

Hops, H., & Cobb, J. A. (1973). Survival behaviors in the educational setting: Their implications for research and intervention. In L. A. Hammerlynk, L. C. Handy, & E. J. Mash (Eds.), *Behavior change* (pp. 193–208). Champaign, IL: Research Press.

Hops, H., & Cobb, J. A. (1974). Initial investigations into academic survival skill training, direct instruction and first grade achievement. *Journal of Educational Psychology, 66,* 548–553.

Hops, H., Fleischman, D. H., Guild, J., Paine, S., Street, A., Walker, H. M., & Greenwood, C. R. (1978). *Program for establishing effective relationship skills (PEERS): Consultant manual.* Eugene: University of Oregon, Center at Oregon for Research in the Behavioral Education of the Handicapped.

Hops, H., & Greenwood, C. R. (1981). Social skill deficits. In E. J. Mash & L. G. Terdal (Eds.), *Behavioral assessment of childhood disorders.* New York: The Guilford Press.

Hops, H., & Lewin, L. (1984). Peer sociometric forms. In T. H. Ollendick & M. Hersen (Eds.), *Child behavioral assessment.* New York: Pergamon Press.

Humphreys, L. E., & Ciminero, A. R. (1979). Parent report measures of child behavior: A review. *Journal of Clinical Child Psychology, 8,* 56–63.

Hymel, S. (1983). Preschool children's peer relations: Issues in sociometric assessment. *Merrill-Palmer Quarterly, 29,* 237–260.

Hymel, S., & Asher, S. (1977, March). *Assessment and training of isolated children's social skills.* National Institute of Child Health and Human Development (NIH), Bethesda, MD.

Inhelder, B., & Piaget, J. (1964). *The early growth of logic in the child, classification and seriation.* New York: Harper and Row.

Izard, C. E. (1977). *Human emotions.* New York: Plenum Press.

Jacobson, E. (1938). *Progressive relaxation.* Chicago: University of Chicago Press.

Jackson, N. F., Jackson, D. A., & Monroe, C. (1983). *Getting along with others.* Champaign, IL: Research Press.

Jewett, J. F., & Clark, H. B. (1976, December). *Training preschoolers to use appropriate dinner time conversation: An analysis of generalization from school to home.*

Paper presented at the Association for the Advancement of Behavior Therapy, New York.

Jones, K. T., & Evans, H. L. (1980). Self-reinforcement: A continuum of external cues. *Journal of Educational Psychology, 72*, 625–635.

Jones, R. T., Nelson, R. E., & Kazdin, A. (1977). The role of external variables in self-reinforcement. *Behavior Modification, 1*, 147–178.

Kagan, J., & Kogan, N. (1970). Individual variation in cognitive processes. In P. H. Mussen (Ed.), *Carmichael's manual of child psychology, vol. 1* (3rd ed.). New York: Wiley.

Kagan, J., & Moss, H. A. (1962). *Birth to maturity*. New York: Wiley.

Kanfer, F. H. (1975). Self-management methods. In F. H. Kanfer & A. P. Goldstein (Eds.), *Helping people change*. Elmsford, NY: Pergamon Press.

Kanfer, F. H., & Saslow, G. (1965). Behavioral analysis: An alternative to diagnostic classification. *Archives of General Psychiatry, 12*, 529–538.

Kanfer, F. H., & Saslow, G. (1969). Behavioral diagnosis. In C. M. Franks (Ed.), *Behavior therapy: Appraisal and status*. New York: McGraw-Hill.

Kaplan, P. G., Crawford, S. K., & Nelson, S. L. (1977). *NICE: Nifty Innovations for Creative Expression*. Denver, CO: Love Publishing Company.

Karoly, P. (1981). Self management problems in children. In E. J. Mash & L. G. Terdal (Eds.), *Behavioral assessment of childhood disorders*. New York: The Guilford Press.

Katz, R. C., & Vinceguerra, P. (1980, November). *Interactions between informational context and reinforcement schedules in the maintenence of behavior change*. Paper presented at the 14th Annual Convention of the Association for Advancement of Behavior Therapy, New York.

Kaufman, L. M., & Wagner, B. R. (1972). Barb: A systematic treatment technology for temper control disorders. *Behavior Therapy, 3*, 84–90.

Keane, S. P., & Tryon, A. S. (1984, November). *The relationship between self-efficacy and children's social status*. Paper presented at the annual meeting of the Association for the Advancement of Behavior Therapy. Philadelphia.

Kendall, P. C. (1978, November). *Self-instructions with children: An analysis of the inconsistent evidence for treatment generalization*. Paper presented at the Association for the Advancement of Behavior Therapy Convention, Chicago.

Kendall, P. C. (1981). Cognitive-behavioral interventions with children. In B. B. Lahey & A. E. Kazdin (Eds.), *Advances in clinical child psychology* (Vol. 4). New York: Plenum Press.

Kendall, P. C., & Braswell, L. (1985). *Cognitive-behavioral therapy for impulsive children*. New York: The Guilford Press.

Kendall, P. C., & Fischler, G. L. (1984). Behavioral and adjustment correlates of problem solving: Validation analyses of interpersonal cognitive problem-solving measures. *Child Development, 55*, 879–892.

Kendall, P. C., & Morison, P. (1984). Integrating cognitive and behavioral procedures for the treatment of socially isolated children. In A. W. Meyers & W. E. Craighead (Eds.), *Cognitive behavior therapy with children*. New York: Plenum Press.

Kent, R. N., & Foster, S. L. (1977). Direct observational procedures: Methodological issues in naturalistic settings. In A. R. Ciminero, K. S. Calhoun, & H. E. Adams (Eds.), *Handbook of behavioral assessment*. New York: Wiley.

Knaus, W. J. (1974). *Rational emotive education*. New York: Institute for Rational Living.

Kohlberg, L. (1969). Stage and sequence: The cognitive–developmental approach to socialization. In D. A. Goslin (Ed.), *Handbook of socialization theory and research.* Chicago: Rand McNally.

Kovacs, M. (1981). Rating scales to assess depression in school aged children. *Acta Paedopsychiatrica, 46,* 305–315.

Krasnor, L. R. (1982). An observational study of social problem solving in young children. In K. H. Rubin & H. S. Ross (Eds.), *Peer relationships and social skills in childhood.* New York: Springer Verlag.

Krasnor, L. R. & Rubin, K. H. (1981). The assessment of social problem-solving skills in young children. In T. V. Merluzzi, C. R. Glass, & M. Genest (Eds.), *Cognitive assessment.* New York: Guilford Press.

Krathwohl, D., Bloom, B., & Masia, B. (1956). *Taxonomy of educational objectives.* New York: David McKay.

Krumboltz, J. D., & Krumboltz, H. B. (1972). *Changing children's behavior.* Englewood Cliffs, NJ: Prentice-Hall.

Ladd, G. W. (1981). Effectiveness of a social learning method for enhancing children's social interactions and peer acceptance. *Child Development, 52,* 171–178.

Ladd, G. W., & Mize, J. (1983). A cognitive-social learning model of social skill training. *Psychological Review, 10* (2), 127–157.

LaGreca, A. M., & Mesibov, G. B. (1979). Social skills intervention with learning disabled children: Selecting skills and implementing training. *Journal of Clinical Child Psychology, 8,* 234–241.

LaGreca, A. M., & Santogrossi, D. A. (1980). Social skills training with elementary school students: A behavioral group approach. *Journal of Consulting and Clinical Psychology, 48,* 220–227.

Lambert, N. M., Windmiller, M., Cole, L., & Figueroa, R. (1974). *AAMD adaptive behavior scale: Public school version (1974 revision).* Washington, DC: American Association on Mental Deficiency.

Lang, M., & Tisher, M. (1978). *Children's depression scale.* Melbourne: Australian Council for Educational Research.

Lefkowitz, M. M., & Tesiny, E. P. (1980). Assessment of childhood depression. *Journal of Counseling and Clinical Psychology, 48,* 43–50.

Lew, M., & Mesch, D. (1984). *Isolated students in secondary schools: Cooperative group contingencies and social skills training.* Paper presented at the Annual Conference of the American Psychological Association. Toronto.

Lewis, M., & Michalson, L. (1983). *Children's emotions and moods.* New York: Plenum Press.

Libet, J., & Lewinsohn, P. M. (1973). The concept of social skill with special references to the behavior of depressed persons. *Journal of Consulting and Clinical Psychology, 40,* 304–312.

Lochman, J. E., Burch, P. R., Curry, J. F., & Lampron, L. B. (1984). Treatment and generalization effects of cognitive-behavioral and goalsetting interventions with aggressive boys. *Journal of Consulting and Clinical Psychology, 52,* 915–916.

Luria, A. (1961). *The role of speech in the regulation of normal and abnormal behaviors.* New York: Liveright.

Mager, R. (1972). *Goal analysis.* Belmont, CA: Fearon.

Mager, R. G., & Pipe, P. (1970). *Analyzing performance problems.* Belmont, CA: Fearon.

Maheady, L., Maitland, G. E., & Sainato, D. M. (1982). *Interpretation of social interactions by learning disabled, socially/emotionally disturbed, educable mentally retarded, and nondisabled children.* Unpublished manuscript.

Mahoney, M. J. (1977). Some applied issues in self-monitoring. In J. D. Cone & R. H. Hawkins (Eds.), *Behavioral assessment*. New York: Brunner/Mazel, Inc.

Mann, R. A. (1976). *Assessment of behavioral excesses in children*. In M. Hersen & A. A. Bellack (Eds.), *Behavioral assessment: A practical handbook*. Elmsford, NY: Pergamon Press.

Marlatt, G. A., & Perry, M. A. (1975). Modeling methods. In F. H. Kanfer & A. P. Goldstein (Eds.), *Helping people change*. Elmsford, NY: Pergamon Press.

Mash, E. J., & Terdal, L. G. (Eds.). (1976). *Behavior therapy assessment*. New York: Springer.

Masters, J. C., & Mokros, J. R. (1974). Self-reinforcement processes in children. In H. Reese (Eds.), *Advances in child development and behavior* (Vol. 9). New York: Academic Press.

Matson, J. L., & Esveldt-Dawson, K. (Undated). *Evaluation of social skills with youngsters (MESSY) (self-rating form)*. Unpublished report, University of Pittsburgh School of Medicine.

Matson, J. L., Esveldt-Dawson, K. & Kazdin, A. E. (1983). Validation of methods for assessing social skills in children. *Journal of Clinical Child Psychology, 12*, 174–180.

Matson, J. L., Rotatori, A. F., & Helsel, W. J. (1983). Development of a rating scale to measure social skills in children: The Matson evaluation of social skills with youngsters (MESSY). *Behaviour Research and Therapy, 21*, 335–340.

McFall, R. M. (1977). Analogue methods in behavioral assessment: Issues and prospects. In J. D. Cone & R. P. Hawkins (Eds.), *Behavioral assessment*. New York: Brunner/Mazel, Inc.

McFall, R. M. (1982). A review and reformulation of the concept of social skills. *Behavioral Assessment, 4*, 1–33.

McFall, R. M., & Lillesand, D. B. (1971). Behavior rehearsal with modeling and coaching in assertion training. *Journal of Abnormal Psychology, 77*, 313–323.

McFall, R. M. & Twentyman, C. T. (1973). Four experiments on the relative contributions of rehearsal, modeling, and coaching to assertion training. *Journal of Abnormal Psychology, 81*, 199–218.

McGinnis, E., & Goldstein, A. P. (1984). *Skillstreaming the elementary school child*. Champaign, IL: Research Press.

McPhail, P. (1975). *Consequences*. Niles, IL: Developmental Learning Materials.

Mehrabian, A., & Epstein, N. A. (1972). A measure of emotional empathy. *Journal of Personality, 40*, 525–543.

Meichenbaum, D. (1975). Self instructional methods. In F. H. Kanfer & A. P. Goldstein (Eds.), *Helping people change: A textbook of methods*. Elmsford, NY: Pergamon Press.

Meichenbaum, D. (1976). A cognitive behavior modification approach to assessment. In M. Hersen & A. S. Bellack (Eds.), *Behavioral assessment: A practical handbook*. Elmsford, NY: Pergamon Press.

Meichenbaum, D. (1977). *Cognitive–behavior modification: An integrative approach*. New York: Plenum Press.

Meichenbaum, D., & Goodman, J. (1971). Training impulsive children to talk to themselves: A means of developing self-control. *Journal of Abnormal Psychology, 77*, 115–126.

Michelson, L., & DiLorenzo, T. M. (1981). Behavioral assessment of peer interaction and social functioning in institutional and structured settings. *Journal of Clinical Psychology, 87*, 499–504.

Michelson, L., Foster, S. L., & Ritchey, W. L. (1981). Social skills assessment of children. In B. B. Lahey & A. E. Kazdin (Eds.), *Advances in clinical child psychology*. New York: Plenum Press.

Michelson, L., Sugai, D. P., Wood, R. P., & Kazdin, A. E. (1983). *Social skill assessment and training with children*. New York: Plenum Press.

Michelson, L., & Wood, R. (1980). *Behavioral assessment and training of children's social skills. Progress in behavior modification* (Vol. 9). New York: Academic Press.

Michelson, L. & Wood, R. (1982). Development and psychometric properties of the Children's Assertive Behavior Scale. *Journal of Behavioral Assessment, 4*, 3-14.

Milburn, J. F. (1974). *Special education and regular class teacher attitudes regarding social behaviors of children: Steps toward the development of a social skills curriculum*. Unpublished doctoral dissertation, The Ohio State University, Columbus.

Milburn, J. F., & Cartledge, G. (1979). Build your own social skills curriculum. *Exceptional Teacher, 1*, 1-8.

Milich, R., & Landau, S. (1984). A comparison of the social status and social behavior of aggressive and aggressive/withdrawn boys. *Journal of Abnormal Child Psychology, 12*, 277-288.

Miller, D. C. (1977). *Handbook of research design and social measurement*. New York: David McKay.

Miller, L. C. (1967). Louisville behavior checklist for males, 6-12 years of age. *Psychological Reports, 21*, 885-896.

Miller, L. C. (1972). School Behavior Checklist: An inventory of deviant behavior for elementary school children. *Journal of Consulting and Clinical Psychology, 38*, 134-144.

Miller, L. C., Barrett, C. L., Hampe, E., & Noble, H. (1971). Revised anxiety scales for the Louisville behavior checklist. *Psychological Reports, 29*, 503-511.

Miller, L. C., Barrett, C., Hampe, E., & Noble, H. (1974). *Louisville fear survey scale for children*. Unpublished manuscript. Louisville, KY: Child Psychology Research Center, Bulletin No. 1.

Miller, W. H. (1975). *Systematic parent training: Procedures, cases and issues*. Champaign, IL: Research Press.

Minskoff, E. (1980a). Teaching approach for developing nonverbal communication skills in students with social perception deficits. Part I. *Journal of Learning Disabilities, 13*, 118-124.

Minskoff, E. H. (1980b). Teaching approach for developing nonverbal communication skills in students with social perception deficits. Part II. *Journal of Learning Disabilities, 13*, 203-208.

Moore, S., & Updegraff, R. (1964). Sociometric status of preschool children related to age, sex, nurturance-giving and dependency. *Child Development, 35*, 519-524.

Morgan, R. G. T. (1980). Analysis of social skills: The behavior analysis approach. In W. T. Singleton, P. Spurgeon, & R. B. Stammers (Eds.), *The analysis of social skill*. New York: Plenum Press.

Morrison, R. L., & Bellack, A. S. (1981). The role of social perception in social skill. *Behavior Therapy, 12*, 69-79.

Moyer, D. M. (1974). *The development of children's ability to recognize and express facially posed emotion*. Unpublished doctoral dissertation, The Ohio State University, Columbus.

Moyer, J., & Dardig, J. (1978). Practical task analysis for special educators. *Teaching Exceptional Children, 11*, 16-18.

Murdock, J. Y., Garcia, E. E., & Hardman, M. L. (1977). Generalizing articulation training with trainable mentally retarded subjects. *Journal of Applied Behavior Analysis, 10*, 717-733.

Nay, W. (1977). Analogue measures. In A. R. Ciminero, K. S. Calhoun, & H. E. Adams (Eds.), *Handbook of behavioral assessment.* New York: Wiley.

Nelson, R. O., & Hayes, S. C. (1981). Theoretical explanations for reactivity in self monitoring. *Behavior Modification, 5*, 3–14.

Newcomb, A. F., & Bukowski, N. M. (1983). Social impact and social preference as determinants of children's peer group status. *Developmental Psychology, 19*, 856–867.

Nicki, R. M., Remington, R. E., & MacDonald, G. A. (1984). Self-efficacy, nicotine-fading/self-monitoring and cigarette-smoking behavior. *Behavior Research and Therapy, 22*, 477–485.

Northrup, J., Wood, R., & Clark, H. B. (1979, June). Social skill development in children: Application of individual and group training. Invited workshop, Association for Behavior Analysis, Fifth Annual Convention, Dearborn, MI.

Novaco, R. (1975). *Anger control: The development and evaluation of an experimental treatment.* Lexington, MA: Lexington Books.

O'Connor, R. D. (1973). Relative efficacy of modeling, shaping and combined procedures for modification of social withdrawal. In C. M. Franks & G. T. Wilson (Eds.), *Behavior therapy and practice.* New York: Brunner/Mazel.

Oden, S., & Asher, S. R. (1977). Coaching children in social skills for friendship making. *Child Development, 48*, 495–506.

O'Leary, S. G., & Dubey, D. R. (1979). Applications of self-control procedures by children: A review. *Journal of Applied Behavioral Analysis, 12*, 449–465.

Olexa, D. F., & Forman, S. G. (1984). Effects of social problem-solving training on classroom behavior of urban disadvantaged students. *Journal of School Psychology, 22*, 165–175.

Ollendick, T. H., & Hersen, M. (1984). *Child behavior assessment.* Elmsford, NY: Pergamon Press.

Palkes, H., Stewart, M., & Kahana, B. (1968). Porteus maze performance after training in self-directed verbal commands. *Child Development, 39*, 817–826.

Patterson, G. R. (1977). *Families: Applications of social learning to family life* (rev. ed.). Champaign, IL: Research Press.

Patterson, G. R., & Gullion, M. E. (1976). *Living with children: New methods for parents and teachers* (rev. ed.). Champaign, IL: Research Press.

Phillips, E. (1978). *The social skills basis of psychopathology: Alternatives to abnormal psychology.* New York: Grune & Stratton.

Piaget, J. (1965). *The moral judgment of the child.* New York: Free Press.

Piers, E. V. (1984). *The Piers–Harris children's self concept scale: (The way I feel about myself)* (1984 ed.). Los Angeles: Western Psychological Services.

Polsgrove, L. (1979). Self-control: Methods for child training. *Behavior Disorders, 4*, 116–130.

Premack, D. (1959). Toward empirical behavior laws, part 1: Positive reinforcement. *Psychological Review, 66*, 219–233.

Premack, D. (1965). Reinforcement theory. In D. Levine (Ed.), *Nebraska symposium on motivation.* Lincoln, NB: University Press.

Prins, P. J. M. (1984). *Children's self-speech and self-regulation in anxiety provoking situations: Toward an integration of process and outcome.* Paper presented at the 18th Annual Convention of the Association for Advancement of Behavior Therapy, Philadelphia.

Prinz, R. J., Swan, G., Liebert, D., Weintraub, S., & Neale, J. M. (1978). Assess: Adjustment scales for sociometric evaluation of secondary-school students. *Journal of Abnormal Child Psychology, 6*, 493–501.

Quay, H. C., & Peterson, D. R. (1975). *Manual for the behavior problem checklist.* Champaign, IL: Children's Research Center, University of Illinois.

Quay, H. C., & Peterson, D. R. (1983). Interim manual for the revised behavior problem checklist (1st ed.). Coral Gables, FL: University of Miami.

Quay, H. C., & Jarrett, O. S. (1984). Predictors of social acceptance in preschool children. *Developmental Psychology, 20,* 793–796.

Quinsey, V. L., & Varney, G. W. (1977). Social skills game: A general method for the modeling and practice of adaptive behaviors. *Behavior Therapy, 8,* 297–281.

Rathus, S. A. (1973). A 30-item schedule for assessing assertive behavior. *Behavior Therapy, 4,* 398–406.

Reardon, R. C., Hersen, M., Bellack, A. S., & Foley, J. M. (1979). Measuring social skill in grade school boys. *Journal of Behavioral Assessment, 1,* 87–105.

Reppucci, N. D., & Saunders, J. T. (1974). Social psychology of behavior modification: Problems of implementation in natural settings. *American Psychologist, 29,* 649–660.

Reynolds, C. R., & Richmond, B. A. (1978). Factor structure and construct validity of "what I think and feel," the revised children's manifest anxiety scale. *Journal of Personality Assessment, 33,* 281–283.

Rhode, G., Morgan, D. P., & Young, K. R. (1983). Generalization and maintenance of treatment gains of behaviorally handicapped students from resource rooms to regular classrooms using self-evaluation procedures. *Journal of Applied Analysis, 16,* 171–188.

Richard, B. A., & Dodge, K. A. (1982). Social maladjustment and problem-solving in school-aged children. *Journal of Consulting and Clinical Psychology, 50,* 226–233.

Richards, C. S., & Perri, M. D. (1978). Do self-control treatments last? An evaluation of behavioral problem-solving and faded counselor contact as treatment maintenance strategies. *Journal of Counseling Psychology, 25,* 376–383.

Rie, E. D., & Friedman, D. P. (1978). *A survey of behavior rating scales for children.* Columbus, OH: Office of Program Evaluation and Research. Division of Mental Health, Ohio Department of Mental Health and Mental Retardation.

Rincover, A., & Koegel, R. L. (1975). Setting generality and stimulus control in autistic children. *Journal of Applied Behavior Analysis, 8,* 235–246.

Rinn, R. C., & Markle, A. (1979). Modification of social skill deficits in children. In A. S. Bellack & M. Hersen (Eds.), *Research and practice in social skills training.* New York: Plenum Press.

Risley, T. R., & Hart, B. (1968). Developing correspondence between the nonverbal and verbal behavior of preschool children. *Journal of Applied Behavior Analysis, 9,* 335–354.

Roberts, N., & Nelson, R. O. (1984). Assessment issues and strategies. In A. W. Meyers & W. E. Craighead (Eds.), *Cognitive behavior therapy with children.* New York: Plenum Press.

Robertson, S. J., Simon, S. J., Pachman, J. S., & Drabman, R. S. (1979). Self control and generalization procedures in a classroom of disruptive retarded children. *Child Behavior Therapy, 1,* 347–362.

Roff, M., Sells, S. B., & Golden, M. (1972). *Social adjustment and personality development in children.* Minneapolis: University of Minnesota Press.

Rogers-Warren, A., & Baer, D. M. (1976). Correspondence between saying and doing: Teaching children to share and praise. *Journal of Applied Behavior Analysis, 1,* 267–295.

Roistacher, R. C. (1974). A micro-economic model of sociometric choice. *Sociometry, 37,* 219–238.

Rose, S. D. (1972). *Treating children in groups*. San Francisco: Jossey-Bass.

Rosenberg, M. (1965). *Society and the adolescent self-image*. Princeton, NJ: Princeton University Press.

Rosenhan, D., & White, G. M. (1967). Observation and rehearsal as determinants of prosocial behavior. *Journal of Personality and Social Psychology, 5*, 424–431.

Ross, A. D., Lacey, H. M., & Parton, D. A. (1965). The development of a behavior checklist for boys. *Child Development, 36*, 1013–1027.

Rothenberg, B. (1970). Children's social sensitivity and the relationship to interpersonal competence, intrapersonal comfort, and intellectual level. *Developmental Psychology, 2*, 335–350.

Rotheram, M. J. (1978, April). *Social skills training programs in elementary and high school classrooms*. Paper presented at Seventh Annual Behavior Therapy Association Conference, Houston, TX.

Rubin, K. H. (1982). Social and social-cognitive developmental characteristics of children. In K. H. Rubin & H. S. Ross (Eds.), *Peer relationships and social skills in childhood*. New York: Springer-Verlag.

Rubin, K. H., Daniels-Beirness, T., & Bream, L. (1984). Social isolation and social problem solving: A longitudinal study. *Journal of Consulting and Clinical Psychology, 52*, 17–25.

Sagotsky, G., Patterson, C. J., & Lepper, M. R. (1978). Training children's self control: A field experiment in self monitoring and goal setting in the classroom. *Journal of Experimental Child Psychology, 25*, 242–253.

Santogrossi, D. A., O'Leary, K. D., Romanczyk, R. G., & Kaufman, K. F. (1973). Self evaluation by adolescents in a psychiatric hospital school token program. *Journal of Applied Behavior Analysis, 6*, 277–287.

Sarason, S. B., Davidson, K. F., Lighthall, F. F., Waite, R. R., & Ruebush, B. K. (1960). Anxiety in elementary school children. New York: Wiley.

Scherer, M. W., & Nakamura, C. Y. (1968). A fear survey schedule for children (FSS-FC): A factor analytic comparison with manifest anxiety (CMAS). *Behavior Research and Therapy, 6*, 173–182.

Schneider, M., & Robin, A. (1975). *The turtle technique: A method for the self-control of impulse behavior*. Unpublished manuscript, State University of New York at Stony Brook.

Schofield, J. W., & Whitley, B. E. (1983). Peer nomination vs. rating scale measurement of children's peer preference. *Social Psychology Quarterly, 46*, 242–251.

Selman, R. L., & Byrne, D. F. (1974). A structural–developmental analysis of levels of role taking in middle childhood. *Child Development, 45*, 803–806.

Selman, R. L., Schorin, M. Z., Stone, C. R., & Phelps, E. (1983). A naturalistic study of children's social understanding. *Developmental Psychology, 19*, 82–102.

Seymour, F. W., & Stokes, T. F. (1976). Self-recording in training girls to increase work and evoke staff praise in an institution for offenders. *Journal of Applied Behavior Analysis, 9*, 41–54.

Shapiro, E. S. (1984). Self monitoring procedures. In T. H. Ollendick & M. Hersen (Eds.), *Children behavior assessment*. Elmsford, NY: Pergamon Press.

Sheslow, D. V., Bondy, A. S., & Nelson, R. O. (1983). A comparison of graduated exposure, verbal coping skills, and their combination in the treatment of children's fear of the dark. *Child and Family Behavior Therapy, 4*, 33–45.

Shneidman, E. S. (1952). *Make a picture story (MAPS)*. New York: The Psychological Corporation.

Shure, M. B., & Spivack, G. (1978). *Problem-solving techniques in childrearing*. San Francisco: Jossey-Bass.

Sines, J. D., Parker, J. D., Sines, L. K., & Owen, D. B. (1969). Identification of clinically relevant dimensions of children's behavior. *Journal of Consulting and Clinical Psychology, 33*, 728-734.

Smith, J. M., & Smith, D. E. P. (1976). *Child management: A program for parents and teachers*. Champaign, IL: Research Press.

Spielberger, C. D. (1973). *State–trait anxiety inventory for children*. Palo Alto, CA: Consulting Psychologist Press.

Spivack, G., Platt, J. J., & Shure, M. (1976). *The problem-solving approach to adjustment*. San Francisco: Jossey-Bass.

Spivack, G., & Shure, M. B. (1974). *Social adjustment of young children. A cognitive approach to solving real-life problems*. San Francisco: Jossey-Bass.

Spivack, G., & Spotts, J. (1966). *Devereux child behavior (DCB) rating scale*. Devon, PA: Devereux Foundation.

Spivack, G., Spotts, J., & Haimes, P. (1966). *Devereux adolescent behavior rating scale*. Devon, PA: Devereux Foundation.

Spivack, G., & Swift, M. (1967). *Devereux elementary school behavior rating scale*. Devon, PA: Devereux Foundation.

Stephens, T. M. (1976). *Directive teaching of children with learning and behavior disorders* (2nd ed.). Columbus, OH: Charles E. Merrill.

Stephens, T. M. (1977). *Teaching skills to children with learning and behavior disorders*. Columbus, OH: Charles E. Merrill.

Stephens, T. M. (1978). *Social skills in the classroom*. Columbus, OH: Cedars Press.

Stephens, T. M. (1980). *Social Behavior Assessment (SBA)*. Columbus, OH: Cedars Press.

Stephens, T. M. (1981). *Social behavior asssessment technical information*. Unpublished manuscript.

Stevenson, H. C., & Fantuzzo, J. W. (1984). Application of the "generalization map" to a self-control intervention with school-aged children. *Journal of Applied Behavior Analysis, 17*, 203-212.

Stokes, T. F., & Baer, D. M. (1977). An implicit technology of generalization. *Journal of Applied Behavior Analysis, 10*, 349-367.

Stokes, T. F., Baer, D. M., & Jackson, R. L. (1974). Programming the generalization of a greeting response in four retarded children. *Journal of Applied Behavior Analysis, 7*, 599-610.

Strain, P. S., Kerr, M. M., & Ragland, E. U. (1981). The use of peer social initiations in the treatment of social withdrawal. In P. S. Strain (Ed.), *The utilization of classroom peers as behavior change agents*. New York: Plenum Press.

Strayer, J. (1980). A naturalistic study of empathetic behaviors and their relation to affective states and perspective taking skills in preschool children. *Child Development, 51*, 815-822.

Tisher, M., & Lang, M. (1983). The children's depression scale: Review and further developments. In D. P. Cantwell & G. A. Carlson (Eds.), *Affective disorders in childhood and adolescence*. New York: SP Medical and Scientific Books.

Trower, P. (1980). Situational analysis of the components and processes of behavior of social skilled and unskilled patients. *Journal of Consulting and Clinical Psychology, 3*, 327-339.

Trower, P., Bryant, B., & Argyle, M. (1978). *Social skills and mental health*. Pittsburgh: University of Pittsburgh Press.

Turnbull, A., Strickland, B., & Brantley, J. (1978). *Developing and implementing individualized education programs*. Columbus, OH: Charles E. Merrill.

Tyler, R. W. (1949). *Basic principles of curriculum and instruction*. Chicago: University of Chicago Press.

Urbain, E. S., & Kendall, P. C. (1980). Review of social–cognitive problem-solving interventions with children. *Psychological Bulletin, 88*, 109–143.

Van Den Pol, R. A., Iwata, B. A., Irancic, M. T., Page, T. J., Neef, N. A., & Whitley, F. P. (1981). Teaching the handicapped to eat in public places: Acquisition, generalization, and maintenance of restaurant skills. *Journal of Applied Behavior Analysis, 14*, 61–69.

Van Hasselt, V. B., Hersen, M., & Bellack, A. S. (1981). The validity of role play tests for assessing social skills in children. *Behavior Therapy, 12*, 202–216.

Van Hasselt, V. B., Hersen, M., Bellack, A. S., & Whitehill, M. B. (1979). Social skill assessment and training for children: An evaluative review. *Behavior Research and Therapy, 17*, 413–438.

Van Houten, R. (1980). *How to motivate others through feedback*. Lawrence, KS: H&H Enterprises, Inc.

Vaughn, B. E., & Langlois, J. H. (1983). Physical attractiveness as a correlate of peer status and social competence in preschool children. *Developmental Psychology, 19*, 516–567.

Vygotsky, L. (1962). *Thought and language*. New York: Wiley.

Waber, B. (1972). *Ira sleeps over*. New York: Scholastic Book Services.

Wahler, R. G. (1969). Setting generality: Some specific and general effects of child behavior therapy. *Journal of Applied Behavior Analysis, 2*, 239–246.

Walk, R. D. (1956). Self ratings of fear in a fear-invoking situation. *Journal of Abnormal and Social Psychology, 22*, 171–178.

Walker, H. M. (1970). *Problem behavior identification checklist*. Los Angeles: Western Psychological Services.

Walker, H. M., & Buckley, N. K. (1974). *Token reinforcement techniques*. Eugene, OR: E-B Press.

Walker, H. M., & Hops, H. (1976). Increasing academic achievement by reinforcing direct academic performance and/or facilitative nonacademic responses. *Journal of Educational Psychology, 68*, 218–225.

Walker, H. M., McConnell, S., Holmes, D., Todis, B., Walker, J., & Golden, N. (1983). *The Walker Social Skills Curriculum*. Austin, TX: Pro-Ed.

Walker, H. M., Street, A., Garrett, B., Crossen, J., Hops, H., & Greenwood, C. R. (1978). *Reprogramming environmental contingencies for effective social skills (RECESS): Consultant manual*. Eugene: Center at Oregon for Research in the Behavioral Education of the Handicapped, University of Oregon.

Walls, R. T., Werner, T. J., Bacon, A., & Zane, T. (1977). Behavior checklists. In J. D. Cone & R. H. Hawkins (Eds.), *Behavioral assessment*. New York: Brunner/Mazel, Inc.

Weissberg, R. P., & Gesten, E. L. (1982). Considerations for developing effective school-based social problem solving (SPS) training programs. *School Psychology Review, 11*, 56–63.

Weissberg, R. P., Gesten, E. L., Liebenstein, N. L. Doherty-Schmid, K., & Hutton, H. (1980). *The Rochester social problem-solving (SPS) program: A training manual for teachers of 2nd–4th grade*. Rochester, NY: University of Rochester.

Weissberg, R. P., Gesten, E. L., Rapkin, B. D., Cowen, E. L., Davidson, E., Flores de Apodaca, R., & McKim, B. J. (1981). Evaluation of a social-problem-solving training program for suburban and inner-city third-grade children. *Journal of Consulting and Clinical Psychology, 49*(2), 251–261.

Wheeler, V. A. & Ladd, G. W. (1982). Assessment of children's self efficacy for social interaction with peers. *Developmental Psychology, 18*, 795–805.

Wiig, E. (1982). *Let's talk: Developing prosocial communication skills*. Columbus, OH: Charles E. Merrill Publishing Company.

Wiig, E. H., & Bray, C. M. (1983). *Let's talk for children*. Columbus, OH: Charles E. Merrill.

Wiig, E. H., & Semel, E. M. (1976). *Language disabilities in children*. Columbus, OH: Charles E. Merrill.

Wildman, B. G., & Erickson, M. T. (1977). Methodological problems in behavioral observation. In J. D. Cone, & R. P. Hawkins, *Behavioral assessment*. New York: Brunner/Mazel, Inc.

Wilson, G. T. (1978). Cognitive behavior therapy: Paradigm shift or passing phase? In J. P. Foreyt & D. P. Rathjen (Eds.), *Cognitive behavior therapy*. New York: Plenum Press.

Winnett, R. A., & Winkler, R. C. (1972). Current behavior modification in the classroom: Be still, be quiet, be docile. *Journal of Applied Behavior Analysis, 5,* 499-504.

Witt, J. C., & Martens, B. K. (1983). Assessing the acceptability of behavioral interventions. *Psychology in the Schools, 20,* 510-517.

Witt, J. C., Martens, B. K., & Elliott, S. N. (1984). Factors affecting teachers' judgments of the acceptability of behavioral interventions: Time involvement, behavior problem severity, and type of intervention. *Behavior therapy, 15,* 204-209.

Wolf, M. M. (1978). Social validity: The case for subjective measurement or how applied behavior analysis is finding its heart. *Journal of Applied Behavior Analysis, 11,* 203-214.

Wolpe, J. (1958). *Reciprocal inhibition therapy*. Stanford, CA: Stanford University Press.

Wolpe, J. (1969). *The practice of behavior therapy*. Elmsford, NY: Pergamon Press.

Wolpe, J., & Lazarus, A. A. (1966). *Behavior therapy techniques*. Elmsford, NY: Pergamon Press.

Wong, B. V. L., & Wong, R. (1980). Role-taking skills in normal achieving and learning disabled children. *Learning Disability Quarterly, 3,* 11-18.

Wood, M. (1975). *Developmental therapy*. Baltimore: University Park Press.

Wood, R., & Flynn, J. M. (1978). A self-evaluation token system vs. an external evaluation token system alone in a residential setting with predelinquent youth. *Journal of Applied Behavior Analysis, 11,* 503-512.

Wood, R., & Michelson, L. (1978). *Children's assertive behavior scales*. Unpublished manuscript.

Wood, R., Michelson, L., & Flynn, J. (1978, November). *Assessment of assertive behavior in elementary school children*. Paper presented at the annual meeting of the Association for the Advancement of Behavior Therapy, Chicago.

Workman, E. A. (1982). *Teaching behavioral self-control to students*. Austin, TX: Pro Ed.

Zimmerman, B. J., & Pike, E. O. (1972). Effects of modeling and reinforcement on the acquisition and generalization of question-asking behavior. *Child Development, 43,* 892-907.

PART 2

# SPECIAL APPLICATIONS OF SOCIAL SKILLS TEACHING

# Introduction to Part 2

The five chapters in part 2 demonstrate ways in which the process of selecting social skills, assessing the child's level of performance, teaching the needed skills, and developing strategies for maintenance and transfer can be applied to a variety of populations. Programs are suggested for children at different age levels, preschool and primary, elementary school-age and adolescence; and at different levels of functioning, normal as well as handicapped. The chapter by Sapon-Shevin is aimed at normal preschool- and school-aged children in the early processes of socialization; Schleien and Wehman define procedures for the severely handicapped child or even adult. Although the program outlined by Bash and Camp was originally developed in research with impulsive, aggressive boys, these authors now see their program as having potential for many learning situations, as well as a help to children with a variety of behavior problems. The actual target population in the article included here is teachers who will be using their procedures. Oden's techniques for teaching peer interaction social skills focus on the child who may be rejected by peers for a variety of reasons related to social skill deficits. The skill-deficient adolescents for whom Goldstein's Structured-Learning approaches are to be applied include those who are labeled *aggressive*, *withdrawn*, and *immature*. Particular emphasis is on aggressive youth, as having the greatest social impact and, thus, the greatest need for intervention.

In the selection of social skills for teaching, there is a need to select skills that are relevant to the child according to a number of different criteria, one of the most salient being the selection of skills that will be reinforced by others in the environment and, thus, maintained over time. A common set of such behaviors is identified by the authors of the chapters oriented to the younger or lower functioning child; that is, those skills that combine to make up the class of behaviors called *cooperation*, clearly an important area for young and severely handicapped children if they are to develop the ability to interact appropriately with their peers. Schleien and Wehman demonstrate the importance for the severely-impaired child of providing basic skills around which to structure interaction, in this case, games and other motor activities that could serve to put the child in proximity to others and enable him to relate to them in the context of the activity. In her approach to teaching cooperation to children, Sapon-Shevin similarly stresses the value of games and provides a number of games that require certain kinds of interaction defined as facilitating cooperation; that is, talking nicely, sharing and taking turns, including others, and gentle physical contact. Oden presents techniques for the teaching of behaviors that will serve to enhance peer acceptance and, thus, either prevent or remedy the problem of social isolation. The concepts she deals with are those of participation, cooperation, communication, and support; that is, giving attention and help. For the population addressed by Bash and Camp, the goal is to reduce impulsivity and increase the child's repertoire of alternative responses. Among the specific skills described are problem solving through self-guiding speech, self-evaluation, recognition of emotions, and the concept of fairness. Goldstein et al. provide an inventory of 50 social skills appropriate to the adolescent. The categories include dealing with feelings, alternatives to aggression, dealing with stress, and planning skills. Their techniques also provide opportunities for the youth participating in the program to identify for themselves the skills relevant to their own lives, a provision particularly necessary for adolescents.

Procedures for assessing social skill deficits are suggested by several contributors. Schleien and Wehman use a task analysis approach to assessment, outlining in detail the sequence of steps involved so the subcomponents of the skill can be identified, the child's ability assessed, and instruction begun at the point of deficit. Oden suggests various approaches to assessing the child to determine the nature of peer relationships, making use of several informants (the peers, the adults, and the child), as well as differing methods (sociometrics, interview, and observation, and several contexts). Goldstein's assessment procedures involve the use of a skill checklist to identify deficiencies and using checklist profiles as a guide for structuring group composition based on common needs for training in particular skills.

The methods used by the contributors in part 2 show both diversity and similarities, suggesting some of the ways in which the same approaches can be used with different populations and, also, some of the ways in which teaching needs to be tailored to the child's level of functioning. The explicit set of teaching instructions in the task analysis approach of Schleien and Wehman provides a step-by-step, individualized program, using verbal instruction, physical guidance, modeling, and reinforcement to teach the motor behaviors that can become the vehicle for social interaction. Although the systematic and detailed approach suggested in this chapter is especially necessary for the severely handicapped, the ability to analyze learning tasks in this form could add to the effectiveness of any teaching effort. The use of games and children's literature proposed by Sapon-Shevin to teach cooperation to groups of children is combined with discussion and application of the concepts to other classroom activities. The games and books presented in her chapter can be particularly useful for introducing a variety of kinds of social skills teaching methods.

Oden presents a "coaching" procedure, designed to be used with individual children in which the adult provides verbal instruction to a child prior to a play session. Following the coaching session on concepts related to positive peer interactions, the child has an opportunity to practice in actual play with a peer, then engages with the instructor in a review of the concepts following the play period. Oden's procedures primarily involve verbal instructions, prompting, and feedback. The Oden chapter provides a coaching scenario that can serve as a model for teaching a variety of concepts. Bash and Camp also present specific scripts demonstrating how the teacher can provide a model through his or her own thinking out loud problem-solving processes. The principal emphasis of the Bash and Camp article is the need for the teacher to understand and master the problem-solving sequences first, in order to be an effective model. The Structured Learning approach of Goldstein et al., as presented here, is structured primarily for use with a group. It makes use of four components: modeling, role playing, feedback, and training for transfer. Models are provided through audiotapes, videotapes, or films. The core of this training is behavioral; however, Goldstein et al. outline affective and cognitive dimensions wherein anger control and moral education interventions are also included. This multimodel approach (i.e., behavioral, cognitive, affective) can also be seen in the Bash and Camp Think Aloud program, as well as, to a lesser extent, in the training sequences provided by Oden.

Programming for maintenance of skills over time and transfer to settings outside the training situation are accomplished in several different ways. The play skills taught by Schleien and Wehman's methods to the severely handicapped, the games suggested by Sapon-Shevin, and the cooperative interactions developed in the Oden program can be said to be those that, by their nature, open the child to the "natural community of reinforcers." Children who master the abilities to share, take turns, talk pleasantly, and help other children will certainly be reinforced by other children, as well as by adults. The cognitive skills in the Bash and Camp program, particularly the self-evaluation procedures and problem-solving strategies, constitute metacognitions or awareness of cognitive activities, the kind of process highly likely to promote generalization. Goldstein et al. suggest a variety of procedures for transfer of social skills from the training to real life, including the structuring of the training setting so it resembles the actual life situation, teaching self-evaluation and self-reinforcement skills, homework assignments in which the skills are practiced outside the training setting, and programming parents and peers to provide reinforcement.

There are adequate data presented to establish the value of the teaching procedures presented in part 2. Schleien and Wehman and Sapon-Shevin cite a variety of studies supporting the kinds of procedures suggested for their populations. Camp and Bash have successfully applied the Think-Aloud procedures in several empirical studies, as have Oden with coaching procedures and Goldstein with Structured Learning. The diversity of approaches presented in part 2, all with evidence of successful application, suggests something of the breadth of methods available for teaching social skills.

# 6

# Teacher Training in the Think Aloud Classroom Program*

## Mary Ann S. Bash and Bonnie W. Camp

Think Aloud is a program designed to increase cognitive and social problem-solving skills in elementary school children. It was originally proposed as a method of improving self-control in young aggressive boys through reducing impulsivity, increasing the repertoire of alternative responses in frustrating situations, and providing skills for successful problem solving. In developing the curriculum and procedures used in the program, the authors leaned heavily on the work of Meichenbaum (Meichenbaum & Goodman, 1971), and Shure & Spivack (1974a).

Previous work with aggressive boys (Camp, 1977; Camp, Zimet, Van Doorninck, & Dahlem, 1977) had demonstrated that they differed from normal boys not only in behavior but in cognitive skills as well. Despite good verbal intelligence, the aggressive boys aged 10 failed to use their verbal skills to think through complex problems. As a result, they reacted impulsively and failed to perform as adequately as might otherwise be expected. It seemed that both their behavior problems and their poor performance on cognitive tests might be improved if they could learn to slow down and use their good verbal skills to guide their behavior.

Several previous studies suggested that this might be accomplished most effectively if they were first trained to think out loud. Meichenbaum and

*Portions of the materials and scripts included in this chapter were developed through the support of a Research Scientist Award No. MK 2047-356 from the National Institutes of Mental Health and Grant No. NEG-00-3-002 from the National Institute of Education. Funds from the Piton Foundation supported preliminary development of the classroom program. Most of the teacher and student anecdotes derive from the implementation of Think Aloud procedures in the Denver Public Schools under the Cognitive Problem Solving Program funded by Title IV-C from the Colorado Department of Education.

Goodman (1971), for example, demonstrated that training in self-guiding speech could assist children in special classes to improve behavior and cognitive test performance. Other research (Hetherington & McIntyre, 1975) suggested that children were unlikely to transfer self-guiding speech into self-discipline unless they witnessed someone else modeling this behavior. In addition, the work of Spivack and Shure (1974) suggested that learning to think of alternative solutions to a problem might be essential for achieving improvement in social behavior.

These features were combined into the Think Aloud program (Camp & Bash, 1981) and were applied to both cognitive and social problems. In early trials with the program, resource room teachers had daily half hour sessions with one or two children for a period of 8 weeks. Children who participated were first- and second-grade boys, identified as having significant aggressive behavior problems. Evaluation of progress achieved with the program indicated significant improvement in cognitive ability and in prosocial behavior (Camp, Blom, Hebert, & Van Doorninck, 1977).

Early in the development of Think Aloud, we recognized that aggressive boys were not the only ones with limited problem-solving skills. Spivack and Shure (1974) had noted that inability to think of alternatives was often encountered in youngsters with many types of behavioral problems. Additionally, ability to think of many alternative solutions to problems has been used in measures of creativity (Torrance, 1966) and cited as critical to successful problem-solving discussions (Maier, 1963).

Both successes and failures with aggressive boys led us to consider the potential value of expanding this program for use in a regular classroom. For the greatest effect, children needed to apply Think Aloud skills in the real life situation of the classroom. Early attempts were made to enlist classroom teachers' assistance. They were willing to complement the resource room program but did not understand what to do. Clearly, we needed a training program for teachers, if we wanted them to reinforce problem-solving skills in the classroom. Moreover, a classroom program would make the training available to a broader range of children, many of whom might have borderline deficiencies easily amenable to a small boost.

The focus of the remainder of this chapter will be on describing our experience with this classroom program, the obstacles encountered in teaching the program to teachers, and our solutions to these problems.

## DESIGNING THE CLASSROOM PROGRAM

Two major problems confronted us from the outset. One concerned the development of materials and procedures that could be used in a group setting to elicit self-guiding speech in dealing with both cognitive and social problems. The second problem concerned how to teach teachers to model verbalization of their own cognitive behavior and to let children develop their own solutions.

The first problem required development of both technique and materials. The core of the Think Aloud program is use of self-guiding speech in problem solving. Overt practice is required before this verbalization is faded to a covert level. How does one get young children to verbalize aloud in this fashion? In the resource room program, we used the "copy cat" game to elicit attention to the teacher's language and gestures as she modeled a task. A similar procedure could be used with groups resulting in unison repetition of standard answers. The copy cat game poses many obvious problems, including the fact that children often repeat mindlessly without thinking about what they are saying. Many educators would look with horror on the situation where 30 children in a classroom are all talking at once, particularly when they are saying different things as they work on a task. We had, however, seen effective use of individual verbalization in small groups at the Exemplary Center for Reading Instruction in Salt Lake City and thought it worth trying.

There was still the problem of finding appropriate materials so that every child in the classroom could participate. The final program drew on a wide variety of materials and procedures to elicit verbalization of plans, alternatives, coping with errors, conceptual shifts, and memory. Each task selected met three criteria: (a) it is amenable to several strategies, (b) it is solvable by means available to the student, and (c) the goal is personally engaging. The problems include increasingly complex tasks such as coloring, finding similarities and differences, mazes, classification, perceptual puzzles, and matrices.

Finally, we decided to try a teacher training program, which lasted one month. This involved one or two preparatory sessions in which modeling was practiced, followed by daily lessons in the classroom during which the trainer and classroom teacher alternated days as teacher and observer.

## Description of the Program

Using the lead of Meichenbaum and Goodman (1971), the initial phase of the program concentrates on developing an organized approach to problem solving. This approach is applied primarily to cognitive problems, and consists of four questions: (a) What is my problem? or, What am I supposed to do? (b) How can I do it? or, What is my plan? (c) Am I using my plan? and (d) How did I do? The students learn to ask themselves these questions to organize their approach to an assignment. They ask and answer the first two questions before they begin their work.

Their answer to the first question ("What is my problem?") guides them to focus on the specific task. In answering the second question ("How can I do it?") the students, as a group, brainstorm a myriad of alternative plans for solving the problem. This repertoire of choices provides students second or third chances to be successful on an assignment if the plan they first choose is ineffective. These alternative strategies might increase the time students spend on-task if, indeed, they follow through with the proposed strategies. To increase the likelihood of follow-through, Think Aloud teaches students to address the third question ("Am I using my plan?") to themselves several times while they work on their task. This question enables students to increase self-control as they change or correct plans on the basis of their performance. Answers to this question might take any of the following directions: (a) Yes, because I'm doing what I planned and it's working; (b) Yes, because I'm doing what I planned, but there must be a better way to get the job done so I'll change my plan; (c) No, because I forgot to do what I planned so I'll start again; or (d) No, because I forgot what I planned, but what I'm doing is working so I'll use this new plan. The students would, in fact, articulate the details of the plan they were and/or were not following instead of verbalizing the general comments described above.

After the work is done, the students direct the fourth question to themselves ("How did I do?"). Self-evaluation might be based on a combination of several criteria: completing the task, effort, efficiency, following the plan, neatness, accuracy, on-task behavior, how they feel about their work. Self-evaluation answers have taken all of the following forms: (a) I did everything you told me to, and I did it quickly and quietly; (b) I was good at following my plan; (c) I was terrific at thinking out loud; (d) I was not good at staying in my seat, but I got my work done; (e) I couldn't figure out the puzzle, but I kept trying; (f) I'm proud because I found a better way than we planned. This self-evaluation precedes teacher assessment and is the means for reducing teacher-student conflict when a teacher might otherwise criticize or overestimate a student's performance by assessing only the final product.

Students learn the four organizational questions effortlessly, but learning to answer the questions is a major hurdle. Young children are introduced to the self-instruction questions by playing "copy cat" on a simple coloring task. Answering the questions on a different task, such as a puzzle, they typically verbalize the plan, "I'll color slowly and carefully and stay inside the lines," that they learned on the coloring problem. It takes several lessons for young children to discover that different tasks require different answers to the four self-instruction questions.

Cognitive tasks of increasing difficulty are introduced to students by teacher modeling. The teacher verbalizes an appropriate plan and the obstacles that interfere with the plan. Following the teacher's model, the students practice self-instruction technique on a different example of the task.

Presented here are two scripts for modeling self-instruction. Note that for both tasks (a) the problem is stated, (b) alternative plans are proposed, (c)

**1**

What is my problem?

**2**

How can I do it?

**3**

Am I using my plan?

**4**

How did I do?

**Figure 6.1.** "What is my problem?"

coping with an error is modeled, (d) the use of the proposed plan is monitored, and (e) the teacher evaluates his or her performance.

Day 2. Think Aloud Introduction and Practice*
*Materials:* Large cue pictures which remind children of the four self-instruction questions [Figure 6.1]

---

*From Bash, M. A. (1978). *Think Aloud Classroom Resource Manual,* grades 1-2. Denver, CO: Denver Public Schools. Used with permission of the author.

>coloring shapes worksheets [Figure 6.2]
>crayons
>clipboard

Review first 2 questions, and add next 2.

Think out loud on coloring shapes.

*Teacher:* *(Show shape papers.)* You are all very good at coloring. Let's practice thinking out loud while we color. *(Point to fattest-bordered circle.)* Our problem is to color this shape the best we can without going outside the lines. Your problem is to be copy cats and copy just what I *say* and *do*. What is your problem? *(Point to cue picture-1.)* Good.

*Teacher:* *(Give children and yourself the paper of shapes to be colored. Select the circle with a fat border first.)* We each have a paper with some shapes on it. The problem is to color this shape the best we can without going outside the lines. Pick a colored pencil and I'll pick one.

*Teacher:* Let's learn to think out loud to help us do this paper. Remember you must copy what I *say* and *do*. Let's try it.

*Teacher:* *(Holding crayon in air. [The questions and answers are all to be copied by the children.])*
Q. What is my problem?
A. I am supposed to color this circle without going outside the lines.
Q. How can I do it?
A. I'll go slowly. I'll be careful. I'll outline the circle first. Then I can go faster in the middle. OK, here I go. *(Begin coloring.)*
*(Note: Children may become so intent on coloring that they fail to copy. Remind them as often as necessary:* Where are my copy cats?*)*

*Teacher:* Q. Am I using my plan?
A. Yes. I'm making a frame around the outside. I'm going slowly. Now I can go faster in the middle. *(Cross line boundary.)* Ooops, I went too fast, I

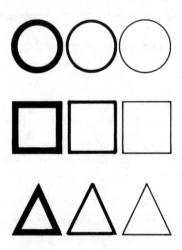

**Figure 6.2.** Coloring shapes worksheet

went outside the line. That's O.K. I'll be more careful. I'll go slower. There
I did it.

Q. How did I do?

A. I tried hard. I went slowly. I usually stayed inside the lines. That makes me
feel good.

*Teacher:* Good, you were good copy cats. And I learned something. Is it a good
idea to color fast?

*Children:* _____

*Teacher: (Ask classroom teacher to model thinking out loud on a different shape
while the kids copy. Then have a child or two think out loud on different shapes
while others copy him.)*

Alternative plans for the coloring task might have included using only one
crayon so coloring doesn't take too long, or using the side of the crayon
instead of the point, or pressing softly to shade the shape lightly.

MAZES*

*Materials:* Bear cue pictures
          Trails A & B
          Picture mazes (Fido, Red Riding Hood, Puddle)

(From: *Activity Fun*, A Whitman Book, Western Publishing Company, Inc.,
Racine, Wisconsin)

*Teacher:* I have a new problem for us today. We are going to make trails. What
is a trail?

*Children:* _____

*Teacher:* Yes, it is like a small road where motorcycles can go or where people
can hike. *(Show Trail A, see Fig. 6.3 for sample trails A and B.)* The problem
is to draw a trail from #1 to #2 to #3 to #4 and so on without lifting your pencil from the paper. I'll try the first one. You be copy cats.

*Teacher: (Looking at task but before picking up pencil.)*

Q. OK. What is my problem?

A. I need to draw a trail to each number in order — like 1, 2, 3, 4 — without lifting my pencil from the paper.

*Teacher:* Q. How can I do it?

A. Before I draw a line, I'll find the next number I have to go to. That's how
thinking out loud will help me. I *could* go fast *but* I might make a mistake,
so I'll go slow.

*Teacher:* Here I go. *(Pick up pencil.)* Here's #1 — that's where I start. Now my
plan — I'll find #2. Good, here it is *(hold finger on #2 and draw line to it).*
#3 — Yep. Good, I'm going slow and I'm planning ahead. *(While looking for
#4 lift pencil off of paper. If children don't catch you, say:)* Oops. I'm sup-
posed to keep my pencil on the paper. That's kind of hard. I better remind
myself — keep my pencil on the paper. *(Holding pencil on paper)* OK, now where
do I go? I'm at #3 so I better find #4. Yep. *(From #4 go directly to #6 without
planning. When recognize error, feign anger and slam pencil on desk.)* I did
it wrong. I didn't plan ahead. I can't even do this. *(Pout, in manner typical*

*From Camp, B. W., & Bash, M. A. (1975). *Think Aloud Group Manual.* ERIC
EDS No. 142024. Used with permission of the authors.

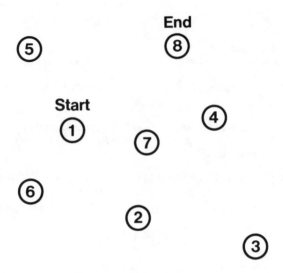

**Figure 6.3.** Sample trails A and B

*of the students, then calm yourself.)* Well I just went too fast. I knew I'd make a mistake if I went too fast. If I slow down I can do all right. *(Place pencil back at #4.)*

Q. Am I using my plan?

A. Yes, I'm looking ahead. There's #5 — that's where I need to go. I feel better now — I'm doing a good job. After 5 comes 6. Good. And that's how we do this trail. I'll let you have a turn now.

*Teacher:*    Q. How did I do?

A. I got kind of mad, but then I slowed down. I did better when I planned ahead. I wasn't very good at keeping my pencil on the paper.

*Teacher:*    You try making a trail. *(Hand children another short trail but turn paper over after brief exposure. Point to cue picture #1 if necessary to initiate verbalizations. If children want to silently verbalize while paper is overturned, that should be sufficient. When mazes become harder, overt verbalizations will be required.)*

*Children:* _____

*Teacher:*    *(When they finish the sample, hand children Trial B with numbers 1 through 15.)* Here's a problem with more numbers. What plan will help you do this problem?

*Children:* _____

*Teacher:*    Is it a good idea to go fast on this problem?

*Children:* _____

*Teacher:*    *(After self evaluation, hand children Fido Maze.)* Now I have a different problem for you. This time I want you to draw a trail, but the numbers won't tell you where to go. I'll give you a picture of a dog. His name is Fido. He is trying to get across the street without being hit by a car. He wants you to find a trail across the street for him. *(Provide no reminders of thinking out loud. See if children talk spontaneously. Place pencil on table beside paper.)*

*Children:* _____

*Teacher:* *(Show Little Red Riding Hood Maze.)* Now it's my turn. What's my problem? I want to get Little Red Riding Hood to her grandmother's house without getting trapped by the wolf and without stepping on any plants. And I can't lift my pencil from the paper.

*Teacher:* How can I do it? I have a new plan. I will look ahead with my eyes and fingers to find the best trail for her. I'll have to go slow so I don't get caught.

*Teacher:* 1. This is one way she could go. *(Trace with finger into wolf trap plus along branches off of it.)* Nope, this way I'll get trapped. 2. *(Eye trace south route from Red Riding Hood.)* Am I using my plan? Yes, I'm planning ahead. I can go this way. *(Set pencil to paper.)* Go slowly because I can't step on any plants. *(Slowly finger trace backwards from house.)* I have to get to the house, right? Good. I can go this way. *(Cut through tree leaf in haste.)* Oh, I knew that would happen if I went fast. Now I made a mistake and I was doing so good at planning ahead. *(Calm self.)* I'll just have to be more careful. Now I'm doing better.

*Teacher:* How did I do? I was good at planning ahead with my finger and eyes. I learned I can plan from the beginning or from the end. But I've got to remind myself to slow down.

*Teacher:* *(Hand children Puddle Maze.)* You are supposed to get Martha to school without stepping in any puddles and without lifting your pencils from the paper. Is it a good idea to plan ahead from the beginning or the end?

*Children:* _____

*Teacher:* *(Turn papers over and wait for thinking out loud.)*

*Children:* _____

*Teacher:* *(At end of task)* What new plan can help us on these problems?

*Children:* _____

*Teacher:* Is it a good idea to plan ahead with your finger and eyes when you do a trail?

*Children:* _____

*Teacher:* Why?

*Children:* _____

(*Note:* Picture mazes from any children's activity book could be substituted in this activity.)

Alternative plans for a maze might include planning a short distance and making the path, or tracing with the eraser end of the pencil to leave a hint of a trail, or tracing with two fingers simultaneously from the start and the end and meeting them in the middle.

Following the teacher-modeled task, the students attempt a different example of the problem while instructing themselves through the four problem-solving questions.

Chart 1 summarizes the organized approach used on cognitive tasks.

*Chart 1*

Problem-Solving Approach to Cognitive Tasks

Step 1. Identify the problem or assignment.

Step 2. Propose several alternative plans for solving problem or assignment.

BeginWork
Step 3. Monitor use of plan: change, correct, or stay with plan.
Step 4. Self-evaluate performance in terms of effort, success, behavior, feelings.

Soon after children have become thoroughly familiar with thinking out loud by asking and appropriately answering the self-instruction questions, interpersonal problems are introduced. Interpersonal problems are conflicts that arise between students and teachers, parents, siblings, or other students.

Most of Think Aloud's interpersonal problem-solving instruction derives from Myrna Shure and George Spivack's (1974a) work with preschool and kindergarten children. In their year-long programs for young children, Shure and Spivack use commercial pictures and games to teach concepts such as and/or, same/different, not. Where possible, Think Aloud introduces concepts such as same/different on cognitive tasks early in the program. Other Shure and Spivack lessons were shortened or combined for use with primary school children. As a result, Think Aloud includes nine interpersonal lessons dealing with (a) identifying and sharing emotions (i.e., How does the child in this picture probably feel?); (b) recognizing physical causality (i.e., What are lots of different reasons why she might have fallen off her bike?); (c) recognizing emotional causality (i.e., What are lots of different reasons why David might be mad?); (d) What might happen next? (i.e., What might happen next if you sit on a broken fence?); (e) Is it a good idea or not a good idea? (i.e., Is it a good idea to call a person a name?); and (f) Problem solving (i.e., What are lots of different things Danny could say or do to get a chance to play with the kite?).

The four-step cognitive problem-solving approach plus this preliminary instruction in consequential thinking prepare students to begin developing a repetoire of alternative solutions for dealing with interpersonal problems. Then, they must learn to evaluate each alternative solution. Here, we found the Shure and Spivack kindergarten program needed expanding to provide children with more explicit concepts for evaluating the outcomes of interpersonal problems. Whereas Shure and Spivack rely primarily on "Is it a good idea?", Think Aloud carries this further and articulates four specific criteria to use in judging if a solution is a good idea: (a) Is it safe? (b) Is it fair? (c) How does it make you and others feel? and (d) Does it solve the problem? Even primary school children are cognizant of safety needs, so little instruction is required on this criterion, though it must be highlighted as an important dimension of problem solving.

Because "fairness" appears to be such an important concept for children, an entire lesson was designed to provoke discussion around this issue. To teach standards of justice, we developed verbal situations to accompany line drawings of situations that provoke frustration. The script that follows is the

Think Aloud lesson introducing the concept of fairness. Frequently, students disagree on the fair solution, and this interaction among students introduces the reality that fairness is not a clear-cut issue and that conditions affect the observer's perception of what is fair.

SOCIAL #7 — Fairness*
(Use mounted Fairness pictures and Dragon & Wolf puppets.

*Teacher:* Today we are going to talk about fairness. Let's look at this picture. *(Show Figure 6.4 — Fairness #1, bike.)*
*Teacher:* This girl took Teresa's bike away from her. Was that a fair thing for her to do?
*Children:* _____
*Teacher:* Why not?
*Children:* _____
*Teacher:* What is the problem? What does the girl want to do?
*Children:* _____
*Teacher:* What could she *say* or *do* that would be fair so she can ride the bike?
*Children:* _____
*Teacher:* Why would that be fair?
*Children:* _____
*Teacher:* How does Teresa feel *(least verbal child)*?
*Child:* _____
*Teacher:* Is that fair?
*Child:* _____
*Teacher:* Let's pretend that *(one child's name)* has Wally *(hand wolf puppet to less demanding child. This action will no doubt provoke a spontaneous social*

---

*From Camp, B. W., & Bash, M. A. (1978). *Think Aloud Group Manual* (rev. ed.), Denver, CO: University of Colorado Medical Center, C250, 80262. Used with permission of the authors.

**Figure 6.4.** Fairness Number 1

*situation that should be dealt with.)* And I have Dilly. You have this toy that Dilly wants. So Dilly grabs it. *(Use Dilly to grab at Wally.)* Is that fair?

*Children:* _____

*Teacher:* Why not?

*Children:* _____

*Teacher:* What does Dilly want?

*Children:* _____

*Teacher:* *(Hand Dilly to noninvolved child).*
Tell Dilly something he could *do* or *say* to Wally that would be fair.

*Child:* _____

*Teacher:* *(Put puppets away.)* Let's look at another picture. *(Show Figure 6.5 — Fairness #2, boy and girl coloring.)* Pretend that Peter and Lisa are coloring. Peter has a box of five crayons, but no red crayon. Lisa has only three crayons, including a red one. Pretend that Peter wants the red crayon. Is it fair for him to take it away from Lisa?

*Children:* _____

*Teacher:* *(If "no" is given)*_____, what does Peter want?

*Child:* _____

*Teacher:* What would be a fair thing he could *do* or *say?*

*Children:*_____

*Teacher:* *(Show Figure 6.6 — Fairness #3, father giving money to girl.)* Father says, "Sally, since you were my helper today, I want to give you some money to buy that record you've been wanting" Is that a fair thing for father to say?

*Children:*_____

*Teacher:* *(If "yes")* Why? *(If child says it is not fair, ask* Why? *and* What would be a fair thing for him to say or do?)

*Children:*_____

*Teacher:* How does Sally feel when father gives her the money?

*Children:*_____

*Teacher:* How does father feel when he makes Sally *(happy)?*

*Children:*_____

*Teacher:* *(Show Figure 6.7 — Fairness #4, big girl with popsicle.)*
The big girl has the last popsicle. Her little sister ran to tell mother. Mother says to the big girl, "Let her have the popsicle because she is little." Is that a

**Figure 6.5.** Fairness Number 2

**Figure 6.6.** Fairness Number 3

**Figure 6.7.** Fairness Number 4

fair thing for mother to say? *(If children are still distracted by presence of pup-pets, address them through puppets to answer the question, i.e., Wally, is that a fair thing for mother to say?)*

Children:_____

*Teacher:* What would be a fair thing for mother to say?

Children:_____

*Teacher: (Show Figure 6.8 — Fairness #5, boy on swinging rope. Point to boy swinging on rope.)*

"I'm going to keep swinging all afternoon." Is that a fair thing for Brian to say?

Children:_____

*Teacher:* How does his friend feel?

Children:_____

*Teacher:* What is something different Brian could say or do that would be fair?

**Figure 6.8.** Fairness Number 5

*Children:*_____
*Teacher:* How would his friend feel if Brian (*repeat one child's response*)?
*Children:*_____
*Teacher:* Let's look at the last picture. (*Show Figure 6.9 — Fairness #6, boys play-*
      *ing baseball.*) These three boys were playing baseball and broke Mr. Blake's
      window. Only Jim got caught. Is it fair for Mr. Blake to punish Jim?
*Children:*_____
*Teacher: (If "no")* What would be fair?
          *(If "yes")* Why is it fair for him to punish Jim?
*Children:*_____
*Teacher:* How does Mr. Blake feel?
*Children:*_____
*Teacher:* He might feel (*repeat child's response*). Why?
*Children:*_____

A different criterion for evaluating if a solution is a good idea or not is to attend to how it makes you and others feel. For example, if a selfish action is committed and other people feel left out or disappointed, students are asked to think of a different solution that would make everyone feel happy.

Finally, a problem solution is judged in terms of effectiveness. If a student wants a toy another child has, ignoring the child is probably not a good idea because it will not solve the problem. However, asking to play with the child probably is a good idea because the student's desire will be satisfied.

The student's understanding of these evaluation criteria is tested when the teacher states the problem "I need a pencil." She proceeds to grab a pencil from a student and claims the solution is a good idea because it solved the

**Figure 6.9.** Fairness Number 6

problem. Consistently, Think Aloud students counter the teacher by explaining that grabbing was not a good idea because it was not really safe, it was not fair, and it made the victim angry. The students make the discovery that effectiveness cannot stand by itself as an evaluation criterion. It must be judged in light of the three other criteria — safety, fairness, and feelings. Once the criteria for evaluating outcomes are established, we post in our classrooms cue cards to remind the children of the criteria (see Figure 6.10). This interpersonal instruction sequence establishes the readiness skills in language and consequential thinking to prepare students to understand responsible behavior. At this point, students require extensive practice in interpersonal problem solving through verbal situations and through role playing before they consistently engage in responsible behavior in their own lives. Chart 2 summarizes the organized approach used with social tasks.

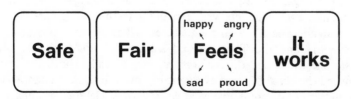

**Figure 6.10.** Evaluation Criteria

*Chart 2*
Interpersonal Problem-Solving Instruction

Step 1. Identify emotions.
Step 2. Physical causality. ⎫ Consequential
Step 3. Emotional causality. ⎬ thinking
Step 4. What might happen next? ⎭
Step 5. Is it a good idea?
       Safety
       Fairness           ⎫ Evaluation of
       How it makes people feel ⎬ possible conflict
       Effectiveness      ⎭ solutions
Step 6. PRACTICE verbal situations and role playing.
Step 7. Application to real-life conflict or conflict resolution.

## TEACHING TEACHERS HOW TO THINK ALOUD

Despite teachers' enthusiasm for Think Aloud concepts, we quickly found that few were able to use the technique in spontaneous classroom situations. Part of the problem seemed to arise from the fact that implementation of Teach Aloud procedures requires some adjustment of philosophies regarding classroom management.

To promote self-control through Think Aloud, a teacher must be able to accept two classroom management philosophies: (a) a noisy classroom may be the product of constructive activity, and (b) students are capable of responding to most questions if given enough time to organize their thoughts.

The first management principle in Think Aloud initially shocks students, teachers, principals, and parents. Think Aloud students are retaught to verbalize what goes on in their minds while they work productively. At the outset of the program, they resist thinking out loud because they have been instilled with the idea from teachers, principals, and parents that they must be quiet to be good workers. We have no evidence that the students will not achieve equally in a quiet classroom but our observations on language development and self-control encourage us to pursue the thinking-out-loud philosophy.

On one occasion, second graders were productively verbalizing as they attempted to organize 12 pictures into a logical matrix. Every student was in his seat and a few students were explaining to their neighbors their rationale for categorizing a few of the pictures. There were no obvious disruptive behaviors and the Think Aloud trainer did not hear any off-task conversation. But when the assistant principal walked into the room he admonished the class: "I want everyone of you to be quiet. There is no reason for all this noise. You know what your work is. Get it done quietly." The powerful effect of self-instruction was blotted from the lesson.

The second classroom management procedure is most difficult to use consistently. Teachers are uncomfortable when they pose a question and it is not answered immediately. So they rephrase the question or provide the answer. Thus, the students have escaped responsibility for doing their own thinking. Think Aloud requires teachers to increase the amount of time between asking a question and repeating it or rephrasing it, so students have enough time to organize their thoughts. This "wait time" may cause unnerving pauses; but students will accept responsibility for thinking, planning, and accepting consequences of their behavior when they must verbalize answers to school and behavior related questions.

Even if they accepted the philosophy behind Think Aloud, teachers often simply did not know how to implement it. We heard teachers phrase giveaway questions so students could mimic an answer. We watched teachers dictate solutions, which was less time consuming (and less effective) than involving the students in problem solving. And most disappointing to us, teachers continued giving or revising directions of modeling when students encountered difficulty with the task.

We tried several strategies to increase teachers' internalization of the Think Aloud technique. First, we wrote more detailed scripts for teachers to practice. Each script was a perfect model of integration of Think Aloud elements. When teacher performance failed to improve, we thought we might be providing too many crutches for teachers. Therefore, our second strategy was to reduce the amount of modeling the Think Aloud staff provided teachers. Whereas the formal curriculum was originally taught alternately by a teacher-in-training and a Think Aloud specialist, we cut back to a maximum of two specialist lessons a week. Still, the results were disappointing. Even increasing the number of inservice hours failed to elicit the result we sought.

Then we realized that, perhaps, some teachers were unable to see more than one way to solve a problem. Generating multiple solutions was a behavior we were trying to develop in students and, yet, some teachers had not mastered the skill. The evidence was clear that many of our teachers needed instruction and practice in this basic aspect of problem solving before they could develop enough proficiency to instruct others.

In addition to lacking skill in thinking of alternative strategies, teachers frequently failed to give adequate directions or neglected to model ways of surmounting obstacles that might block the way to task completion.

These experiences led us to develop a teacher training program that begins with exercises in the three problem-solving skills that trouble teachers the most: (a) emphasizing process, not end product; (b) generating and accepting alternatives equally; and (c) predicting obstacles. Teachers usually assess students' performance based on their end products: the completed workbook page, the typed composition, the varnished table. Think Aloud teachers are asked to put more emphasis on the thinking process that leads to the end product. To practice recognizing "process," teachers complete modified Chinese tangrams (Puzzle Grams No. 6042, Ideal School Supply Company, Oak Lawn, Illinois 60453), which provide five geometric shapes (two small triangles, a large triangle, a square, and a parallelogram) that can be arranged to form many different figures. The thinking process is emphasized by having the teachers verbalize the task strategies they use to help them organize the pieces into the prescribed shape. They are stopped before they have time to finish the tangram, and successful strategies are reviewed. The end product is not evaluated.

A different "process" exercise gives teachers practice in asking questions for information. Again, the exercise focuses on "process" instead of end product. In this task, teachers are allowed 20 questions to help them determine what an object is. Each question must be phrased so that it can receive a "yes" or "no" response. Most important, when the teachers ask questions, they must tell why they asked that question or how they can use the information from the question. Twenty questions rarely provide enough information to determine the use for the plastic items pictured in Figure 6.11. The second problem-solving behavior—generating and accepting alternatives equally—is developed through an "elaborative thinking" exercise. Teachers in Think Aloud training work together to think of all the different reasons why Lucy Anchor, a retired millionnaire, might not want to take a Caribbean cruise. No condition of reality versus fantasy is prescribed. The teachers are encouraged to accept each idea as a "different" idea without indicating a preference. This neutral response by the teacher will be important during classroom instruction.

Finally, teachers practice another element of effective problem solving—predicting obstacles. One exercise teachers practice to develop this skill is to write the part of a story that connects its beginning to the prescribed end.

Figure 6.11.

The teachers are instructed to write about several "means" used to reach the "end" of the story and to change means that might be blocked by obstacles. The obstacles might derive from traits of the story's characters or they might be external to the characters. This ability to develop several ways to overcome obstacles on the way to a goal is described by Platt and Spivack (1975) as means-ends thinking. Another exercise requires teachers to predict the obstacles that will prevent their students from completing a task successfully. They test their predictions by giving the task to their students.

Once teachers have developed some skill in the preliminary exercises, the training program moves toward helping them incorporate these skills into mastery of the Think Aloud teaching methodology. They still need a great deal of practice which comes largely from presenting Think Aloud's problem content to children.

At this point, many teachers still find it difficult to (a) model the thinking "process," (b) withhold judgment of students' performance until students have evaluated themselves, and (c) teach emotions.

Teachers are so practiced at giving directions that they often misunderstand the difference between giving directions and modeling. The following examples will illustrate the distinction that is critical to Think Aloud teaching proficiency.

## Task 1

This task is a primary reading worksheet on alphabetizing first letters only (Figure 6.12). Often this type of task prompts a teacher to give directions such as: "On this worksheet, you must circle the word before or after to answer the questions. Use the letters along the side of the paper to help you remember the order of the alphabet. If the word comes before the other word, circle 'before.' If the word comes after the other word, circle 'after.'"

In the Think Aloud program, however, modeling might take the following form: "*What is my problem?* I have to figure out if a word comes before or after another and to circle the word 'before' or 'after' to show the answer. *How can I do it?* First I'll write the letters next to each other the way I'm used to: a b c d. Then I'll write the words next to the letters. Before means first so, if the word comes first, I'll circle 'before.' The question is about the word 'boy.' I'll underline 'boy' to help me remember it is the important word."

## Task 2

This is a math task of coloring only triangles among many shapes to find a hidden picture.

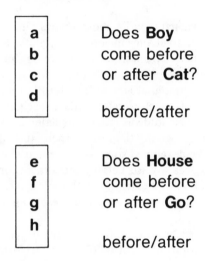

| a |
|---|
| b |
| c |
| d |

Does **Boy**
come before
or after **Cat?**

before/after

| e |
|---|
| f |
| g |
| h |

Does **House**
come before
or after **Go?**

before/after

**Figure 6.12.** Reading worksheet

Again, the teacher who directs rather than models may say: "On this paper you are to color only the triangles. When all the triangles are colored you will see a hidden picture."

The teacher who models her thinking might say: "*What is my problem?* I have to color only the triangles to find a hidden picture. *How can I do it?* First, I will put a triangle at the top of my page to help me remember just to color triangles. Then I will count the sides of each shape to be sure it is a triangle. I see some places on the paper where two triangles come next to each other and share a side. I had better make a plan that will help me remember to count the same side for both of the triangles." This last plan illustrates how predicting obstacles can be incorporated into modeling to reduce the risk of student failure because of unforeseen obstacles.

Intrusion of evaluative responses too early in the problem-solving procedure is one of the hardest habits for teachers to change. Praise is important reinforcement for most students when it is well timed and task specific. However, when the goal of a lesson is to engage many students in discussion, it is imperative that the teacher accept each response without evaluation. When the teacher says to one student "That's a good idea" during discussion, other students commonly respond, "My idea isn't as good as his," "He took my idea," or "That's just what I was going to say." If the goal is to encourage responses from many students or to encourage students to judge the quality of their own responses, the teacher should reinforce the fact of contributing rather than assessing a value on the contribution. An appropriate teacher response might be, "You are coming up with lots of different ideas. Who can add a third idea?"

Withholding judgment of a student's performance offers another opportunity to increase the student's self-discipline and to contribute to a positive classroom climate. When a student has practiced self-evaluation, he learns to evaluate his performance fairly. Gradually, he can own up to off-task behavior and can plan more appropriate activity. This skill of students to evaluate themselves gives teachers a way of avoiding confrontation when students are not performing up to the teacher's expectations. When a student works on a paper haphazardly or participates disruptively in a group activity, for example, the teacher may ask the student to monitor his use of his plan more carefully or to reassess his plan. If the student is able to plan a more appropriate behavior, he will be more committed to following the plan than if the teacher dictates the behavior in a reprimand. In the case where the student is not yet capable of appropriate self-evaluation, the teacher must continue to serve as a model.

The third difficult aspect of Think Aloud for teachers to internalize is teaching emotions. Young children typically recognize and have the verbal labels for only a few emotions: happy, glad, sad, bad, and mad. To increase the breadth of their understanding, Think Aloud defines a wide range of emotions, provides the verbal labels, and encourages students to describe occasions when they felt the emotion.

Whereas teachers frequently use or elicit from children words to describe how a character in a story might feel, they rarely define the feeling in words. Nor do they stress how the feeling causes us to react to others or how we might reduce a negative feeling or intensify a positive one. We have developed a sequence for teaching an emotion that includes a definition, examples of emotional responses, and strategies for altering the emotion.

1. Identify need for recognizing a particular emotion.
2. Show facial expression that characterizes emotion.
3. Label emotion for students.
4. Define emotion.
5. Provide personal example.
6. Restate definition.
7. Show picture. What might have provoked the emotion?
8. Show different picture. What might have provoked the emotion?
9. What's something the person could say or do to lessen or to intensify the emotion.
10. Follow up by using the emotion label during class or by identifying the emotion in literature.

We have used this sequence to teach anxiety, pride, disappointment, jealousy, confidence, and embarrassment. Following is the Think Aloud anxiety script.

| 20-minute lesson | |
|---|---|
| Object: | Introducing the "feeling" — anxious, nervous, worried. |
| Rationale: | Anxiety is a common feeling children experience. However, many times they are unable to talk about this feeling because they lack the necessary language. Children also need to know what they can do to help themselves feel better when they are feeling anxious. |
| Student Objectives: | The children will be able to identify people showing feelings of anxiety; suggest causes for feeling this way; and identify ways of reducing "anxious" feelings. |
| Materials: | Pictures from: |
| | *AWARE Activities for Social Development* by Phyllis Elardo & Mark Cooper, Menlo Park, California: Addison-Wesley Publishing Company: 1977, pages 42 and 86. |
| | *Understanding Our Feelings* study prints, Instructo Corporation, Paoli, PA 19301: woman chewing on kleenex |
| | *Moods and Emotions* teaching pictures, David C. Cook Publishing Co., 850 N. Grover Avenue, Elgin, Illinois 60120: picture #7 and story from guide page 16 "All Alone." |
| | Word cards for anxious, nervous, worried. |
| Follow-Up: | *Moving Day* by Tobi Tobias, Knopf, 1976. |

*Teacher:* *(show anxiety picture — page 42)* All of these children feel the same way. Are they smiling?
*Children:* _____
*Teacher:* How do you think these children feel?
*Children:* _____
*Teacher:* Here's a word to describe how these children feel. *(Show word card — anxious.)* These children feel anxious. How do these children feel?
*Children:* _____
*Teacher:* When we feel anxious, we usually are worried about what might happen to us in the future. Today I felt anxious because I didn't know if my car was going to start this morning. Thumbs up if you have ever felt anxious. Thumbs down if you don't know if you have ever felt anxious.
*Children:* _____
*Teacher:* We can use other words to describe this feeling of not knowing what might happen in the future. The other words are nervous and worried. *(Show word cards.)* Sometimes the word anxious can also mean excited. *(Give examples.)* I am anxious to go to the movies or I am anxious to finish my work so I can go to the art center. But today we are only going to talk about anxious as meaning nervous or worried about what might happen to us in the future. *(Show Understanding our Feelings picture.)* How does this woman probably feel?
*Children:* _____
*Teacher:* Yes, this woman might feel anxious *(nervous, worried)*. What's one thing that might make her feel anxious.

*Children:* _____
*Teacher:* That's one idea. *(Repeat idea.)* Or, she might feel anxious because . . .
*Children:* _____
*Teacher:* That's a different idea. *(Encourage children to make complete statements using because. If children have difficulty thinking of ideas, ask them if their mother has ever looked like this and what caused her to look worried or anxious.)*
*Children:* _____
*Teacher:* *(Show boy picture from AWARE, page 86.)* This boy is at school. How do you think he feels?
*Children:* _____
*Teacher:* He might feel anxious because . . .
*Children:* _____
*Teacher:* That's one idea of what might make this boy feel anxious. Let's think of lots of different ideas. *(If children have difficulty in suggesting ideas, ask* "How many of you have ever felt anxious when you had to read out loud in front of the class?")
*Children:* _____
*Teacher:* *(Accept three or four different ideas.)* Let's listen to a story about a girl named Cindy. *(Read story— "All Alone" from Moods and Emotions Guide, page 16. In the first sentence substitute the word* nervous *for* afraid: "Cindy was nervous." *End story after* "Maybe something dreadful had happened.") *(Show Moods and Emotions picture #7—Cindy.)*
*Teacher:* This is Cindy. How does Cindy Feel?
*Children:* _____
*Teacher:* Why does Cindy feel anxious?
*Children:* _____
*Teacher:* What does feeling anxious mean?
*Children:* _____
*Teacher:* Our problem is to think of lots of different things Cindy could say or do so she doesn't feel so anxious. Let me hear you think out loud.
*Children:* _____
*Teacher:* That's one idea. *(List ideas on board.)* What are some different ideas? *(Continue in this manner until children have exhausted their supply of ideas. Add your own ideas to stimulate student responses when necessary.)*
*Children:* _____
*Teacher:* *(Guide children to self-evaluate their work.)*
*Children:* _____
*Follow-up:* *(Read story "Moving Day." Half way through story ask how the girl is feeling and why she is feeling that way. Continue story to its end. Discuss ways the little girl handled her anxious feelings. What did she do? What did she say?)*

## GENERALIZATION OF THINK ALOUD SKILLS

The success of Think Aloud has been assessed both formally through testing and informally through observation and reported anecdotes. Because the classroom program is both newer and more difficult to evaluate than the individual program, most evaluation to date has been on students with aggressive behavior problems working in a one-to-one or two-to-one situation.

With the basic individual program, the most consistent differences from control populations have been registered on cognitive test performance, where Think Aloud graduates have surpassed all types of controls (Camp, Blom et al., 1977; Camp, 1980). Prosocial behavior in the classroom has increased more among Think Aloud graduates than untreated controls (Camp, Blom et al. 1977) and equivalent to that of children in a self-esteem training program (Camp, 1980). Aggressive behavior problems have also decreased significantly, but no more than in control groups (Camp, Blom et al., 1977; Camp, 1980). One study with learning disabled children (Watson & Hall, 1977) has also reported significant improvement in both achievement and behavior following Think Aloud training as compared to other types of training.

Formal evaluation of the classroom program to date is consistent with results of the individual program. In the earliest version, which did not contain lessons in social problem solving, children exposed to Think Aloud registered significantly more improvement in cognitive test performance than unexposed children (Camp & Bash, 1978). Participants in the classroom version, which includes the social problem-solving lessons, have also demonstrated significant increases in nonaggressive solutions on the Preschool Interpersonal Problem-Solving Test of Shure and Spivack (1974b).

Informal observations by trainers and teacher reports have produced a rich volume of anecdotes, which reflect unique responses from students and teachers as a result of Think Aloud instruction. The first level at which this appears is often during actual Think Aloud lessons. For example, one aspect of the interpersonal problem-solving training is to teach students to identify other people's feelings and to empathize with others. Even first graders readily apply these social skills to ease their teacher's frustration and embarrassment.

When one Think Aloud teacher became very discouraged because she could not complete a geometric puzzle, several students quickly offered help: "Don't worry, Miss Allen, we'll help you do it." "Why don't you find the pieces that go in the corner before you work on the middle." In another first grade, the teacher raised her hand for the trainer to help her when she was unsure of herself in teaching a Think Aloud lesson. The students identified with her discomfort and said, "Mrs. Riley, you're a student too. You're learning how to think aloud with us."

Empathy for other students was also observed during a Think Aloud lesson in a second-grade classroom. During the lesson, felt-backed pictures would not adhere to a felt board while the teacher and students worked to classify the pictures. The last student to work at the felt board evaluated himself: "How did I do? Terrible because I kept knocking the pictures off the board. But I'm sure I know how the pictures go together if I could think of a different plan for making them stay on the board." However, one main-streamed learning disabled student refused to let Kenneth downplay his own effort: "You really did a good job because you kept trying even when you felt mad when the pictures kept falling off. You ought to feel proud."

Think Aloud's self-instruction questions teach students to monitor the use of their plans and develop an understanding that making mistakes is part of the problem-solving process. Jack, a sixth grader, dashed to the teacher for a second paper any time he made a mistake. During Think Aloud training he began spontaneously to verbalize a change in plan to prevent errors and to eliminate the need for fresh paper.

A second level in generalizing Think Aloud skills occurs when the teacher restructures a typical school situation into a problem-solving lesson in which students assume some responsibility for planning a solution. Lining up for gym is one of the first situations in which teachers commonly apply Think Aloud. Prior to Think Aloud training, teachers often call children by table or by row to line up for gym. After exposure to Think Aloud, several teachers have reported approaching this issue in the following manner. "My prob-lem is to get children to the gym quickly and safely without disturbing other classes. How can I do it? I could call each child by name but that would take too long. What are some other plans which would help me solve my problem?"

Another common school problem develops on Halloween, when some chil-dren lack costumes for the annual Halloween parade. Typically, children without costumes are jeered at by costumed students. In one second-grade Think Aloud classroom, the teacher prevented the taunting by identifying a class problem and its corresponding solution: to design costumes for any stu-dent without one. The costumed students enthusiastically helped create innovative garb that eliminated the potential for heckling.

Before Think Aloud training, teachers often took on student problems as their own. For example, a student who bothered other students was told how to get along with others. Or when money was stolen, teachers employed new procedures for storing money. In both cases, the teacher attempted to solve the problem, but the problem persisted. Some teachers have used Think Aloud to engage the class in looking together for the cause of the behavior. In one class discussion, it was determined that the student pest might be seek-ing friends or attention by bothering peers. The Think Aloud teacher set up the following puppet situation to help the student pest find more appropri-ate ways of getting attention: Peter wants people to talk to him and to be his friends. What are different things for Peter to do or say to get people to pay attention to him? The class suggested many solutions that they would accept as motions of friendship. The unidentified pest listened attentively and came to school the next day with a toy he was willing to share.

In another classroom, it was decided that the thief might be stealing money in order to buy something. The teacher set up a role play situation to reduce the need for stealing money: Rita wants to give her sister a birthday present but she does not have any money. What are different things she could do or say so she can get a present for her sister? The children verbalized alternative solutions as to how Rita could make or get a present for her sister. The stealing in the classroom was not repeated.

One goal of Think Aloud is to teach students to evaluate their own work spontaneously. For them to develop this spontaneity, the teacher must first model self-evaluation and then structure situations wherein the students practice such self-evaluation. One first-grade teacher modeled self-evaluation for the problem of getting children to the gym quickly and safely. "How did I do? My plan to call children by the month of their birthday didn't work because some students weren't sure of their birth date. When I changed my plan to call children by colors of the clothes they were wearing, all children knew when to line up and all children listened for directions. That plan worked and I feel good."

A student in the class had a chance to practice evaluating his performance later in the day. Mark was talking when he was supposed to be completing math seatwork and was required to self-evaluate when the period ended. "How did I do? I was messing around so I didn't do my paper, but I know how to do the problems. I might as well stay in from recess and do it." The student was angry for having to stay inside, but he was mad at himself as the offender not at the teacher as a punisher.

Finally, when teachers present a lesson in the style of Think Aloud they talk less. As students gain proficiency at identifying problems, generating plans, and monitoring their adherence to plans, teachers make fewer repetitions of task directions and fewer task reminders. A teacher was awed when her second graders produced their best art projects after thinking out loud. A student explained the miracle: "This time we really knew what our problem was." This time the students had been required to articulate the problem statement rather than simply hearing the teacher rephrase it for them.

Evidence of the third level of generalization comes from anecdotes about children using Think Aloud skills independently, without prompting. Students frequently report their own think aloud triumphs. A first grader chattered quietly at her seat as she completed a music task. Her assignment was to listen to melodies and to circle an arrow that indicated the direction the tune took. When she finished, she beamed and proudly reported to her teacher how thinking out loud helped her do her work. She reviewed for the class each of the answers she gave to the four Think Aloud questions.

Another first grader who was assigned to a resource room for disruptive behavior reported to her teacher that she knew she was behaving better because "Ralph* whispers in my ear to be quiet and raise my hand whenever I forget my plan."

In one case, a mother recounted how her second grader improved the climate at home. When the family's 5-year-old was unresponsive to traditional toilet training, the second grader suggested posting Ralph's questions on the bathroom wall. The problemsolver proceeded to instruct the younger child to think out loud. The plan worked and the story's ending was a happy one.

Teachers love to report occasions when students have relieved them from intervening in potential conflict situations. During reading seatwork, one boy was wandering aimlessly around the room. The teacher heard a student admonish the boy: "You better use a different plan to get your work done before the teacher catches you."

Another second-grade teacher overheard the following dialogue between two students during an art lesson:

*Alex:* This stitchery is boring!
*Ellen:* What's wrong with it?
*Alex:* It's too hard.
*Ellen:* You planned your own thing. Maybe you need a new plan. What's a different idea?

The same teacher was excited by the empathy and attention to feelings that Ruth expressed in the following hall scene:

*Mark to Susan:* I don't like you. Nobody likes you!
*Ruth to Mark:* Does that make her feel good?
*Mark:* It's true.
*Ruth:* Yes, but there's something better you could say. You didn't have to make her feel bad.

Finally, students actively seek opportunities to recognize problem situations and to plan solutions. Planning even begins to appear in students' creative writing. The examples that follow were written by first-grade Think Aloud students.

### SAM'S SLED

Nip ran up the hill and the sled is there. Nip got on the sled and the sled moved. I can't get off the sled. The milkman is down there. I hope Nip can get off the sled. Sam has a plan. I think this will work if I can get this over here. Here is a sled. I hope this will work. Yes, it worked. I am glad.

---

*Ralph is the name children have given the bear who illustrates the four self-instruction questions. All Think Aloud students have a copy of Ralph and his questions at their desks.

RALPH AND THE BERD HOUS

One day Ralph dsidide too bild a berd hous. But he had a polbem. He did not know WHAT! too do beacas he did not have the rite aqupment. But THENE! he had a ideea. How can I do it. He sied if I only had a rooler. "I cood do it." The end.

Think Aloud instruction can also occur outside the classroom. For example, while monitoring the lunchroom, a Think Aloud teacher restructured a problem situation so that the students took responsibility for resolving the dilemma. The school had designated a Captain's Table to recognize students who cleaned their plates, showed good manners, and talked softly. The monitor was pleased to find a table of six fifth graders who each merited a seat at the Captain's Table. However, he told the girls it was too hard for him to pick just one representative. He asked the girls to help him. The girls agreed that feelings might be hurt if only one of them were chosen, so they planned that each girl could sit at the Captain's Table one day of the week and they wrote out a schedule. But the dilemma had two parts. A roster had to be signed for the week. The girls identified two plans: sign all the names or pick a group name. The girls chose to sign the roster, "The Six Angels."

Teachers might be immortalized by the words "Walk, don't run!" The Think Aloud skill of requiring students to plan alternate ways of behaving has helped more than one teacher avoid such immortality. One Think Aloud teacher asked her sixth grader who was running up the stairs, "What's a different way you could go up the stairs?" John answered that he could walk up, and did so. The next day, both John and the teacher saw another boy bounding up the steps. This time, John said to the other boy, "What's a different way to go up the stairs?" The other boy responded to John by walking up the stairs.

## COMPARISON WITH OTHER PROGRAMS

Many teachers have encountered a number of programs designed to improve their management of interpersonal conflict among students. They have often asked for explanations regarding the differences between Think Aloud and these other programs. In this context, the work of Glasser (1969), Gordon (1970), and Kohlberg (see Mattox, 1974, and Galbraith & Jones, 1976) have come up most often. In this section, we would like to review each of these briefly and to contrast them with the Think Aloud program.

Kohlberg has been concerned with describing and classifying the reasons children give for what they do. He has grouped these into six stages which he believes reflect moral development: Stage I—primary motivation is to avoid punishment; Stage II—motivation is primarily What's in it for me?; Stage III—a desire to please or conform emerges; Stage IV—emphasis is placed on social order; Stage V—stresses the rights of the individual; Stage

VI—conscience and self-chosen principles determine decisions. Kohlberg has been interested in trying to facilitate growth from one stage to another through group discussion of moral dilemmas.

An example of a moral dilemma that may be used in such discussion follows (Fenton, 1976, pp. 189–190):

### JOE'S MORAL DILEMMA

Joe is a 14-year-old boy who wanted to go to camp very much. His father promised him he could go if he saved up the money for it himself. So Joe worked hard at his paper route and saved up the $40 it cost to go to camp and a little more besides. But just before camp was going to start, his father changed his mind. Some of his friends decided to go on a special fishing trip, and Joe's father was short of the money it would cost. So he told Joe to give him the money he had saved up from the paper route. Joe didn't want to give up going to camp, so he thought of refusing to give his father the money.

Teachers may be prepared for these discussions by general training in discussion skills, which may consist of discussions and modeling of taking an "open, nonjudgmental attitude" and preparing "what if" and "probe" questions to keep the discussion going. Because the discussion focuses on what we would call the final evaluation stage, it presupposes an understanding of cause and effect. Acceptance and internalization of higher moral stage solutions are expected to occur without explicit instruction, presumably through the power of peer models.

In the Think Aloud program, no formal stages have been posited. However, we have accepted Shure and Spivack's notion that children need to have an understanding of cause and effect before they can consider the question of what someone should do. In addition, Think Aloud discussions emphasize the idea derived from Shure and Spivack (1974a), Maier (1963), and others that immediate evaluation of solutions often curbs development of alternatives. Kohlberg's discussions of moral dilemmas could easily be included as one part of the Think Aloud program, particularly for children who have already developed skill in problem analysis or an understanding of cause and effect. Story dilemmas are already included in the Think Aloud program, as the Fairness lesson presented earlier. Plans for a program in upper grades include the use of moral dilemmas such as Kohlberg's beginning in early lessons.

However, Think Aloud is a much broader program than can be covered in the discussion of moral dilemmas alone. At this stage in the development of the Think Aloud program, training for teachers involves, in particular, a more far-reaching development of skill in taking a nonjudgmental attitude and promoting discussions that stimulate multiple student contributions. Discussion of moral dilemmas can, like most of the Think Aloud program, be used in a preventive sense as well as in analyzing on-the-spot problems.

The other two programs are designed primarily to assist teachers in developing skill in resolving conflicts as they arise. Gordon's (1975) film, *Teacher Effectiveness Training in the Classroom*, starts with the premise that resolution of conflicts is impaired by faulty communication. Teacher Effectiveness Training is designed to improve communication skills of teachers through what Gordon describes as a "no lose" method of communication. This method attempts to cut the flow of resentment that interferes with resolution or problem solving. Elements of this method that are discussed in his film include (a) establishing problem ownership; (b) active listening characterized by giving feedback and listening for feelings; (c) use of "I" messages; (d) identifying roadblocks to communication (directing, threatening, moralizing, advising, lecturing, judging, praising, name calling, interpreting, reassuring, probing, withdrawing, sarcasm); and (e) practice in the "no lose" method.

Gordon's use of the "no lose" method of communication in a conflict situation shares much in common with Think Aloud and includes the following steps: (a) defining the problem in terms of needs; (b) generating possible solutions; (c) evaluating and testing the various solutions; (d) deciding on mutually acceptable solutions; (e) implementing the solution; and (f) evaluating the solution. Gordon's approach and Think Aloud both emphasize defining the problem, but Think Aloud does not restrict definition to "needs." On the other hand, Think Aloud does not deal only with conflict as it arises; rather, much of the Think Aloud program is preventive. The two methods are similar in emphasis on generating many possible solutions and evaluating and testing them. Think Aloud goes beyond Gordon's program, however, in helping children to develop a repertoire of alternatives, to think in terms of alternatives, and to understand concepts of cause. On the other hand, development of good communication has not been dealt with as completely and systematically in Think Aloud training as in the Gordon program. The Gordon program tends to be more immediately applicable to the problems teachers have in dealing with children, while Think Aloud requires building a good deal of background skill before its tenets are readily applicable.

In general, however, the Gordon training in communication would seem to be an excellent background for teacher development of the type of attitudes and discussion skills needed by both the Think Aloud program and for developing the nonjudgmental attitudes proposed by Kohlberg.

Like Gordon's Teacher Effectiveness Training, Glasser's use of reality therapy in the school situation is directed primarily toward providing teachers with a method of dealing with situational crises. Glasser proposes eight steps toward dealing effectively with interpersonal problem situations. These are (a) make friends, be personal; (b) deal with the present, ask "What are you doing now?"; (c) deal with behavior (not feelings), ask "Is it helping?"; (d) make a plan to do better; (e) get a commitment; (f) do not accept excuses; (g) do not punish, but do not interfere with reasonable consequences; (h) never give up. This approach can be applied in counseling students, classes, teachers, and parents to achieve appropriate resolution of problem situations. Teacher training involves instruction in Glasser's background psychological theory of motivation, needs, and desirable goals in human growth. For example, Glasser suggests that people are "ill" because they act irresponsibly, and treatment needs to be directed toward helping them act more responsibly. Camp would say that behavior is likely to persist in being maladaptive if the person does not have alternative methods of coping with different situations. The two positions are not in conflict but put emphasis on different aspects of behavior. Glasser's approach can also be applied in a preventive fashion, though it has not been presented primarily for this purpose.

Glasser's first three steps can be viewed as setting the stage for problem solving and defining the problem. It begins directly with discussion and involves no modeling of cognitions. Altogether, the eight steps outlined by Glasser are much broader and far reaching than the Think Aloud program. However, Think Aloud could be viewed as concentrating primarily on Glasser's Step 4 — Make a plan. The advantage of Think Aloud in this stage is that it provides children with a method of developing alternatives to their usual behavior and builds an understanding of cause and effect. Although it may be argued that a more haphazard approach may accomplish the same thing, Think Aloud may help develop planning skills and evaluating skills more rapidly, thereby shortcutting some of the negative consequences that may have to be experienced otherwise. In addition, the emphasis on modeling in the Think Aloud program has some theoretical advantage in assisting with internalization of verbal regulation of behavior. Again, the amount of discussion contained in the Glasser program and the way in which it is carried out, probably, in the long run, achieve results similar to Think Aloud. Glasser's Steps 5–8 go well beyond the Think Aloud program and involve suggestions regarding direct management of problem situations, especially those that occur repeatedly despite plans and commitments.

Viewing all of these approaches together, it is conceivable that a very powerful curriculum for teacher training could be developed using all four. For example, one could envision training teachers by beginning with Gordon's communication skills, followed by the preliminary problem-solving exercises that introduce the Think Aloud technique. This could be followed by training in the Think Aloud program with inclusion of Kohlberg's moral dilemmas toward the end of the program for younger children or early in the program for older children. Finally, all of the preceding could easily be incorporated into an overall management approach based on Glasser's eight steps.

## REFERENCES

Camp, B. W. (1977). Verbal mediation in young aggressive boys. *Journal of Abnormal Psychology*, *86*, 145–153.

Camp, B. W. (1980). Two psychoeducational training programs for aggressive boys.

In C. Whalen & B. Henker (Eds.), *Hyperactive children: The social ecology of identification and treatment.* New York: Academic Press.

Camp, B. W., & Bash, M. A. (1978, August). *The classroom "Think aloud" program.* Paper presented at the American Psychological Association Convention, Toronto.

Camp, B. W., & Bash, M. A. (1981). *Think aloud.* Champaign, IL: Research Press.

Camp, B. W., Blom, G. E., Hebert, F., & Van Doorninck, W. J. (1977). "Think aloud": A program for developing self-control in young aggressive boys. *Journal of Abnormal Child Psychology, 5,* 157–169.

Camp, B. W., Zimet, S. G., Van Doorninck, W. J., & Dahlem, N. W. (1977). Verbal abilities in young aggressive boys. *Journal of Educational Psychology, 69,* 129–135.

Fenton, E. (1976). Moral education: The research findings. *Social Education, 40,* 189–193.

Galbraith, R. E., & Jones, T. M. (1976). *Moral reasoning: A teaching handbook for adapting Kohlberg to the classroom.* Anoka, MN: Greenhaven Press.

Glasser, W. (1969). *Schools without failure.* New York: Harper & Row.

Gordon, T. (1970). *Parent effectiveness training.* New York: Peter H. Wyden.

Gordon, T. (1975). *Teacher effectiveness training in the classroom.* Hollywood, CA: Media Five Film Distributors.

Hetherington, E. M., & McIntyre, C. W. (1975). Developmental psychology. *Annual Review of Psychology, 26,* 97–136.

Maier, N. R. F. (1963). *Problem-solving discussions and conferences.* San Francisco: McGraw-Hill.

Mattox, B. A. (1974). *Getting it together: Dilemmas for the classroom.* La Mesa, CA: Pennant Educational Materials.

Meichenbaum, D. (1975). Theoretical and treatment implications of developmental research on verbal control of behavior. *Psychologie Canadienne/Canadian Psychological Review, 16,* 22–27.

Meichenbaum, D., & Goodman, J. (1971). Training impulsive children to talk to themselves: A means of developing self-control. *Journal of Abnormal Psychology, 77,* 115–126.

Platt, J. J., & Spivack, G. (1975). *Manual for the means-ends problem solving procedure (MEPS): A measure of interpersonal cognitive problem solving skill.* Philadelphia: Department of Mental Health Sciences, Hahnemann Community Mental Health/Mental Retardation Center.

Shure, M. B., & Spivack, G. (1974a). *A mental health program for kindergarten children: A cognitive approach to solving interpersonal problems.* Philadelphia: Department of Mental Health Sciences, Hahnemann Community Mental Health/Mental Retardation Center.

Shure, M. B., & Spivack, G. (1974b) *Preschool Interpersonal Problem Solving (PIPS) test: Manual.* Philadelphia: Department of Mental Health Sciences, Hahnemann Community Mental Health/Mental Retardation Center.

Spivack, G., & Shure, M. B. (1974). *Social adjustment of young children: A cognitive approach to solving real-life problems.* San Francisco: Jossey-Bass.

Torrance, P. (1966). *Torrance tests of creative thinking.* Columbus, OH: Ginn.

Watson, D. L., & Hall, D. L. (1977). *Self-control of hyperactivity.* La Mesa, CA: Pupil Services Division, La Mesa-Spring Valley School District.

# 7
# Severely Handicapped Children: Social Skills Development Through Leisure Skills Programming

Stuart J. Schleien and Paul Wehman

The purpose of this chapter is to discuss assessment techniques, instructional procedures, and intervention strategies in leisure skills programming that can be utilized to facilitate social skill development in severely handicapped children. Individualized programs in four recreational program areas (toy play, games, hobbies, sports) are also presented in the latter part of the chapter to assist in the acquisition of leisure and social skills. The material presented in this chapter provides the basis for the systematic programming of social development in severely handicapped children. The task analyses presented are not meant to be comprehensive but, instead, are representative of group-oriented leisure skills that severely handicapped children can master through systematic instruction.

## A RATIONALE FOR LEISURE EDUCATION

### Abundance of Leisure Time

All too often, severely handicapped persons have not developed the necessary skills to use their free time creatively or constructively. They will participate in an educational program for a small part of their day and have nothing to do during its remainder. Unoccupied time must cease to be the dominant quality of the child's life style. Constructive activities can be offered to the individual to fill this void. The development of nonwork-, nonschool-related skills must be encouraged and systematically programmed to resolve the critical problem of free time. The child's use of leisure time and his attitude toward recreation may determine the degree of success he will experience through the educational efforts. Constructive use of free time has become a vital aspect of healthy, normal living, especially in these times, when leisure time has become increasingly available for all people. For severely handicapped children, learning leisure-time activities can facilitate the development of interpersonal relationships and social skills.

## Means of Teaching Social Skills

The development of leisure skills in severely handicapped children will enhance social skill development. Involvement in recreational activities offers some of the most effective means for children to acquire and develop these skills.

Social skill development is facilitated through group play. Children who fail to develop the necessary skills to engage in play are considered handicapped. The development of cooperative play behavior and participation in leisure activities will lead to making friends; getting along with others; learning to share, compete, cooperate, and take turns; and a generally more satisfactory social adjustment. An adequate social adjustment is required for successful daily living, including time on the job, in the community, and with friends and family.

In a national survey of families with handicapped children, it was found that only a small portion of the subjects, the hearing impaired, had used at least one recreational service (Brewer & Kakalik, 1979). Of the families that did use recreational services, the parents favorably regarded leisure as an end in itself, in that the parents were most satisfied that their children learned independent living skills and made new friends. This study provides just one example of the interplay between participation in recreation and socialization. There is widespread agreement among educators concerning this interaction between the two disciplines. The fact that social development could be increased through interaction with peers and adults during leisure education was also revealed by Verhoven and Goldstein (1976). A major reason for inappropriate behavior at play by handicapped children is their limited cooperative play skills and lack of social interaction among peers (Wehman & Schleien, 1981). Paloutzian, Hasazi, Streifel, and Edgard (1971) also noted an inordinate amount of isolated play among severely handicapped young children, reinforcing the association between play and social skills.

Independent, or isolated, play is a lower stage of social development than cooperative play. In fact, children fail to develop higher level social behaviors, such as cooperative play when they have little peer interaction during play (Wehman, 1979). Effective feedback cannot be obtained until there are social interactions between children. As an individual becomes more proficient at recreating with others, socialization skills will be acquired (Paloutzian et al., 1971). Sharing, taking turns, and teamwork are aspects of social interaction that constitute cooperative play (Knapczyk & Yoppi, 1975; Samaras & Ball, 1975).

In her rationale for leisure education as a process rather than a specific service in education, Collard (1981) identified the many roles that leisure education can play in assisting in the development of needed social skills. Handicapped individuals can learn valuable and critical social skills to facilitate appropriate functioning in the school, on the job, and in the community. Zigmond (1978) insisted that handicapped individuals must be socially competent to attain maximum benefit from classroom instruction in all curriculum areas. Several other authors have cited the importance of proficiency in socialization among handicapped individuals to perform successfully on the job (Neal, 1970; President's Committee on Mental Retardation, 1974; Wehman, 1977) and within the community (Collard, 1981; Novak & Heal, 1980; Wehman & Schleien, 1981).

A publication of the Alcohol, Drug Abuse, and Mental Health Administration of the U.S. Department of Health and Human Services (1979) outlines how play teaches children to relate to other people and helps them learn how to live in a particular place in the particular way the culture expects. Social rules and morals are learned in this manner. Practicing principles of give and take, sharing similar space, and exchanging information with other playmates through play can assist in preparation for adult life.

## Systematic Instruction Required for Appropriate Leisure Activity

Without systematic instruction in leisure skills programming, severely handicapped children will not learn the skills necessary to play appropriately. At times, even after the child has acquired the skill, without systematic instructional strategies (e.g., external positive reinforcement), he may never maintain, generalize, or initiate the skill into other environments. Besides emphasizing the provision of activities that build on the present capabilities of the youth and prevent further disability, systematic instruction must be provided to foster engagement in appropriate leisure activity. Instruction of this sort may include assessing the leisure skill competencies of the individual, careful selection of materials and skills for instruction, and implementation techniques or specific training methods to assist in the acquisition, maintenance, and generalization of the skills.

## Reduction of Inappropriate Social Behaviors

Severely handicapped children often engage in seemingly inappropriate, unacceptable social behavior. Children who are constructively using their leisure time do not exhibit the behaviors (i.e., body rocking, head banging, violent actions, social withdrawal) typically characteristic of these individuals. Research has clearly indicated that there is an inverse relationship between acquisition of play skills and self-stimulated or abusive behavior. Recreational activity of a social nature provides opportunities through which the participant can learn to adjust to the social demands of society.

Schleien, Kiernan, and Wehman (1981) conducted a leisure skills training program in a group home for six moderately mentally retarded residents. An inverse relationship was found between high-quality (e.g., goal-directed, age-appropriate) leisure behaviors and inappropriate (e.g., stereotypic or age-inappropriate) behaviors. The training program included leisure counseling, reinforcement, and making materials available. In another study, prompting and positive physical reinforcement were provided to three severely handicapped children for appropriate toy play (Favell, 1973). Instructor guidance and reinforcement for toy play were correlated with an increase in appropriate play and a decrease in stereotypic behaviors.

Wuerch and Voeltz (1982) also found increased frequencies of positive behaviors when individuals were systematically trained in leisure activities. They measured the effects of leisure instruction on the behaviors of four severely handicapped adolescents attending a private special education school. Two students exhibited increased constructive, exploratory, and attending behavior during downtime as a result of the training. A third student decreased self-stimulation when using the materials, but increased it when she had no objects to manipulate. The authors viewed the results as offering cautious support for associating play training with positive collateral effects.

## Acceptance in Community and Reduction of Institutionalization

One of the major goals of any recreation program for severely handicapped persons is to contribute to the individual's ability to function independently in the community. By fostering the child's capability for independent living (e.g., transportation, self-help skills), the need for institutionalization is significantly reduced. Unfortunately, many of these individuals are isolated from peers and the community in general because of untidy appearance, nonacceptable social behavior, and negative attitudes of community members. It is nearly impossible for them to develop any social relationships, and they are typically excluded from normal contacts. Every recreational experience has a contribution to make in social skill development and community living. One of the more effective ways to reduce the attitudinal barriers prevalent within the mainstream of community living is for handicapped children to play with normal peers, allowing all to notice the similarities, not the differences, between them as they play.

## PLAY SKILL VARIABLES FOR INITIAL ASSESSMENT

Once a commitment to leisure education has been made, teachers and other practitioners are faced with the following question: Which leisure skills should be selected for instruction? With the large number of leisure skills (games, toys to manipulate, sports, hobbies) available, and the recreation skill deficits characteristic of most severely handicapped children, assessment of these individuals' leisure skill strengths and weaknesses is a process critical to efficient instruction.

Initial assessment will help determine which skills the participant can perform independently and which skills require verbal, gestural, or physical assistance. Fortunately, within the last few years, two criterion-referenced recreation curriculum guides have been developed that are sensitive to the unique needs and problems of individuals with severe handicaps (Wehman & Schleien, 1981; Wuerch & Voeltz, 1982). Both curricula use task analysis, activity modifications, and applied behavior analysis to develop recreation and social skills in severely handicapped participants. In addition to appropriate instructional strategies, Wehman and Schleien and Wuerch and Voeltz describe leisure skill inventories, activity checklists, and assessment techniques to assist the instructor with activity selection. The variables that will be examined highlight important leisure skill areas for functional assessment.

## Proficiency of Leisure Skill: Task Analytic Assessment

Although a number of areas can be assessed in a recreation environment, an initial consideration must be, does the individual know how to interact with the materials? Stated another way, when given leisure skill materials, can the participant use them appropriately? If not, then systematic instruction is required.

What is required for evaluating leisure skill proficiency is task analytic assessment (Knapczyk, 1975). An instructional objective must be written for a given material. The objective should reflect the specific skill that the teacher wants the child to learn. An example of a task analytic assessment for playing with a spinning top is provided in Table 7.1. The recording form indicates that, for the first 5 days of assessment (baseline), the child performed a total of three, three, two, four, and four steps, independently. This indicates that instruction should begin at step four in the task analysis.

There are multiple advantages of this type of observational assessment. First, the information collected about the child on this particular play skill helps the teacher to pinpoint the exact point at which instruction should begin. In this way, the child does not receive instruction on skills in which he is already proficient. Second, this facilitates step by step individualized instruction for children with complex learning problems. Evaluation of the child's proficiency with different toys over an extended period of time will also be more objective, precise, and less subject to instructor bias.

## Duration of Activity

As suggested by the findings of Reid, Willis, Jarman, and Brown (1978), if the individual has some degree of proficiency with leisure materials, then the instructional variable of interest may be the duration or length of time the participant engages in the activity. This is assessed by recording the length of time devoted to different activities. Because this may be an extremely time consuming measure to use with several individuals, the teacher may elect to observe only half the participants one day and the other half the next. Another option would be to record activity involvement only twice a week instead of daily.

The length of independent leisure activity is particularly important to assess because of its relevance to most home situations, where parents cannot constantly occupy time with their handicapped child. A frequently heard request from many parents is to teach the child to play independently, thereby relieving the family of continual supervision. A careful assessment of the child's duration of leisure activity before instruction will help the teacher and parents set realistic independent leisure goals for the child. Figure 7.1 presents a sample data collection sheet.

## Appropriate Versus Inappropriate Object Manipulation

Another assessment issue faced by instructors and researchers is differentiating between appropriate actions with objects versus actions that would not be considered appropriate. Several play studies failed to address this issue (Burney, Russell, & Shores, 1977; Favell & Cannon, 1977; Wehman, 1977). Those behaviors typically considered as inappropriate play actions are harmful or destructive to the child, peers, or materials. However, many profoundly mentally retarded and autistic children will exhibit high rates of repetitive, self-stimulated behavior with toys (e.g., banging, pounding, slamming) that are not necessarily harmful or destructive, yet, are still inappropriate. Furthermore, the problem is compounded because, with certain objects, banging or slamming actions may actually be appropriate. Many children will do unusual things with toys that *might* be considered appropriate by other observers (Goetz & Baer, 1973).

Hence, instructors are faced with how to assess the qualitative nature of object manipulation. There are several ways of coping with this difficulty. The first one involves using two or three observers periodically and having these observers rate the appropriateness of the action. Objective judging provides a check and balance system for the teacher. A second method of assess-

**Table 7.1.** Task Analytic Assessment for Playing with a Top

|  | M | T | W | Th | F |
|---|---|---|---|---|---|
| 1. S approaches top | + | + | + | + | + |
| 2. S places hands on top | + | + | + | + | + |
| 3. S finds handle of top | + | + | − | + | + |
| 4. S pushes handle down on top once | − | − | − | + | + |
| 5. S brings handle up | − | − | − | − | − |
| 6. S brings handle down on top twice | − | − | − | − | − |
| 7. S brings handle up each time | − | − | − | − | − |
| 8. S brings handle down on top three times | − | − | − | − | − |
| 9. S brings handle up each time | − | − | − | − | − |
| 10. S brings handle down on top four times | − | − | − | − | − |
| 11. S brings handle up each time | − | − | − | − | − |
| 12. S brings handle down on top five times | − | − | − | − | − |
| 13. S brings handle up each time | − | − | − | − | − |
| 14. S stops top from spinning | − | − | − | − | − |
| 15. S puts top away | − | − | − | − | − |

ing appropriateness of object manipulation is to identify the principle actions that a nonhandicapped child of comparable mental age might carry out with each object (Fredericks et al., 1978). These actions may serve as guidelines.

Identifying a number of fine-motor categories for object manipulation is yet another means of coding the qualitative nature of responses. This requires generating a fine-motor classification system that observers can use as a basis for recording actions. Tilton and Ottinger (1964, p. 968) provided nine categories, which are self-explanatory and were identified after extensive observational analysis of normal, trainable retarded, and autistic children:

1. Repetitive manual manipulation
2. Oral contacts
3. Pounding
4. Throwing
5. Pushing or pulling
6. Personalized toy use
7. Manipulation of movable parts
8. Separation of parts of toys
9. Combinational uses of toys

## Leisure Preference Evaluation

Public Law 94-142 mandated a crucial role for parents and students in the planning of individualized educational programs for handicapped students. Curriculum developers are expected to encourage maximum parental and student participation in the selection of goals and methods to best meet the needs of such students. Unfortunately, educators and recreation professionals are

| Leisure Skill Object | Minutes/Seconds Engaged with Object | Type of Action |
| --- | --- | --- |
| 1. Waterpaints | | |
| 2. Record | | |
| 3. Plants | | |
| 4. Autoharp | | |
| 5. Ball | | |
| 6. Magazine | | |
| 7. Target Game | | |
| 8. Lincoln Logs | | |
| 9. Viewfinder | | |
| 10. Pinball machine | | |

**Figure 7.1.** Initial object assessment

accustomed to making unilateral decisions in the planning process and, consequently, may lack the inclination or skills to honor student preferences. Interestingly, in Matthews' (1982) study, a comparison of the recreational preferences of mentally retarded and nonmentally retarded children revealed many similarities between the two groups.

Assessing favorite leisure activities is an important step in initiating a recreation program. The goal in this process is to identify which, if any, activities are preferred by the participant. This is a fairly easy task. By employing duration assessment, the amount of minutes or seconds spent with each leisure material can be recorded. This observation and recording should take place for at least a week.

A second means of assessing leisure preferences is through presenting a small number of different materials and determining the amount of time before the participant responds. This is referred to as a *latency measure of behavior.* McCall (1974) has used latency as a measure of length of time that elapsed before infants acted on a variety of objects, each possessing different stimulus attributes such as configural complexity or sound potential. Through measuring passage of time until a response, teachers may be able to evaluate the relative attractiveness of and preferences for certain materials with severely handicapped individuals.

## Frequency of Interactions

For many severely handicapped children, an important instructional goal is to initiate and sustain more frequent interactions with peers. A relatively common occurrence may be the presence of several handicapped children each playing in isolation during free play (Fredericks et al., 1978). When this happens, the potential benefits of social interaction are not accrued.

One way of assessing social interaction is a simple count of the number of times one child (a) initiates an interaction, (b) receives an interaction, and (c) terminates interaction. Duration assessment may be used to measure the length of the interaction between peers or between the child and adults in the room.

A second means of gathering more information on social interactions is the coding of specific types of interactions. Carney and her associates (1977, p.67) detailed the following social interaction skills:

1. Receives Interaction
   Receives hug
   Returns smile
   Gives object to other who has requested it
   Returns a greeting
   "Receives" cooperative play
   Answers questions
   Recognizes peers, teachers by name
   Shows approval
   Discriminates appropriate time, place, situation before receiving
2. Initiates Interaction
   Greets another person
   Requests objects from another person
   Initiates cooperative play
   Seeks approval
   Seeks affiliation with familiar person
   Helps one who has difficulty manipulating environment
   Initiates conversation
3. Sustaining Interactions
   Attends to on-going cooperative activity
   Sustains conversation
4. Terminates Interactions
   Terminates cooperative play activity
   Terminates conversation

This sequence provides an important step toward detailing the specific skills that teachers should be attempting to elicit in delayed children. In addition to providing sequence, these skills may be task-analyzed and the child's proficiency on selected behaviors assessed. These four categories of interaction can be employed to code the qualitative nature of the interaction (Hamre-Nietupski & Williams, 1977).

## Direction of Interaction

Analyzing to whom interactions are directed may also be helpful in assessing which individuals in the play environment are reinforcing to the child. As Beveridge, Spencer, and Miller (1978) observed, child–teacher interactions occur more frequently than child–child interactions, especially with severely delayed children. Structured intervention by an adult is usually required to increase child–child interactions (Shores, Hester, & Strain, 1976).

When making home visits and observing the child playing with siblings or neighborhood children, the direction of interactions should be assessed. This should be done not only with handicapped children but also with nonhandicapped peers. This type of behavioral analysis can be revealing, since most nonhandicapped children do not include handicapped children in play unless prompted and reinforced by adults (Apolloni & Cooke, 1978).

In conducting a behavioral assessment of social interactions, the checklist below might be utilized as a means of coding a number of interactions:

| NAME | INITIATED INTERACTION | RECEIVED INTERACTION |
|------|----------------------|---------------------|
| Herman | | |
| Roselyn | | |
| Dorene | | |
| Sydney | | |

This form, however, would not allow for analyzing the direction of interactions. The following checklist would facilitate assessing which peers or adults the child interacted with:

| | Herman | Roselyn | Dorene | Sydney | Instructor |
|------|--------|---------|--------|--------|-----------|
| Herman | X | | | | |
| Roselyn | | X | | | |
| Dorene | | | X | | |
| Sydney | | | | X | |

## Free Play Assessment

In some cases, there may be little interest or time to collect the specific types of information just discussed. Some teachers may want to consider using a simpler method of assessing the level of free play at which the child is functioning.

One such strategy makes use of Parten's (1932) developmental sequence:

autistic–unoccupied–independent–observing–attempt–associative–cooperative interaction. With this strategy, the teacher clearly defines the types of behaviors that are characteristic of the different developmental levels of play. For example, in the autistic play stage, characteristic behaviors might include not touching or physically acting on any play materials during free play periods or nonfunctional repetitive actions for long periods of time. Independent play might be considered as any appropriate play behaviors exhibited alone or away from other peers. Cooperative or social play would be another skill level in the basic developmental sequence and would include such skills as physical or verbal interaction with other peers and teachers (Fredericks et al., 1978).

This assessment strategy is convenient and economical in terms of time expended and can allow for ease in collecting fairly accurate information provided the categories are clearly defined and, therefore, easy to discriminate. This type of behavioral assessment does not, however, capture many of the collateral skills that are clearly associated with play skill development such as fine-motor skills, changes in emotionality, and social behavior.

Schleien (1982) demonstrated the use of this assessment approach in a study with severely learning disabled children. The study attempted to determine whether an individualized leisure education instructional program could produce significant gains in cooperative leisure time use during free play in the classroom.

Twenty-three students in two classrooms were assessed to determine their leisure skill competencies, repertoires, and activity/material preferences. Four categories of developmental levels of play (i.e., inappropriate, isolate, parallel, cooperative) were derived from the Social Interaction Rating Scale, an eight-point scale used to measure the level of social behavior of young severely mentally retarded children in a free play setting (Paloutzian et al., 1971). Paloutzian's levels were adapted from those used by Parten and Newhall (1943) for intellectually average children. The operational definitions of the modified developmental levels of play (adapted by Schleien) follow.

### Inappropriate Play

Percentage of time student plays or uses free time inappropriately: manipulates or uses toys, objects, or recreation materials incorrectly; engages in socially inappropriate behavior (e.g., verbal/physical abuse of others); manipulation of chronological age-inappropriate toys, objects, or recreation materials (determined by manufacturer's age level recommendation); non-goal directed, nonfunctional, purposeless behavior; stereotypic behavior (e.g., self-stimulation).

### Isolate Play

Percentage of time student plays/manipulates toys, objects, or recreation materials appropriately, but in a solitary manner (not within 5 feet of another peer).

*Parallel Play*

Percentage of time student plays with or manipulates toys, objects, or recreation materials appropriately, in the presence of a peer, but not cooperatively: although other peers are within 5 feet, student does not interact with them (i.e., makes no attempt to talk to, hand toy to, touch, etc.)

*Cooperative Play*

Percentage of time student plays with or manipulates toys, objects, or recreation materials in an appropriate and cooperative fashion (i.e., interacts socially with peers, engages in play with another and joins in a cooperative, give-and-take manner; no hitting or yelling at each other; also, shares toys, objects, or game).

The leisure education instructional program, including exposure to cooperative games and materials and leisure skills instruction, using applied behavior analysis (e.g., modeling, social reinforcement), was an effective means of facilitating cooperative leisure skills. The intervention program was shown to have a functional relationship with socially appropriate activity; concurrently, inappropriate social behaviors were reduced in all of the students. Results from this study indicated that children with severe learning disabilities can acquire a more diverse repertoire of social and cooperative leisure skills than has been previously demonstrated in the literature.

## PROGRAMMING FOR COOPERATIVE PLAY: STATE OF THE ART

There have been a number of studies describing the development of cooperative play with severely handicapped persons. A limitation related to the population studied is that these efforts often fall far short of the sustained cooperative play documented by the early childhood researchers, such as Parten and Newhall (1943), Gesell (1940), and more recently, Barnes (1971).

Whitman, Mercurio, and Caponigri (1970), for example, trained two severely mentally retarded children to roll a ball back and forth. Extensive physical guidance and modeling were required before the children performed the skill under the trainer's verbal cues. Generalization was achieved through phasing in two other peers and having them enter into the ball rolling game.

A similar study, but with a greater emphasis on comparing the effects of a higher functioning peer model versus an adult model, has also been carried out with an extremely withdrawn, profoundly mentally retarded boy (Morris & Dolker, 1974). Ball rolling was also the skill being trained. Results indicated that no significant differences were found between models and that extensive behavior shaping, e.g., physical guidance, was required in addition to modeling for the behavior to develop.

In a study with TMR students (Knapczyk & Peterson, 1975), nonmentally retarded, older children were integrated into the playroom with the TMR children and encouraged to interact through cooperative play. It was discovered that substantially increased rates of cooperative play occurred with the normal models. This was empirically evaluated in a reversal design with the results that cooperative play levels decreased to baseline levels when these models were removed.

A second study carried out by the same investigators was equally revealing. Introduction of nonmentally retarded, preschool children of equivalent mental ages but younger chronological ages (3- and 4-year-olds) led to few changes in cooperative play levels of the same TMR students. Knapczyk and Peterson (1975) interpret these findings as an indication that competence in models, when viewed by less competent observers, influences the likelihood of behavior being imitated.

A recent study illustrates the potential of arranging the environment in such a way to promote playful activity (Strain, 1975). In this program, eight severely mentally retarded preschoolers listened while the teacher read stories to them; each child was then given an opportunity to pretend he or she was one of the characters in the story. Immediately after story-telling time was over, the children were encouraged to engage in cooperative play. Evaluation through a reversal design revealed that socio-dramatic storytelling increased the frequency of cooperative play responses.

Imitation has proven to be an effective means of training severely mentally retarded children and adolescents in cooperative play skills. This is further supported in the often cited study by Paloutzian and his colleagues (1971). Imitation training was given to 10 severely and profoundly mentally retarded children. With the development of generalized imitation skills, cooperative play behaviors were acquired. Children were trained through modeling to pull peers in wagons, engage in cooperative ball games, and share play materials.

This general strategy of extensive modeling and direct intervention has also been carried out with severely handicapped adolescents and adults (Wehman, 1976). Workshop clients were shaped into different cooperative play experiences by adult trainers with the use of physical guidance.

One of the most comprehensive efforts at analyzing the instructional components of social interaction training can be found in the excellent work by Williams and his associates (Williams, 1975) with TMR students. These workers analyzed social interaction into four components: initiates interaction; receives interaction; sustains interaction; and terminates interaction. Peer functioning level, task availability, and training across environmental settings were major points considered by these programmers when arranging an appropriate environment for social interaction. Several task analyses for leisure time programs (e.g., use of a Viewmaster, playing Old Maid) were also presented. What makes this research unique is the explicit instructional direction given for carrying out the program. Also, supportive data was given for each program that was completed by the student.

There are numerous strategies through which the goal of cooperative play and social interaction between two or more peers can be attained. Some of these include

1. A child can be paired with an adult trainer and trained in different play situations.
2. A child can be paired with a higher functioning, although still retarded, peer, who engages in appropriate play (Morris & Dolker, 1974).
3. A child can be paired with a nonmentally retarded peer, who engages in appropriate play.
4. Two equivalent (low functioning) peers can be paired and trained by one or more adult trainers (Wehman, 1976).
5. A group of severely handicapped children can be integrated with non-mentally retarded peers (Knapczyk & Peterson, 1975).
6. Any of the previous combinations can be used and different types of reinforcement given; i.e., points, edibles, or praise for instances of cooperative play.
7. Environmental arrangements preceding the onset of play sessions may be manipulated through toy selection, room size, or background music.

These different strategies have yet to be exhaustively examined by programmers or researchers. It is frequently believed by many teachers and therapeutic recreation specialists that severely handicapped individuals do not and will not interact socially or play cooperatively. It should be emphasized that verbal language is not required for cooperative play; nonverbal language can be a most efficient means of communication for children with severe handicaps, provided training is given. Toys and play materials are excellent vehicles for communication between peers as well as between student and teacher. Many institutionalized severely mentally retarded individuals have no desire or reason to communicate after years in a dismal and apathetic ward environment. Stimulating and attractive play materials that are associated with positively reinforcing play sessions can alter this limited incentive to communicate.

## LEISURE CURRICULUM FACILITATING SOCIAL INTERACTION

The balance of this chapter will provide selected individualized programs designed for severely handicapped children. These programs have been adopted from work on leisure skill curriculum development (Wehman & Schleien, 1981) and emphasize leisure skills that facilitate social interaction. The skills depicted are representative of the four program areas and are chronologically age appropriate for the preschool (0–6 years) and school-age (7–15 years) child.

## Toy Play

Toy play involves a participant's interaction with an inanimate object, either as an individual or as a member of a group. When two or more persons are involved, toy play can stimulate social and cooperative activity, allowing the participants to express themselves creatively and develop progressively higher skilled competencies. Because rules generally do not exist during toy play, the participants have the freedom to design activities commensurate to their own individual needs and interests.

### Preschool

Matchbox cars are a favorite with preschoolers. These are miniature cars, trucks, and motorcycles with wheels that turn, several with opening doors and hoods. These car models are inexpensive and relatively sturdy. By allowing the players to race their cars, an activity requiring cooperation, social skill development could be significantly enhanced. Besides the enjoyment from racing the cars, participants will gain an interest in collecting and trading them (see Figure 7.2).

### School Age

A frisbee is a saucer-shaped disc with a diameter of 10–12 inches. The frisbee has a rounded outer edge that is grooved and curves under for easy grasping. The frisbee could be tossed back and forth in a game, requiring each player to throw and catch it. A frisbee game is an excellent means to teach the participant to share, take turns, listen to others, and cooperate. Several players can participate simultaneously (see Figure 7.3).

## Games

Games are perhaps the purest form of recreation, with sheer pleasure being the primary motivating factor. Individuals engage in games because they particularly enjoy a given activity and appreciate the company of the other players. Games follow definite rules and may involve a wide range of functioning competencies, ranging from simple to complex levels of participation in cooperative and/or competitive interactions. Manipulation of an object or toy, taking turns, following rules, and the concept of winning and losing may all be learned through recreational games. Games can include board and table games, social (get acquainted) games, gross motor games, musical/rhythmical games, and card games.

### Preschool

London Bridge is a musical game that has been a favorite with children for years. The game is played in a group with two youngsters joining hands

*Name of Activity*: Race Matchbox Cars

*Instructional Objective*: Given a matchbox car and a second participant with a matchbox car, the participant will race the cars by pushing them forward 24″.

*Materials*: Two matchbox cars

| Task Analysis | Correction Procedures/Activity Guidelines/ Special Adaptations |
|---|---|
| 1. Assume squatting position: bending knees, lowering rear to ground. | 1. Teacher gives verbal cue to participant; if participant responds correctly, teacher provides reinforcement immediately. |
| 2. Extend dominant arm downward toward matchbox car, palm facing down. | 2. If participant does not respond correctly, then teacher repeats verbal cue and models correct response. |
| 3. Lower dominant arm until palm makes contact with top (roof) of matchbox car. | 3. If participant still does not respond correctly, then teacher repeats verbal cue and physically guides participant through correct response. |
| 4. Curl fingers around one side of matchbox car. | |
| 5. Wrap thumb around other side of matchbox car. | 4. This instructional sequence is repeated several times in each training session with participant. |
| 6. Apply inward pressure between thumb and fingers to grasp car firmly. | 5. The teacher may need to explain the meaning of the action verbs *go* and *stop* before the race begins. Subsequently, the participant will be able to follow the commands independently. |
| 7. Bend elbow, raising car off ground. | |
| 8. Position matchbox car 6″ from and parallel with second participant's car (both cars facing forward). | |
| 9. On verbal command "Go!", extend arm outward, applying downward and forward pressure onto car with hand, pushing car forward. | 6. Electric race car and track sets are available, which would require a minimum of motor activity to move cars around the track. |
| 10. When arm is fully extended, extend fingers and thumb, releasing car, causing car to "race" with second car. | 7. Weights attached to the bottoms of matchbox cars could prevent the participant from throwing the car rather than rolling it. |
| 11. Race car 6″. | |
| 12. Race car 12″. | |
| 13. Race car 24″. | |

**Figure 7.2.** "Race matchbox cars" activity

and holding them high above their heads to represent a bridge. The other players march around in a circle and underneath the bridge simultaneously with their singing of the song "London Bridge is Falling Down." When the words "my fair lady" are sung, the bridge falls on a player. That person then

*Name of Activity*: Catch Frisbee

*Instructional Objective*: Given a frisbee thrown by another person, the participant will catch the frisbee from 5' away.

*Materials*: Frisbee

| Task Analysis | Correction Procedures/Activity Guidelines/ Special Adaptations |
|---|---|
| 1. Stand 5' away from and the facing other player, feet parallel and shoulder's width apart. | 1. Teacher gives verbal cue, "Catch the frisbee," to participant; if participant responds correctly, teacher provides reinforcement immediately. |
| 2. Extend both arms outward toward other person, palms faced outward, fingers extended. | 2. If participant does not respond correctly, teacher repeats verbal cue and models correct response. |
| 3. Eye track path of frisbee through air. | 3. If participant still does not respond correctly, teacher repeats verbal cue and physically guides participant through correct response. |
| 4. As frisbee approaches, position palms directly parallel with frisbee. | |
| 5. When frisbee makes contact with palms, curl fingers inward toward palms until they are resting on top of frisbee, thumbs resting on underside of frisbee. | 4. Repeat instructional sequence, as needed, several times in each training session. |
| | 5. Participant may practice catching the frisbee as it is slid across the floor; as proficiency develops, the frisbee may be thrown through the air as the distance is gradually increased. |
| 6. Apply inward pressure between fingers and thumbs to grasp frisbee firmly, catching frisbee. | 6. Frisbees come in several sizes and weights and should be selected according to individual preference and skill level. |
| | 7. Initially, a Nerf frisbee could be used to prevent injury and to facilitate grasping. |
| | 8. Several players may play this game to increase opportunity for social interaction. |

**Figure 7.3.** "Catch frisbee" activity

joins the two players to enlarge the bridge. The children will acquire the ability to follow game procedures, work together in forming the bridge and will enjoy singing this popular tune together (see Figure 7.4).

*School Age*

As a chronologically age-appropriate active game for school-age children and older, musical chairs facilitates social development, as all players must march together and attempt to sit in a chair at the same time. Music is played and the children walk in a circle around the chairs (one less chair than number of players) until the music stops. When the music does stop, all players try to sit in the chairs. One person is left standing, and a chair is removed. Players do not have to be eliminated, but could remain seated without removing a chair. Players will learn to cooperate and gain an understanding of win and lose (see Figure 7.5).

## Community Activity/Hobbies

Activities and hobbies carried out in the community have potential for contributing to the development of life-long leisure skills. An individual may pursue a community activity or hobby as a youngster and continue to excel in and use those skills with increasing degrees of sophistication throughout his or her lifetime. Participation in community activities and hobbies tends to be less active than in either sports or other physical games and may include such activities as playing a musical instrument in a home rhythm band and a wide variety of arts and crafts activities. Participation in a community activity or hobby is usually of a noncompetitive nature, without the concepts of win and lose. Although we would hope that an interest in many of the different leisure skills would certainly develop throughout a person's lifetime, the skills in this activity area are typically most enduring for the individual.

*Preschool*
The ringing of an approaching ice cream truck is one of the most welcomed sounds a child will hear outdoors. The process of buying ice cream from a vendor requires the participant to wait his turn, learn to communicate and interact with others, receive an item from the ice cream vendor, pay for it, and possibly share it with a friend. All these component skills facilitate social development in some manner and, therefore, are important social skills. Throughout life, the child will be expected to take turns, wait in lines, purchase goods, and request assistance from others. Buying ice cream could be an enjoyable way to acquire essential social and daily living skills of relating and responding to others. This activity could be part of a leisure walk program (see Figure 7.6).

*School Age*
Fooseball, an enjoyable, age-appropriate form of entertainment for both school-age children and adults, is a table game that helps develop cooperative and competitive interactions. Requiring a minimum of two players, a social interaction is automatically arranged. Played like soccer, with a goal at either end of the board, the players stand at opposite sides of the board and manipulate levels that cause the fooseball men to block or kick the ball through a goal. To successfully engage in this game, each participant must be responsive to the opponent's actions, as well as work cooperatively with other team members (see Figure 7.7).

*Name of Activity*: London Bridge

*Instructional Objective*: Given knowledge of the London Bridge song, the participant will sing and continue to walk under the bridge until the bridge falls.

*Materials*: Five or More Players

| Task Analysis | Correction Procedures/Activity Guidelines/ Special Adaptations |
|---|---|
| *To Build Bridge*:<br><br>1. Stand facing other player.<br><br>2. Keeping arms extended, raise arms upward and outward until palms meet with other player's hands.<br><br>3. Interlock hands with other player by curling fingers through spaces of other player's fingers until participant's fingers touch back of other player's hands.<br><br>4. Maintain above stance allowing players to pass under bridge until bridge falls down catching one player.<br><br>*To Catch Player*:<br><br>5. Keeping hands clasped with other player, lower arms concurrently as one player is passing directly under bridge, until arms are surrounding caught player at waist.<br><br>6. Rock caught player by swaying arms first to one side and then to the other side of caught player's body.<br><br>7. Release hand grips by extending fingers and lowering arms toward body to make bridge fall.<br><br>8. Caught players become part of bridge until all players have been caught. | 1. Teacher gives verbal cue to participant; if participant responds correctly, teacher provides reinforcement immediately.<br><br>2. If participant does not respond correctly, then teacher repeats verbal cue and models correct response.<br><br>3. If participant still does not respond correctly, then teacher repeats verbal cue and physically guides participant through correct response.<br><br>4. This instructional sequence is repeated several times in each training session with participant.<br><br>5. This musical game is an excellent facilitator of social skill development, as all players must work cooperatively to form bridge.<br><br>6. To make game more realistic for participants, the name of the bridge could be changed from London Bridge to another name of a bridge in the player's hometown (e.g., in New York, Brooklyn Bridge).<br><br>7. Players unfamiliar with game could be paired with more competent individuals to form bridge.<br><br>8. Players should be encouraged to sing along after they have learned the motions of the game. Participants physically unable to play could be singers, therefore, all may be participating in one way or another.<br><br>9. Players forming bridge should be encouraged to be gentle when catching a player, making sure not to hit a player's head as the bridge falls. |

**Figure 7.4.** "London Bridge" activity

# Sports

The distinction between sports and games is often characterized by a time line. Although activities falling in both categories employ a definite set of rules, sports tend to contain greater sophistication in the rules and equipment

*Name of Activity*: Musical Chairs

*Instructional Objective*: Given several participants and one less chair, arranged in a circle with backs of chairs toward inside of circle, and a source of music that can be turned on and off, participants will walk around the chairs to the music, sitting down in a chair when the music stops.

*Materials*: Record player, record, 5 (or more) participants, 1 less chair than the number of players.

| Task Analysis | Correction Procedures/Activity Guidelines/ Special Adaptations |
|---|---|
| 1. Listen for music to begin. | 1. Teacher gives verbal cue to participant; if participant responds correctly, teacher provides reinforcement immediately. |
| 2. Walk around chairs in clockwise direction as music plays. | 2. If participant does not respond correctly, then teacher repeats verbal cue and models correct response. |
| 3. Sit in closest chair as soon as music stops. | 3. If participant still does not respond correctly, then teacher repeats verbal cue and physically guides participant through correct response. |
| 4. Participant who is unable to find vacant chair must leave circle. | 4. This instructional sequence is repeated several times in each training session with participant. |
| 5. Remove chair from circle. | 5. Game may be played by nonambulatory persons by merely outlining areas on floor with tape that participants move to when music stops. |
| 6. Continue to play until one participant (winner) is remaining. | 6. A cassette tape player may be used allowing a participant to stop and start the music by merely pressing a button on the deck. |
| | 7. Players who have left the game should be encouraged to cheer or otherwise stay involved so as to maintain interest in the game. A player who is "out" can control the music or could remain seated without removing a chair so as not to be eliminated. |
| | 8. Players should be encouraged to march with their knees raised high to avoid running around the chairs. |

**Figure 7.5.** "Musical chairs" activity

used, with greater emphasis placed on the competitive aspects of the activity. An individual's skill repertoire should include both individual and team sports requiring various degrees of social and motor coordination. Severely handicapped children are becoming more active in sports nationwide as can be observed by the increased interest in Special Olympics and wheelchair sports and games.

*Name of Activity*: Buy Ice Cream from Ice Cream Truck

*Instructional Objective*: Given an ice cream truck, the participant will purchase ice cream from the vendor.

*Materials*: Ice cream truck, money.

| Task Analysis | Correction Procedures/Activity Guidelines/ Special Adaptations |
|---|---|
| 1. Walk to ice cream truck, holding money in dominant hand using palmar grasp. | 1. Teacher gives verbal cue to participant; if participant responds correctly, teacher provides reinforcement immediately. |
| 2. Stand opposite vendor's window. | 2. If participant does not respond correctly, then teacher repeats verbal cue and models correct response. |
| 3. When asked, name or point to desired ice cream item. | |
| 4. Release money onto counter by extending fingers. | 3. If participant still does not respond correctly, then teacher repeats verbal cue and physically guides participant through correct response. |
| 5. Grasp ice cream with dominant hand using palmar grasp. | 4. This instructional sequence is repeated several times in each training session with participant. |
| 6. Wait for change, if appropriate. | 5. This activity could be simulated in the classroom using a large piece of cardboard as the ice cream truck, and a bell. Pictures of various ice cream items could be painted on the cardboard. Have participants walk up to the window (cut a section out of cardboard) and purchase ice cream using poker chips. A quantity of ice cream cones could be bought and hidden behind the cardboard, so that each participant is reinforced with ice cream during the practice session. |
| 7. Walk away from ice cream truck, carrying change, and eat ice cream. | |
| | 6. The teacher could contact the local ice cream vendor and request a special trip to the playground for the benefit of participants. Perhaps this could become a weekly summer treat for them. |
| | 7. Participants will probably learn very quickly to associate the sound of the bell with the approaching ice cream truck. |

**Figure 7.6.** "Buy ice cream" activity

## Preschool

A seesaw is a piece of recreational equipment found in playgrounds and schoolyards across the nation. It requires the cooperation of two individuals, one to raise and the other to lower their ends of the board concordantly.

*Name of Activity:* Fooseball

*Instructional Objective:* Given a fooseball table and another player, the participant will manipulate the two rows of playing men to hit the ball into the opponent's goal to score 1 point (first player to score 7 points wins the game).

*Materials:* Fooseball table.

| Task Analysis | Correction Procedures/Activity Guidelines/ Special Adaptations |
|---|---|
| 1. Stand facing levers on side of fooseball table. | 1. Teacher gives verbal cue to participant; if participant responds correctly, teacher provides reinforcement immediately. |
| 2. Grasp levers with both hands using palmar grasp. | 2. If participant does not respond correctly, teacher repeats verbal cue and models correct response. |
| 3. Eye track path of ball across table. | |
| 4. Position one row of playing men directly in path of ball by either extending arm or bending it at elbow, pushing or pulling appropriate lever to move row of men laterally across table. | 3. If participant still does not respond correctly, teacher repeats verbal cue and physically guides participant through correct response. |
| | 4. Repeat instructional sequence several times as needed in each training session. |
| 5. When ball makes contact with playing man and has been stopped, quickly rotate wrist counterclockwise to turn appropriate lever, causing playing man to make contact with ball, hitting ball forward toward opponent's goal. | 5. Levers can be enlarged with adhesive tape or sponge to facilitate grasping. |
| | 6. For participants in wheelchairs, the table can be lowered to a comfortable level and the levers lengthened by attaching wooden dowels to them. |
| 6. Opponent attempts to block ball. | 7. A heavier ball, the same size as a standard fooseball, can be used to slow down the pace of the game. |
| 7. Hit ball into goal, scoring 1 point. | |
| 8. Continue playing until one player scores 7 points to win game. | 8. Since each side of the table has four levers, with proficiency, two teams of two players each can compete against each other. |

**Figure 7.7.** "Play fooseball" activity

Participants take turns raising their side of the seesaw off the ground. Several games could be played on the seesaw, as the participants must work cooperatively to gain success. If one player does not cooperate, success will not be reached. Children learn to trust each other and take turns.

*School Age*

    Volleyball, a team sport, is an excellent facilitator of both motor and social skill development. As it promotes jumping, striking, and locomotor skills,

*Name of Activity*: Seesaw Play

*Instructional Objective*: Given an 8' seesaw, the participant will raise and lower the seesaw while sitting on it, in concordance with another player, three consecutive times.

*Materials*: Seesaw

| Task Analysis | Correction Procedures/Activity Guidelines/ Special Adaptations |
|---|---|
| 1. Stand facing left side of seesaw, feet parallel and 6" apart. | 1. Teacher gives verbal cue to participant; if participant responds correctly, teacher provides reinforcement immediately. |
| 2. Bend knee of right leg, lifting foot over seat of seasaw. | 2. If participant does not respond correctly, then teacher repeats verbal cue and models correct response. |
| 3. Lower rear to seesaw. | |
| 4. Lower right foot to ground. | 3. If participant still does not respond correctly, then teacher repeats verbal cue and physically guides participant through correct response. |
| 5. Extend arms outward toward handles of seesaw, palms faced down. | |
| 6. Lower arms until palms make contact with handle. | 4. This instructional sequence is repeated several times in each training session with participant. |
| 7. Curl fingers around handle. | 5. If it is believed that the participant cannot hold onto the handle and remain seated when lifted into the air on the seesaw, the teacher may initially sit on the seesaw with the participant. In this way, the danger of participant falling off is diminished and the range of motion is still experienced. |
| 8. Wrap thumbs around opposite side of handle. | |
| 9. Apply inward pressure between thumbs and fingers to grasp handle firmly. | |
| 10. Extend knees, pushing off from feet, raising seesaw into air. | 6. Before a conventional playground seesaw is used, a miniature one should be practiced on. A Gym-Dandy space rocker works the same way except that the participants are not raised into the air and the danger of falling to the ground is reduced. This space rocker seats three persons (one in the center), and is an excellent means for participants to learn appropriate seesaw body movements. |
| 11. As seesaw descends, lower feet onto ground, bending knees as seesaw touches ground. | |
| 12. Go up and down on the seesaw second time. | |
| 13. Go up and down on seesaw third time. | |

**Figure 7.8.** "Seesaw play" activity

volleyball also encourages cooperation and teamwork as each player depends on his or her teammates to get the ball over the net without letting it hit the ground. The rotation of players also facilitates social interaction and allows each player to share equally in the opportunity to play each position, including the serving position.

*Name of Activity*: Volleyball: Underhand Serve

*Instructional Objective*: Given a volleyball and a volleyball net, the participant will serve the ball over the net in an underhand fashion from 10' away.

*Materials*: Volleyball, net

| Task Analysis | Correction Procedures/Activity Guidelines/ Special Adaptations |
|---|---|
| 1. Stand at back right corner of court behind end line, feet parallel and shoulder's width apart, facing net 10' away. | 1. Teacher gives verbal cue to participant; if participant responds correctly, teacher provides reinforcement immediately. |
| 2. Grasp ball with both hands on either side of ball. | 2. If participant does not respond correctly, teacher repeats verbal cue and models correct response. |
| 3. Rotate hands and ball counterclockwise so that dominant hand is resting on top of ball and nondominant hand is supporting ball on the bottom. | 3. If participant still does not respond correctly, teacher repeats verbal cue and physically guides participant through correct response. |
| 4. Release ball with dominant hand allowing ball to rest in palm of nondominant hand. | 4. Repeat instructional sequence several times, as needed in each training session. |
| 5. Extend arm of nondominant arm, moving ball outward to front of body. | 5. Underhand serve may be performed with a close-fisted hand or with an open hand (hitting ball with heel of palm). Ball will usually travel farther when fist is used. |
| 6. Curl fingers of dominant hand inward to palm, making a fist. | 6. Initially, participant should serve ball a short distance from net to assure success. As skill develops, participant may gradually back up to end line. |
| 7. Extend arm of dominant arm, bringing fist downward to side of body. | 7. As lead-up activity to underhand serve, participant could throw ball required distance over net (as in "Newcomb" game). |
| 8. Quickly flex elbow, raising fist upward and outward toward lower half of ball. | 8. To improve eye-hand coordination and to simplify task, participant may practice serving balloon or beach ball instead of standard volleyball. |
| 9. Continue to raise fist upward against ball, hitting it forward, serving ball 2'. | |
| 10. Serve ball 4', 6', 8', then 10' over net. | |

**Figure 7.9.** "Underhand serve" activity

## SUMMARY

The purpose of this chapter has been to discuss the implementation and development of social and leisure skills in severely handicapped children. With appropriate assessment techniques, skill selection, instructional strategies and skill adaptations, severely handicapped children will learn to play cooperatively and, as a consequence, develop socially.

A section of this chapter described several areas of leisure skill competency that can be assessed in severely handicapped children: the *proficiency* with which toys, objects, or materials were engaged; the *length* of self-initiated action; materials *preferred* by clients; and frequency and direction of social *interactions*.

When these assessment and intervention strategies are used in conjunction with a logically sequenced recreation curriculum and instructional technology, the application of the systematic instruction process to leisure skill development is complete.

The latter part of the chapter presented a series of recreational programs that have been task-analyzed and specially adapted for implementation with severely handicapped preschoolers and school-age children. The ultimate goal of any such recreational program is for the individual to develop an age-appropriate leisure skill repertoire, in order to use leisure time constructively and acquire the necessary social skills that facilitate daily independent living within the community, home, or agency.

## REFERENCES

Apolloni, T., & Cooke, T. (1978). Integrated programming at the infant, toddler, and preschool levels. In M. Guaralnick (Ed.), *Early intervention and the integration of handicapped and nonhandicapped children*. Baltimore: University Park Press.

Barnes, K. (1971). Preschool play, norms: A replication. *Developmental Psychology, 5,* 99-103.

Beveridge, M., Spencer, J., & Miller, P. (1978). Language and social behavior in severely educationally subnormal children. *British Journal of Social and Clinical Psychology, 17,* 75-83.

Brewer, G., & Kakalik, J. (1979). *Handicapped children: Strategies for improving services.* New York: McGraw-Hill.

Burney, J., Russell, B., & Shores, R. (1977). Developing social responses in two profoundly retarded children. *AAESPH Review, 2,* 53-63.

Carney, I., Clobuciar, A., Corley, E., Wilcox, B., Bigler, J., Fleisler, L., Pany, D., & Turner, P. (1977). Social interaction in severely handicapped students. In *The severely and profoundly handicapped child.* Springfield, IL: State Department of Education.

Collard, K. (1981). Leisure education in the schools: Why, who, and the need for advocacy. *Therapeutic Recreation Journal, 15,* 8-16.

Favell, J. (1973). Reduction of stereotypes by reinforcement of toy play. *Mental Retardation, 11,* 21-23.

Favell, J., & Cannon, P. R. (1977). Evaluation of entertainment materials for severely retarded persons. *American Journal of Mental Deficiency, 81,* 357-361.

Fredericks, H., Baldwin, V., Grove, D., Moore, W., Riggs, C., & Lyons, B. (1978). Integrating the moderately and severely handicapped preschool child into a normal day care setting. In M. Guaralnick (Ed.), *Early intervention and the integration of handicapped and nonhandicapped children*. Baltimore: University Park Press.

Gesell, A. (1940). *First five years of life.* New York: Harper.

Goetz, E., & Baer, D. (1973). Social control of form diversity and the emergence of new forms in children's blockbuilding. *Journal of Applied Behavior Analysis, 6,* 209–217.

Hamre-Nietupski, S., & Williams, W. (1977). Implementation of selected sex education and social skills programs with severely handicapped students. *Education and Training of the Mentally Retarded, 12,* 364–372.

Knapczyk, D. (1975). Task analytic assessment of severe learning problems. *Education and Training of the Mentally Retarded, 16,* 24–27.

Knapczyk, D., & Peterson, N. (1975). Task analytic assessment of severe learning problems. *Education of Mentally Retarded, 10,* 74–77.

Knapczyk, D., & Yoppi, J. (1975). Development of cooperative and competitive play responses in developmentally disabled children. *American Journal on Mental Deficiency, 80,* 245–255.

Matthews, D. (1982). Some recreation preferences of the mentally retarded. *Therapeutic Recreation Journal, 16,* 42–47.

McCall, R. (1974). *Exploratory manipulation and play in the human infant.* Monograph of Society for Research on Child Development. Chicago, IL: University of Chicago Press.

Morris, R., & Dolker, M. (1974). Developing cooperative play in socially withdrawn retarded children. *Mental Retardation, 12,* 24–27.

Neal, L. (1970). *Recreation's role in the rehabilitation of the mentally retarded.* Eugene, OR: University of Oregon Rehabilitation and Training Center in Mental Retardation.

Novak, A., & Heal, L. (Eds.). (1980). *Integration of developmentally disabled individuals into the community.* Baltimore: Paul H. Brookes Publishing.

Paloutzian, R., Hasazi, J., Streifel, J., & Edgard, C. (1971). Promotion of positive social interactions in severely retarded young children. *American Journal of Mental Deficiency, 75,* 519–524.

Parten, M. B. (1932). Social play among school children. *Journal of Abnormal Psychology, 28,* 136–147.

Parten, M., & Newhall, S. (1943). Social behavior of preschool children. In R. Barker, J. Kounin, & H. Wright (Eds.), *Child behavior and development.* New York: McGraw-Hill.

President's Committee on Mental Retardation. (1974). *America's needs in habilitation and employment of the mentally retarded.* Washington, DC: U.S. Government Printing Office.

Reid, D., Willis, B., Jarman, P., & Brown, K. (1978). Increasing leisure activity of physically disabled retarded persons through modifying resource availability. *AAESPH Review, 3,* 78–93.

Samaras, M., & Ball, T. (1975). Reinforcement of cooperation between profoundly retarded adults. *American Journal on Mental Deficiency, 80,* 63–71.

Schleien, S. (1982). Leisure education for the learning disabled student. *Learning Disabilities, 1,* 105–122.

Schleien, S., Kiernan, J., & Wehman, P. (1981). Evaluation of an age-appropriate leisure skills program for moderately retarded adults. *Education and Training of the Mentally Retarded, 16,* 13–19.

Shores, R., Hester, P., & Strain, P. (1976). The effects of amount and type of teacher–child interaction on child–child interaction during free play. *Psychology in the Schools, 13,* 171–175.

Strain, P. (1975). Increasing social play of severely retarded preschoolers through social dramatic activities. *Mentally Retarded, 13,* 7–9.

Tilton, J., & Ottinger, D. (1964). Comparison of toy play behavior of autistic, retarded and normal children. *Psychological Reports, 15*, 967–975.

U.S. Department of Health and Human Services. (1979). *Plain talk about children with learning disabilities.* Rockville, MD: Alcohol, Drug Abuse, and Mental Health Administration.

Verhoven, P., & Goldstein, J. (1976). *Leisure activity participation and handicapped populations.* Arlington, VA: National Recreation and Park Association.

Wehman, P. (1976). A leisure time activities curriculum for the developmentally disabled. *Education and Training of the Mentally Retarded, 11*, 309–313.

Wehman, P. (1977). Research on leisure time and the severely developmentally disabled. *Rehabilitation Literature, 38*, 98–105.

Wehman, P. (1979). Toward a recreation curriculum for developmentally disabled persons. In P. Wehman (Ed.), *Recreation programming for developmentally disabled persons.* Baltimore: University Park Press.

Wehman, P., & Schleien, S. (1981). *Leisure programs for handicapped persons: Adaptations, techniques, and curriculum.* Baltimore: University Park Press.

Whitman, T., Mercurio, J., & Caponigri, V. (1970). Development of social responses in severely retarded children. *Journal of Applied Behavioral Responses, 3*, 133–138.

Williams, W. (1975). Procedures of task analysis as related to developing instructional programs for the severely handicapped. In L. Brown, T. Craivner, W. Williams, & R. York (Eds.), *Madison alternatives to zero exclusions: A book of readings.* Madison, WI: Madison Public Schools.

Wuerch, B., & Voeltz, L. (1982). *Longitudinal leisure skills for severely handicapped learners: The Ho'onanea curriculum component.* Baltimore: Paul H. Brookes Publishing.

Zigmond, N. (1978). A prototype of comprehensive service for secondary students with learning disabilities: A preliminary report. *Learning Disabilities Quarterly, 1*, 39–49.

# 8
# Developing Social Skills Instruction for Peer Interaction and Relationships

Sherri Oden

Considering the growth of research supporting the usefulness of social skills instruction to children's learning, the educational applications of this research should receive enthusiastic attention from parents and teachers. Earlier research showed that a child's peer acceptance is partly a function of peer values and receptivity to the child's gender, racial or cultural membership, physical attractiveness and skill, and achievement (see Asher, Oden, & Gottman, 1977). Whether a child will actually be neglected or rejected by peers also appears to be influenced by the various characteristics and opportunities inherent in the educational context and by the child's own social competence (see Oden, 1982b).

In general, children who are disliked by peers have been found to be more aggressive, disruptive, and inappropriate in their actions, whereas children who are neglected or less known by peers (often referred to as withdrawn or isolated) are found to lack skills for social initiative and participation (Coie, Dodge, & Coppotelli, 1982; Dodge, 1983; Gottman, 1977). Low peer status, without intervention, has been found to have considerable stability over a period of several years (Coie & Dodge, 1983) and even until young adulthood (Cowen, Pederson, Babigian, Izzo, & Trost, 1973). Children with negative social behaviors appear to be especially likely to maintain low peer acceptance over time (Coie & Dodge, 1983). Studies to be discussed here demonstrate that social skill instruction methods can be used to intervene in cases of low peer acceptance.

It is not clear exactly why social skill instruction can be effective. The methods appear to foster social knowledge, behavioral enactment, and rehearsal of social strategies that are normative; that is, generally valued and expected in peer interaction and relationships. The methods also appear to foster social judgment as children are asked to evaluate their behavior in terms of its consequences for them and their partners by weighing the behavior in reference to specific situations and peers. The methods can be compared to those used by parents with young children, who are coached to enter peer groups, make friends, and resolve disputes.

An educator or parent should bear in mind some very general guidelines, prior to planning a social skill intervention approach or curriculum. First, attention must be given both to the quantity and quality, or appropriateness, of social behaviors to be learned (Asher & Renshaw, 1981; Ladd & Oden, 1979). One should not look for many absolutes here, because peer groups will differ with age, cultural, and situational factors. Rather, it is proposed that there may be a *threshold for acceptance* by peers in typical situations or particular kinds of relationships. A child may need to learn how to discover when his or her behavior falls short of the threshold, as in low assertiveness, initiative, or verbal interaction, *or* goes beyond the threshold to violate the peer norms or expectations, in being too aggressive or overly competitive. For example, Putallaz (1983) found that young boys' future peer status prior to entry in the first grade could be predicted, in part, by how well they understood general peer expectations for social behavior.

Some children need to learn new social behaviors and also gain in their attention to and skill in evaluation of peer feedback and consequences of their behavior in various situations and relationships. Thus, we should not be expecting children who are given social skill instruction to change their personalities or to become overly concerned with peer acceptance, but to learn to become more aware of when their behavior is outside the threshold for acceptance. In this conceptualization, a child who is very aggressive and not well-liked might only need to become aggressive to a lesser extent, less frequently, or only in certain circumstances to gain peer acceptance. Some evidence indicates that peers' negative attitudes towards a child will change when the child's behavior improves (Singleton, 1982). We can all think of someone of whom we would be more accepting, if only they would talk just a little less or help out sometimes. The selection of social skills for focus thus can be tailored to individual children's general social functioning or specific behaviors that need change.

A second major guideline refers to the diversity of social situational considerations. Some social situations or tasks (e.g., resolving a dispute, meeting new peers) may require particular types of skills, which may be a focus for one or many children in a classroom. Another major consideration should include social behavior pertaining to general social interaction situations *and* social behavior particular to a diversity of peer relationships, such as acquaintances, close friendships, social friends, and activity partnerships, that exist in classroom dyads and small groups (see Oden, Herzberger, Mangione, & Wheeler, 1984). We have tended to characterize children's peer relations both inside and outside the classroom as friends or not friends (e.g., Gottman, 1983).

Too often, research has been restricted to assessment of peer interaction in group situations without regard for the relationships that exist as parameters in these interactions. In research by Gottman and Parkhurst (1980) with young preschool children, it was demonstrated that young children do have close friendships. In research by Putallaz and Gottman (1981) and Gottman and Parkhurst (1980), as well as Newcomb and Brady (1982), it was observed that, compared to stranger and acquaintance interactions, best friend interactions exhibited intimacy, including sharing personal information, secrets, and fantasy play to a greater extent. Still, we have tended to overlook the study of nonfriends. We know children make distinctions, even if their articulation is not complex. Cooper and Marquis (1983) collected data in classrooms and observed that primary and elementary school children acted as collaborators in activities by providing information, instruction, and evaluation to each other.

Hallinan and Tuma (1978) asked children to sort classmates' names into best friends, friends, and nonfriends. About 25% of the children were identified as nonfriends. Do nonfriends have some type of relationships with each other, for example, acquaintances, activity partners, enemies? Fine (1981) found that 18% of all possible relationships in a Little League were close friends, 31% were friends, 2% disliked, and 47% neither liked nor disliked. In a study of primary school-age children becoming acquainted in dyads (Oden et al., 1984), children's behavior was compared to that of friend dyads from a similar age group in the same art activity (Wheeler, 1981). Differences were observed in their social interaction. For example, friends took significantly more turns than the newly acquainted dyads, and their disputes were significantly lower in duration. In the study of the newly acquainted dyads, children were quite involved in facilitating each other's art activities and setting down plans and rules for use of materials. While the children were becoming acquainted, few dyads seemed oriented towards making friends, but rather they appeared to behave more like activity partners. More research is needed to establish the existence of activity partnerships in the classroom, but it is important to bear in mind that children need social skills for a variety of peer relationships, not only friendship.

In summary, social skill instruction may be developed for individuals or groups for diverse purposes: specific behaviors of individuals or groups that appear to be outside the threshold of peer acceptance; skills for specific critical situations; and skills for diverse types of peer relationships, such as friendships and activity partners. The following sections will include discussion of assessment of peer relationships, recent research on social skill instruction, and guidelines and examples for developing social skill instruction.

## ASSESSING A CHILD'S PEER RELATIONSHIPS

Key questions must be answered prior to intervention: Are a child's social difficulties considerably outside the realm of the problems in which other children are engaged? Are the peer relationships in a given classroom or group constructive for both individual and group development? Although there is a general understanding of the factors that contribute to children's peer status, parents and professionals often do not have a firm ground upon which to make decisions about whether or not to intervene to enhance a child's social competence or peer status.

An assessment of children's peer relationships should include a focus on the context in which they occur. The child may first be evaluated as a social being; that is, across a variety of contexts, such as the home, classroom, playground, or neighborhood. The child may then be evaluated by specifically focusing on the group context. Does the child have knowledge and skill in relating to peers in groups; for example, participating in games or activities with appropriate cooperation, competition, and awareness of the norms and conventions of the peer group? In a peer group that has continuity, does the child contribute as a member of the group and play a role in constructing the group's rules, activities, and agenda? Finally, is the child able to relate in a dyadic context (with another child)? The dyadic context is potentially a friendship or activity partnership in which children have been observed to create their own structure and in which they can explore similarities and differences, provide mutual reinforcement and feedback, resolve conflicts, and seek to sustain the relationship over time (Gottman & Parkhurst, 1980; Oden et al., 1984). Similarly, we can assess a group or classroom in terms of its cohesiveness at a dyadic level. For example, are there friendships and best friendships that emerge and sustain within classroom groups?

Three major perspectives provide resources for the teacher, parent, or counselor for gathering information about children's social skills and group and dyadic relationships: the peer perspective, the adult perspective, and the child's perspective. Sociometric methods, observation, and interviews are the methods often used by researchers and other professionals to gain insight into each of these perspectives.

## Sociometric Techniques

Sociometric methods, discussed in greater detail in chapter 2, are useful in determining the degree of a child's peer acceptance and participation in a range of peer relationships, including play or social friends, activity partner, close friends, and acquaintances. In using these techniques, it is a good idea to first develop a picture of the classroom as a whole. A classroom is a social group, which may vary in how easy or difficult it is to develop and maintain positive peer relationships. What is the average of peer acceptance scores or nominations? How spread out is the distribution of scores? It is helpful to look for cliques or close friendship groups to determine where cohesiveness exists and plan to observe the openness of these groups or friends to entry and participation from others. In studying the rating scores and nominations of children who are not well liked, there may be important information for intervention. According to research by Dodge (1983), some children are *controversial*, that is, they receive low scores from some children and higher scores from others; although Newcomb and Bukowski (1983) did not find this classification to be particularly reliable. By using sociometric methods that ask children to name or rate the peers they like the most and least, neglected and rejected peers can be differentiated.

In general, on sociometric scales, the children who simply receive the lowest scores are thought to include both the least-liked children and children who are not well known (Asher & Hymel, 1981). The latter peer status difficulty is thought to indicate that the child is overlooked, not well known, or in popular usage, appears "shy." According to research by Coie and Dodge (1983) with third- and fifth-graders over a 5-year period, these neglected children are more likely to become accepted over time than children who are disliked. After sociometric assessment has revealed which, if any, children in a classroom have these types of social isolation or difficulties, further study of the situation is needed through observation and discussion with the child or children.

## Observing Children

For more systematic assessment, what to observe can be determined from a sociometric technique or from talking with teachers, parents, or other children. From observing children often, we can learn some of the social skills of most children at a given developmental level or age. Thus, we have some guidelines for what to focus on with children who lack these skills. Furthermore, we may find that a specific child is quite skilled but is not welcomed due to the types of activities in the classroom or the attitudes in peer group cliques that have developed. When children are socially isolated but are socially skilled, the intervention should be at the level of program intervention so that more opportunities are created in which more children can get to know each other. Furthermore, classmates may lack social skills for helping some children to become included. For example, in a study with hard-of-hearing children by Vandell, Anderson, Ehrhardt, and Wilson (1982), although the hearing-impaired children improved in their social skills from a coaching social skills approach, they were still not well accepted by classmates. The authors suggested that the peer group would need some type of intervention to better enable them to overcome their attitudes or difficulties in interacting with these children.

Observing can be useful, informally, as well as systematically. By observing children in different situations, at different times, and over a period of time, a teacher can determine which social skills appear to be important for social interaction and relationship-building in the classroom, in other groups, or in the dyadic context. Children's typical responses to a given setting, activity, or section of the classroom can also be a useful guideline. Are there activities that result in frequent conflicts and struggles for most children; whereas in other activities, children are more likely to coordinate their activities with others? Some activities may tend to result in exclusiveness from a given peer group versus openness to new members. If alert, we can observe the processes by which a child tries to join a group and the responses he or she tends to receive from peers. We can witness friendships developing and the conflicts that ensue and need resolution. We can spot the child who "hovers" on the periphery (e.g., Gottman, 1977) and the children who are frequently in a fight or struggle.

To evaluate the activity and identify the peer groups and dyads within the classroom, children can be observed in terms of who is present and for how long in a given activity. From observing individuals and determining their activities and skills, the observer can make up a random list of the children and spotcheck for a few seconds to see what each child is doing, then go to the next child and so on; or, observe a given child for a longer period of time and then go to the next and so on. Another procedure allows the observer to scan the entire group for a few seconds and mark behavior on a few dimensions, such as positive socializing versus playing alone, constructively or unconstructively. Many of these procedures take considerable practice, yet much can be learned from simply trying to master them. An essential skill is learning to describe children's behavior according to actions, rather than according to the observer's impressions of unobservable feelings or personality characteristics (e.g., "He yelled out" rather than "He was disgusted," and "He did not answer" rather than "He is shy."). To determine one's objectivity and the validity of the types of behaviors being assessed, another person should sometimes observe independently but along with the observer, and their results should be compared. Several reviews of observational procedures are available and provide examples, explanations, and instructions for application; for example, Cartwright and Cartwright (1984) and Irwin and Bushnell (1980). See chapter 2 for an additional discussion of direct observation.

Through the information gained from sociometrics and observations, the teacher has a more objective basis for evaluating a classroom for its quality of social context for all the children and for individuals who appear to lack positive peer relationships. The teacher should also create opportuni-

ties for informal conversations with children about the classroom and interacting with peers in the classroom. It is especially important to talk with any
child who appears to be having difficulties in his perceptions and feelings
about the classroom and his peer activities. Some children may not be very
positively oriented toward their peers or toward making friends with the particular children in the classroom. A child might have interests that take up
his energies, and friends in another classroom or in the neighborhood. Some
children may value competing with peers more than cooperating. Still, a reasonable objective might be to learn how to be assertive without undermin-
ing the efforts of others. It does seem in a child's best interest to learn to
participate constructively in peer interactions in the classroom and thereby
acquire social skills that are useful throughout life in working with others.

Talking with the parents to gain further insight is a critical step to include,
especially if any individual interventions will be offered. Parental support
may result in increasing parent interest and/or skills in supporting the child's
peer relationships.

## INTERVENING IN CHILDREN'S PEER RELATIONSHIPS

### Educational Curricula

Several educational methods have been developed for the social adjustment problems of individual children and groups in schools. These curricula or specially designed programs differ in the kinds of experiences they
provide for children: activities that allow the full participation of children
who have diverse skills or abilities, for example, pairing a child of less
mature social skills with younger children (Furman, Rahe, & Hartup, 1979);
design of activities to enhance group cooperation (Johnson & Johnson,
1979); and problem-solving activities and instruction for individual children
or small groups of children (Rubin & Clark, 1983; Shure & Spivack, 1978).
First, we will discuss curriculum approaches to foster more positive peer relationships in the classroom. We will examine methods of social skill training
and social problem solving found to be effective in intervention with individuals who have problematic peer relationships.

There is a curriculum for children's social development in every classroom,
even if the teacher is not explicit or is not really aware of it (Cartledge & Milburn, 1980; Johnson, 1981). The types of activities that comprise the academic curriculum define the parameters of children's peer interactions. Some
activities may encourage children to get to know each other, whereas others
would not. Some situations may encourage children to focus on looking the
best or winning rather than trying to do one's best (Dweck & Bempechat,
1983). Such a classroom atmosphere might not only undercut many individuals' attempts to achieve but interfere in children's collaborative efforts as

well. Some curricula would tend to rely heavily on certain social or individual processes, while neglecting others. A curriculum balanced for social processes would include both adequate opportunity for group discussion and group activities that do not require discussion, for example, sports, art, language arts. There should be opportunities for pairs and triads as well as small groups to work together. Partners and small groups will inevitably become established as the children wish, but teachers should not build curriculum activities around exclusive cliques that exist. Instructional activities could be set up in ways that allow opportunity for friendships to form and thrive and yet time for children to get to know all classmates better.

Although all activities should be examined for academic, social, and individual processes, some appear to be especially fruitful for enhancing positive peer relationships. For example, language arts activities, including music, art, and reading children's literature, can be especially important in helping children to express individual feelings, ideas, and creativity and, at the same time, enhance their involvement with many children they might not ordinarily seek out due to differences in race, sex, age, and physical or learning ability (see Oden, 1982a). Studies have found that reading and discussing stories about children who differ on some characteristic, such as physical disability, help children to have more receptive attitudes toward peers who are different in some way (e.g., physically handicapped). Through examining stories, children are thought to gain greater awareness of feelings and motivations in others as well as differences in perspective, that is, seeing things from another's point of view (Moss & Oden, 1983).

Academic projects may also be constructed specifically so that children learn more about cooperative group effort. The goal structures of activities can be planned for cooperation as well as individual assertiveness. Subjects such as math, spelling, vocabulary, geography, and so forth can be structured for group cooperation. Some research evidence indicates that these changes foster children's cognitive abilities and academic achievements, as well as peer relations (Johnson, 1981). Although more limited for preschoolers, group discussion on issues of interest for primary and elementary school-age children may include controversial subjects. Such discussion can enhance peer group communication (Johnson & Johnson, 1979). Topics of controversy, handled by discussion, can be extended to activities such as a classroom newspaper or debate. Discussions and debates can take place in relation to a television program, movie, play, story, or current event. Role playing a situation or event as a reenactment might be a vehicle for setting the stage for a discussion. Discussion of issues in human relations can be useful in helping children to examine prejudicial or stereotyped judgment versus greater objectivity. Such experience should help children's overall education and their social-cognitive development. With experience, discussions could extend to more immediate interpersonal issues (such as helping a child who is new in the classroom or a child who is left out of activities), difficulties in a peer conflict incident, appreciation of differences in classmates, understanding different values or perspectives, or developing fair ways to utilize space and resources.

## Social Skills Instruction: Research Findings

Although the research evidence is not sufficient to pinpoint how an individual child who lacks peer acceptance or friendships arrives at his or her given status, some studies have demonstrated that such a child can benefit from further socialization; that is, from verbal instruction and behavioral "rehearsal" (Covill-Servo, 1982; Ladd & Oden, 1979; Oden & Asher, 1977) and from modeling (Gresham & Nagle, 1980; O'Connor, 1972). These procedures are based largely on Bandura's (1977) theory of how humans learn in social settings. Parents and other adults in a child's early experience frequently provide the child with considerable modeling, verbal instruction, prompting, and feedback, as children learn to join a peer group at the sandbox, settle a fight during a game in the backyard, or share or take turns in the classroom. Some children may have received less social skill instruction, including feedback and suggestions from parents and teachers, when a situation is problematic. Some children might have lacked the cognitive, social, or language ability to use this information adequately when it was provided at an earlier point. Other children may have lacked the opportunities to try new behaviors with peers. They may have lived in a neighborhood with few peers, moved a great deal, or been in a family whose activities rarely included other children.

Oden and Asher (1977) found that providing instruction in social skills was helpful even for third- and fourth-grade children. In this study, 11 classrooms of children were asked to respond to two sociometric techniques: a roster and rating scale questionnaire and a friendship nomination method. Children who were the lowest-rated and received just one or no friendship nominations were selected for participation in the study. The purpose of the study was to assess the effects of "coaching" social skills to children who were socially isolated; that is, children who had few or no friends and/or lacked general peer acceptance because they were disliked, neglected, or less known by peers.

The social skill training method, referred to as *coaching*, included three components during each of five sessions: verbal instruction was given individually to each child by an adult, followed immediately with an opportunity to "practice" while playing with another child who was randomly selected from the class and was at least moderately well accepted by classmates, and finally, an individual postplay review session was conducted with the same adult. The content of the instruction consisted of social skill concepts and examples that were proposed to the child as ideas for how to make a game fun or enjoyable to play with another person: (a) participating in a game or activity; (b) cooperating (e.g., taking turns and sharing materials); (c) communicating (e.g., talking and listening); and (d) supporting (e.g., giving attention or help).

Three experimental conditions were included in the study: coaching, peer pairing, and control. Each condition or "group" was formed by randomly selecting one of the three lowest-rated children from each classroom for each condition, resulting in 11 children in each group. Children in each condition were provided with six play sessions over a 4-week period. (No instruction was given for the first session.) They played with a different classmate each time. Six different games (e.g., dominoes, Blockhead, picture drawing) were used. In the peer-pairing condition, each low-accepted child was paired with the same peer partners and played the same games as in the coaching condition, but these children received no coaching instruction or postplay review. A control condition was included to examine the possible prestige effects of simply being taken out of the classroom by the experimenter along with more-liked peers to play games. The control children were, therefore, taken out of the classroom with the same peer partners as in the other conditions, but they played solitary games and did not interact.

The sociometric measures were again administered to the 11 classrooms approximately 10 days after the experimental period had ended. The results were that children in the coaching condition had significantly increased on the sociometric measure of acceptance for playing with peers, but not for working with peers. Although some children made gains in friendships, the gains for the group overall were not statistically significant. In contrast, children in the peer-pairing group declined on all measures, and children in the control group remained unchanged. A follow-up assessment was made approximately 1 year later to determine the endurance of these initial increases in peer acceptance for playing with peers. Of the 33 children in the original sample of isolated children, 22 remained in the district 1 year later and were distributed among 11 different classrooms with eight from the coaching group, seven from the peer-pairing group, and seven from the control group. The coached children had continued to improve with an average score that was only somewhat below the classroom average. The peer-pairing group also made some gains, recovering from their previous initial loss of peer status, and the control group made no significant gains. The results demonstrate the potential for lasting effects of social skill instruction. This study served to initiate further research that addressed numerous questions: the effects of different "coaches"; the effects of coaching more than one child at a time; the contributions of receiving attention from an adult; the effect of more guided behavioral rehearsal and feedback; the effects of variations in content of skill learning; the contributions of age differences;

and the contributions of peer pairing with classmates compared to pairing with nonclassmates. In general, subsequent work has served to both clarify and refine the Oden and Asher work as well as replicate its major finding. Children do appear to benefit from social skills instruction that includes information and guidance in evaluating their interactions with their peers and opportunities to interact with classmates.

A study by Ladd (1981) presents corroborative evidence with third-graders who were found to be low in peer acceptance on the sociometric measure of playing with peers and also low in frequency of specific social skills in a natural play context. The skills included asking positive questions, leading or offering useful suggestions, and being helpful to another. Three conditions were used in this study: verbal social skill training, attention control, and no treatment control. In the group that received skill training, pairs of children were given verbal instruction from an adult along with immediate guided rehearsal during a game. Across the eight sessions, this guidance was gradually withdrawn and each child was individually asked to evaluate his or her own behavior. In the latter sessions, two additional peers were included. The children in this condition received a more specific set of skills than in the Oden and Asher study, and they were given more direct guidance and feedback with respect to their behavior in practicing the skills. They gradually practiced and critiqued their own behavior independently. The second condition was an attention control group, which was included to assess the attentional effects of receiving instruction from an adult. These children received instruction and practice in how to play games according to the rules. Finally, a control group was included that did not participate in any instruction or activity in the study. The results were that both the verbal skill training group and the attention control group made initial gains in peer acceptance and general social behavior, while only the skill training group made gains in two of the specific behaviors in which they had been instructed. The control group did not change. Furthermore, at follow-up assessment 1 month later, the control group remained unchanged, and the attention control group had dropped back to the levels of peer acceptance and social behavior observed prior to the intervention portion of the study. In contrast, the skill training group continued to improve by making further gains in peer acceptance, general positive social behavior, and the specific social skills that had been instructed.

Studies by Covill-Servo (1982) and Gresham and Nagle (1980) also utilized a method highly similar to that of Oden and Asher, with basically similar results. These studies, however, included experimental conditions that further examined the reasons for the gains in peer status and/or strengthened the effect. These studies successfully programmed the teaching of the social skills by introducing one basic type in a session or every other session. In the Ladd study, the social skills included were more specific and observable than in Oden and Asher (i.e., asking questions of peers, instructing, leading or directing peers, and giving praise, encouragement, and support). In addition, the social skill instruction was done first with pairs of target children, with a pair of more liked children added in later sessions as the experimenter or coach faded out his role in giving "guided rehearsal," that is, direction and feedback of the instructed social skills. The results of this study found gains for the coaching procedure in general social participation, in the specific social skills instructed, and in peer status. The degree of the effects of this procedure compared with controls appears stronger than Oden and Asher's findings and may indicate that the alterations, especially for difficult children, may be helpful. The total amount of time in the intervention is nearly twice that of Oden and Asher's procedure. More research is needed to evaluate the time factor.

Covill-Servo's study employed two major differences from the other studies. One half of the subjects were given instruction by one coach and one half by another. No differences in results were found for the two groups. Further, low-accepted children in one experimental condition were paired for peer play activity sessions with children from a different classroom. These children made fewer gains than children who had been paired with classmates. Several interpretations are possible. The stigma of being poorly accepted may not be that difficult to overcome given changes in behavior, along with exposure to the children affecting the peer perception changes toward the children. It may also be that the children have difficulty generalizing their new skills to interactions with their classmates. More research is needed.

The effects of a modeling procedure were examined and compared to coaching social skills by Gresham and Nagle (1980). This study included a group of low-accepted children who were exposed to the same content through videotape and narration as children who received coaching of the social skills depicted in the videotape. The results found no additional effects for the modeling plus coaching versus the coaching alone, and the modeling alone group was less effective. Still, modeling would appear to be a useful alternative to coaching since it was effective in enhancing the children's peer acceptance. It might also be more easily applied in some educational situations. Some social skills would seem to be especially well suited to instruction by modeling. For example, teaching initiating strategies (e.g., approaching a group), using conversational openers, and simple kinds of cooperation such as taking turns or sharing materials, could be made concrete through videotape, play acting, or role play. In contrast, communication that is effective would be difficult to depict and convey clearly without some additional instruction. The potential of modeling may also be considered when constructing methods for younger children as found in studies by O'Connor (1972) and Chittenden (1942). These earlier studies showed that difficult and withdrawn or low-interacting children would increase their positive social initiatives and interactions from either modeling through a film or with puppets along with a narrative or instruction. These early studies did not gather data on the children's social behavior from the perspective of their peers so it is difficult to examine whether their increased sociability was effective from the peers' point of view.

A child who does not play well with classmates may respond more effectively with younger peers. This was demonstrated by Furman, Rahe, and Hartup (1979) with younger children (preschool age) who were assessed as socially isolated. Preschoolers who were well accepted were paired for 10 play sessions with socially isolated children who were 1 year older, with resulting gains in peer interaction in the classroom by the low-status children. No gains were found for children who had only been paired with agemates. Several interpretations might be made. Perhaps interaction with younger children is facilitating because the children have more in common in their level of skills or types of interests. Perhaps the younger child allows the older child to be more assertive or dominant. The older child thereby gains experience in social skills that he does not have the opportunity to practice with his or her classmates.

An alternative perspective that takes into account the developmental level of the preschool-age child has been developed by Scarlett (1980). This investigator maintains that isolated children in the preschool play a large role in their isolation by the fact that they play less than nonisolated children and are thus less interesting and attractive as social partners. In developing any intervention with preschool age children, it would be important to keep in mind that the young child almost always plays with some object, game, or other type of play activity whether alone or with another peer or peers. When a child simply watches other peers or is uninvolved in any play activity, he is not likely to be sought out by peers, and he lacks some vehicle for including others even if he were to become more assertive toward possible playmates. Scarlett advocates that teachers spend time with such children as "co-players" in games and activities to facilitate the children's play activity. His research indicates that this strategy does facilitate children's subsequent peer interactions. Clearly, the developmental level of the child must be taken into consideration in developing a suitable social skills instruction or experiential approach for children. Teachers who are experienced with the developmental level of their children, however, can be very good judges of how to adapt any procedure that seems to have some potential for children of a given developmental level.

Recent research on social skill instruction by Bierman (1983) and Bierman and Furman (1984) includes a peer activity with somewhat older children (fifth- and sixth-graders). They found that coaching instruction that included a focus on conversational skills as a peer activity, with one low-accepted and two accepted peers (making a videotape), was effective in enhancing the children's conversational skills, positive behavioral peer responses, and peer acceptance as later measured by peer ratings. In another interesting study, Coie and Krehbiel (in press) found that tutoring low-achieving, disliked children in academic skills enhanced both their achievement and peer acceptance. The study also found that social skills training similar to the Oden and Asher and Ladd procedures showed reading achievement gains and peer acceptance improvement as well. However, the use of a combined skill training program (academic and social) was not superior and appeared to require further investigation.

An important consideration with children of all ages appears to be the social contexts or situations in which the children interact and the kinds of relationships that may develop. Thus, with younger children, fantasy play and role play may be especially important areas for focus, whereas older children may participate in developing complex tasks or projects as collaborators. Prior to developing a social skill intervention, the goals of the social skill instruction need to be established according to the developmental level of the children, the range of participation of an individual child in diverse peer relationships (e.g., close friends, activity partners), skills necessary for various social and academic situations or tasks, and specific behavioral difficulties (e.g., overly aggressive or quiet) of individual children.

The following section will present a discussion of the coaching social skills procedures that have been developed and examples based on scripts that have been used. Suggestions for adapting these procedures for use by teachers and parents will also be provided.

## Developing Social Skills Instruction

As discussed thoroughly by Ladd and Mize (1983), the procedures typically referred to as *coaching social skills* include the *instruction* of concepts or rules, the opportunity for *practicing or rehearsing* related behavior, and *feedback* on the new learning. Coaching may be thought of as the provision of a conceptual framework that provides a model for behavior and a social context in which behavior may be modeled, shaped, and responded to with feedback. The coach also tends to elicit positive attention and motivation. Coaching should be built around the context of an opportunity for rehearsal or practice. Without potentially stressful evaluation, learning is further enhanced from the coaching instruction and feedback. Many of the creative arts experiences and children's games are particularly appropriate contexts for social learning. As previously discussed, the teacher or parent should evaluate, however, whether the properties or requirements of activities allow a child to participate and experience a range of behaviors. Many games, for example, exclude children due to the requirements of the game, or the requirements exclude the very behaviors to be encouraged, or negative behaviors are encouraged. In the instruction and feedback components of coaching, the teacher or parent provides information through language labels or concepts that refer to types of behavior to be kept in memory by the child for use when appropriate.

The child is first instructed in social concepts (e.g., cooperation) by an adult, who encourages the child to suggest specific behavioral examples and adds examples when a child does not provide any. Throughout, the coach repeats and reviews the concepts and gives feedback on how well the child understands their applicability. More general social reality concepts may be included, such as taking into consideration the perspectives or viewpoints of others and considering the consequences of various behaviors for all persons involved. Spivack and Shure (1974) have demonstrated the effectiveness of instruction in additional problem solving and social reasoning skills.

*Guidelines for Planning Instruction*

In research and consultant work, we found that even a well-engineered plan or script can fall flat if delivered to children in a lecture style. To achieve an effective communication process between adult and child, the teacher or parent has to have the selected social skill concepts and specific examples for each concept well in mind. The teacher or parent should also avoid the role of judge or disciplinarian, if possible, and strive to assume the role of a guide, who is a supportive and knowledgeable adult, in how to make friends and get along with others. In social skill instruction sessions, the child's task is to develop skill as a "cognizer," planner, and evaluator of his or her social experiences.

The following is a list of guidelines for preparing for social skill instruction with a child or a peer group.

*Skill Focus.* Following one or more of the assessment methods described in previous sections of this chapter, select the social skill or skills to be instructed (e.g., cooperation).

*Organization.* The content should be organized in a consistent fashion from skill to skill. The particular language used to refer to the social skills depends on the developmental level of the child or children. With younger children, use simpler language and more concrete examples. Props also help (e.g., puppets, cartoons). With older children, the language used to refer to the social skills can be organized from more abstract and general concepts to ones with more specific behavioral examples (e.g., cooperation—sharing, taking turns).

*Preparation.* Thoroughly review what will be said to the child or children before each session. A script may help, but it should be memorized fairly well so that it can be presented or delivered in a fluid, conversational manner. A list of social skill examples should be handy for reference during the session. The list may be extended to include the children's appropriate examples given during the session. Focus on one or two social skill concepts may be sufficient for a given session.

*Presentation.* Basic instructional skills for teaching any content to children are applicable. Included are maintaining the children's attention and interest by a positive, well-paced approach and by listening and responding positively and constructively (e.g., "Right," "Okay," "That's one idea, but how about . . .") to the children's responses. At the same time, basic skills in behavior management (e.g., setting limits for acting out behavior, see Ginott, 1972) are important to ensure that the social skill instruction is not undermined.

*Activities and Peer Participants.* The social skill instruction may be built around normal activities in the classroom (e.g., prior to an art activity) or may include introduction of a new activity or game that the teacher or parent believes has a high likelihood of being a positive experience. Highly competitive games should be avoided at first.

The selection of particular children who will participate should also be considered (e.g., friend, several children who rarely interact, a class activity partner), or children may wish to select their own playmates or work partners. However, the pairing of two long-standing enemies is not a good peer context in which to try out newly learned behaviors! Finally, social skill instruction may be integrated into a related curriculum activity (e.g., reading children's literature, see Moss & Oden, 1983).

*Feedback and Review.* Feedback should be positive and constructive, and aimed at helping the child to make the association between language conceptions of social skills and his or her behavioral enactment of these skills. The feedback and review may consist of simple prompts as well as directions. The instructional style often used by a sports coach or a theatrical director is quite appropriate (see Strauss, 1966). For example, if a given child initiates some action (e.g., offering to share materials) that would be a step in the right direction toward learning cooperation but is off course a bit (e.g., taking up too much space on the art table), the child should receive some corrective direction or redirection. The child's positive examples and reasoning about a social skill and its application should be confirmed (e.g., "That's right") and the negative or inappropriate examples should be redirected (e.g., "No, that's not an example of cooperation, but how about taking turns? Is that an example of cooperation?").

In the Oden and Asher (1977) research, the following social skills categories and list of examples were used for focus with the low-accepted children.

- *Participation:*
  get involved
  get started
  pay attention to the game or activity
  try to do your best
- *Cooperation:*
  take turns
  share the game or materials
  make a suggestion if you have a problem with the game
  give an alternative if you disagree about the rules
- *Communication:*
  talk with the other person
  say things about the game or yourself
  ask a question about the game
  ask a question about the person
  listen when the other person talks
  look at the other person to see how he's doing
- *Friendly; Fun; Nice (or Supportive; Helpful):*
  give some attention to the other person
  say something nice (or positive) when the other person does well
  smile sometimes
  have fun in the game
  offer some help or suggestions
  give some encouragement

In the research, each child received instruction individually from an adult in each of these categories or concepts. The latter category was originally based on language gained from various interview studies with children. More recent research (e.g., Ladd, 1981) has focused on helpful or supportive as a category. In other studies since Oden and Asher's work, children have been effectively instructed in dyads and small groups rather than individually (e.g., Ladd, 1981; Bierman, 1983). In the Oden and Asher study, a 5–7 minute period of individual social skill instruction was provided prior to the second–sixth play sessions, in which each child who was low-accepted by peers played a different activity with a different well-accepted classmate (of the same sex) each time. The adult first asked the child about the game or activity played at the prior session and why or why not he or she found it to be enjoyable. The adult then said, "I have some ideas I'd like to discuss with you about what makes it fun to play a game with another person" (Oden & Asher, 1977, p. 500). In order not to stigmatize the child in any way, no specific mention was made of the child's low peer acceptance or need to learn social skills. Although each of the skills was covered with at least a few examples each time, more time was spent in later sessions on those skills that appeared to need more attention by a given child. Other studies have found it to be effective to focus on adding one major new skill concept each session or every other session. The same steps were followed for each skill instructed each time. See Table 8.1 for an example of the process used in Oden and Asher's study and specific examples based on the script and children's typical responses.

In general, the elements of the process should include providing instruction by probing the child's understanding of concepts and their opposites through exploring specific examples, probing the child's understanding of social consequences of each type of example behavior, and providing feedback and direction regarding the children's understanding of concepts, behaviors, and consequences. In the Oden and Asher research, the script was closely adhered to and the adult would simply listen in a receptive way to any diversions or elaborations from the child, then quickly continue. In consulting with teachers, we found this style was sometimes necessary, but other times, it was useful to make more attempts to draw out the child's ideas more fully in regard to a specific incident or type of behavior. It is also an approach that tends to encourage future communication between the teacher or parent, which would seem to be an important goal for adults and children who have ongoing relationships.

In the 3–5 minute postplay review, the adult asked the child, "Did you get a chance to try out some of the ideas we talked about?" (Oden & Asher, 1977, p. 500). The child was then asked to evaluate how well the other child felt about playing the game with him or her. "Do you think _____ liked playing the game with you?" The child was then asked if he or she played or tried out each of the major social skills by reviewing each one with a couple of examples. "Let's see, did you *cooperate* when you played the game, did you take turns, share?" and so forth.

After several of the instructional sessions revealed that a particular child appeared to have mastered his or her understanding of the skills, *generalization to the classroom* was encouraged. The child was asked to think about games and activities in his or her classroom, which are played with other children. The games or activities that the child suggested were then used for the focus of the social skill concepts and specific examples. The child was then encouraged to try out some of these behaviors (e.g., sharing, taking turns) in the games and activities in the classroom with peers, to see how well they worked there and if they made a game or activity fun or enjoyable to play with another person. The child would then be asked about how well these ideas worked in subsequent instructional sessions.

In applying social skills instruction, it is important not to call undue attention to a child or children. Otherwise, the child may become stigmatized by peers or lose his or her self-esteem because of the instruction. In order to minimize undue attention to individuals, a teacher or parent should plan for

**Table 8.1.** Social Skill Instructional Process

| STEP | EXAMPLE DIALOGUE |
|------|------------------|
| 1. Propose Skill or Concept | *Adult:* Okay, I have some ideas about what makes a game fun to play with another person. There are a couple of things that are important to do. You should *cooperate* with the other person. |
| 2. Probe Understanding | *Adult:* Do you know what *cooperation* is? Can you tell me in your own words?<br>*Child:* Ahh . . . sharing. |
| 3. Provide Feedback/Direction | *Adult:* Yes, sharing. (If child gives an inaccurate example, say, "I was thinking of something like sharing.") |
| 4. Probe Understanding/Give Specific Examples | *Adult:* Okay, let's say you and I are playing the game you played last time. What was the game?<br>*Child:* Drawing a picture.<br>*Adult:* Okay, tell me, then, what would be an example of sharing when playing the picture drawing game?<br>*Child:* I'd let you use some pens, too. |
| 5. Provide Feedback/Direction | *Adult:* Right. You would share the pens with me. That's an example of cooperation. (If child gives an inaccurate example, redirect as in Step 3.) |
| 6. Probe Understanding of Consequences | *Adult:* Would sharing the pens with me make the game fun to play? (You may add "with another person" or "for both you and the other person?") |
| 7. Probe Understanding of Opposites | *Adult:* Now, let's say you and I are playing the picture-drawing game, can you give me an example of what would *not* be cooperating?<br>*Child:* Yeah, taking all the pens! |
| 8. Provide Feedback/Direction | *Adult:* Right, taking all the pens is an example of *not* cooperating. (If child gives an inaccurate example, redirect as in Step 3.) |
| 9. Probe Understanding of Consequences | *Adult:* Would taking all the pens make the game fun to play? (You may add "for both you *and* the other person?")<br>*Child:* No! |
| 10. Provide Feedback/Direction | *Adult:* So, you wouldn't take all the pens. Instead, you'd cooperate by sharing them with me. |
| 11. Probe Understanding of Further Examples | *Adult:* Okay, let's say you and I are playing the picture-drawing game. Can you tell me another way you could cooperate?<br>*Child:* Umm . . . I don't know.<br>*Adult:* How about taking turns? That's another example of cooperation. How could we take turns while playing the game?<br>*Child:* You could go first. Then I could wait. |

*continued*

**Table 8.1.** continued

| STEP | EXAMPLE DIALOGUE |
|---|---|
| 12. Provide Feedback/Direction | *Adult:* Yes, that's an example of taking turns. |
| 13. Probe Understanding of Consequences | *Adult:* Would taking turns make the game fun to play? (You may add "with another person?" or "for *both* you and the other person?")<br>*Child:* Yes, I think so. |
| 14. Probe Understanding of Opposites | *Adult:* Can you give me an example of *not* taking turns? What would that be like?<br>*Child:* One person would keep drawing and not let the other person draw. |
| 15. Probe Understanding of Consequences | *Adult:* Would that make the game fun to play? (You may add "for *both* you and the other person?")<br>*Child:* No. Someone might get mad. |
| 16. Provide Feedback/Direction | *Adult:* Right. If I wouldn't let you draw you might get angry and wouldn't like playing the game. So instead, we could take turns drawing. |
| 17. Probe Understanding of Further Examples | *Adult:* Can you think of any more ideas for cooperating?<br>*Child:* No. |
| 18. Prompt Trying Out Ideas | *Adult:* Okay, I'd like you to try out some of these ideas when you play  (game)  with  (other child)  . |
| 19. Inform Child of Postplay Feedback/Direction | *Adult:* Let's go and get  (other child)  and after you play, I'll talk with you again for a minute or so and you can tell me if these ideas seem to help to make a game fun (or enjoyable) to play with another person. Okay?<br>*Child:* Okay. |
| 20. Postplay Feedback/Direction | *Adult:* Did you get a chance to try out some of the ideas we talked about to see how they worked? Let's see, did you *cooperate* by *sharing* and *taking turns*? How did that work? |

full participation, if possible, of classmates or playmates in the various peer interaction activities provided. Every child should also have some opportunity to have some discussions with the adult. In the Oden and Asher study, this was accomplished by asking each child who played each game to evaluate how much fun or how enjoyable it was as a game in school.

The administration of these social skill instructional procedures may present many practical problems for teachers and parents. In schools, the aid of a coteacher, assistant, counselor, or parent may be especially helpful. Modified versions of the social skill instruction can also be integrated into existing activities or curricula. The generalization of children's social learning may also be increased by alterations in the curriculum or activities of a particular setting. These methods may also need to be combined with other procedures for application with children who have more severe emotional or behavioral problems or have some learning or physical disability. Finch and Hops (1982) and their colleagues developed effective behavioral procedures that include use of concrete reinforcers and that may be combined with social skill instruction. In a recent survey of special education programs and clinical programs, we found that social skill instructions were being effectively combined with behavioral approaches and also group therapy experiences (Oden, 1982a).

## SUMMARY AND CONCLUSION

Research indicates that children who lack peer acceptance can benefit from social skills instruction that include instruction and opportunities for peer interaction or rehearsal. Various kinds of intervention have been employed, including curriculum approaches and direct social skills instruction. A teacher or parent should be careful to make an assessment of the type of social skill development that is needed for a particular child. Various methods of assessment were discussed. The selection of particular social skills may be accomplished by focus on particular types of situations that may be problematic, particular types of behaviors that may be a source of peer rejection or neglect, general positive social behaviors that are expected and/or normative for peers of this age, and skills important for various types of peer relationships, such as friendships or activity partnerships. Although more research is indicated to establish the more effective aspects of various types of social skills interventions, several types of formats seem useful and may be adapted to the developmental level and cultural background of the children. Furthermore, combinations of methods may be especially effective with children who have severe peer relationship difficulties.

## REFERENCES

Asher, S. R., & Hymel, S. (1981). Children's social competence in peer relations: Sociometric and behavioral assessment. In J. D. Wine & M. D. Smye (Eds.), *Social competence*. New York: Guilford Press.

Asher, S. R., Oden, S. L., & Gottman, J. M. (1977). Children's friendships in school settings. In L. G. Katz (Eds.), *Current topics in early childhood education* (No. 1, pp. 33–61). Norwood, NJ: Ablex.

Asher, S. R., & Renshaw, P. D. (1981). Children without friends: Social knowledge and social skill training. In S. R. Asher & J. M. Gottman (Eds.), *The development of children's friendships*. New York: Cambridge University Press.

Bandura, A. (1977). *Social learning theory*. Englewood Cliffs, NJ: Prentice Hall.

Bierman, K. L. (1983). *The effects of social skills training on the interactions of unpopular and popular peers engaged in cooperative tasks.* Paper presented at the meeting of the Society for Research in Child Development, Detroit, MI.

Bierman, K. L., & Furman, W. (1984). The effects of social skills training and peer involvement on the social adjustment of preadolescents. *Child Development, 55,* 151–162.

Cartledge, G., & Milburn, J. F. (1980). *Teaching social skills to children: Innovative approaches.* Elmsford, NY: Pergamon Press.

Cartwright, C. A., & Cartwright, G. P. (1984). *Developing observational skills,* 2nd ed., New York: McGraw-Hill.

Chittenden, G. F. (1942). An experimental study in measuring and modifying assertive behavior in young children. *Monographs of the Society for Research in Child Development, 7* (1, Serial No. 31).

Coie, J. D., & Dodge, K. A. (1983). Continuities and changes in children's social status: A five-year longitudinal study. *Merrill-Palmer Quarterly, 29,* 261–282.

Coie, J. D., Dodge, K. A., & Coppotelli, H. (1982). Dimensions and types of social status: A cross-age perspective. *Developmental Psychology, 18,* 557–570.

Coie, J. D., & Krehbiel, G. (in press). Effects of academic tutoring on the social status of low-achieving, socially rejected children. *Child Development.*

Cooper, C. R., & Marquis, A. (1983). *Conceptualizing children's classroom discourse and its consequences.* Paper presented at meeting of the Society for Research in Child Development, Detroit, MI.

Covill-Servo, J. (1982). *A modification of low peer status from a sociopsychological perspective.* Unpublished doctoral dissertation, University of Rochester, Rochester, NY.

Cowen, E. L., Pederson, A., Babigian, H., Izzo, L. D., & Trost, M. A. (1973). Long-term follow-up of early detected vulnerable children. *Journal of Consulting and Clinical Psychology, 41,* 438–446.

Dodge, K. A. (1983). Behavioral antecedents of peer social status. *Child Development, 54,* 1386–1399.

Dweck, C. S., & Bempechat, J. (1983). Children's theories of intelligence: Impact on learning. In S. G. Paris, G. M. Olson, & H. W. Stevenson (Eds.), *Learning and motivation in the classroom.* Hillsdale, NJ: Lawrence Erlbaum.

Finch, M., & Hops, H. (1982). Remediation of social withdrawal in young children: Considerations for the practitioner. *Child and Youth Services, 5,* 29–42.

Fine, G. A. (1981). Friends, impression management, and preadolescent behavior. In S. R. Asher & J. M. Gottman (Eds.), *The development of children's friendships.* New York: Cambridge University Press.

Furman, W., Rahe, D. F., & Hartup, W. W. (1979). Rehabilitation of socially withdrawn preschool children through mixed-age and same-age socialization. *Child Development, 50,* 915–922.

Ginott, H. G. (1972). *Between teacher and child.* New York: Avon Books.

Gottman, J. M. (1977). Toward a definition of social isolation in children. *Child Development, 48,* 513–517.

Gottman, J. M. (1983). How children become friends. *Monographs of the Society for Research in Child Development, 48* (3, Serial No. 20).

Gottman, J. M., & Parkhurst, J. T. (1980). A developmental theory of friendship and acquaintanceship processes. In W. A. Collins (Ed.), *Minnesota Symposia on Child Psychology,* (No. 13). Hillsdale, NJ: Lawrence Erlbaum.

Gresham, F. M., & Nagle, R. J. (1980). Social skills training with children: Responsiveness to modeling and coaching as a function of peer orientation. *Journal of Consulting and Clinical Psychology, 18,* 718–729.

Hallinan, M. T., & Tuma, N. B. (1978). Classroom effects on change in children's friendships. *Sociology of Education, 51*, 270–282.

Irwin, D. M., & Bushnell, M. M. (1980). *Observational strategies for child study.* New York: Holt, Rinehart & Winston.

Johnson, D. W. (1981). Student–student interaction: The neglected variable in education. *Educational Researcher, 10*, 5–10.

Johnson, D. W., & Johnson, R. (1979). Conflict in the classroom: Controversy and learning. *Review of Educational Research, 49*, 51–70.

Ladd, G. W. (1981). Effectiveness of a social learning method for enhancing children's social interaction and peer acceptance. *Child Development, 52*, 171–178.

Ladd, G. W., & Mize, J. (1983). A cognitive-social learning model of social skills training. *Psychology Review, 90*, 127–157.

Ladd, G. W., & Oden, S. (1979). The relationship between peer acceptance and children's ideas about helpfulness. *Child Development, 50*, 402–408.

Moss, J. F., & Oden, S. (1983). Children's story comprehension and social learning. *The Reading Teacher, 36*, 784–789.

Newcomb, A. F., & Brady, J. E. (1982). Mutuality in boys' friendship relations. *Child Development, 53*, 392–395.

Newcomb, A. F., & Bukowski, W. M. (1983). Social impact and social preference as determinants of children's peer group status. *Developmental Psychology, 19*, 856–867.

O'Connor, R. D. (1972). Relative efficacy of modeling, shaping, and the combined procedures for modification of social withdrawal. *Journal of Abnormal Psychology, 79*, 327–334.

Oden, S. (1982a). The applicability of social skills training research. *Child and Youth Services, 5*, 75–89.

Oden, S. (1982b). Peer relationship development in childhood. In L. G. Katz (Ed.), *Current topics in early childhood education*, No. 4. Norwood, NJ: Ablex.

Oden, S., & Asher, S. R. (1977). Coaching children in social skills for friendship making. *Child Development, 48*, 495–506.

Oden, S., Herzberger, S. D., Mangione, P. L., & Wheeler, V. A. (1984). In J. Masters & K. L. Yarkin-Levin (Eds.), *Boundary areas in social and developmental psychology.* New York: Academic Press.

Putallaz, M. (1983). Predicting children's sociometric status from their behavior. *Child Development, 54*, 1417–1426.

Putallaz, M., & Gottman, J. (1981). Social skills and group acceptance. In S. R. Asher & J. M. Gottman (Eds.), *The development of children's friendships.* New York: Cambridge University Press.

Renshaw, P. D., & Asher, S. R. (1982). Social competence and peer status: A distinction between goals and strategies. In K. H. Rubin & H. S. Ross (Eds.), *Peer relationships and social skills in childhood.* New York: Springer Verlag.

Rubin, K. H., & Clark. M. L. (1983). Preschool teachers' ratings of behavioral problems: Observational, sociometric, and social-cognitive correlates. *Journal of Abnormal Child Psychology, 11*, 273–285.

Scarlett, W. G. (1980). Social isolation from agemates among nursery school children. *Journal of Child Psychology and Psychiatry, 21*, 231–240.

Shure, M. B., & Spivack, G. (1978). *Problem-solving techniques in childrearing.* San Francisco: Jossey-Bass.

Singleton, L. G. (1982). *Peer perception of social behavior change in popular and unpopular children.* Unpublished doctoral dissertation, University of Illinois at Urbana-Champaign.

Spivack, G., & Shure, M. B. (1974). *Social adjustment of young children.* San Francisco: Jossey-Bass.

Strauss, A. (1966). Coaching. In B. J. Biddle & E. T. Thomas (Eds.), *Role theory: Concepts and research.* New York: Wiley.

Vandell, D. L., Anderson, L. D., Ehrhardt, G., & Wilson, K. S. (1982). Integrating hearing and deaf preschoolers: An attempt to enhance hearing children's interactions with deaf peers. *Child Development, 53,* 1354–1363.

Wheeler, V. A. (1981). *Reciprocity between first-grade friend and nonfriend classmates in a conflict-of-interest situation.* Unpublished doctoral dissertation, University of Rochester, Rochester, NY.

# 9
# Teaching Cooperation

Mara Sapon-Shevin

## INTRODUCTION

The teaching of social skills to children has only recently begun to receive the attention it warrants. There have been several major impediments to the recognition that children's social behavior can be established systematically, and these have arisen from a variety of sources. Each of these impediments will be examined and then followed by reports of the recent research and changes in educational philosophy that have made the teaching of social skills, such as cooperation, both a reasonable goal and a valued process.

The first impediment stems from *developmental frameworks*, in which rigid adherence to stage theories of development has led teachers and researchers to view social development as an inevitable, natural process in which systematic teaching is seen as fruitless or unnecessary. For example, many followers of Piaget have stated that the young child is incapable of interpersonal communication because he lacks the ability to take the role of the other child. Flavell (1963) writes that the preoperational child, who is primarily egocentric, "repeatedly demonstrates a relative inability to take the role of the other person, that is, to see his own viewpoint as one of many possible and to try to coordinate it with these others" (p. 156). He goes on to state, "The young child is . . . the unwitting center of his universe. Only his own point of view, his schemas, his perceptions, etc., can really figure in his various activities, since he is unaware that others see things differently, i.e., that there are points of view of which his is only one" (p. 274).

Piaget's (1965) work states that not until at least age 11 do children abandon some of their egocentricity, seeing rules as emanating from the agreement of those involved, susceptible to change, rather than as immutable. Kohlberg's work (Reimer, Paolitto, & Hersh, 1983) on the development of moral judgment places most children up to age 12 at Stage 1 or Stage 2 of his schema. Both of these are described as *preconventional* and are primarily egocentric, individualistic, and as such, preclude taking the perspective of other individuals. These assumptions have implied to many people that systematic teaching of interpersonal social skills to young children represents an inappropriate, doomed endeavor.

A second major impediment has been the *global* way in which affective curriculum goals and objectives are stated (Lillie, 1975, p. 21).

> Goals are vague: "educating the whole child," "Providing for emotional and social growth," "developing a feeling of self worth," "providing the child-oriented curriculum," and "developing creativity and independence" are phrases often cited by early children educators as objectives for preschool, day care, or nursery school programs. Although these are all important educational goals, they do not clarify the instructional tasks ahead for the teacher.

Even when social learning milestones are elaborated more fully, these descriptions are often viewed as checklists for achievement (i.e., the teacher marks off those children who have attained a specific level or criterion) instead of teaching goals or objectives, for which the teacher accepts the responsibility. Although some curriculum guides list the social skills that children are expected to master; that is, "The child participates in group activities without dominating the group;" "The child is willing to help others;" "The child interacts with a number of different children each day" (Broman, 1978, p. 242), the provision of specific strategies for reaching these goals is less common.

Another impediment has originated from *psychological theories* that have maintained the inevitability and even the value of aggressive interpersonal interaction. Problems of aggression often confront teachers in educational settings, and considerable research attention has been focused on the origins and control of aggressive behavior. Many common assumptions about aggression center on its innateness as a biological trait, including the Freudian notion that aggression inevitably dominates over personal and communal activity. Lorenz (1966) contends that aggression represents an instinctive biological disposition.

The psychoanalytic approach to controlling aggression has been through catharsis, or purging, of aggressive activity. Many still advise that children and adults need to express their anger and hostility openly in order to remain psychologically "healthy" (Caldwell, 1978). Again, these assumptions lead away from efforts to systematically establish prosocial behavior.

Several types of "mythology" have also impeded the serious study of cooperation and its establishment. Combs (1979) identifies *myths* as beliefs that are generally held, sometimes contain a germ of truth, justify behavior, and often become institutionalized. Two types of mythology have maintained a strong emphasis on competition in our schools.

Widely held educational mythology maintains that students achieve more academically in competitive settings, that competition is a great motivator, and that creating more cooperative, humane environments may promote social behavior but does so *at the cost of academic achievement.* Slavin (1983) writes: "The essentials of the traditional instructional system are so similar from school to school and even from country to country that we often forget that there is nothing sacred or immutable about them" (p. 2).

Another set of sociological and cultural myths maintains that "schools should prepare young people to live in our competitive society," that this must be done through competition, and that "failure is good for people, that experiencing failure is somehow strengthening and ennobling" (Combs, 1979, p. 121).

Fortunately, many of these impediments are being removed, and recent research in many areas of child development, group processes, cross-cultural anthropology, and learning theory have offered support to the feasibility and positive outcomes of directly teaching children cooperative skills.

## Challenges in Child Development

The "egocentric child" concept has been effectively challenged recently (Cairns, 1979). Garvey and Hogan (1973) conducted studies showing that children in the age range $3\frac{1}{2}$–5 spend considerable time in social interaction and much of that interaction involves talking. Yarrow and Waxler (1977) conducted a study on prosocial behaviors in very young children, particularly in response to the discomfort or pain expressed by someone else in the environment. They report (p. 79):

> While in the youngest children others' crying tended to elicit contagious cry-ing as well as amusement, crying began to decrease, and as it waned, it was replaced by serious or worried attending. Around 1 year most of the youngest cohort first showed comfort to a person crying or in pain by patting, hugging, or presenting an object. Among $1\frac{1}{2}$- and 2-year-olds, comforting was some-times sophisticated and elaborate, e.g., fixing the hurt by trying to put a Band-aid on, covering mother with a blanket when she is resting, trying to locate the source of the difficulty. Children also began to express concern verbally and sometimes gave suggestions about how to deal with the problem. Such pre-cocity on the part of the very young gives one pause. The capabilities for com-passion, for various kinds of reaching out to others in a giving sense are viable and effective responses early in life. How such behaviors develop and change in the process of socialization in various cultures and subcultures are issues to which science has addressed little investigation.

Cross-cultural studies further support the hypothesis that even very young children are capable of empathic responses to other individuals. Borke (1973) studied children in both America and China and found that "Chinese and American children by 3 to 3.5 years of age were able to differentiate easily between social situations which evoke happy and unhappy responses in other people. These results . . . provide further evidence that the capacity for social sensitivity and empathic awareness develops at a very early age" (p. 107).

The crumbling of previously accepted notions of fixed developmental stages has been accompanied by growing data that support the crucial role played by teachers and by the general social environment in establishing and maintaining social behaviors in children. Smith, Neisworth, and Greer (1978) state, "Teachers are all too quick to assume that a child's inappropriate behaviors must be the result of problems at home or due to immaturity. Teachers need to realize that these behaviors are, at least partially, a consequence of their own actions" (p. 84).

## Challenges in Psychological Development

Much of the early work that focused on children's social behavior concerned itself with the factors that generate and maintain aggressive behavior in children. Bandura and Walters (1963) pointed out the need for a close examination of aggression and its relation to the environment. Subsequent experimentation confirmed the notion that it was indeed possible to shape aggressive behavior in children. In an experiment by Walters and Brown (1963), the following hypothesis was tested: "Children rewarded for hitting responses in an impersonal play situation subsequently show more interpersonal physical aggression than children who have not been rewarded" (p. 564). An experiment was carried out in which 7-year-old boys played with a toy doll that dispensed marbles and lit up when punched. In subsequent game playing, these boys showed more physical aggression than those who had not experienced the training session.

A study by Wahler (1967) addressed the possibilities of strengthening and weakening different kinds of play (aggressive play, solitary play, cooperative play) through the use of contingent peer attention. This study confirmed the notion that social behavior could be brought under the control of the social environment and, more important, that the other children in the classroom represented part of the social environment and could, therefore, be seen to be controlling properties of children's social behavior.

A study by Allen, Hart, Buell, Harris, & Wolf (1965) established that social reinforcement (in this case, teacher praise and attention) could bring about prominent changes in the social behavior of an "isolated" nursery school child. In this study, the teacher presented systematic attention to the child whenever she interacted with other children. This was followed by a marked increase in the amount of time this child spent interacting with other children.

In a further attempt to assess relevant aspects of the environment, particularly in terms of their potential for providing the occasion for different types of social behavior, Quilitch and Risley (1973) undertook a study that assessed the role of different kinds of toys in affecting social behavior. This experiment established that "The type of toys given to children within a free-play setting has a pronounced and dramatic effect on their social play and the amount of time spent playing cooperatively with each other" (p. 577). Quilitch and Risley (pp. 577–578) concluded their study with the following recommendations:

> Schools and child-care centers can now take charge to maximize children's opportunity to practice social and cooperative play behaviors. This social training, traditionally left to chance, could be planned so that all children have the maximum possible opportunity to develop their social skills. . . . Play materials that set the occasion for aggressive play, verbal behavior, sharing behavior or competition might be used with groups of children suffering certain behavioral play deficits. . . . Thus, the study of the effects of toys upon children's social behaviors allows the applied psychologist to create developmental or therapeutic play environments that promote social behaviors previously found amenable only to individual remediation programs.

The Quilitch and Risley article is important in that it identified activities (such as games and toys) as part of the environment that can affect social behaviors.

These studies established experimentally the possibility of shaping certain social behaviors in children through systematic reinforcement procedures. Various programs have been developed to assist the parent, teacher, or therapist in applying these principles to the socialization of young children in natural settings (Asher & Renshaw, 1981; Becker, 1971; Michelson, Sugai, Wood, & Kazdin, 1984; Patterson & Guillion, 1976; Sheppard, Shank, & Wilson, 1972; Strain, 1981).

With specific reference to the inevitability of aggressive behavior in children, recent research has seriously weakened some underlying assumptions. Some recent investigations describe aggression in ways more compatible with the development of systematic strategies for decreasing aggressive behavior and with teaching more socially desirable responses to conflict. Sears, Whiting, Nowlis, and Sears (1953) and Eron, Walder, Toigo, and Lefkowitz (1963) report positive correlations between the amount of physical punishment a child receives at home and the amount of aggressive behavior children display in school. In other words, children who are themselves punished tend to punish other children. Sears, Maccoby, and Levin (1957, p. 766) state:

> the way for parents to produce a nonaggressive child is to make abundantly clear that aggression is frowned upon, and to stop aggression when it occurs, but to avoid punishing the child for his aggression.

Caldwell (1978) reviews relevant research in the area and makes the following suggestions: (a) physical punishment of aggression is not the answer; (b) ignoring aggression in children is not the answer; and (c) nonpermissiveness in our attitudes toward aggression may be as important as punishment for aggressiveness.

Recent observations made by educators of nursery and day care schools in China have also cast doubt on the presumption that aggression in young children is inevitable and to be expected. Kessen (1976, p. 56) reports

> The children were generally docile and *conforming*, displaying little of the restlessness, rough and tumble play, grabbing of property, or the pushing and striking of peers that are common in American homes and nursery schools.

Sidel (1976, p. 114) reports a similar observation

> What is so amazing, of course, in walking the streets of Peking or Shanghai, or visiting a commune or urban neighborhood, is that we never saw aggression among the children. No doubt it exists, but we never witnessed it.

In analyzing these findings and contrasting them with a much higher rate of aggressive behaviors found among kibbutz-raised children in Israel, Sidel (1976, p. 168) comments

> Part of the reason for this difference might stem from acceptance on the part of those who live in the Kibbutz of Freudian psychology and of aggression as a natural component of man, possibly one which is better acted out than repressed. The Chinese, of course, do not study Freud and those who are aware of his teachings do not believe they are relevant to their setting. That the Chinese do not believe that aggression is necessarily inevitable seems evident. (p. 168)

In challenging the psychoanalytic notion of aggression as a health catharsis, Berkowitz (1973, p. 135) after reviewing the literature on controlling aggression in children concludes

> He [the child] should not be encouraged to attack someone to express his hostility in the hope that he will drain some hypothetical energy reservoir. The catharsis notion is an outmoded theoretical conception lacking adequate empirical support which also has potentially dangerous social implications. Violence ultimately produces more violence.

Other studies have also indicated that exposure to aggression may stimulate and increase aggression rather than reduce it (Cohen, 1976).

## Challenges in Learning Theory/Educational Research

Extensive recent research in the area of cooperative learning has countered the notion that children learn best under competitive conditions and that competition is essential in maintaining high rates of performance. In a meta-analysis of 122 studies conducted by Johnson, Maruyama, Johnson, Nelson, and Skor (1981), the authors found that cooperation is superior to both competition and individualistic efforts in promotion achievement and productivity and that cooperation without intergroup competition will promote higher achievement and productivity than will cooperation with intergroup competition. Both Slavin (1980; 1983) and Sharan (1980), in extensive reviews of the literature, documented the effectiveness of cooperative learning methods in producing high levels of achievement; in promoting more positive race relations in desegregated schools; in facilitating the integration of mainstreamed students in regular classrooms; and in improving students' self-esteem, their liking of their classmates and teacher, and their feelings of internal locus of control.

The notion that high achievement can only be accomplished at the expense of social/emotional development has been successfully challenged. Research in the area of cooperative learning supports the notion that cooperative learning can facilitate *both* academic achievement and the development of positive interpersonal skills by using models that make use of positive peer pressure and positive social interaction in order to achieve academic objectives.

## Challenges in Social/Cultural Mythology

It is more difficult to challenge cultural mythology with research, because mythology is not data based. Strong arguments have been raised, however, to counter some of the widely held beliefs often advanced in support of competition. Combs (1979) challenges the notion that schools must be competitively organized in order to prepare students for a competitive world. He states that we are, as a world, increasingly *dependent* upon one another and that, while there are instances in which we do compete with one another, mostly we cooperate with others in order to allow society to function smoothly. Combs (p. 19) states

> Advocating competition as a way of life also produces a concomitant belief that, of necessity, someone must win and someone must lose in life's activities. Few of us would be willing to accept such a dog-eat-dog concept as a basic guideline for living together in our democratic, cooperative society.

In responding to the myth that competition is a great motivator, Johnson and Johnson (1978) and others have found that competition is only effective when each child feels that he has a chance to win; clearly, in many school situations, this is not the case. And, finally, in responding to the belief that students must experience failure in order to grow and be able to deal with failure in the future, Sapon-Shevin (1978) argues that the best preparation for subsequent failure is a long history of successes, positive self-esteem, and a realistic assessment of one's own skills and abilities. In other words, even if there are aspects of competitiveness and failure out in the "real world," we do not have evidence to support the belief that schools must mirror that world as preparation.

# METHODS OF TEACHING COOPERATION

There are numerous ways of systematically establishing cooperative behaviors in students; these vary in terms of their formality (restructuring an entire curriculum as opposed to initiating a single activity) and in terms of their resemblance to typical classroom organization and activities. There are also less formal, less intensive ways of structuring classroom activities that promote cooperative behavior; the use of cooperative learning games and children's literature that focuses on cooperative themes are two ways in which teachers can incorporate activities designed to foster cooperation into their existing daily structure. The advantage of these strategies is the ease with which they can be adopted in limited form with a minimum of training and preparation and without significantly altering existing structures in the classroom.

This chapter will briefly review several of the more formal, intensive models for cooperative learning and will then focus on the use of cooperative games and the use of children's literature to assist in the establishment of cooperative social interaction in children.

## Academic Approaches

The Jigsaw Method (Aronson, 1978), Teams Games Tournaments (De-Vries & Edwards, 1973), and various Small Group Learning models (Johnson & Johnson, 1975; Sharan, 1980) are examples of systematic ways of restructuring academic curricula through the use of cooperative learning techniques. The strength of such models is in their comprehensiveness and their adaptability to various subject areas.

### The Jigsaw Method

In Aronson's (1978) Jigsaw Method, students are assigned to six-member teams; the material to be learned is divided into six parts, and each student is responsible for learning and then teaching his portion of the material to each of his groupmates. Members of different groups who have been assigned the same section of material meet in "expert" groups to discuss their own sections. Each group member is tested on all of the material, so that there is a forced interdependence between group members. For example, if the topic being studied is the life of Abraham Lincoln, one group might be given information on his early years, another group information on Lincoln's Civil War experiences, another group information on the assassination, etc. Originally designed to mitigate the problems and tensions that had developed between students of different racial groups following desegregation, evaluative data on the efficacy of the Jigsaw Method have been mixed.

Sharan (1980) reports that in some cases, the use of the method resulted in positive changes in students' attitudes toward themselves, toward classmates, and toward school, and some significant gains in achievement for minority group pupils.

### Competitive Cooperative Groups: TGT, STAD

In Teams Games Tournaments (TGT) (DeVries & Edwards, 1973; DeVries & Slavin, 1978), students are divided and assigned by the teacher to four- or five-member groups, which are heterogeneous according to ability and reflect the ethnic/racial mix of the classroom. The students tutor one another in preparation for weekly tournaments in which students compete with members of other teams who performed comparably in the past. After the tournaments, team scores are figured and a newsletter is used to recognize high-scoring teams and individuals.

In Student Teams-Achievement Divisions (STAD), students are also assigned to teams made up of high-, average-, and low-performing students. After new material has been presented by the teacher, teams help one another to go over worksheets and learn the material. Following this team practice, students take individual quizzes on the new material. Individual scores are combined into team scores based on an improvement score (how much the student's quiz score exceeds his past quiz average).

In a new variation, Team-Assisted Individualization (TAI) (Slavin, Leavey, & Madden, 1982), students are assigned to four- or five-member heterogeneous teams and then work through programmed mathematics units. Teammates work in pairs of their choice, helping each other with the material. Students who have completed a unit take checkout tests and a team score is derived from individual student test scores and the number of tests completed in a week.

In reviewing the research on TGT and STAD, Sharan (1980) summarized the effects of these methods on academic achievement as follows: "It appears that the team tasks [peer tutoring] and scoring systems are not critical components for the TGT and STAD methods . . . but the team reward [group scoring] and the underlying structure of instructional activities do account for achievement gains" (pp. 247–248). TGT and STAD experiments have produced positive effects on a variety of measures assessing social and affective variables, including increases in pupils' perceptions of mutual concern among peers, more positive attitudes toward subject matter, and an increase in the number of friends as measured on a sociometric test.

### Small Group Learning: Learning Together and Group Investigation

In Learning Together (Johnson and Johnson, 1975), teacher-assigned heterogeneous groups work on a single product as a group, following specific guidelines from the teacher. The teacher's role consists of assigning students to heterogeneous groups, arranging the classroom to facilitate peer interaction, providing appropriate materials, explaining the task and the cooperative goal structure to the students, observing the student–student interaction, intervening as needed, and evaluating the group products using a criterion-referenced evaluation system. Group members are trained to observe and monitor the social interactions within their own group and to provide feedback to group members concerning the extent to which they have praised, supported, asked questions, clarified, or paraphrased one another during the group work time.

Sharan's (1980) Group-Investigations model (G-I) involves two to six students working in groups on subtopics, which are part of a general problem delineated by the teacher. For example, if the area being studied is the Renaissance, one group might investigate the music of the time, another group the art of the period, another group the scientific investigations of the time, etc. Teachers and students cooperatively plan the goals and expected outcomes of the group, and each group works together on a project that is subsequently presented to the class as a whole. The method stresses having students share their individual perspectives with the group as a whole and having groups broaden the perspective of the whole class through their presentations.

Johnson and Johnson (1978) report positive outcomes for academic achievement as well as increased attraction, trust, interpersonal liking, sense of being accepted by teachers and peers, and more positive attitudes toward school and towards the learning situation. Sharan (1980) reports the efficacy of the G-I method for promoting learning on a high level of cognitive function, without a loss in the acquisition of basic information, and in substantially improving the social climate of the classroom.

*General Comments*

Although all of these methods share the thread of group cooperation, there are prominent differences in the extent to which competition is also utilized (as in TGT), the extent to which the actual group processes are monitored by the teacher, and the ways in which group outcomes are measured. More recent research has addressed itself to detailing the precise nature of the social interaction that takes place in small groups (Webb, 1982) and to answering certain remaining key questions regarding the appropriateness of equating group outcomes with individual learning and the effects of the division of responsibility on individual responsibility and learning.

# Cooperative Games

One strategy for establishing cooperative behaviors is the use of games, especially those that stress cooperation rather than competition. Games are a way of providing children with "fun"; games represent activities chosen for their appeal to children and their general acceptance as a standard part of childhood programming. Games, however, can be examined as ways of structuring the environment for a brief period of time according to very specific "rules." During the game, children can be observed to engage in specific social interactions: touching each other in various ways, repeating set words or phrases, choosing and/or excluding other children, and so forth.

Teachers must exercise caution, however, in the games they select to play with children; a careful analysis reveals that many games provide for social interactions that are considered undesirable in other (nongame) settings and that often contradict the social behavior likely to be proposed by a teacher at other times in the school day. For example, Simon Says is ostensibly a game to teach listening and discrimination skills. However, when examined from a viewpoint of what actually happens during the game, it also appears to provide the opportunity for one child to cause other children's elimination from the game through attempts to mislead or trick. Teachers who have worked hard to establish positive social relationships among children in their classrooms may find a need to look critically at the games they organize or allow to be played in their classes.

In a previous study (Sapon-Shevin, 1976), I examined several hundred children's games in terms of the social behaviors initiated by the games and found numerous games that provided for the display of a wide range of social behaviors generally considered undesirable. For example,

1. *Taunting/teasing:* Children are required to call another player a name or to repeat in chant-like fashion some mocking refrain (examples: Lame Wolf, King of the Castle).

2. *Grabbing or snatching in scarcity situations:* A situation is presented in which there are more children than objects (chairs, clubs, etc.) and children who are able to secure the scarce object may remain in the game while other children are eliminated (examples: Musical Chairs, Steal the Bacon).

3. *Monopolizing or excluding other children:* A situation is organized so that some children are in control (of a ball or a situation) and use their energy to keep other children from participating (examples: Keep Away or circle games in which children try to keep other children from breaking through the circle).

4. *Physical force:* Situations in which children are asked to hit another player with a ball, pull another player across a line, slap another child with one's own hands or with a ruler, or push another child out of the circle (examples: Spud, Tag Ball, King of the Castle).

Inasmuch as such game behaviors can be viewed as incompatible with the establishment of the desirable social skills identified earlier, teachers must carefully analyze the behavioral components of the games they select.

Because not all games are of equal value in teaching appropriate social skills, teachers who are seeking consistency in the models they present to children and in the behaviors in which children engage during schooltime will want to seek out games that will help strengthen, rather than contradict, the establishment of certain social behaviors.

One way of examining games relates to the extent to which they foster competitive or cooperative behaviors. Competitive situations are those in which children work against one another, thus producing losers as well as winners, and often many losers and only one winner. In cooperative situations, the obstacle to be overcome is not another player, but rather the inherent difficulty of the task itself or some external obstacle, such as time. For example, two children attempting to build a tall tower of 12 blocks are confronting the obstacles of gravity and balance; if they succeed, they have triumphed over these obstacles rather than over each other.

Many teachers already have extensive repertoires of cooperative activities, but may not refer to them as *games.* To many people, a game must be, by definition, a competitive activity in which there are winners and losers. Children themselves become socialized at a very young age to consider only certain kinds of activities to be games. A 7-year-old, after watching a group of 4-year-olds play a cooperative game, exclaimed to me, "Hey, that's not fair, that's an everybody wins game; somebody's gotta lose." For this reason, educational settings represent ideal locations for teaching children that "fun" does not have to mean one winner only and that "winning" need not necessarily be the desirable or only objective of an activity.

Cooperation, however, is not simply a "mind set" or an inclination. Rather, there are very specific skills and strategies that children need to be taught in order to cooperate successfully. These skills include listening to one another, coordinating one's movements and energies with those of other children, and engaging in those social behaviors that will facilitate and prolong interacting with other children rather than driving them away.

This chapter will focus on two kinds of cooperative games: those designed primarily for promoting positive social interaction and those designed to develop academic, cognitive skills through a cooperative framework.

## Cooperative Games for Fun

Although numerous cooperative behaviors can be structured and strengthened by cooperative games, the games selected for inclusion here focus on four specific behaviors, which can be identified as teaching objectives for social interaction:

1. Including children who have been left out; opening one's games or activities to others; finding a part for another child to play.
2. Sharing and taking turns.
3. Touching other children gently; helping other children who have fallen down or who are experiencing difficulty.

4. Talking nicely to classmates; calling classmates only by names they like; noticing and commenting on classmates' strengths rather than weaknesses.

Each game is described in terms of how it is played, the social behaviors structured by the game, and how the game can be modified or adapted. The games all fit into one or more of the categories, although there is considerable overlap and crossover between the games.

*Including Others/Sharing, Taking Turns.* The following games are examples that fit this category.

*Cooperative Tale* (Arnold, 1972) — One player starts a story and each player adds a little piece to the story, moving around the circle.

*Because* (Arnold, 1972) — The first player describes an event, the second player must give a reason for the occurrence of that event, and the third player must give a probable effect of that event, such as "The toast burned"; "Because the toaster was too hot"; "So everyone had charcoal for breakfast."

Social Behaviors: Listening to others; taking turns; coordinating one's efforts with those of other children. Notes/Suggestions: These games required the systematic inclusion of many children. Children less able may be given prompts or help by the adult or by other children, but may still participate in the activity.

*Cooperative Shapes, Numbers, or Letters* (Orlick, 1978) — Groups of children are asked to use their bodies to form various shapes (circle, square), letters, or numbers.

Social Behaviors: Gentle physical contact; inclusion; problem solving. Notes/Suggestions: In order for this activity to be successful, children must find a way to decide collectively how to form the shape/letter and how to use all of the children. This can be seen as a crucial antecedent to subsequent discussions of "What part can you find for Johnny to play?" or "How can Suzie be part of this game?"

*Nonverbal Birthday Line-up* (Harrison, 1976) — In this activity, the leader gives only the following instructions: "Without talking, line yourselves up according to the month and day you were born. The idea is to have one line starting with January and ending with December with everyone in the right order." The participants themselves must figure out a way to communicate without words so that they know where to begin and end the line and where everyone fits.

Social Behaviors: Including others, nonverbal communication, gentle touching. Notes/Suggestions: It is always fascinating to see a group working on this activity. Groups often hold up fingers for months and days, some have stamped their feet different numbers of times, acted out their month, etc. This author generally urges the group to do an internal, nonverbal check on themselves before the oral count-down at the end. This often results in much heated gesturing, repositioning, etc. Sometimes one or more "leaders" emerge, who attempt to get the group in the right order. This sometimes is the occasion for silent negotiating and compromise, as there can only be one beginning to the line and one end.

*Musical Laps* (Harrison, 1976) — This is a cooperative version of *Musical Chairs*. The whole group forms a circle all facing in one direction, close together, each with hands on the waist of the person ahead. When the music starts, everyone begins to walk forward. When the music stops, everyone sits down in the lap of the child to the rear. If the whole group succeeds in sitting in laps without falling to the floor, the *Group* wins. If children fall down, gravity wins. It works best with more than 10 children about the same size.

*Nonelimination Musical Chairs* (Orlick, 1978) — The object is to keep everyone in the game even though chairs are systematically removed. As in the competitive version, music is played, and more and more chairs are removed each time the music stops. In this game, though, more children have to sit together to keep everyone in the game.

Social Behaviors: Gentle physical contact; sharing, inclusion; group problem solving. Notes/Suggestions: These two games are unique in that they represent crucially different alternatives to traditional musical chairs, in which pushing, shoving, and grabbing lead to success. In Musical Laps, the obstacle is gravity; this game is ideal because it rarely works the first time, as children tend to stand too far apart. When everyone falls down, the group must then engage in problem solving; that is, "What can we try to make it work?" Even young children playing this game have been observed to engage in elaborate planning and hypothesis testing. When the group finally succeeds, there is general rejoicing. An additional positive feature of this game is the fact that when the group collapses, it cannot be identified as "Billy's fault" but, because many children fall, is usually seen as a failure of the group.

In Nonelimination Musical Chairs, rather than the pushing and exclusionary tactics of traditional Musical Chairs, children must find ways to make room for more and more children. The verbal behavior heard during this game is generally of the form "Come sit on/with me" or "Make room for Johnny."

This game represents an ideal starting point for exploring issues of "limited resources" with children; rather than confirming the "each child must have his own material" notion. Teachers can explore ways in which children can find creative alternatives to exclusion. For example, on the playground, if more than two children want to use the seesaw, how could that be done?

(For example, two children on each end; two children count, while two see-saw, then switch places, etc.).

*Barnyard* (Harrison, 1976) — People stand in a large circle, choose six animals (less for a group of fewer than 20) and count off by animals. Then, with everyone's eyes closed, each person finds all the others of his or her kind by constantly calling the animal sounds, "Baa-a-a," "Meow, meow," etc. When two of the same animals come across each other, they hold hands and find others until they are all together. It is a very funny game. *Note:* The idea is not to finish first, but merely to find your own kind.

Social Behaviors: Gentle touching; inclusion; listening. Notes/Suggestions: This game can be used as a way of structuring interaction between *specific* children. For example, by naming Billy and Sam (who don't generally interact) both "Horses," the adult ensures that the two boys will "find each other" and become a part of the same group. Animals can also be assigned in such a way as to pair an out-going, active child (who can be predicted to participate freely) with a withdrawn or quiet child who seldom participates, thus ensuring the involvement of *both* children.

*Big Snake* (Orlick, 1978) — The children start by stretching out on their stomachs and holding the ankles of the person in front of them to make a two-person snake, which slithers across the floor on its belly. They soon connect up for a four-person snake, an eight-person snake, and so on, until the child group is one Big Snake. At various lengths, the children like to see if they can turn the whole snake over on his back without coming apart. The snake can also go over "mountains" through "holes" or up "trees," or may curl up and go to sleep. It takes a coordinated snake to perform these last two feats.

Social Behaviors: Taking turns; coordinating movements; following requests; sharing limited materials; communicating and taking cues from other children; gentle physical contact. Notes/Suggestions: In this activity, children must work together to accomplish a given task. It also structures a situation that attempts to include a varying number of children and to use the bodies/energies of all of the children.

After children have successfully played these games, teachers can refer back to them as examples when situations arise that require the cooperation and/or collaboration of numerous children. "Remember how you all worked together to make the big snake move in the same direction?" A game like the Big Snake presents a situation in which any single individual's idea of which direction to move must give way to the wishes of others for this activity to succeed. This fact can be used as a discussion starter to explore (a) Who decided what to do? (b) How could you tell that person what *you* wanted to do? (c) Could you decide together? If not, how did you take turns deciding? (d) How did you feel about being the one to decide about going along with the others' ideas?

*Helping Others.* The following games fall into this category.

**Frozen Bean Bag** (Orlick, 1978) (Help Your Friends) — This is an active game of helping. All the children begin by moving around the area at their own pace, each balancing a bean bag on his or her head. The leader can change the action or pace by asking the children to try to skip, hop, go backwards, go slower, go faster, etc. If the bean bag falls off a child's head, he or she is frozen. Another child must then pick up the bean bag and place it back on the frozen player's head to free him, without losing his own bean bag. The object of the game is to help your friends by keeping them unfrozen. At the end of the game, the children can be asked how many times they were helped or helped others. If desired, a quick count of helping acts can be taken.

Social Behaviors: Being attentive to and finding those who need help; providing assistance; gentle physical contact; insuring the continued participation of all children. Notes/Suggestions: This game serves as an introduction to several crucial concepts: (a) How can one tell when someone needs help? (b) What are some ways of helping? (c) How does one respond *after* she or he has been helped?

Following this game, the teacher might introduce a role playing situation in which one child is working or playing at some activity and somehow gets "stuck"; children can then brainstorm ways of helping that child continue; that is, help him find his missing puzzle piece, help him carry over a stool so he can reach the top of this building, etc.

**Hot or Cold** (Arnold, 1972) — An object is hidden while one player, chosen to be "it" is not in the room. He is then brought back and asked to find it. Other players tell him when he is "hot" or "cold," depending on whether he is approaching or going away from the place where the object is hidden. When the player has found the object, he then takes his turn at hiding it and joins the rest in directing the next player. This game can also be played by having children clap (loudly for "near," softly for "far") to guide another child to a hidden object.

Social Behaviors: Following directions, giving directions accurately. Notes/Suggestions: Unlike many activities that involve an "it" player, in this game all of the individuals are engaged in a facilitative activity for that "it" player; that is, they are all working directly for his or her success. Games of this type represent the epitome in cooperation: The success of the individual and the success of the group are not only compatible, but one is the function of the other. All of the players are working for the success of one child.

*Gentle Physical Contact.* This type of game includes:

**Knots** (Harrison, 1976) — Everyone closes eyes and moves together, each child taking a different child's hand in each of his or her hands. When each child has two hands, they all open their eyes and try to untangle themselves without dropping hands. The group must work together to get out the knots. It leads to very amusing situations because, although the group may end up in one big circle, most of the time there will be a knot or two in the circle, and even two or more circles, either intertwined or separate.

*Mile of Yarn* (Orlick, 1978) — This is an interesting way to "knit" young children together. One child starts with a bright ball of thick yarn (or a strip of material), wraps the end of the yarn around her waist, and passes it to another child, and so on. Once the whole group has been intertwined in yarn, the whole process is reversed. The last player begins to rewind the ball, passes it to the next child, and so on until the fully wound ball reaches the first child.

*Touch Blue* (Harrison, 1976) — The leader announces, "Everyone touch blue!" (or another color, object, etc.). Participants must touch something on another person. "Touch a sandal!" or "Touch a bracelet!" ensures physical contact. There are endless variations, such as "Touch a knee with your left thumb."

*Ha Ha* (Harrison, 1976) — Lots of floor space is needed or a lawn under a warm sun. Someone lies down and the next child lies down putting his or her head on the stomach of the first child. The third child puts his or her head on the stomach of the second child, and so on. Then the first child says "Ha!" Second child, "Ha Ha!" Third child, "Ha Ha Ha!" and so on, increasing the number of Has. The laughter is infectious.

Social Behaviors: Group problem solving; gentle physical contact. Notes/Suggestions: Many children have experienced few opportunities to engage in activities in which they touch other children in gentle, nonaggressive ways. Although gentle physical contact is not in and of itself a sufficient antecedent for cooperation, it does establish relationships between children that are more likely to lead to continuing physical proximity and social interaction. Adults use these games to introduce the ideas of making people feel better by touching them. Children who observe that another child looks sad or is crying can be encouraged to offer hugs, touching, and other physical contact, *already* a part of their repertoire from the game. For many children for whom touching is not encouraged at home, particularly boys, games provide a safe, structured way of insuring contact.

*Talking Nicely.* In this category examples include:
*Make Me Laugh* (Harrison, 1976) — Participants get in a circle. In turn, each child turns to the child on his or her left and attempts to say or do something to make that child smile or laugh. This can be done by saying something funny or complimentary to the other child, by making a funny face, or by any other means suggested by the teacher.

Social Behaviors: Saying nice things to someone; problem solving.

Notes/Suggestions: This activity is useful because it represents a systematic effort to teach children how to work at making each other happy. Many children already possess elaborate rituals for making other children (especially specific other children) miserable. This activity can also be viewed as a link to the procedures described by Spivack and Shure (1974) for problem solving around the question "How could he make Bill happy?"

*Introductory Name Game* (Prutzman, Burger, Bodenhamer, & Stern, 1977)—Have children sit in a circle to foster group feeling and to allow everyone to see and pay attention to the child speaking. Ask a simple, interesting question. "What is your favorite dessert?" or "What is a game you enjoy?" or "What is your favorite soup?" Go around the circle and have everyone say his or her name and answer the questions. Children can then be asked what they remember about each child; for example, "What is Billy's favorite toy?" Participation should be voluntary. Some children may choose not to answer the question.

*The Affirmative Interview* (Prutzman et al., 1977)—An activity for a large group, where one child is interviewed and given special attention in front of the whole group. The questions should be simple, nonthreatening, and interesting enough to hold the attention of those listening. Some examples are What is your favorite sandwich? What place would you like to visit? What is something you enjoy doing? on Saturday morning? after school? What good movie have you seen lately?

The interviewer should look directly at the child being interviewed and ask questions that seem appropriate to that child. The interviewer should be very positive, praising the interviewee as much as possible. Also, only one or two children should be interviewed in one time block, so that everyone is able to enjoy an equal amount of attention from those listening.

Social Behaviors: Asking and answering questions; listening to others; taking turns. Notes/Suggestions: These activities can be easily adapted to the age and maturity levels of the children involved. They represent systematic ways for teaching children to "make conversation" and to say nice things about each other.

Simply playing a game that incorporates cooperative behaviors does not ensure that children will generalize those behaviors into other situations. The teacher will need to follow the games with other activities that help the child to develop an awareness of the process in which he was engaged and ways in which the game behaviors apply to other parts of his life. The teacher may want to conduct discussions after the game, asking children to remember what happened, why the game turned out well or poorly, what could have been improved, and pointing out the specific positive behaviors that occurred.

The children can also be helped to identify other situations where those behaviors are appropriate; for example, following the Frozen Bean Bag game with a discussion of ways we help others at school, at home, on the playground, etc. Helping others could then be used as a theme over a period of 1–2 weeks, during which "helping others" projects could be generated. The teacher can use the games as a basis for problem solving and role playing similar real-life situations; for example, "We have 15 children and only 10 packages of crayons, what can we do?" or "Mary and Elaine are playing hospital and Karen wants to join them—what part could she have?" Having children engage in cooperative play can help teachers to establish a consistency in their classroom regarding *what* solutions are considered acceptable and *how* these solutions can be reached.

For sources of cooperative games, see *The New Games Book* (Fluegelman, 1976) and *More New Games* (Fluegelman, 1981), *For the Fun of It* (Harrison, 1976), *The Cooperative Sports and Games Book* (Orlick, 1978), *The Second Cooperative Sports and Games Book* (Orlick, 1982), *Everybody Wins* (Sobel, 1983), *Playfair* (Weinstein & Goodman, 1980).

*Cooperative Instructional Games*

In addition to games that are strictly for fun, teachers can structure instructional games to be cooperative as well. The following games present a basic format, and each is adaptable for students of different ages and to different subject matter. Each game description includes an itemization of what materials are needed and what needs to be prepared in advance, how the game is played, what cooperative behaviors and what cognitive skills are structured by the game, and how the game can be modified with regard to skill and/or subject matter. These games are particularly useful for practice and reinforcement of material learned in a more formal setting.

*What Am I?* — Prepare in Advance: Cards or sticky labels to be attached to people's backs on which are printed the names of famous people, parts of the body, different animals, famous events in history, etc.

How to Play: (a) Pin one card on each player's back. (b) Participants circulate asking only yes–no questions of others trying to guess what/who is on their back. Participants can ask only one question of a person before going on to another player. (c) When players know who they are, they continue to circulate, answering questions for other players.

Academic/Social Skills: Students must know how to phrase questions that can be answered by "yes" or "no" and that yield productive information. Students must talk to and interact with a broad range of people because of the one-question-per-person rule. There is likely to be laughter and amusement as people ask and answer questions and general congratulations when players figure out who/what they are. Students who experience difficulty asking questions can be identified to the group so that other players can rally around them. (Although it is not considered "standard" to *give* players the answers, it is okay for players to help others know in which areas to ask questions; i.e., "Why don't you ask me if you're dead or alive?" "Why don't you ask if you fought on the side of the Allies or the Axis"?) Students who experience difficulty *answering* someone's questions can be encouraged to consult with another player ("Bill just asked me if the person on his back has ever held public office; has he?" "Is what's on Diane's back a mammal or not?") or to check with the teacher or another reference. The emphasis is consistently on pooling information and cooperating to find out the answer.

Modifications/Adaptations: Depending on the age and level of the pupils, the hidden cards could have names of people in the news ("Am I a man or a woman?" "Am I in politics?"); kinds of fruit ("Am I red?" "Am I a citrus fruit?"); parts of the body ("Am I part of the circulatory system?" "Do people have two of me?"); holidays ("Am I a national holiday?" "Are there parades on my day?"); or any set of items that belong to a general category. This game can be played with all ages, even with preschoolers, using pictures of the object to be guessed rather than the word(s).

*Sequence Games* – Prepare in Advance: A set of cards on which a story or sequence has been written so that each card provides the clue for what follows it. For example, one card says "When someone jumps, you say 'boo'." The next card says, "When someone says 'boo,' you faint." And the next card might say, "When someone faints, you say 'There s(he) goes, down for the count.'" The cues can be words, actions, gestures, or anything else that would be visible or audible to other players. One card must indicate who starts; for example, "You go first by _____", or say something like "When everyone is quiet, you say '_____.'"

How to Play: (a) Have people sit in a circle, in chairs or on the floor. (b) Shuffle the cards and distribute them to the players. Every player should have at least one card, although it is all right for players to have more than one. (c) The player whose card signals the beginning does whatever is on his or her card. (d) Each other player watches, follows the sequence, and does what is on his or her card, until all the cards have been used and the sequence is completed.

Academic/Social Behaviors: Students must attend closely to the words and/or movements of their classmates. They must coordinate their part of the sequence with that of other players. Like a play, the sequence will probably not work smoothly the first time. Students generally want to repeat the sequence over and over after redistributing the cards until the sequence flows smoothly and quickly. As much or as little academic content can be incorporated into the sequence as desired (see Modifications/Adaptations).

Modifications/Adaptations: This game is infinitely variable according to the age, level, reading ability (or lack thereof) of the students. More advanced students often enjoy writing their own sequence games for other class members. For example, one group of youngsters (four or five) prepares

a sequence game for the rest of the class. These can be written just for fun
or covering any subject matter. A sequence game on Eskimo culture might
have sequences like "When someone tells their dog to 'mush,' you pretend
to be preparing seal skins"; one on different kinds of rocks might have lines
like "When someone says 'the volcano is erupting,' you shout 'here comes
the molten lava, get out of the way.'" Cards for nonreaders can have two
pictures on them. The top picture (someone combing their hair) is their clue
for when to go; the bottom picture (brushing their teeth) is their clue for
what to do. In other words, when they see someone combing their hair, they
brush their teeth. Cards can have jokes on them: each card has the punch
line of the previous joke and the introduction to the next joke, players have
to figure out which punchline goes to which joke. Cards can have pieces of
a story or a rhyme that ends on one card and is continued on another; one
card says "If you lived in Holland then you would be Dutch, a rabbit is an
animal that lives in a _____" and the next card says "Hutch." "If you lived
in Finland then you'd be a Finn, a word that means the opposite of out is
_____."

With children who lack experience in following directions or reading, the
teacher can go over all the cards with the whole group before playing the
game, can focus on key vocabulary items before beginning the game, can
pair a good reader with a good "actor" as a team, or use other strategies.

*Cooperative Equations or Word Sentences* — Prepare in Advance: a set of
cards with different words on them. These might be separated by parts of
speech (i.e., nouns on red cards, adjectives on green cards, pronouns on yellow cards, etc.) or, for cooperative equations, a set of cards with different
numerals and numerical symbols or operations on them. Again, these might
be color-coded.

How to Play: There are various possibilities. The cards can either be dealt
out so that each player (4–6 players works best) has some of each kind of
card or so that each player has cards of one kind; i.e., Billy has all the verbs,
Allison all the adjectives, etc. Players can either take turns or cooperate to
make the longest possible sentence (or equation), the funniest sentence, a
sentence in which there is at least one, two, or three, of each part of speech,
etc. After a sentence has been written, all the players read it, or after an
equation has been done, all the players attempt to solve it. Rules can be varied according to the teacher's objectives for the game: make as many equations as you can that solve to be equal to 10; see how many verbs you can
use in one sentence; see if it's possible to write a question without using who,
what, or why, etc.

Academic/Social Behaviors: The cognitive skills involved in writing, reading, and/or solving sentences are self-explanatory and could be modified
according to the level of the players. The cooperation involved in deciding
what to write, what should go where, who can add something, etc., are the

most important cooperative behaviors likely to be observed. Teachers can add rules designed to encourage greater degrees of cooperation; that is, any sentence the group wants credit for must include at least one of each person's cards (thus ensuring that everyone is included and no one takes over) or that every member of the group must be able to read the sentence to the teacher to get credit, etc. Teachers will also want to experiment with determining what constitutes the optimum number of players in a group in order to intensify cooperation.

Modifications/Adaptations: The level of difficulty of the words on the cards, the rules that the teacher generates as constituting an acceptable sentence or equation, and the way the teacher credits acceptable sentences or equations can all be varied to increase or decrease the difficulty level of the game.

*Cooperative Concentration* — Prepare in Advance: A large set of cards that can be matched. The cards can have exact matches (i.e., two cards with the numeral *2* written on them), two cards can match because they are equivalent (one card has *3 × 4* on it and another *12*), cards can correspond in some way (one card has *casa* on it and another the word *house*, or one card can provide the answer to the other (one card has *invented the telephone* on it and another has *Alexander Graham Bell*).

How to Play: (a) Players sit or stand in a circle, each holding one (possibly two) cards, which they keep hidden against their chests. (b) One player begins by calling on a player to reveal his or her card, and then calling on another player (or himself) to reveal his or her card, attempting to make a match. (c) If the player successfully makes a match (group consensus), the two cards are placed in the center. (d) If the player is not successful, the players again conceal the cards and the next player takes a turn. (e) The players on both sides of the person taking his or her turn are designated as "helpers" and may provide assistance if asked for. (f) The game is "won" when all matches have been made and placed in the center. (g) Players continue to take turns even after they are no longer holding a card themselves.

Academic/Social Behaviors: The skills involved in being able to read what is on the cards and match it are self-evident. The level of difficulty of the game can be varied infinitely depending on the players (see Modifications/ Adaptations). Because the game is won when the whole group has succeeded, there is likely to be general cooperation in the group, and specific help displayed by the designated helpers. Because the role of "helpers" changes with each turn, every player is given the chances to be a solver and a helper. The rules of the game can be varied to allow any other player to volunteer help, to allow players to signal to each other concerning the placement of the cards, or any other variation that facilitates solving the puzzle and helping one another. As this is a cooperative activity, no form of help can be labeled *cheating*, and the academic outcomes of the game, which come from recognizing what matches what and understanding the relationship between cards, will be achieved regardless of the way in which cards are matched.

Modifications/Adaptations: This game has been successfully used in preschool classes and in high school physics classes. Virtually any subject matter can be used: colors can be matched with color words, sentences with the piece of punctuation they miss, equations with their solutions, clock faces with times, names of rocks with rock types, states and their capitals, presidents and their terms, chemicals and their symbols, etc. Younger, less advanced players can match exact duplicates: a picture of a dog with an identical picture of another dog; more advanced players can match riddles and their answers, excerpts from literature with the book from which they were drawn, French sentences with their English translations, etc.

Another, related game can be played using the same cards. Each player is given one card, and the players all circulate trying to find their match. This involves going up to different people, comparing cards, and judging whether they do in fact match. Again, the difficulty of this can be varied by what is on the cards — if near-perfect (but not exact) matches are possible, then players will find out that someone doesn't have a match, and a renegotiation of cards must take place. After all the cards have been matched, pairs of students can read aloud their matches or otherwise share them with the entire group. (In matching riddles and answers, for example, one member of the pair might read the riddle, the other the answer.)

*Cooperative $20,000 Pyramid* — Prepare in advance: Large cards with six *categories* written on them (one category per card). For example, holidays, tools, citrus fruits, presidents who were assassinated, things found in a bathroom, etc.

How to Play: This cooperative game is a take-off on the popular television game show. The object of the game is for one group of players to devise clues that they will give to other players, in an attempt to get them to say the name of the category. The clues will be *members* of the category. One group of players takes the large cards (or another list of the categories) and sits down together. As a group, they generate clues that they think will get the other players to say the name of the category. For example, for the category citrus fruits, they might come up with clues such as lemons, limes, oranges, tangerines, grapefruit, etc. For the category tools, they might come up with screwdriver, hammer, saw, pliers, wrench, etc. A group member records the clues for the group. After the group has come up with what they hope will be enough clues for each category, a number of players who were *not* part of this group are selected to receive clues. They sit facing the class on chairs. The clue givers hold up the large card with the category written on it for the rest of the class (but not the clue-receivers) to see and begin reading off their clues for the first category. As soon as any member of the clue-receivers thinks he knows the category, he consults with his fellow-receivers, and when they agree, they guess. If they are right, they go on to the next category. If they are wrong, they continue getting additional clues.

Academic/Social Behaviors: The skills involved in generating a list of members of the set without giving additional clues can be challenging. Many teachers have reported that although many young students know about Christmas, Halloween, etc., they do not know the generic term *holiday*. The clue givers must also think carefully about what clues might be misleading and in what order clues should be given. For example, for the category things found in the bathroom, the clues a toilet, a sink, a bathtub, soap, etc., might work in that order. If, however, the clues given were soap, toothpaste, deodorant, hairspray, etc. (all of which *are* found in the bathroom), the clue-receivers might very logically *mis*guess the category to be drugstore items or things you use on your body. The group of clue-givers must work cooperatively to generate a good list. Any single contribution must be considered and considerable discussion is likely to take place: "Is a nectarine a citrus fruit?" "Was Robert Kennedy an Assassinated President"? Although members of the group may contribute *un*equally to the total list of clues, single contributions count, and thus a child who thinks of only one clue, but a good one, will be appreciated in the group.

Modifications/Adaptations: Clearly, the level of difficulty of the categories will alter the game substantially. Very young players might have categories like fruit or animals, while more advanced players might have categories like words with silent letters, terms used on a job application, or what Joan of Arc might have said. Categories can be designed for any subject: in math, prime numbers; in history, famous battles of World War II; in literature, Shakespearian plays; in geography, state capitals, etc.

The rules of the game can also be modified to change the level of difficulty. As a challenge, a time limit can be set (let's see if all the categories can be guessed in X number of minutes) or by giving only five or fewer clues for any one category. Students can attempt to set records for the fewest number of clues required or the shortest amount of time needed. The exciting thing about this game is that it epitomizes cooperation: If the clues are good, the guessers are successful and, thus, everyone wins.

Because children are likely to respond positively to the suggestion "Let's play a game!" teachers can use these opportunities to have children interact in cooperative (and perhaps novel) ways. Both cooperative recreational games and cooperative academic games can be used in the classroom to substantially change the classroom atmosphere and to add a new flavor to ways in which children interact with one another.

## CHILDREN'S LITERATURE

Children's books provide another potential source for teaching children cooperative skills. Because most children enjoy story time and reading and because many educators already include a story or reading assignments in their daily activities, the use of children's books to teach about cooperation can easily be incorporated into many ongoing programs.

Streibel (1977) reviewed recent children's books in an effort to see how these books handled the resolution of conflict and to explore the potential of using children's books to teach alternatives to fighting. She presents the following goals and guidelines for analyzing and evaluating young children's books:

> Problem solving/Conflict resolution—The goal of peace education is teaching children methods of creative problem solving. The following questions were used to facilitate evaluation of the books in this category: (a) Who, if anyone, accepts responsibility for finding a solution to the problem/conflict? (b) How are fears of rejection/failure or needs to save face resolved? (c) Is the problem solved? How do you know it is solved? What are the implied standards for a "successful" solution? (d) Is the solution "realistic"? (Could the same behaviors in "real life" lead to similar resolutions?) (e) Is the solution a direct consequence of someone's actions, or does it occur by chance or by magic? Does the story imply that actions have consequences, or that things happen regardless of any plan or problem-solving approach? (f) What is the role of adults in the story? What does this teach about children's abilities to solve problems; what does it teach about adult problem solving? Are children encouraged to depend on adults or authority figures for solutions to conflicts? (g) Are there patterns along age, sex, ethnic lines in passivity–activity, leadership, decision making, or power in dealing with conflict? (h) What is the role of aggression or violence (either physical or verbal)? (i) What is the role of cooperation or competition? (j) Is any decision-making PROCESS shown? Does this process include exploring alternatives, or is only one solution presented? Are consequences of actions visualized before the solution is enacted? Are any standards presented for evaluating the best alternative? (k) Are everyone's needs taken into account in the solution? (pp. 2-3).

These broad questions can serve as the basis for adults to evaluate the potential of various books for teaching cooperation to children. The following selected books can be used as the starting point for teaching.

## Books for Young Children

*Two Good Friends* (Dalton, 1974) provides an excellent example of a book that could be used as part of a teaching unit on cooperation. Bear and Duck are very good friends, but they are very different: Duck is a meticulous housekeeper, whose house is always clean and neat, but he often has no food in the house; Bear, however, is an excellent cook, and his house is always full of good things to eat, but he is a terrible housekeeper and his house is always very dirty. After some initial difficulties in reconciling their differences, they reach a perfect solution: Duck cleans Bear's house for him and Bear bakes delicious things for Duck to eat.

Teachers might read the story aloud to children and then have them discuss the following:

1. What was Duck good at?
2. What was Bear good at?
3. What wasn't Duck good at?
4. What wasn't Bear good at?
5. How did Duck and Bear feel about each other's weaknesses? (anger, frustration)
6. What did they decide to do?

Several other books share the theme that people have unique talents, which can be combined to serve the best interests of the group as a whole. In *Mr. Tall and Mr. Small* (Brenner, 1966), a giraffe and a mouse meet in the forest and each thinks the other looks funny. The two animals argue and debate who is quicker, stronger, etc. In the end, a fire threatens both of them and they must combine their special strengths to save themselves. *My Friend John* (Zolotow, 1968) tells the story of a boy and his best friend, John. The two boys know and respect each other's strengths and weaknesses, cooperate whenever they can, and each boy has strengths that compensate for the other's weaknesses.

A whole class of children cooperate in *Doing Things Together* (Barkin & James, 1975) to plan a party for Parents' Day. One child does the decorations, another coordinates the entertainment, and the party is a big success. This book would be a natural introduction to actually planning and having a class party, which stresses the collaborative, cooperative nature of such an endeavor and rewards such efforts with the fun of a party.

As a follow-up activity, teachers might then have children identify one or two things they were good at and one or two things they were not good at. (Although children may be asked to help identify other children's strengths, it is highly preferable for children to identify only their own weaknesses.) The teacher can then ask students to try out the solution in the book by finding someone they can help with something and someone who can help them. For example, if Mary identifies herself as good at jumping rope and singing and not very good at remembering her library book and Billy identifies himself as good at remembering things but not good at jumping rope, the children can be encouraged to engage in some exchange of skills. Such exchanges, of course, need not be limited to two children; it is hoped they will involve children interacting with several other children. Children can be encouraged to explore solutions that involve both helping people learn how to do things better themselves *and* doing things for people, and teachers can explore with children the implications of each.

Once this helping/cooperation model has been established, the teacher can attempt to fade out such structure until the children are able independently to seek the help of other children and offer to help in areas of difficulty. Teachers can do this by following a sequence such as the following:

1. If Billy needs help with something, teacher offers him help and also verbally identifies another child who might be able to help ("I bet next time Karen could help with that").
2. The next time Billy needs help, the teacher either encourages Karen to help him ("Karen, I bet you could help Billy with that") or encourages Billy to seek Karen's help ("I wonder if Karen might be able to help you with that").
3. The next time a similar situation arises, the teacher steps even further into the background, perhaps by saying to the class, "Billy's having trouble with 'x'. What do you suppose you could all do about it?" and by encouraging other children to do the matching; that is, "Steven, why don't you help Billy find someone who can help him."

After each of these stages, the teacher should praise all of the participants, not just the helper. The teacher must be sure to model that admitting that one doesn't know or can't do something and asking for help are appropriate and expected behaviors. He or she can do this both by praising the child who asks for help appropriately; for example, "Billy had a problem, but he sure found a good way to get help," and by modeling behavior himself or herself, "I'm having a lot of trouble moving this desk—who could help me?" Following such a progression should allow the teacher to structure cooperative interactions systematically *and* to gradually withdraw herself or himself as the exclusive source of help and information.

Another book suggested by Streibel (1977) can also form the beginning of an exercise in cooperation. *That's Mine* (Winthrop, 1977) is the story of a boy and a girl who are playing with blocks. At first they are extremely competitive and verbally abusive, which leads to a fight in which both of their structures tumble to the ground. When they realize that they can work together, they are able to build something even more elaborate and exciting than they could alone. This book can be read to children and discussion can focus on the advantages of cooperation: "How did the children feel about each other when they were building separate buildings?" "What happened when both children wanted the same block?" "What made the children decide to work together?" "What kind of a building were they able to make together?" In *The Snowman* (Erskine, 1978), Berkley, a young bear, and his friend Calvin attempt to build a big snowman together. In fighting over who owns the snowman, they ruin it. Later, they come back and build some little snowmen and go sledding together. Like *That's Mine*, *The Snowman* stresses that fighting is counterproductive, while cooperation pays off. After reading and discussing either of these books, discussion can proceed to an elaboration of activities best accomplished cooperatively. A follow-up book, *Some Things You Just Can't Do By Yourself* (Schiff & Becky, 1973), can be shared with the children. This very brief book details things you can't do by yourself: hug, play checkers, play hide and seek, shake hands, ride in a wagon, kiss, etc. It ends by asking children to think of some additional things that can't be done alone. Children could be asked to draw or cut out pictures of other activities, and a book of cooperative activities might be assembled.

After this activity, the teacher may wish to select some of the cooperative games previously identified, particularly those that involve active sharing, to play with the children as further reinforcement of the notion of cooperation. Teachers may also wish to maintain an ever-alert posture toward instances of cooperation in their own classrooms and to reward such behavior; for example, by allowing the children involved to record their cooperation by dictating or drawing in the class book of cooperative activities.

Other books for use with young children include *Swimmy* (Lionni, 1963), in which a band of little fish decide to swim together to avoid being eaten by bigger fish; *I Can't Said the Ant* (Cameron, 1961), in which a tiny ant, with the help of many friends with different talents, solves a difficult dilemma; *Harlequin and the Gift of Many Colors* (Charlip and Supree, 1973), in which each child contributes a small piece of material from his own costume in order to make a costume for Harlequin; and *Jungle Day or How I Learned to Love My Nosey Little Brother* (Bottner, 1978), in which 7-year-old Jackie, who initially scorns her little brother's offer of help on an art project she's struggling with, later collaborates with him and by pasting the *best* parts of all her pictures together successfully creates a new, exciting animal.

## Books for Older Children

Books for older children can also be used to teach about cooperation, although the format for sharing such books with children may be somewhat different. In addition to reading aloud to children (a practice many teachers of older students *do* continue), teachers may assign selected books to individual children or to the whole class, followed by discussion or an assignment of some sort, including a cooperative sharing time with the class.

*The Blind Man and the Elephant: An Old Tale from the Land of India* (Quigley, 1959) might be used as an example of the value (and sometimes the necessity) of working together to figure something out. In this fable, six blind men approach an elephant and try to figure out what it is and what it looks like. Each man feels a different part of the elephant and, on the basis of what he feels, tries to infer what an elephant is. They learn that they have each touched *only a part* of the elephant and that in order to find out the truth, they must all put together their information. Teachers could follow up this story with both discussion and group exercises in which each child knows or has access to only a piece of a "whole" (a puzzle, a story, etc.), and all the children must combine their perspectives in order to develop the whole picture. This could be done on a very limited basis as follows: One child has the clue *red*, another the clue *fruit*, another the clue *round*, and another the clue *vine*. Different combinations of clues are tried and guesses are made: red and round could be a ball; red and fruit could be a strawberry; fruit and vine could be grapes; round and fruit could be an orange. Only when *all* of the clues are shared does the correct answer *tomato* emerge (yes — a tomato is a fruit, not a vegetable).

On a broader level, an exercise such as those described in the Jigsaw Method (Aronson, 1978) or the Group Investigation Method (Sharan, 1980) could be designed in which students have to combine what they each have learned or investigated in order to understand the whole picture. For example, Larry is charged with finding out what people wore in the Middle Ages, Susan with what kinds of housing they lived in, Karen with what music was like at the time, and Lamont with what jobs people held. All the students combine their information to write a class play, design scenery, find appropriate music, etc.

Another aspect of interpersonal cooperation is touched on in *The Quitting Deal* (Tobias, 1975), in which 7-year-old Jenny and her mother cooperate in order to help each other break bad habits: Jenny wants to stop sucking her thumb, her mother wants to stop smoking. By planning out different "cures" for one another — the "holding hands cure" in which they will hold each other's hands until the urge passes — and a series of positive contingencies they set for each other — they actively attempt to help each other overcome a problem in an atmosphere of love, trust, and cooperation.

This book might be used as an exploration of the ways in which children can learn to help one another with personal objectives through mutual support and positive peer pressure. It is possible to structure a classroom in which the achievement of any one child's objective becomes the opportunity for the whole class to celebrate. If the entire class gets extra free time when Michael finishes his spelling and if students have been taught specific positive ways to help Michael get done (encouraging him, not distracting him, etc.), then Michael's accomplishment becomes the source of celebration, and other students have the satisfaction of having assisted Mike. Teachers must be careful to structure such group contingencies in ways that are positive (i.e., never "everyone loses free time if Michael doesn't finish") and to help students learn positive ways to manage each other's behavior ("If you see Michael working, tell him he's doing a good job"). Teachers must also closely monitor the social behaviors that occur in such situations, being ever alert to make sure that the peer interactions are supportive and not punitive.

On a less formal level, opportunities abound for creating situations in which any child's success constitutes the group's success. For example, each child gets to color in one square on a big chart for each problem he got right, and when the whole grid is filled, something special happens for the whole class. In this way, Carol's five right answers contribute, as do Alice's ten and Darrel's ten adjusted, easier problems.

Other books for older readers with cooperation as a theme include *Where the Good Luck Was* (Molarsky, 1970), in which four 9-year-old boys work together to earn money to buy crutches for a friend with a broken ankle; *Sail, Calypso!* (Jones, 1968), in which two boys both find an abandoned sailboat, fight over its ownership, and eventually work together to renovate the boat; and *The Street of the Flower Boxes* (Mann, 1966), in which 9-year-old Carlos and his 5-year-old brother, Luis, rip up a neighbor's flowers, then replant the flowers, make and sell flower boxes to the whole neighborhood, and then plan a street carnival in order to cover unexpected expenses. Any of these books might be used as the take-off for discussions, projects, and elaboration on the themes of cooperation, friendship, conflict resolution, and working together.

The potential for using children's books to model cooperation is an exciting one, worthy of future exploration by educators who work with children. (For a subject matter index of children's books that includes cooperation as a listing, see Dryer, 1977.)

## SUMMARY

This chapter focused on two major strategies for establishing appropriate social skills in children, games and literature, with particular emphasis on cooperation and conflict resolution.

The research reviewed supported the notion that stopping aggression is not enough. Children need to be taught specific repertoires for dealing with those situations of conflict and stress that invariably present themselves in social environments. Although it is ultimately desirable that children be able to articulate the reasons for various social behaviors, children *can* be taught to display those behaviors even at ages when their limited verbal skills do not lend themselves to such articulation. Thus it is not necessary to wait until a child can explain "why we apologize when we hurt someone" or "why it's nice to share with people" before teaching them to apologize and share. It is appropriate with children of any age group to teach through activities that specify directly the social behaviors to be displayed; for example, patting the person on your left, saying something nice to someone in the circle. The use of children's games and children's books has been proposed because of their potential for establishing socially appropriate behavior and because game time and story time are already a part of most school curricula.

## REFERENCES

Allen, K. E., Hart, B. M., Buell, J. S., Harris, F. R., & Wolf, M. M. (1965). Effects of social reinforcement on isolate behavior of a nursery school child. In L. P. Ullman and L. Krasner (Eds.), *Case studies in behavior modification*. New York: Holt, Rinehart and Winston.

Arnold, A. (1972). *A World Book of Children's games.* New York: T. Y. Crowell.

Aronson, E. (1978). *The jigsaw classroom.* Beverly Hills, CA.: Sage.

Asher, S. R., & Renshaw, P. D. (1981). Children without friends: Social knowledge and social skill training. In S. R. Asher and J. M. Gottman (Eds.), *The development of children's friendships.* New York: Cambridge University Press.

Bandura, A., & Walters, R. H. (1963). *Social learning and personality development.* New York: Holt, Rinehart.

Barkin, C., & James, E. (1975). *Doing things together.* Milwaukee: Raintree Publishers.

Becker, W. C. (1971). *Parents are teachers.* Champaign, Ill: Research Press.

Berkowitz, L. (1973). Control of aggression. In B. Caldwell & H. Ricciuti (Eds.), *Review of child development research,* vol. III. Chicago: University of Chicago Press.

Borke, H. (1973). The development of empathy in Chinese and American children between three and six years of age: A cross-cultural study. *Developmental Psychology, 9,* 102–108.

Bottner, B. (1978). *Jungle day or how I learned to love my nosey little brother.* New York: Delacorte Press.

Brenner, B. J. (1966). *Mr. Tall and Mr. Small.* Reading, MA.: Addison-Wesley.

Broman, R. L. (1978). *The early years in childhood education.* Chicago: Rand McNally College Publishing.

Cairns, Robert B. (1979). *Social development: The origins and plasticity of interchanges.* San Francisco: W. H. Freeman and Company.

Caldwell, B. M. (1978). Aggression and hostility in young children. In C. Torriero (Ed.), *Readings in early childhood education.* Guilford, CT: Dushkin.

Cameron, P. (1961). *I can't said the ant.* East Rutherford, NJ: Coward McCann Georgian.

Charlip, R., & Supree, B. (1973). *Harlequin and the gift of many colors.* New York: Parents' Magazine Press.

Cohen, S. (1976). *Social and personality development in childhood.* New York: Macmillan.

Combs, A. W. (1979). *Myths in education.* Boston: Allyn and Bacon.

Dalton, J. (1974). *Two good friends.* New York: Crown.

DeVries, D. L., & Edwards, K. J. (1973). Learning games and student teams: Their effects on classroom process. *American Educational Research Journal, 10,* 307–318.

DeVries, D. L., & Slavin, R. E. (1978). Teams-Games-Tournament (TGT): Review of ten classroom experiments. *Journal of Research and Development in Education, 12,* 28–38.

Dryer, S. S. (1977). *The Bookfinder, vols. I and II.* Circle Pines, MN: American Guidance Services.

Eron, L. D., Walder, L. O., Toigo, R., & Lefkowitz, M. M. (1963). Social class parental punishment for aggression and child aggression. *Child Development, 34,* 849–867.

Erskine, J. (1978). *The snowman.* New York: Crown Publishers.

Flavell, J. N. (1963). *The developmental psychology of Jean Piaget.* New York: Van Nostrand Reinhold.

Fluegelman, A. (1976). *The new games book.* Garden City, NY: Dolphin Books/Doubleday.

Fluegelman, A. (1981). *More new games.* Garden City, NY: Dolphin Books/Doubleday.

Garvey, C., & Hogan R. (1973). Social speech and social interaction: Egocentrism revisited. *Child Development, 44*, 562–568.

Greene, F. (1962). *China.* New York: Ballantine Books.

Harrison, M. (1976). *For the fun of it: Selected cooperative games for children and adults.* Philadelphia: Nonviolence and Children Series. Friends Peace Committee.

Johnson, D. W., & Johnson, R. T. (1975). *Learning together and alone.* Englewood Cliffs, NJ: Prentice-Hall.

Johnson, D. W., & Johnson, R. T. (1978). Cooperative, competitive and individualistic learning. *Journal of Research and Development in Education, 12*(1), 3–15.

Johnson, D. W., Maruyama, G., Johnson, R. T., Nelson, D., & Skor, L. (1981). Effects of cooperative, competive, and individualistic goal structures on achievement: A meta-analysis. *Psychological Bulletin, 89*, 47–62.

Jones, A. (1968). *Sail, Calypso!* Boston: Little, Brown and Co.

Kessen, W. (1976). *Childhood in China.* New Haven, CT: Yale University Press.

Lillie, D. L. (1975). *Early childhood education: An individualized approach to developmental instruction.* Chicago: Science Research Association.

Lionni, L. (1963). *Swimmy.* Westminister, MD: Partheon.

Lorenz, K. (1966). *On aggression.* New York: Harcourt, Brace World.

Mann, P. (1966). *The street of the flower boxes.* New York: Coward, McCann and Geoghegan.

Michelson, L., Sugai, D. P., Wood, R. P., & Kazdin, A. E. (1984). *Social skills assessment and training with children.* New York: Plenum Press.

Molarsky, O. (1970). *Where the good luck was.* New York: Henry Z. Walck.

Orlick, T. (1978). *The cooperative sports and games book: Challenge without competition.* New York: Pantheon Books.

Orlick, T. (1982). *The second cooperative sports and game book.* New York: Pantheon Books.

Patterson, A. R., & Gullion, M. E. (1976). *Living with children: New methods for parents and teachers,* rev. ed. Champaign, IL: Research Press.

Piaget, J. (1965). *The moral judgment of the child.* New York: Free Press. [Originally published in 1932].

Prutzman, P., Burger, M. L., Bodenhamer, G., & Stern, L. (1977). *The friendly classroom for a small planet: Handbook of the children's creative response to conflict program.* New York: Quaker Project on Community Conflict.

Quigley, L. F. (1959). *The blind man and the elephant: An old tale from the land of India.* New York: Charles Scribners Sons.

Quilitch, H., & Risley, R. R. (1973). The effects of play materials on social play. *Journal of Applied Behavior Analysis, 6*, 573–578.

Reimer, J., Paolitto, D., & Hersh, R. (1983). *Promoting moral growth: From Piaget to Kohlberg.* New York: Longman.

Riley, S. (1971). Joey comes to class. *Early Years, 8*, 42–43; 55–57.

Sapon-Shevin, M. (1976). Formal group contingencies and games as the occasions for social interactions between children. Unpublished doctoral dissertation, University of Rochester, Rochester, NY.

Sapon-Shevin, M. (1978, October). Another look at mainstreaming: Exceptionality, normality and the nature of difference. *Phi Delta Kappan, 60*, 119–121.

Schiff, N., & Becky, S. (1973). *Some things you just can't do by yourself.* Stanford, CA: New Seed Press.

Sears, R. R., Maccoby, E. E., & Levin, H. (1957). *Patterns of child rearing.* Evanston, IN: Row, Peterson.

Sears, R. R., Whiting, J. W. M., Nowlis, V., & Sears, P. S. (1953). Some child-rearing antecedents of aggression and dependency in young children. *Genetic Psychological Monographs, 47,* 135–234.

Sharan, S. (1980). Cooperative learning in small groups: Recent methods and effects on achievement, attitudes, and ethnic relations. *Review of Educational Research, 50*(2), 241–271.

Sheppard, W. C., Shank, S. B., & Wilson, D. (1972). *How to be a good teacher: Training social behavior in young children.* Champaign, IL: Research Press.

Sidel, R. (1976). *Women and child care in China: A firsthand report.* New York: Penguin Books.

Slavin, R. E. (1980). Cooperative learning. *Review of Educational Research, 50*(2), 315–342.

Slavin, R. E. (1983). *Cooperative learning.* New York: Longman.

Slavin, R. E., Leavey, M., & Madden, N. A. (1982). *Effects of student teams and individualized instruction on student mathematics achievement, attitudes, and behaviors.* Paper presented at the annual convention of the American Educational Research Association, New York.

Smith, R. N., Neisworth, J. T., & Greer, J. G. (1978). *Evaluating educational environments.* Columbus, OH: Charles E. Merrill.

Sobel, J. (1983). *Everybody wins: Non-competitive games for young children.* New York: Walker and Co.

Spivack, G., & Shure, M. B. (1974). *Social adjustment of young children: A cognitive approach to solving real-life problems.* San Francisco: Jossey-Bass.

Strain, P. S. (1981). *The utilization of classroom peers as behavior change agents.* New York: Plenum Press.

Streibel, B. (1977). *Conflict resolution in children's literature.* Madison, WI: Center for Conflict Resolution.

Tobias, T. (1975). *The quitting deal.* New York: Viking Press.

Wahler, R. G. (1967). Child–child interactions in free field settings: Some experimental analyses. *Journal of Experimental Child Psychology, 5,* 278–293.

Walters, R. H., & Brown, M. (1963). Studies of reinforcement of aggression III: Transfer of responses to an interpersonal situation. *Child Development, 34,* 563–571.

Webb, N. (1982). Student interaction and learning in small groups. *Review of Educational Research, 52*(3), 421–445.

Weinstein, M., & Goodman, J. (1980). *Playfair.* San Luis Obispo, CA: Impact Publishers.

Winthrop, E. (1977). *That's mine.* New York: Holiday.

Yarrow, M. R., & Waxler, C. Z. (1977). The emergence and functions of prosocial behaviors in young children. In R. C. Smart & M. S. Smart (Eds.), *Readings in child development and relationships.* New York: Macmillan.

Zolotow, C. S. (1968). *My friend John.* New York: Harper Row.

# 10

# The Adolescent: Social Skills Training Through Structured Learning

Arnold P. Goldstein, Robert P. Sprafkin,
N. Jane Gershaw, and Paul Klein

Structured Learning, a skills training approach developed for use with certain adolescent and other skill-deficient populations, is the focus of the present chapter. We will present, in some depth, the nature of our target adolescent populations—who they are, how they are optimally identified and classified, and how they have been dealt with in treatment and skill remediation efforts in the past. Structured Learning will then be presented in detail. Its history, specific procedures, target skills, and research evaluation outcomes will each be described. In all, our effort will be to familiarize the reader with the substance of this approach, highlight its strengths and weaknesses and, in doing so, encourage both its further application and continued research examination.

## THE SOCIAL SKILL DEFICIENT ADOLESCENT

A number of diverse attempts have been undertaken to develop classification systems that adequately describe children and adolescents exhibiting behavior disorders. Prior to 1966, 24 such systems had been proposed (Group for the Advancement of Psychiatry, 1966). Unfortunately, most were essentially lacking in evidence of sufficient reliability, as well as evidence that the system related meaningfully to decisions about the types of remedial treatment best recommended. The group's own classification system made some beginning strides at dealing with these chronic deficiencies. But a truly useful system of classifying behavior disorders, perhaps of technological necessity, awaited the development of multivariate statistical techniques. By means of such techniques, investigators in recent years have been able to bring together and simultaneously draw upon very diverse types of information on a broad range of behaviorally disordered adolescents. In this regard, Quay, Peterson, and their colleagues have used observational behavior ratings by teachers, parents, clinic staff, and correctional workers; case history materials, the responses of adolescents themselves to personality testing, and other types of information — all obtained from and about adolescents in public schools, child guidance clinics, institutions for delinquents, and mental hospitals. In the research of these investigators, as well as several others (Achenbach, 1966; Achenbach & Edelbrock, 1978; Hewitt & Jenkins, 1946; Patterson & Anderson, 1964; Peterson, Quay, & Tiffany, 1961; Ross, Lacey, & Parton, 1965), a three-category classification pattern has consistently emerged. The three patterns — aggression, withdrawal, and immaturity — account for the vast majority of behaviors typically included under the term *behavior disorders.*

## Aggression

Quay (1966, p. 9) comments:

Almost without exception multivariate statistical studies of problem behaviors . . . reveal the presence of a pattern involving aggressive behavior, both verbal and physical, associated with poor interpersonal relationships with both adults and peers. This pattern has received a variety of labels: e.g., unsocialized aggressive (Hewitt & Jenkins, 1946); conduct problem (Peterson et al., 1961; Quay & Quay, 1965); aggressive (Patterson & Anderson, 1964); unsocialized psychopath (Quay, 1964); psychopathic delinquency (Patterson, Quay, & Cameron, 1959); antisocial aggressiveness and sadistic aggressiveness (Dreger et al., 1964); and externalizing (Achenbach, 1966).

This classification reflects such specific behaviors as fighting, disruptiveness, destructiveness, profanity, irritability, quarrelsomeness, defiance of authority, irresponsibility, high levels of attention seeking and low levels of guilt feelings. In Quay's research, youngsters in this category typically answer affirmatively to such questionnaire items as (Quay, 1966, pp. 10–11):

I do what I want to whether anybody likes it or not.
The only way to settle anything is to lick the guy.
If you don't have enough to live on, it's OK to steal.
It's dumb to trust other people.
I'm too tough a guy to get along with most kids.

Quay observes that the essence of this pattern is an active antisocial aggressiveness almost inevitably resulting in conflict with parents, peers, and social institutions. Children and adolescents extreme on this pattern seem likely to be in such difficulty as to be involved in the courts and institutions for delinquents.

# Withdrawal

Numerous researchers have also consistently identified a behavior disorder pattern characterized by withdrawal and variously labeled overinhibited (Hewitt & Jenkins, 1946); personality problem (Peterson et al., 1961), disturbed neurotic (Quay, 1964), internalizing (Achenbach, 1966), and withdrawn (Patterson & Anderson, 1964; Ross et al., 1965). Quay (1966, p. 11) describes this pattern further:

> These behaviors, attitudes, and feelings clearly involve a different pattern of social interaction than do those comprising conduct disorder; they generally imply withdrawal instead of attack. In marked contrast to the characteristics of conduct disorder are such traits as feelings of distress, fear, anxiety, physical complaints, and open and expressed unhappiness. It is within this pattern that the child who is clinically labeled as an anxiety neurotic or as phobic will be found.

In addition, as the relevant studies demonstrate, the behavior disorder pattern characterized centrally by withdrawal is also marked by depression, feelings of inferiority, self-consciousness, shyness, anxiety, hypersensitivity, seclusiveness, and timidity.

# Immaturity

As is true of aggression and withdrawal, immaturity has frequently emerged as a third prominent class of adolescent behavior disorder. It has been identified as such in samples of adolescents studied in public schools, child guidance clinics, and institutions for delinquents. Behaviors forming a significant component of the immaturity pattern include short attention span, clumsiness, preference for younger playmates, passivity, daydreaming, and incompetence. As Quay notes, this pattern represents a persistence of behaviors that largely were age appropriate earlier in the youngster's development, but that have become inappropriate in view of the chronological age of the adolescent and of society's expectations of him.

Quay's (1966) reflections on the three patterns of behavior disorders are most relevant to our skill deficiency focus. He comments (pp. 13–14):

> The characteristics of the three . . . patterns may all be said to be clearly maladaptive either from the social or individual viewpoint. Extremes of such behaviors are at variance with either the expectations of self, parents, or educational and other social institutions. . . . Each of the previous patterns also involves interpersonal alienation with peers, attack in the case of conduct disorders, withdrawal in the case of personality disorder, or lack of engagement in the case of immaturity.

To describe the aggressive, withdrawn, or immature adolescent as we have just done is to focus on what each youngster is and does. But, it will be profitable from a skill deficiency viewpoint to examine correspondingly what each such youngster is not and does not do. Thus, the aggressive adolescent is not only often proficient in fighting, disruptiveness, destructiveness, and similar antisocial skills; he is also deficient in such prosocial skills as self-control, negotiating, asking permission, avoiding trouble with others, understanding feelings of others, and dealing with someone else's anger. The withdrawn youngster, in an analogous manner, lacks proficiency in such prosocial skills as having a conversation, joining in, dealing with fear, decision making, dealing with being left out, responding to persuasion, and dealing with contradictory messages, as well as skills relevant to expressing or receiving apologies, complaints, or instructions. The parallel skill deficiency pattern for the immature adolescent typically involves a lack of competence in sharing, responding to teasing, responding to failure, dealing with group pressure, goal setting, and concentration. The illustrative prosocial skills we have enumerated here are a brief sampling of the skill training targets that form the major focus of Structured Learning.

## DEVELOPMENTAL HURDLES

We have proposed that behavior-disordered youngsters are primarily of three types and that each may be described not only in terms of the presence of a repertoire of dysfunctional and often antisocial behaviors, but also in terms of the absence of a repertoire of prosocial or developmentally appropriate behaviors. It is our belief that a treatment oriented toward the explicit teaching of prosocial skills can function as an optimal treatment approach for such adolescents. Desirable, functional skills missing from their behavioral repertoires can, we propose, be taught successfully. However, it is not only the aggressive, withdrawn, or immature youngster with whom we are concerned. Many other adolescents (those less likely to come to the attention of school, clinic, or institution personnel) are, we feel, appropriate potential targets for skill training efforts. Manster (1977), in his book, *Adolescent Development and the Life Tasks*, describes very well the sequence of life tasks that all adolescents must successfully master. In school, at work, in the community, and with peers, family, authority figures, the developing adolescent meets, must cope with, and master a wide and increasingly more complex series of personal and interpersonal life tasks. These tasks are many and varied. In the realm of love, sex, and peer relationships, the skills demanded may include social skills (e.g., having a conversation, listening, joining in), skills for dealing with feelings (e.g., dealing with fear, expressing affection, understanding the feelings of others), and skills useful for dealing with stress (e.g., dealing with embarrassment, preparing for a stressful conversation, responding to failure). School-related tasks demand proficiency at yet other skills. Certainly, primary here are planning skills (e.g., goal setting, gathering information, decision making). School settings also require daily success at tasks involving both peers (e.g., dealing with group pressure) and authority figures (e.g., following instructions). The work setting similarly is multifaceted in its task demands and, hence, in its requisite skills—again involving planning and stress management competencies in particular. For many youngsters, whether in school, at work, or elsewhere, the skill demands placed upon them frequently involve the ability to deal satisfactorily with aggression—either their own or someone else's. In these instances, skills to be mastered include self-control, negotiating, and dealing with group pressure.

The developmental sequences hinted at here are rarely smooth, and efforts at aiding their progression appear to be a worthy goal. It is in this sense, therefore, that the clinically "normal" adolescent experiencing the need for assistance over certain developmental hurdles is also a potential target trainee for the skill training approach that forms the substance of this chapter.

## TREATMENT APPROACHES

We now wish to turn to an examination of the diverse treatment approaches in use for skill-deficient adolescents. In doing so, we will place heaviest emphasis upon efforts to remediate the aggressive youngster. We will not slight the withdrawn, the immature, or the normal adolescent. Techniques applied to these latter youngsters, and the effectiveness of these techniques, will, indeed, be examined. But in terms of its impact on society, altering the overt behavior of aggressive adolescents and reorienting such behavior in more prosocial directions are goals of prime importance—and, thus, clearly deserving of our special attention.

### A Prescriptive Viewpoint: What Works for Whom?

A number of diverse approaches exist for the training, treatment, and rehabilitation of aggressive, withdrawn, immature, and other seriously skill-deficient youngsters. These include such putatively correctional, rehabilitative procedures as incarceration and probation; an array of traditional types of individual and group psychotherapy; several less psychodynamic group-oriented approaches, such as use of positive peer culture or guided group interaction procedures; a series of newer behavioral techniques, mostly centering around efforts to alter overt maladaptive or antisocial behavior by the management of reinforcement contingencies; and, very recently, certain psychoeducational therapies in which the treatment goal is usually to increase the adolescent's proficiency in prosocial skills and, by implication, decrease

his reliance on antisocial behaviors. Each of these approaches has its propo-
nents and opponents. For each there are testimonials, critics, and, in some
instances, research supporting its value.

Our own view regarding these several correctional, rehabilitative, counseling, psychotherapeutic, behavioral, and psychoeducational procedures is
prescriptive. By this we mean that none of them may be viewed as good or
bad or effective or ineffective in any absolute sense. Let us, for example,
consider the recent history of psychotherapy. In the 1950s, when research
on the effectiveness of psychotherapy was just beginning, investigators asked
Does treatment A work? or Is treatment A better than treatment B? But
answers to such questions, even when positive, proved next to useless. Little
or no information was provided by answers to such global questions, either
about how to improve the effectiveness of the particular treatment (because
it was studied as a whole, with no attention to its separate components) or
how to use the research findings to help any individual person (because only
group effects were studied).

In response to such shortcomings and the companion awareness that none
of the treatments can yet be sufficiently powerful to help all or almost all
types of people, clinicians and researchers have come more and more to ask
a new, more differential type of outcome question: Which type of patient,
meeting with which type of therapist, for which type of treatment, will yield
which outcome? This customized, differential, or prescriptive view of the
helping enterprise leads to avoiding the assignment of all types of patients
to any given treatment; to acknowledging that a given psychotherapist or
counselor may be therapeutic for one type of patient but may be unhelpful
or even psychonoxious for another; to steps that counteract the patient
uniformity myth, the therapist uniformity myth, and the treatment uniformity myth. Mostly, this view leads to positive efforts to match patients, therapists, and treatments to maximize the likelihood of a beneficial outcome.
We and others have elaborated this prescriptive viewpoint in considerable
detail elsewhere (Goldstein, 1978; Goldstein & Stein, 1976).

In 1974, Martinson published an article titled "What Works?", a review
of diverse efforts to alter the deviant behavior of juvenile offenders.
Research on the treatments and correctional efforts examined by Martinson
focused upon a large number of rather diverse intervention procedures. His
conclusion was unequivocal: "With few and isolated exceptions, the
rehabilitative efforts that have been reported so far have had no appreciable effect on recidivism" (p. 25). This singularly negative conclusion, however, has been effectively shown by Palmer (1976) to rest on Martinson's
reliance upon what we called the "one-true-light-assumption" (Goldstein &
Stein, 1976). This assumption, the antithesis of a prescriptive viewpoint,
holds that specific treatments are sufficiently powerful to override substantial
individual differences and aid heterogeneous groups of patients. Research

in all fields of psychotherapy has shown the one true light assumption to be erroneous (Goldstein, 1978; Goldstein & Stein, 1976), and Palmer (1976) has shown it to be especially in error with regard to aggressive and delinquent adolescents. Palmer returned to the data that Martinson had examined and from which he drew his "nothing works" conclusion. In each of literally dozens of the studies thus reexamined by Palmer, there were homogeneous subsamples of adolescents for whom the given treatments under study did work. Martinson's error was to be unresponsive to the fact that when homogeneous subsamples are combined to form a heterogeneously composed full sample; positive, negative, and no-change treatment outcome effects of different subsamples will cancel one another out. This makes the full sample appear no different in average change than an untreated control group. But, to repeat, when smaller, more homogeneous subsamples are examined separately, many treatments work. Our task, then, is not to continue the futile pursuit of the one true light, the one treatment that works for all; but, instead, to discern which treatments administered by which treaters work for whom, and for whom they do not.*

## Incarceration

It is one thing to espouse a prescriptive clinical strategy regarding the treatment of disturbed and disturbing adolescents, but quite another to implement such a strategy. Our state of prescriptive knowledge is primitive. Most investigators and correctional practitioners, for example, view incarceration as the least desirable alternative treatment for juvenile offenders. "Locking them up" as a correctional treatment is seen as often leading to more and not less eventual antisocial behavior. Yet, in almost every instance, holders of this essentially anti-incarceration viewpoint simultaneously acknowledge, directly or by implication, that there is likely a yet-to-be specified subsample of offenders, probably chiefly characterized by a high prior rate of recidivism, for whom incarceration may well be the optimal intervention (Achenbach, 1974; Bailey, 1966; Empey, 1969; Kassenbaum, Ward, & Wilner, 1972; McClintock, 1961; Robinson & Smith, 1976).

---

*The reader involved in elementary or secondary education will find the reasoning we have put forth here to be familiar, in that what we have described as a growing orientation toward prescriptiveness in the practice and investigation of psychotherapy parallels quite directly a very similar movement in the field of education. The work of Cronbach and Snow (1977) on aptitude treatment interactions, Hunt's (1971) behavior–person–environment matching model, and Klausmeier, Rossmiller, and Saily's (1977) individually guided education are but three of several emerging examples in recent years of growing attention in educational theory and practice to a prescriptive intervention strategy.

## Probation

Probation, too, has its champions as a differentially offered treatment. Evidence exists that probation may be an appropriate intervention for adolescent offenders who are neurotic (Empey, 1969); who display some reasonable level of prosocial behavior (Garrity, 1956) or social maturity (Sealy & Banks, 1971); or who are, in interpersonal (I-level) maturity terminology, Cultural Conformists (California Youth Authority, 1967). In differential contrast, however, probation may well be a considerably less than optimal prescription when the youth is nonneurotic (Empey, 1969); manipulative (Garrity, 1956); or low in social maturity (Sealy & Banks, 1971).

## Individual Psychotherapy

A clearly analogous differential position may be taken regarding the appropriateness of other treatment interventions for disturbed and disturbing adolescents. Depending on which type of youngster is involved, a given treatment may or may not be prescriptively appropriate. Individual psychotherapy, for example, has been shown to be effective with highly anxious adolescents (Adams, 1962); the socially withdrawn adolescents (Stein & Bogin, 1978); those displaying, at most, a moderate level of psychopathic behavior (Carney, 1966; Craft, Stephenson, & Granger, 1964); and youngsters, displaying a set of characteristics summarized by Adams (1961) as "amenable." More blatantly psychopathic youngsters, low anxious youngsters, or those "nonamenable" in Adam's (1961) terms are appropriately viewed as prescriptively poor candidates for individual psychotherapy interventions. Thus, we see once again that depending on which type of youngster is involved, a given treatment may or may not be prescriptively appropriate.

## Group Approaches

Many group approaches have been developed in attempts to aid aggressive, withdrawn, or immature adolescents. Some of the more popular have been activity group therapy (Slavson, 1964), guided group interaction (McCorkle, Elias, & Bixby, 1958), and positive peer culture (Vorrath & Bendtro, 1974). Research evidence demonstrates that such approaches are, indeed, useful for older, more sociable and person-oriented adolescents (Knight, 1969), for those who tend to accept confrontations (Warren, 1972) and the more neurotic-conflicted (Harrison & Mueller, 1964), or acting-out neurotic (California Youth Authority, 1967). Youngsters who are younger, less sociable, or more delinquent (Knight, 1969), who avoid confrontations (Warren, 1972) or are psychopathic (Craft, 1964) apparently are less likely to benefit from group interventions.

## Behavior Modification

In recent years, a host of therapeutic procedures have been developed and proffered under the rubric *behavior modification.* Although withdrawn (O'Connor, 1972) and immature (Stumphauser, 1972) youngsters have been the recipients of some behavioral treatment efforts, much of it has focused upon the aggressive, oppositional, or delinquent adolescent (Bernal, Duryea, Pruett, & Burns, 1968; Braukmann & Fixsen, 1976; Drabman, Spitalnik, & O'Leary, 1973; Patterson & Reid, 1973; Stumphauser, 1972; Wahler, 1969). As Braukmann & Fixsen (1976) note, the more effective of these behavior modification programs typically include (a) a teaching component (e.g., modeling, shaping) designed to add the desired behavior to the adolescent's repertoire; (b) an incentive component (e.g., token economy, behavioral contract) to motivate him; and (c) the actual delivery of reinforcement contingent upon performance of the desired behavior. Literally dozens of specific techniques incorporating one or more of these components have been developed. Even though behavior modification has been the focus of much more experimental scrutiny than any other orientation, a very great deal of evaluative research is still to be done before the effectiveness of such interventions is firmly established. We would add to their admonition by proposing that the outcomes of such research are much more likely to be positive if the treatments thus considered are conceived, implemented, and evaluated prescriptively.

## Summary

This very brief prescriptive view of the array of interventions currently in use for adolescents — incarceration, probation, individual and group psychotherapy, other group approaches, and a number of behavior modification efforts — all converge on the same conclusion. Bailey (1966), Martinson (1974), Vinter & Janowitz (1959), Kassenbaum et al. (1972) and others who have similarly reviewed the (especially aggressive) adolescent research literature and concluded, in essence, that "nothing works" are, in our view, simply wrong. In considering relevant research literature they have succumbed to the joint influence of the one-true-light assumption and the patient uniformity myth. It is not correct that "nothing works." It is correct that almost everything works but, in each instance, only for certain youngsters. To be sure, our prescriptive sophistication for the treatment of adolescents is at a mere beginning. The relatively few adolescent characteristics we were able to point to in connection with each treatment considered above clearly shows the very rudimentary level of prescriptive matching now possible. But it is, indeed, a beginning. Our task, therefore, is to develop and continuously refine an array of treatment offerings, and to engage in the types of prescriptive research that enables us to make even better matches of treaters, youngsters, and treatment approaches. How such research is optimally planned, executed, and evaluated has been considered by us elsewhere (Goldstein, 1978; Goldstein & Stein, 1976), and the interested reader is referred to these sources. The remainder of this chapter is devoted to a presentation of one prescriptive approach, Structured Learning. It is a psychoeducational intervention, designed specifically to enhance the prosocial, interpersonal, stress management, and planning skills of the aggressive, withdrawn, immature, and "normal" but developmentally lagging adolescent—all of whom are, by our definition, skill deficient.

## WHAT IS STRUCTURED LEARNING*

Structured Learning consists of four components—modeling, role playing, feedback, and transfer training—each of which is a well-established behavior change procedure. *Modeling* refers to providing small groups of trainees with a demonstration of the skill behaviors we wish youngsters to learn. If the skill to be learned were negotiating, we would present youngsters with a number of vivid, live, audiotaped, videotaped, or filmed displays (geared to maximize attention and motivation to learn) of adolescents who use the skill effectively. In the display, the skill of negotiating would be broken down into a series of behavioral steps that make up negotiation, and each example presented or modeled would illustrate the use of these behavioral steps. Thus, trainees would see and hear the models negotiating successfully in a variety of relevant settings: at home, at school, and with peer groups.

Once the modeling display has been presented, the next step in learning the skill is role playing. *Role playing* is behavioral rehearsal or practice for eventual real-life use of the skill. To use our example of the skill of negotiation, individuals in the group are asked to think about times in their own lives when they would benefit from using the skill they have just seen modeled or demonstrated. In turn, each youth is given the opportunity to practice using the skill (i.e., the steps that make up the skill) as he or she might eventually use it in real life. This role playing is accomplished with the aid of other group members, as well as the trainers, who simulate the real-life situation. The teenager who wishes to practice negotiation with a friend regarding where to go after school might role play the scene with another group member who acts out the part of the friend.

---

*A further examination of the background and content of this approach appears in Goldstein, Sprafkin, Gershaw, and Klein (1979). This source also contains a detailed presentation of the Structured Learning skills taught to adolescents and the forms (Checklist, Grouping Chart, Homework, etc.) used in selecting and grouping trainees, as well as recording their skill acquisition progress.

*Feedback*, the third component in Structured Learning, refers to providing the youngster with an evaluation of the role played rehearsal. Following each role play, group members and trainers provide the role player with praise (and sometimes material rewards) as his or her behavior becomes more and more like that of the model. During this part of the group session, adolescents are given corrective instruction, which will enable them to continue to improve their skill use.

The last element in Structured Learning is *transfer of training*. This refers to a variety of procedures used to encourage transfer of the newly learned behaviors from the training setting to the real-life situation. Homework assignments, use of real or imaginary props and procedures to make role playing realistic, and rerole playing a scene even after it is learned well (i.e., overlearning) are some of the several transfer enhancing procedures that are part of Structured Learning. Several additional means of potential usefulness for increasing transfer of training are described in detail in Goldstein and Kanfer (1979). In a real sense, transfer of training is the most important, and often most difficult aspect of Structured Learning. If the newly learned behavior does not carry over to the real-life environment, then a lasting and meaningful change in the youngster's behavior is extremely unlikely to occur.

## ORGANIZING THE STRUCTURED LEARNING GROUP

### Selecting Participants

Each Structured Learning group should consist of trainees who are clearly deficient in whatever skills are going to be taught. If possible, trainees should also be grouped according to the degree of their deficiency in the given skill. Trainees can be selected who are all deficient on certain common groups of skills, as assessed by the Structured Learning Skill Checklist. Defining which skills to work on are the *behavioral objectives* for the trainees in the class. The optimal size group for effective Structured Learning sessions consists of five to eight trainees plus two trainers.* The trainees selected for a Structured Learning group need not be from the same class or even the same grade. However, since behavioral rehearsal or role playing in the group is most beneficial when it is as realistic as possible, it is often useful to include

---

*We recognize that most classes in schools are much larger than is desirable for a Structured Learning class. Often it is possible for two or more teachers to combine their classes for a period or two and have one teacher take the larger group while a smaller group of five to eight students participates in Structured Learning. Other means for organizing Structured Learning groups in regular classes are described in Goldstein et al. (1979).

trainees whose social worlds (family, school, peer groups) have some important elements of similarity. In this way, when a participant is asked to role play a part, this can be done in a reasonably accurate fashion.

There are times when it will not be possible to group trainees according to shared skill deficits. Instead, the trainer may want to group according to naturally occurring units, such as school classes, residential cottages, etc. If the trainer decides to use naturally occurring units, the group members will probably reflect some range of skill strengths and weaknesses. In this case, it will be helpful to fill out a Skill Checklist for each trainee in order to obtain a group profile. Starting skills should be those in which many of the group members show a deficiency. In such a potentially divergent group, it is likely that one or two members will be proficient in the use of whatever skill might be taught on a given day. In that case, these more skillful youngsters can be used in helper roles, such as co-actors or providers of useful feedback.

## Number, Length, and Spacing of Sessions

The Structured Learning modeling displays and associated procedures typically constitute a training program, which can be broken into segments matching part or all of the semesters of the school or training setting. It is most desirable that training occur at a rate of one or two times per week. Spacing is crucial. Most trainees in skill training or other programs learn well in the training setting. However, most fail to transfer this learning to where it counts – at home, in school, with friends, in the community. In order to provide ample opportunity for trainees to try out in real life what they have learned in the training setting, there must be ample time and opportunity for skill use between sessions.

Typically, each training session should focus on learning one skill. As such, it should include one sequence of modeling, several role plays, feedback, and assignment of homework. Each session should be scheduled for 1 hour in length. Session length should be determined by a number of factors, such as attention span, impulsivity, verbal ability. If most trainees in a given group show particularly brief attention spans; the session can be as brief as 20 minutes. In such cases, more frequent sessions are advisable. Sessions longer than an hour are possible for trainees whose capacity for sustained attention is greater. Since Structured Learning is intensive, we recommend that sessions not last beyond $1\frac{1}{2}$ hours, as learning efficiency tends to diminish beyond that length of time.

## Trainer Preparation

The role playing and feedback activities that make up most of each Structured Learning session are a series of "action–reaction" sequences, in which effective skill behaviors are first rehearsed (role play) and then critiqued (feedback). As such, the trainer must both lead and observe. We have found that one trainer is hard pressed to do both of these tasks well at the same time; thus, we recommend strongly that each session be led by a team of two trainers.

Two types of trainer skills appear necessary for successful Structured Learning leadership. The first might best be described as General Trainer Skills — i.e., those skills requisite for success in almost any training or teaching effort. These include

1. Oral communication and listening skills;
2. Flexibility and capacity for resourcefulness;
3. Enthusiasm;
4. Ability to work under pressure;
5. Interpersonal sensitivity; and
6. Broad knowledge of human behavior, adolescent development, etc.

The second type of requisite skills are Specific Trainer Skills — that is, those germane to Structured Learning in particular. These include

1. Knowledge of Structured Learning — its background, procedures, and goals;
2. Ability to orient both trainees and supporting staff to Structured Learning;
3. Ability to initiate and sustain role playing;
4. Ability to present material in concrete, behavioral form;
5. Ability to deal with management problems effectively; and
6. Sensitivity in providing corrective feedback.

For both trainer selection and development purposes, potential trainers should first participate, in the role of trainees, in a series of Structured Learning sessions. These sessions are led by two experienced trainers. After this experience, beginning trainers can then colead a series of sessions with an experienced trainer. In this way, trainers can be given several opportunities to practice what they have seen and, also, receive feedback regarding their performance. In effect, we recommend the use of the Structured Learning procedures of modeling, role playing, and feedback as the method of choice for training Structured Learning techniques appropriately.

## THE STRUCTURED LEARNING SESSIONS

### The Setting

One major principle for encouraging transfer from the classroom or clinical situation to the real-life setting is the rule of identical elements. This rule states that the more similar or identical the two settings (i.e., the greater number of physical and interpersonal qualities shared by them), the greater the transfer from one setting to the other. We urge that Structured Learning be conducted in the same general setting as the real-life environment of most participating youngsters and that the training setting be furnished to resemble or simulate as much as possible the likely application settings. In a typical classroom, one can accomplish this, in part, through the creative use of available furniture and supplies. Should a couch be needed for a particular role play, several chairs can be pushed together to simulate the couch. Should a television set be an important part of a role play, a box, a chair, or a drawing on the chalkboard can, in imagination, approximate the real object. If actual props are available (for example an actual TV set, store counter, living room furniture), they should certainly be used in the role play scenes.

A horseshoe seating arrangement is one good example of how furniture might be arranged in the training room. Participating trainees sit at desks or tables so that some writing space is provided. Role playing takes place in the front of the room. Behind and to the side of one of the role players is a chalkboard displaying the behavioral steps that make up the skill being worked with at that time. In this way, the role player can glance up at the steps during the role play. If film strips or other visual modeling displays are used, the screen should be easily visible to all.

## Premeeting Preparation of Trainees

Preparation of trainees individually may be helpful prior to the first meeting of the Structured Learning class. This orientation, or structuring, should be tailored to the individual needs and maturity level of each trainee. It should be designed to provide each group member with heightened motivation to attend and participate in the group, as well as to provide the trainee with accurate expectations of what the activities of the group will be like. Methods of trainee preparation might include

1. Mentioning what the purposes of the group will be, as they relate to the specific skill deficits of the youngsters; for example, the trainer might say, "Remember when you got into a fight with Billy, and you wound up restricted for a week? Well, in this class you'll be able to learn how to stay out of that kind of trouble so you don't get restricted."
2. Mentioning briefly and generally what procedures will be used. The trainee must have an accurate picture of what to expect and not feel as if he or she has been tricked. The trainer might say, "In order to learn to handle (these kinds of) situations better, we're going to see and hear some examples of how different kids do it well, and then actually take turns trying some of these ways right here. Then, we'll let you know how you did, and you'll have a chance to practice them on your own."

3. Mentioning the benefits to be gained from participation, stating that the group will help the trainee work on particular relevant issues, such as getting along in school, at home, and with peers.
4. Mentioning the tangible or token (e.g., points, credits, etc.) rewards that trainees will receive for participation.
5. Using the trainer–trainee relationship to promote cooperation; for example, the trainer might ask the youngster to "Give it a try. I think you'll get something out of it."
6. Presenting the Structured Learning class as a new part of the curriculum in which the trainee is expected to participate. Along with the message of expected participation, trainees should also understand that the group is not compulsory and that confidentiality will be respected. A verbal commitment from the youngster to "give it a try" is useful at this point.
7. Mentioning the particular skills that the youngster is likely to identify as his or her major felt deficiency, and how progress might be made in working on such skills.

## The Opening Session

The opening session is designed to create trainee interest in the group as well as to educate the group regarding the procedures of Structured Learning. The trainers open the session by first introducing themselves and having each trainee do likewise. A brief familiarization period or warm-up follows, with the goal of helping trainees to become comfortable interacting with the trainers and with one another in the group. Content for this initial phase should be interesting as well as nonthreatening. Next, trainers introduce the Structured Learning program by providing trainees with a brief description of what skill training is about. Typically, this introduction covers such topics as the importance of interpersonal skills for effective and satisfying living, examples of skills which will be taught, and how these skills can be useful to trainees in their everyday lives. It is often helpful to expand upon this discussion of everyday skill use, so as to emphasize the importance of the undertaking and its personal relevance to the participants. The specific training procedures (modeling, role playing, etc.) are then described at a level that the group can easily understand.

New trainers should note that, although this overview is intended to acquaint trainees with Structured Learning procedures, frequently trainees will not grasp the concepts described until they actually get involved in the training process. Because of this, we do not advise trainers to spend a great deal of time describing the procedures. Instead, we recommend that trainers describe procedures briefly, as introduction, with the expectation that trainees will actually experience and understand the training process more fully once they have actually started.

## Modeling

As the first step, the trainer describes the skill to be taught and hands out cards (Skill Cards) on which the name of the skill and its behavioral steps are printed. The first live modeling display of the skill is then enacted. Trainees are told to watch and listen closely to the way the actors in each vignette portray the behavioral steps. The skills taught by Structured Learning are listed in Figure 10.1.

Modeling displays should begin with a narrator setting the scene and stating the name of the skill and the behavioral steps that make up that skill. The trainers then portray a series of vignettes in which each behavioral step is clearly enacted in sequence. Content in the vignettes should be varied and relevant to the lives of the trainees. We have described in detail elsewhere (see Goldstein, Sprafkin, & Gershaw, 1976) those characteristics of modeling displays that usually enhance or diminish the degree of learning. Model characteristics are also discussed in chapter 3 of this volume.

Examples of Structured Learning skills for adolescents, and the behavioral steps that constitute each skill, include

1. Starting a Conversation:
   Greet the other person.
   Make small talk.
   Decide if the other person is listening.
   Bring up the main topic.
2. Giving Instructions:
   Decide what needs to be done.
   Think about the different people who could do it and choose one.
   Ask that person to do what you want done.
   Ask other person if he or she understands what to do.
   Change or repeat your instructions if necessary.
3. Understanding the Feelings of Others:
   Watch the other person.
   Listen to what the person is saying.
   Figure out what the other person might be feeling.
   Think about ways to show you understand what he or she is feeling.
   Decide on the best way and do it.
4. Negotiation:
   Decide if you and the other person are having a difference of opinion.
   Tell the other person what you think about the problem.
   Ask the other person what he or she thinks about the problem.
   Listen openly to his or her answer.
   Think about why the other person might feel this way.
   Suggest a compromise.

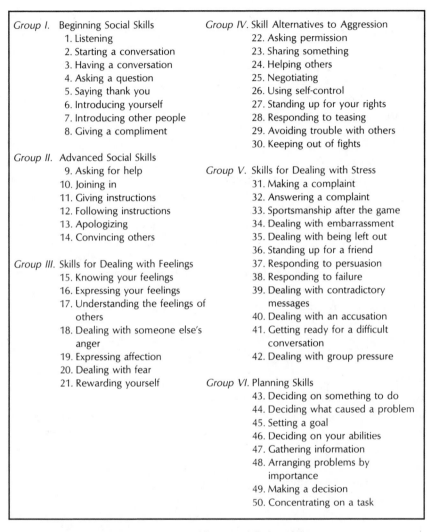

| Group I. | Beginning Social Skills | Group IV. | Skill Alternatives to Aggression |
|---|---|---|---|
| | 1. Listening | | 22. Asking permission |
| | 2. Starting a conversation | | 23. Sharing something |
| | 3. Having a conversation | | 24. Helping others |
| | 4. Asking a question | | 25. Negotiating |
| | 5. Saying thank you | | 26. Using self-control |
| | 6. Introducing yourself | | 27. Standing up for your rights |
| | 7. Introducing other people | | 28. Responding to teasing |
| | 8. Giving a compliment | | 29. Avoiding trouble with others |
| | | | 30. Keeping out of fights |
| Group II. | Advanced Social Skills | | |
| | 9. Asking for help | Group V. | Skills for Dealing with Stress |
| | 10. Joining in | | 31. Making a complaint |
| | 11. Giving instructions | | 32. Answering a complaint |
| | 12. Following instructions | | 33. Sportsmanship after the game |
| | 13. Apologizing | | 34. Dealing with embarrassment |
| | 14. Convincing others | | 35. Dealing with being left out |
| | | | 36. Standing up for a friend |
| Group III. | Skills for Dealing with Feelings | | 37. Responding to persuasion |
| | 15. Knowing your feelings | | 38. Responding to failure |
| | 16. Expressing your feelings | | 39. Dealing with contradictory |
| | 17. Understanding the feelings of | | messages |
| | others | | 40. Dealing with an accusation |
| | 18. Dealing with someone else's | | 41. Getting ready for a difficult |
| | anger | | conversation |
| | 19. Expressing affection | | 42. Dealing with group pressure |
| | 20. Dealing with fear | | |
| | 21. Rewarding yourself | Group VI. | Planning Skills |
| | | | 43. Deciding on something to do |
| | | | 44. Deciding what caused a problem |
| | | | 45. Setting a goal |
| | | | 46. Deciding on your abilities |
| | | | 47. Gathering information |
| | | | 48. Arranging problems by |
| | | | importance |
| | | | 49. Making a decision |
| | | | 50. Concentrating on a task |

**Figure 10.1.** Structured learning skills for adolescents

## Role Playing

The trainer should direct discussion following the modeling display toward helping trainees relate the modeled skill use to their own lives. The trainer invites comments on the behavioral steps and how these steps might be useful in the real-life situations that trainees encounter. Focus should be placed on dealing with specific current and future skill use by trainees, rather than only general issues involving the skill.

It is important to remember that role playing Structured Learning is viewed as behavioral rehearsal or practice for future use of the skill. As such, trainers should be aware that role playing of past events that have little relevance for future situations is of limited value to trainees. However, discussion of past events involving skill use can be relevant in stimulating trainees to think of times when a similar situation might occur in the future. In such a case, the hypothetical future situation rather than the past event would be selected for role playing.

Once a trainee has described a situation in his or her own life in which skill usage might be helpful, that trainee is designated the main actor. He or she chooses a second trainee (co-actor) to play the role of the significant person (e.g., mother, peer, etc.) in his or her life who is relevant to the skill problem. The trainee should be urged to pick as a co-actor someone who resembles the real-life person in as many ways as possible. The trainer then elicits from the main actor any additional information needed to set the stage for role playing; for example, a description of the physical setting, a description of the events immediately preceding the role play, a description of the co-actor's mood or manner.

It is crucial that the main actor seek to enact the behavioral steps that have been modeled. The trainer should go over each step as it applies to the role play situation prior to any actual role playing being started, thus aiding the main actor in making a successful role play effort. The main actor is told to refer to the skill card on which the behavioral steps are printed. As noted previously, the behavioral steps should also be written on a chalkboard visible to the main actor during role playing. Before the role playing begins, the trainer should remind all of the participants of their roles: the main actor should be told to follow the behavioral steps; the co-actor, to stay in the role of the other person; and the observers, to watch carefully for the enactment of the behavioral steps. For the first several role plays, it is helpful for the trainer to coach the observers as to what kinds of cues to observe; for example, posture, tone of voice, content of speech. This also provides an opportunity to set a positive example for feedback from the observers.

Next, the trainer instructs the role players to begin. It is the trainer's main responsibility, at this point, to provide the main actor with whatever help or coaching he or she needs in order to keep the role playing going according to the behavioral steps. The trainer urges trainees who "break role" and begin to explain or make comments to get back into role and explain later. If the role play is clearly going astray from the behavioral steps, the trainer may stop the scene, provide needed instruction, and begin again. One trainer should be positioned near the chalkboard and point to each behavioral step, in turn, as the role play unfolds, thus helping the main actor (as well as the other trainees) to follow each step in order.

The role playing should be continued until all trainees have had an opportunity to participate (in either role) and preferably until all have had a chance to be the main actor. Sometimes, this will require two or three sessions for a given skill. We again suggest that each session begin with two or three modeling vignettes for a skill, even if the skill is not new to the group. It is important to note that, while the framework (behavioral steps) of each role play in the series remains the same, the actual content can and should change from role play to role play. The problem as it actually occurs, or could occur, in each youngster's real life should be the content of the given role play. When completed, each trainee will, thus, be better armed to act appropriately in a real situation requiring skill use in his or her own life.

There are a few further procedural matters relevant to role playing that will increase its effectiveness. Role reversal is often a useful role play procedure. A trainee role playing a skill may, on occasion, have a difficult time perceiving his or her co-actor's viewpoint and vice versa. Having them exchange roles and resume the role playing can be most helpful in this regard. The trainer can assume the co-actor role, in an effort to expose youngsters to the handling of types of reactions not otherwise role played during the session. For example, it may be crucial to have a difficult adult role realistically portrayed in the role play. It is here that trainer flexibility and creativity will certainly be called upon. This may be particularly helpful when dealing with less verbal or more hesitant trainees.

## Feedback

A brief feedback period should follow each role play. This helps the main actor to find out how well he or she followed or departed from the behavioral steps, to explore the psychological impact of his or her enactment on the co-actor, and to provide encouragement to try out the role play behaviors in real life. To implement this process, the trainer should ask the main actor to wait until he or she has heard anyone's comments before talking. The trainer then asks the co-actor about his or her reactions first. Next, the trainer asks the observers to comment on the behavioral steps and other relevant aspects of the role play. The trainers should comment in particular on how well the behavioral steps were followed and provide social reinforcement (praise, approval, encouragement) for close following. To be most effective with the use of reinforcement, trainers should follow the guidelines listed below.

*Guidelines for Positive Reinforcement*

1. Provide reinforcement at the earliest appropriate opportunity after role plays that follow the behavioral steps.
2. Always provide reinforcement to the co-actor for being helpful, cooperative, etc.
3. Provide reinforcement only after role plays that follow the behavioral steps.
4. Vary the specific content of the reinforcements offered; that is, praise particular aspects of the performance, such as tone of voice, posture, phrasing.
5. Provide enough role playing activity for each group member to have sufficient opportunity to be reinforced.
6. Provide reinforcement in an amount consistent with the quality of the given role play.
7. Provide no reinforcement when the role play departs significantly from the behavioral steps (except for "trying" in the first session or two).
8. Provide reinforcement for an individual student's improvement over his or her previous performance.

After the main actor hears all the feedback, the trainer invites him or her to make comments regarding the role play and the comments of others. In this way, he or she can learn to evaluate the effectiveness of his or her skill enactment in the light of evidence from others as to its success or lack of success.

In all aspects of feedback, it is crucial that the trainers maintain the behavioral focus of Structured Learning. Trainer comments must point to the presence or absence of specific, concrete behaviors, and not take the form of general evaluative comments or broad generalities. Feedback, of course, may be positive or negative in content. Negative comments should always be followed by a constructive comment as to how a particular fault might be improved. At minimum, a "poor" performance (major departures from the behavioral steps) can be praised as "a good try" at the same time as it is being criticized. Trainees should be given the opportunity to rerole play these same behavioral steps after receiving corrective feedback. At times, as a further feedback procedure, we have audiotaped or videotaped entire role plays. Giving trainees later opportunities to observe themselves on tape can be an effective aid to learning, enabling them to reflect on their own behavior.

Because a primary goal of Structured Learning is skill flexibility, role play enactment that departs markedly from the behavioral steps may not be "wrong." That is, a different approach to the skill may in fact "work" in some situations. Trainers should stress that they are trying to teach effective alternatives, and that the trainees would do well to have the behavioral steps in their repertoire of skill behaviors available to use when appropriate. As the final optional feedback step, after all role playing and discussion is completed, the trainers may enact one additional modeling vignette or replay portions of the modeling tape. This step, in a sense, summarizes the session and leaves trainees with a final review of the behavioral steps.

## Transfer of Training

Several aspects of the training sessions we describe have, as their primary purpose, augmenting the likelihood that learning in the training setting will transfer to the youngster's real-life environment. We would suggest, however, that even more forthright steps need to be taken to maximize transfer. When possible, we would urge a homework technique that we have found to be successful with most groups. Trainees should first be told how important (i.e., the most important step of all) this transfer aspect is and instructed in how best to implement it. Trainees should be instructed to try, in their own real life, the behaviors they have practiced during the session. The name of the person(s) with whom they will try it, the day, the place, etc., are all discussed. The trainee is urged to take notes on his or her first transfer attempt on the Homework Report form provided by the trainers. This form requests detailed information about what happened when the trainee attempted the homework assignment, how well he or she followed the relevant behavioral steps, the trainee's evaluation of his or her performance and thoughts about what the next assignment might appropriately be.

It has often proven useful to start with relatively simple homework behaviors and, as mastery is achieved, work up to more complex and demanding assignments. Often it is best to make a first homework assignment something that can be done close by; that is, in the school, community center, or wherever the class is meeting. It may then be possible to forewarn and prepare the person(s) with whom the youngster is planning to try out the new skill, in order to ensure a positive outcome. For example, a trainee's homework assignment might be to ask the gym teacher a particular question. The trainer might then tell the gym teacher to expect the trainee's question so that he or she is prepared to answer in a positive way. Trainers should be cautioned, however, that breach of confidentiality can damage a teenager's trust in the trainer. If persons outside of the group are to be informed of specific training activities, youngsters should be told of this, and their permission should be asked, early in the group's life.

These experiences of success at beginning homework attempts are crucial in encouraging the trainee to make further attempts at real-life skill use. The first part of each session is devoted to presenting and discussing these homework reports. When trainees make an effort to complete their homework assignments, the trainers should provide social reinforcement (praise, approval, encouragement). Trainers should meet trainee's failure to do their homework with some chagrin and expressed disappointment. It cannot be stressed too strongly that without these, or similar attempts to maximize transfer, the value of the entire training effort is in severe jeopardy.

## External Support and Self-Reward

Of the several principles of transfer training for which research evidence exists, the principle of performance feedback is clearly most consequential. A youngster can learn very well in the training setting and do all his or her transfer homework, and yet the training program can be a performance failure. "Learning" concerns the question: Can he do it? "Performance" is a matter of: Will he do it? Trainees will perform as trained if—and only if—there is some "payoff" for doing so. Stated simply, new behaviors persist if they are rewarded, diminish if they are ignored or actively challenged.

We have found it useful to implement several supplemental programs outside of the Structured Learning training setting, which can help to provide the rewards or reinforcements trainees need so that their new behaviors are maintained. These programs include providing for both external social reward (provided by people in the trainee's real life) and self-reward (provided by the student himself or herself).

In several settings, we have actively sought to identify and develop environmental or external support by holding orientation meetings for school staff and for relatives and friends of youngsters—that is, the real-life givers of rewards and punishment. These meetings acquaint significant others in the youngster's life with Structured Learning, the skills being taught, and the steps that make up these skills. The most important segment of these sessions involves presenting the procedures whereby staff, relatives, and friends can encourage and reward trainees as they practice their new skills. We consider these orientation sessions to be of major value for transfer of training. In such sessions, the trainers should provide the significant others with an overview of Structured Learning, much like the overview previously described for use with a new group of trainees. An accurate picture of what goes on in a Structured Learning class—what procedures are typically used, and why—should be provided. Most important, participants should be informed as to how they might help in the transfer effort, and why their contributions are so necessary to the success of the program. Typically, such potential reward givers should be given instructions in how to reinforce appropriate behaviors or the approximations of such behaviors. One might tell them what specific responses on their part would be appropriate for the skills being covered in the Structured Learning class. It is often worthwhile to engage these significant others in role playing the kinds of responses they might make, so they can have practice and feedback in these behaviors.

Frequently, environmental support is insufficient to maintain newly learned skills. In fact, many real-life environments in which youngsters work and live actually actively resist a youngster's efforts at behavior change. For this reason, we have found it useful to include in our transfer efforts a method through which students can learn to be their own rewarders — the method of self-reinforcement or self-reward.

Once a new skill has been practiced through role playing, and once the trainee has made his or her first homework effort and received group feedback, we recommend that trainees continue to practice their new skill as frequently as possible. It is at this time that a program of self-reinforcement can and should be initiated. Trainees can be instructed in the nature of self-reinforcement and encouraged to "say something and do something nice for yourself" if they practice their new skill well. Self-rewards may be both things that one says to one's self and things that one does for one's self. The trainee should be taught to evaluate his or her own performance, even if his or her efforts don't meet with the hoped for response from others. For example, the youngster who follows all of the steps of a particular skill well might be taught to reward himself or herself by saying something ("I'll play basketball after school") as a special reward. It is important that these self-rewards are indeed special; that is, not things that are said or done routinely, but things that are done to acknowledge and reinforce special efforts. Trainees' notes can be collected by the trainer in order to keep abreast of independent progress made by trainees, without consuming group time. A trainer should advance a trainee to this level of independent practice only when it is clear that he or she can successfully do what is being asked.

As an additional aid to transfer, it is important to acknowledge the power of peer group pressure on the behaviors of adolescents. The natural peer leader often is far more influential in a youngster's life than any adult trainer could hope to be. In this regard, it is sometimes possible to capitalize on the natural leadership qualities of some adolescents. Hence, the trainer may want to select a peer (adolescent) cotrainer, who can be trained and used instead of a second adult trainer. The peer cotrainer selected, of course, must be proficient in the particular skill being taught.

## TRAINEE MOTIVATION

We believe that psychological skills training research and practice have not given sufficient attention to the relevance of trainee motivation for skill competency and its development. It is as if, in the Hullian terms of several years ago, our focus has been almost exclusively on habit strength at the expense of drive, in a context in which, as Hull (1943) amply demonstrated, behavior was a multiplicative function of both. We feel it important that future investigative efforts in this domain seek to redress this imbalance and, thus, examine means for the substantial enhancement of skill competency motivation — a matter very often of special relevance for aggressive adolescents. In addition to appropriate contingent reinforcement, whose functioning in a skills training context is well established, trainee motivation may be enhanced in conjunction with three different events, which unfold sequentially during the skills training process: (a) the establishment of the trainer–trainee relationship, (b) selection of appropriate target skills, and (c) establishment of certain motivation relevant group parameters.

## Trainer–Trainee Relationship

It is a truism in such interpersonal influence contexts as psychotherapy, counseling, and education that client or student motivation to do "the work" of the process, is in part driven by the steam of a positive relationship with the change agent involved. Ladd and Mize (1983, p. 153) comment in this regard

> as in any pedagogical undertaking, it is likely that a success of a social skill training program also depends on the quality of the relationship established between the child and the instructor. Even the most well-designed and all-inclusive training program may be rendered ineffective if it is conducted in an overly didactic, mechanical, and uninviting manner. Rarely, however, have previous social skill training investigators alluded to instructor characteristics or the instructor–child relationship as important aspects of the skill training process.

Thus, it might seem, we ought to appropriately conclude — consistent with the prevailing truism for other change endeavors — that a warm, close, personal, empathic, trainer–trainee relationship may well substantially potentiate skill acquisition in aggressive adolescent trainees. But all truisms are not necessarily true and, in fact, by their very comprehensiveness may deny or minimize the opportunity for a differentiated, prescriptive perspective on such matters. A host of clinicians have speculated that therapeutic progress of diverse sorts with aggressive adolescents would, in fact, be advanced by a different kind of (especially initial) helper–helpee relationship — one of *low* empathy, high impersonality, and careful avoidance of emotional exploration (Dean, 1958; Goldstein, Heller, & Sechrest, 1966; Redl & Wineman, 1957; Schwitzgebel, 1967; Slack, 1960). Edelman & Goldstein (1984) examined this proposition empirically, and indeed found quite substantial support for the prescriptive utility in such pairings of low empathy (plus high genuineness) helper behavior. Thus, we indeed support the generalization that trainee motivation and consequent skill acquisition are likely influenced substantially by the quality of the trainer-trainee relationship. But precisely what kind(s) of relationships are optimal in this context remains very much an open question — with considerable speculation and some beginning evidence combining to point to a type of relationship quite different from that characteristically aspired to in most other change endeavors.

## Skill Selection

Which skills shall be taught, and who will select them? This is as much a motivational as a tactical question, for to the degree that the youngster is enabled to anticipate learning skill competencies *he* feels he needs, *he* discerns as presently deficient but of likely utility in his real-world relationships, his motivation is correspondingly enhanced. We have operationalized this perspective in our Structured Learning skills training by means of a process we call *negotiating the curriculum*. First, we avoid the option of serving as unilateral skill selector for the trainee. In doing so, we concur with Schinke (1981, p. 81) who observes

> Seldom recognized in interpersonal skills training with adolescents is how values influence client referral and problem definition. Decisions about desirable skills are weighted by personal preferences, moral judgments, and ethical constraints.

We similarly avoid the cafeteria-like option of denying the potential value of our skill-relevant expertise and knowledge and laying out, as it were, the entire skill curriculum and simply asking the trainer to select those he or she wishes. Either unilateral approach, we feel, is inadequate: the first delimits trainee motivation, the second denies trainer expertise. Instead, we utilize a means that allows both parties to actively participate. We begin by having the trainer (if he or she knows the trainee well) and the trainee each *independently* complete their respective versions of the Structured Learning Skills Inventory (Goldstein et al., 1979). Then, much the same as a meeting between an academic advisor and a student meeting to juxtapose and reconcile their respective tentative course programs for the next semester for the student, skills trainer and trainee mutually compare, contrast, examine, and select a program from their Skills Inventories that reflects both the trainer's beliefs about what the trainee needs and the trainee's beliefs about what are his or her own deficiencies and desired competencies. Such is our applied procedure. We feel it to enhance motivation. Whether it in fact serves this important function is indeed an investigative question worth careful examination.

## Group Procedures

Our concern in optimizing trainee participation in the skill selection process is an example of seeking to enhance the trainee's task-associated intrinsic motivation. But extrinsic task characteristics may also profitably be mobilized toward the goal of maximizing inducements for active, on-task trainee participation. Although we as yet have little empirical evidence in support of the group procedure recommendations we are about to make, they indeed appear to us to be reliable extrinsic means for enhancing trainee motivation.

Where are the group sessions held? In most schools and institutions we try to seek a special place, associated in the trainee's thinking with particular privileges or opportunities (e.g., teacher's lounge, student center, recreation area) and yet not a place so removed in its characteristics from the typical skill application settings in which trainees function as to reduce the likelihood of skill transfer.

When will the group meet? If it is not judged to be too great an academic sacrifice, we attempt to schedule skills-training sessions when what the youngsters will have missed in order to attend the sessions is an activity he or she does not especially enjoy (including certain academic subjects), rather than free play, lunch, gym or the like.

Who will lead the group? For our initial, program-initiating groups in particular, we seek to utilize as trainers those teachers, cottage parents, members of the institutional staff, or others who we deem to be most stimulating, most tuned to the needs and behaviors of aggressive adolescents (but not the most overtly empathic, for the reasons described earlier), and in general, most able to capture and hold the attention of participating youngsters. Because the impact of the first meeting(s) of the initial group bears upon not only the motivation and performance of trainees in *that* group, but also, rapidly through the school or institution's grapevine, upon the interest, motivation and, eventually, performance of youngsters who constitute subsequently formed groups, the group leadership skills of the first trainers employed can have far-reaching motivational consequences.

Which skill shall be taught first? This is a crucial decision, one of special relevance to trainee motivation. In addition to reflecting the give and take of the negotiated skill curriculum, the first skill taught is optimally one very likely to yield immediate, real-world reward for the trainee. It must "work"; it must pay off. Whereas some trainers prefer to begin with the simpler conversational skills, as a sort of warm up or break in, our preference is to try to respond to both simplicity and reward potential. The "felt need" of the trainee for the near-future value of a given skill, therefore, weighs especially heavily in our initial, skill selection decisions.

## RESEARCH EVALUATION

We have conducted a number of investigations designed to examine the skill acquisition efficacy of Structured Learning with adolescents. In most of these studies, the youngsters involved were aggressive, disruptive, or, in similar ways, antisocial. Table 10.1 presents the substance of this research program. As can be seen from this information, consistently positive findings have emerged. Structured Learning successfully trains adolescents in such prosocial skills as empathy, negotiating, assertiveness, following instructions, self-control, and perspective taking.

Beyond initial demonstrations that Structured Learning "works" with aggressive adolescents, these beginning studies have also highlighted other aspects of the teaching of prosocial behaviors. D. Fleming (1976), in an effort to capitalize upon adolescent responsiveness to peer influence, demonstrated that gains in negotiation skill are as great when the Structured Learning group leader is a respected peer as when the leader is an adult. Litwack (1977), more concerned with the skill-enhancing effects of an adolescent anticipating that he will later serve as a peer leader, showed that such helper role expectation increases the degree of skill acquired. Apparently, when the adolescent expects to teach others a skill, his own level of skill acquisition benefits, a finding clearly relevant to Reissman's helper therapy principle (1965). Trief (1976) demonstrated that successful use of Structured Learning to increase the perspective-taking skill (i.e., seeing matters from other people's viewpoint) also leads to consequent increases in cooperative behavior. The significant transfer effects both in this study and in the Golden (1975), Litwack (1976), and Raleigh (1977) investigations have been important signposts in planning further research on transfer enhancement in Structured Learning.

As in our earlier efforts with adult trainees, we have begun to examine the value of teaching certain skill combinations. Aggression prone adolescents often get into difficulty when they respond with overt aggression to authority figures with whom they disagree. Golden (1975), responding to this, successfully used Structured Learning to teach such youngsters "resistance-reducing behavior," defined as a combination of reflection of feeling (the authority figure's) and assertiveness (forthright but nonaggressive statement of one's own position). Others in our research group have examined Structured Learning in other ways relevant to aggressive adolescents. Jennings (1975) was able to use Structured Learning successfully to train adolescents in several of the verbal skills necessary for satisfactory participation in more traditional, insight-oriented psychotherapy. And Guzzetta (1975) was successful in providing means to help close the gap between adolescents and their parents by using Structured Learning to teach empathic skills to parents.

Subsequent to these several demonstrations of the skill acquisition efficacy of Structured Learning, our research evaluation program took two significant directions. The first concerned the central skills training issue of skill transfer. In a series of investigations, reported at length in the book *Psychological Skill Training* (Goldstein, 1981), evidence is presented in support of the transfer-enhancing value in the context of skills training of such procedures as overlearning, identical elements, general principles, stimulus vari-

**Table 10.1.** Structured Learning Research with Adolescent and Preadolescent Trainees

| INVESTIGATOR | TARGET SKILL | TRAINEES | SETTING | RESULTS |
|---|---|---|---|---|
| Berlin, 1976 | Empathy | Aggressive adolescents (JD and PINS)[a](N=58) x̄ age=13.6 | Residential Center | 1. SL with conflict content > SL with nonconflict content 2. SL with conflict content > no treatment 3. I level 3 and 4 > I level 2 |
| D. Fleming, 1976 | Negotiation | Aggressive preadolescents (N=80) x̄ age=10.5 | Regular classes in elementary urban schol | 1. No difference between high and low self-esteem trainees 2. No difference between adult-led and peer-led SL groups 3. All SL groups: significant acquisition but nonsignificant transfer |
| L. Fleming, 1976 | Negotiation | Aggressive (N=48) and passive (N=48) educable mentally retarded preadolescents x̄ age=10.5 | Special education classes in urban elementary school | SL > Attention control for aggressive and passive trainees |
| Golden, 1975 | Resistance reduction with authority figure | Aggressive adolescents (N=60) x̄ age=15.2 | Regular classes in urban senior high school | 1. SL = Discrimination training ("good" versus "bad" models) 2. SL > No treatment control on acquisition and transfer criteria |
| Greenleaf, 1977 | Self-control | Aggressive preadolescents (N=60) x̄ age=14.6 | Regular classes in urban junior high school | In progress (testing the effect of peer reinforcement of skill behavior on transfer) |
| Hummel, 1977 | Self-control | Aggressive adolescents (N=60) x̄ age=15.8 | Regular classes in rural senior high school | In progress (testing the effect of training in self-instructional skills on transfer) |
| Jennings, 1975 | Interviewee behaviors (initiation, elaboration, etc.) | Emotionally disturbed adolescents (N=40) x̄ age=13.7 | Children's unit of state mental hospital | 1. SL > Minimal treatment control on subskills of initiation and termination of silence |

| Author, year | Skill | Subjects | Setting | Results |
|---|---|---|---|---|
| | | | | 2. SL > Minimal treatment control on attractiveness to interviewer |
| Litwack, 1976 | Following instructions | Passive resistive adolescents (N = 53) $\bar{x}$ age = 14.10 | Regular classes in urban junior high school | SL + anticipate serving as peer trainer > SL alone > No treatment on both acquisition and transfer criteria |
| Raleigh, 1977 | Assertiveness | Aggressive (N = 37) and passive (N = 37) adolescents $\bar{x}$ age = 13.5 | Regular classes in urban junior high schools | SL (in groups)>SL (individual), discussion (groups), discussion (individual), no treatment on assertiveness or acquisition and transfer criteria |
| Swanstrom, 1977 | Self-control | Aggressive preadolescents (N = 42) $\bar{x}$ age = 9.0 | Regular classes in urban elementary school | 1. SL = Structured discussion 2. SL > No treatment control on acquisition criteria |
| Trief, 1976 | Perspective-taking (PT) cooperation[b] | Aggressive adolescents (JD PINS)[a] (N = 58) $\bar{x}$ age = 15.5 | Residential center | 1. SL (affective + cognitive focus) >SL placebo control and brief instruction control on PT[b] 2. SL (affective focus) > SL placebo control and brief instruction control on PT[b] 3. SL (cognitive focus) > SL placebo control and brief instruction control on PT[b] 4. SL (combined focus) > SL placebo control and brief instruction control on cooperation |
| Wood, 1977 | Assertiveness | Aggressive and passive adolescents (N = 70) $\bar{x}$ age = 14 | Regular classes in urban senior high school | In progress (testing the effect of "identical elements" between SL and application setting on transfer) |

[a]JD = juvenile delinquents; PINS = persons in need of supervision.
[b]Acquisition and transfer.

ability, and additional techniques. This emerging technology is in our view *the* prime research direction for future skills training studies.*

In our experience, however, there are groups of adolescents who may appropriately be characterized as especially "transfer-resistent" and for whom transfer-enhancing interventions must be on a particularly potent and broad spectrum. In response to this challenge, we have designed and begun evaluating (with 60, hardcore incarcerated adolescents) a three-part skills training program, one we posit may be particularly effective in facilitating skill generalization across settings and time for such youngsters. To reflect its aspiration, we have labeled this program *Aggression Replacement Training* (Goldstein, Glick, Zimmerman, Reiner, Couttry, & Gold, in press). Its component procedures are (a) Structured Learning, to teach prosocial skill behaviors; (b) Anger Control Training, to teach anger management and reduction techniques; and (c) Moral Education, to enhance moral reasoning level. Our goal here is a comprehensive intervention, behavioral (Structured Learning), affective (Anger Control Training), and cognitive (Moral Education) in substance. Such a multimodal effort, implemented over an extended period of time, has the potential, we feel, to substantially enhance the impact on transfer and maintenance of gains, even when the target youngsters involved have returned to an environment generally nonsupportive of prosocial behavior or indifferent. Our ongoing empirical tests of this assertion will, it is hoped, reveal whether this is wish or reality.

## REFERENCES

Achenbach, T. M. (1966). The classification of children's psychiatric symptoms: A factor-analytic study. *Psychological Monographs, 80* (Whole No. 615).

Achenbach, T. M. (1974). *Developmental psychopathology.* New York: Ronald Press.

Achenbach, T. M., & Edelbrock, C. S. (1978). The classification of child psychopathology: A review and analysis of empirical efforts. *Psychological Bulletin, 85,* 1275–1301.

Adams, S. (1961). Assessment of the psychiatric treatment program, phase I: Third interim report. *Research Report No. 21. California Youth Authority.*

Adams, S. (1962). The PICO project. In N. Johnson, L. Savits, & M. E. Wolfgang (Eds.), *The sociology of punishment and correction.* New York: Wiley.

Bailey, W. (1966). *Correctional outcome: An evaluation of 100 reports.* Unpublished manuscript, University of California at Los Angeles.

---

*Two texts examining the full array of demonstrable and potential transfer-enhancing techniques are *Maximizing Treatment Gains: Transfer Enhancement in Psychotherapy* (Goldstein & Kanfer, 1979) and *Improving the Long Term Effects of Psychotherapy* (Karoly & Steffen, 1980).

Berlin, R. J. (1976). *Teaching acting-out adolescents prosocial conflict resolution through structured learning training of empathy.* Unpublished doctoral dissertation, Syracuse University.

Bernal, M. E., Duryee, J. S., Pruett, H. L., & Burns, B. J. (1968). Behavior modification and the brat syndrome. *Journal of Consulting and Clinical Psychology, 32*, 447–456.

Braukmann, C. L., & Fixsen, D. L. (1976). Behavior modification with delinquents. In M. Herson, R. M. Eisler, & P. M. Miller (Eds.), *Progress in behavior modification.* New York: Academic Press.

California Department of the Youth Authority (1967). James Marshall treatment program: Progress report.

Carney, F. J. (1966). Summary of studies on the derivation of base expectance categories for predicting recidivism of subjects released from institutions of the Massachusetts Department of Corrections. Boston: Massachusetts Department of Corrections.

Craft, M., Stephenson G., & Granger, C. (1964). A controlled trial of authoritarian and self-governing regimes with adolescent psychopaths. *American Journal of Orthopsychiatry, 34*, 543–554.

Cronbach, L. J., & Snow, R. E. (1977). *Aptitudes and instructional methods.* New York: Irvington.

Dean, S. I. (1958). Treatment of the reluctant client. *American Psychologist, 13*, 627–630.

Drabman, R. S., Spitalnik, R., & O'Leary, K. D. (1973). Teaching self-control to disruptive children. *Journal of Abnormal Psychology, 82*, 10–16.

Dreger, R. M., Lewis, P. M., Rich, T. A., Miller, K. S., Reid, M. P., Overlade, D. C., Taffel, C., & Flemming, E. L. (1964). Behavioral classification project. *Journal of Consulting Psychology, 28*, 1–13.

Edelman, E., & Goldstein, A. P. (1984) Prescriptive relationship levels for juvenile delinquents in a psychotherapy analog. *Aggressive Behavior.*

Empey, L. T. (1969). Contemporary programs for convicted juvenile offenders: Problems of theory, practice and research. In D. J. Mulvihill & M. M. Tumin (Eds.), *Crimes of violence* (Vol. 13). Washington, DC: U.S. Government Printing Office.

Fleming, D. (1976). *Teaching negotiation skills to pre-adolescents.* Unpublished doctoral dissertation, Syracuse University.

Fleming, L. (1976). *Training passive and aggressive educable mentally retarded children for assertive behaviors using three types of structured learning training.* Unpublished doctoral dissertation, Syracuse University.

Garrity, D. (1956). *The effects of length of incarceration upon parole adjustment and estimation of optimum sentence. Washington State Correctional Institution.* Unpublished doctoral dissertation, University of Washington.

Golden, R. (1975). *Teaching resistance-reducing behavior to high school students.* Unpublished doctoral dissertation, Syracuse University.

Goldstein, A. P. (Ed.) (1978). *Prescriptions for child mental health and education.* Elmsford, NY: Pergamon Press.

Goldstein, A. P. (1981). *Psychological skill training.* Elmsford, NY: Pergamon Press.

Goldstein, A. P., Glick, B., Zimmerman, D., Reiner, S., Coultry, T., & Glad, D. (in press). Aggression replacement training. *Journal of Correctional Education.*

Goldstein, A. P., Heller, K., & Sechrest, L. B. (1966). *Psychotherapy and the psychology of behavior change.* New York: Wiley.

Goldstein, A. P., & Kanfer, F. H. (1979). *Maximizing treatment gains: Transfer enhancement in psychotherapy.* New York: Academic Press.

Goldstein, A. P., Sprafkin, R. P., & Gershaw, N. J. (1976). *Skill training for community living.* Elmsford, NY: Pergamon Press.

Goldstein, A. P., Sprafkin, R. P., Gershaw, N. J., & Klein, P. (1979). *Skill-streaming the adolescent: A structured learning approach to teaching prosocial behavior.* Champaign, IL: Research Press.

Goldstein, A. P., & Stein, N. (1976). *Prescriptive psychotherapies.* Elmsford, NY: Pergamon Press.

Greenleaf, D. (1977). *Peer reinforcement as transfer enhancement in structured learning therapy.* Unpublished masters thesis, Syracuse University.

Group for the Advancement of Psychiatry, Psychopathological disorders in childhood: Theoretical considerations and a proposed classification: *GAP Report No. 62.*

Guzetta, R. A. (1974). *Acquisition and transfer of empathy by the parents of early adolescents through structured learning training.* Unpublished doctoral dissertation, Syracuse University.

Harrison, R. M., & Mueller, P. (1964). Clue hunting about group counseling and parole outcome. Sacramento: California Department of Corrections.

Hewitt, L. E., & Jenkins, R. L. (1946). *Fundamental patterns of maladjustment: The dynamics of their origins.* Springfield, IL: State of Illinois.

Hull, C. L. (1943). *The principles of behavior.* New York: Appleton-Century-Crofts.

Hummel, J. W. (1977). *An examination of structured learning therapy, self-control, negotiation training and variation in stimulus conditions.* Unpublished doctoral dissertation, Syracuse University.

Hunt, D. E. (1961). *Matching models in education: The coordination of teaching methods with student characteristics.* Toronto: Ontario Institution for Studies in Education.

Jennings, R. L. (1975). *The use of structured learning techniques to teach attraction enhancing interviewee skills to residentially hospitalized, lower socioeconomic emotionally disturbed children and adolescents: A psychotherapy analogue investigation.* Unpublished doctoral dissertation, University of Iowa.

Karoly, P., & Steffan, J. (1980). *Improving the long-term effects of psychotherapy.* New York: Gardner Press.

Kassenbaum, G., Ward D., & Wilner, D. (1972). *Prison treatment and its outcome.* New York: Wiley.

Klausmeier, H. J., Rossmiller, R. A., Saily, M. (Eds.). (1977). *Individually guided elementary education.* New York: Academic Press.

Knight, D. (1969). The Marshall program: assessment of a short-term institutional treatment program. *Research Report 56.* Sacramento: Department of the Youth Authority.

Ladd, G. W., & Mize, J. (1983). A cognitive-social learning model of social-skill training. *Psychological Review, 90,* 127–157.

Litwack, S. E. (1976). *The use of the helper therapy principle to increase therapeutic effectiveness and reduce therapeutic resistance: Structured learning therapy with resistant adolescents.* Unpublished doctoral dissertation, Syracuse University.

Manster, G. J. (1977). *Adolescent development and the life tasks.* Boston: Allyn & Bacon.

Martinson, R. (1974). What works? Questions and answers about prison reform. *The Public Interest. 0,* 22–54.

McClintock, F. (1961). *Attendance centres.* London: Macmillan.

McCorkle, L. W., Elias, A., & Bixby, F. (1958). *The Highfields story.* New York: Holt, Rinehart and Winston.

O'Connor, R. D. (1972). Relative efficacy of modeling, shaping, and the combined procedures for modification of social withdrawal. *Journal of Abnormal Psychology, 79,* 327-334.

Palmer, T. (1976). Final report to the California Community Treatment Project. Sacramento: California Youth Authority.

Patterson, G. R., & Anderson, D. (1964). Peers as social reinforcers. *Child Development, 35,* 951-960.

Patterson, G. R., & Reid, J. B. (1973). Intervention for families of aggressive boys: A replication study. *Behavior Research & Therapy, 11,* 383-394.

Peterson, D. R., Quay, H. C., & Cameron, G. R. (1959). Personality and background factors in juvenile delinquency as inferred from questionnaire responses. *Journal of Consulting Psychology, 23,* 392-399.

Peterson, D. R., Quay, H. C., & Tiffany, T. L. (1961). Personality factors related to juvenile delinquency. *Child Development, 32,* 355-372.

Quay, H. C. (1964). Dimensions of personality in delinquent boys as inferred from the factor analysis of case history data. *Child Development, 35,* 479-484.

Quay, H. C. (1966). Patterns of aggression, withdrawal and immaturity. In H. C. Quay & J. S. Werry (Eds.), *Psychopathological disorders of childhood.* New York: Wiley.

Quay, H. C., & Quay, L. C. (1965). Behavior problems in early adolescence. *Child Development, 36,* 215-220.

Raleigh, R. (1977). *Individual vs. group structured learning therapy for assertiveness training with senior and junior high school students.* Unpublished doctoral dissertation, Syracuse University.

Redl, R., & Wineman, D. (1957). *The aggressive child.* New York: Free Press.

Reissman, F. (1965). *The culturally deprived child.* New York: Harper.

Robinson, J., & Smith, G. (1976). The effectiveness of correctional programs. In R. Giallombardo (Eds.), *Juvenile delinquency.* New York: Wiley.

Ross, A. O., Lacey, H. M., & Parton, D. A. (1965). The development of a behavior checklist for boys. *Child Development, 36,* 1013-1027.

Schinke, S. P. (1981). Interpersonal-skills training with adolescents. In *Progress in Behavior Modification* (Vol. 11). New York: Academic Press.

Schwitzgebel, R. L. (1967). Short term operant conditioning of adolescent offenders on socially relevant variable. *Journal of Abnormal Psychology, 72,* 134-142.

Sealy, A. & Banks, C. (1971). Social maturity, training, experience, and recidivism amongst British borstal boys. *British Journal of Criminology, 11,* 245-264.

Slack, C. W. (1960). Experimenter–subject psychotherapy: A new method of introducing intensive office treatment for unreachable cases. *Mental Hygiene, 44,* 238-256.

Slavson, S. R. (1964). *A textbook in analytic psychotherapy.* New York: International Universities Press.

Stein, N., & Bogin, D. (1978). Individual child psychotherapy. In A. P. Goldstein (Ed.), *Prescriptions for child mental health and education.* Elmsford, NY: Pergamon Press.

Stumphauser, J. S. (1972). Increased delay of gratification in young prison inmates through imitation of high-delay peer models. *Journal of Personality and Social Psychology, 21,* 10-17.

Swanstrom, C. (1977). *Training self-control in behavior problem children.* Unpublished doctoral dissertation, Syracuse University.

Trief, P. (1976). *The reduction of egocentrism in acting-out adolescents by structured learning therapy.* Unpublished doctoral dissertation, Syracuse University.

Vinter, R., & Janowitz, M. (1959). Effective institutions for juvenile delinquents: A research statement. *Social Service Review, 33,* 118–130.

Vorrath, H. H., & Brendtro, L. K. (1974). *Positive peer culture.* Chicago: Aldine.

Wahler, R. G. (1969). Setting generality: Some specific and general effects of child behavior therapy. *Journal of Applied Behavior Analysis, 2,* 239–246.

Warren, M. Q. (1972). *Classification for treatment.* Paper presented at Seminar on the Classification of Criminal Behavior. Washington, D.C.: National Institute of Law Enforcement and Criminal Justice.

Wood, M. (1977). *Adolescent acquisition and transfer of assertiveness through the use of structured learning therapy.* Unpublished doctoral dissertation, Syracuse University.

# Appendix A
# Resource Materials for Teaching Social Skills

The following section presents materials that could be employed by the teacher or clinician as stimuli to set the stage for social skills instruction, as vehicles for teaching, or as ways to provide practice and generalization of skills. The list is organized into categories corresponding to the principal medium through which the material is presented. These include: Curriculum Programs and Kits, Printed Materials and Books, Audio-Visual Presentations, Dramatic Play Materials and Games. The list is organized as nearly as possible into age levels. The list is not exhaustive, and the intent is to make the reader aware of materials available rather than to endorse any specific items.

## CURRICULUM PROGRAMS AND KITS

*My Friends and Me*
Preschool. Kit includes teacher's guide, 2 activity manuals containing instructions for 190 activities; metal carrying case; 24" × 32" freestanding activity board; six 23" × 29" full-color activity pictures; 59 magnetic shapes in various forms and colors; two 10" × 12" story books with 40 stories and 232 color illustrations; two fuzzy 12" dolls; three inked print blocks of adults, children, and above-mentioned doll figures; five cassettes or twelve 7" records containing 16 recorded activities, narration, dialogue, and 23 songs; miscellaneous equipment of ink pad, ink, sponge, four liquid-chalk pens, eraser; song cards (7" × 9¾"); and spirit masters of 38 illustrated family activities. Kit assists personal and social development. (American Guidance Service)

*Step Text*
Preschool. Twenty-two-book sequenced program designed to develop cognitive skills, language ability, and social adaptability in children, ages 3–6. Teacher's guide and self-storing container included. Contains 400 color pho-

tographic illustrations. Some titles are: "All About Me," "Friends," and "Rainy Day Pals." (Advanced Learning Concepts, Inc.)

## DUSO Kit D-1 (Revised)

Kindergarten and lower elementary. Activities designed to aid in learning words for feelings; learning that feelings, goals, values, and behavior are dynamically related; and learning to talk more freely about feelings, goals, values, and behavior. Materials are manual, 2 story books, 33 posters with easel, 21 records or 5 cassettes, 6 hand puppets, 11 puppet props, 2 character puppets, 33 puppet activity cards, 5 group-discussion cards, 33 role playing activity cards. (American Guidance Service)

## DUSO Kit D-2 (Revised)

Upper primary to grade 4. Activities to develop understanding and valuing of oneself; understanding of interpersonal relationships and purposive nature of human behavior; understanding of interrelationships among ideas, feelings, beliefs, behavior, and competence. Materials include: manual, 33 posters with easel, 27 records or 5 cassettes, 6 hand puppets, 2 character puppets, 33 puppet activity cards, 5 group discussion cards, 33 role playing activity cards. (American Guidance Service)

## Getting Along with Others: Teaching Social Effectiveness to Children

Elementary. Instructional program consisting of guide, skill lessons and activities, and videotapes. A skills training model is employed to help elementary-aged children develop specific skills pertaining to introductions, following directions, verbal and nonverbal communication, sharing, helping, problem solving, giving and responding to feedback, responding to teasing, and resisting peer pressure. (Research Press)

## Startline: Social Education/Communication

Elementary. Social skills program consisting of six early readers, posters, photoface cards, photobody cards, and relationship cards. Book titles include: "What Should I Do?," "Growing Up, Out and About," "Getting It Right," "Working Things Out," and "Friendship." (DLM Teaching Resources)

## Think Aloud: Increasing Social and Cognitive Skills—A Problem-Solving Program for Children

Elementary. Structured learning activities are provided, designed to help children think through social situations and cope with various problems. Children are trained in problem-solving techniques and ways to use self-speech to direct social behavior. Program divided into three levels: (a) grades 1–2, (b) grades 3–4, (c) grades 5–6. (Research Press)

*Toward Affective Development (TAD)*

Grades 3 to 6. A social skills program consisting of 191 sequenced lessons, posters, discussion pictures, audio cassettes, and pupil worksheets. Emphasis is on feelings and peer relationships. Activities include role playing, modeling, simulations, problem solving, and games. Organized into five sections:

1. Reaching In and Reaching Out—sensory awareness and creative thinking.
2. Your Feelings and Mine—labeling and interpreting feelings.
3. Working Together—cooperative participation.
4. Me: Today and Tomorrow—relating personal traits to world of work.
5. Feeling, Thinking, Doing—conflict resolution.

(American Guidance Service)

*Transition*

Elementary and junior high. Emphasizes social and emotional growth of middle school and junior high school student. Appreciation of human differences is stressed by presenting a wide range of racial, ethnic, and economic groups and physical handicaps. Students write out and act out scenarios about personal conflicts and decision making; simulated encounters; directed observation and analysis of human behavior; and large and small group discussions. Program consists of five units entitled: (a) Communication and Problem Solving Skills; (b) Encouraging Openness and Trust; (c) Verbal and Nonverbal Communication of Feelings; (d) Needs, Goals, and Expectations; and (e) Increasing Awareness of Values. (American Guidance Service)

*Asset: A Social Skills Program for Adolescents*

Adolescents. A social skills training program that addresses giving and receiving feedback, resisting peer pressure, problem solving, negotiating, following instructions, and conversing. The program consists of 8 films or videocassettes, leader's guide, and program materials. (Research Press)

*Social Perceptual Training Kit For Community Living*

Prevocational, oriented toward developmentally disabled. Kit contains book with 50 lessons for developing social comprehension, 425 photographic slides, cassette, 31 drawings for preparation of spirit masters or transparencies. Subunits include: introduction to signals; numbers as signals; places as signals; making a good impression; shopping–buying; a big store; living on our own; getting and keeping a job; after hours; and getting along with others. Complete kit. (Educational Activities, Inc)

*The Walker Social Skills Curriculum: The Accepts Program*

Handicapped children. A social skills curriculum, employing the skills training model, to ease the integration of handicapped children into less-restrictive settings. Specific instructional scripts are provided according to the following classes of behavior: 1. Classroom skills; 2. Basic interaction skills; 3. Getting along skills; 4. Making friends skills; and 5. Coping skills. Program also includes videotape that provides an overview of curriculum program and a videotape that demonstrates positive and negative modeling of target skills for trainees. (Pro-Ed)

*Arizona Basic Assessment and Curriculum Utilization System (ABACUS)*
Handicapped—developmental ages 2 to $5\frac{1}{2}$. Comprehensive program designed to screen, assess, program, and monitor the progress of handicapped children relative to body management, self-care, communication, preacademic and social skills. Socialization: (a) awareness of self and others, (b) awareness of feelings, (c) social information, (d) play behavior, and (e) interactive behavior. (Love Publishing Co.)

*Developing Social Acceptability*
Special Education—all ages. Training program for helping the handicapped child interact smoothly in the community. Emphasis is placed upon personal health care and grooming and basic social skills. Includes a 208 page manual and 67 picture cards. Primarily designed for parents. (Walker Educational Book Corp.)

# PRINTED MATERIALS AND BOOKS

## Printed Materials

*I Have Feelings*
4 to 9 years. Pictures and narrative of boy experiencing different emotions. (Human Sciences Press, Inc.)

*Happy Thinking*
Elementary. Forty-two reproducible activity cards help increase a child's awareness and appreciation of the positive in his surroundings. Suitable for individuals, small groups, or entire class. (Opportunities for Learning, Inc.)

*Caring, Belonging, Coping, Feelings, Appreciating*
Grades 2 to 8. Series of reproducible instructional materials focused on the child's affective and social development.
1. *Caring:* designed to help students develop a more concerned, respectful attitude toward themselves, family and others.
2. *Belonging:* emphasizes importance of social interactions within the community, family and peer group.
3. *Coping:* ways to cope with childhood stress.

4. *Feelings:* dealing with personal feelings and those of others in a positive way.
5. *Appreciating:* developing and expressing a sense of appreciation.
(Kino Publications)

*Consequences*
Junior and Senior High. 12″ × 6″ colorful illustrated cards present 71 problems of social responsibility. Some issues dealt with are personal safety, concern for "left-out" people, one-to-one cooperation, furthering welfare of all society, and protecting the environment. Teacher's manual included. (Developmental Learning Materials)

*Sensitivity*
Junior and Senior High. Set of 46 cards containing scenarios for various social situations. Students are encouraged to think out appropriate responses to these problems. (DLM Teaching Resources)

*Human Relations Fundamentals*
Secondary. Covers verbal and nonverbal communication, self-concept role enactment, responsibility, active listening, supportive and nondefensive climates for interaction, and self-expression. Set of 22 transparencies, teacher guide, article reprints. (Lansford Publishing Co., Inc.)

*Activities for Exploring Conflict and Aggression*
Secondary. Instructional activities focused on means for conflict resolution. Can be used as separate unit or integrated into regular curriculum. (J. Weston Walch, Publisher)

*Essential Social Skills*
Secondary. A variety of exercises and activities addressing social situations typically experienced by most teenagers, for example, dating, sex-roles. Spirit duplicating masters. (EBSCO Curriculum Materials)

*People Need Each Other*
Special Education. A variety of activities to teach social awareness and the interdependence of people in modern society. (Opportunities for Learning, Inc.)

## Books—Trainer

*The Bookfinder*
Ages 2 through Adolescence. Three volumes: Volume 1—through 1974, Volume 2—1975 through 1978, Volume 3—1979 through 1982. Provides references and descriptions for children's books according to more than 450

psychological, behavioral, developmental topics. The referenced books may be useful in helping the reader to develop insight and possible alternatives for problem situations. (American Guidance Service)

*Human Development Program Theory Manual and Activity Guides*
Preschool, Kindergarten, Levels I to V. Curriculum guides to be used in implementing the Human Development Program (Magic Circle), a preventive mental health program focused on facilitating self-growth and interpersonal relationships. (Human Development Training Institute)

*Rational Emotive Education: A Manual for*
*Elementary School Teachers,* Knaus
Elementary. A curriculum guide that adapts the principles of Rational Emotive Therapy for application in the elementary classroom. The program includes the principles of RET, irrational belief systems, feelings of inferiority, learning, catastrophizing, responsibility, perspective taking, stereotyping, teasing, bullying, protesting, and friendships. (Institute for Rational Living, Inc.)

*Talking, Listening, Communicating*
Elementary. Curriculum guide designed to teach social communication skills through group activities. The chapters are: (a) Preparing Yourself, (b) Understanding Self, (c) Communication, (d) Building Groups, (e) Relating to Others, (f) Developing Creativity, (g) Making Decisions, (h) Solving Problems, (i) Ending a T.L.C. Group. Skills to be developed include group leadership, social interaction, creativity, problem solving, decision making, and how to end the group positively. (Pro-Ed)

*A Rational Counseling Primer*
Elementary. Young, H.S. (Institute for Rational Living)

*Teaching Children Self Control: A Fable Mod Manual to Deal with*
*Behavior Problems of Elementary School-age Children,* Stawar, T.
Elementary. (Institute for Rational Living, Inc.)

*200 Ways to Enhance Self-concept in the Classroom*
Canfield & Wells. Elementary. (Prentice-Hall, Inc.)

*Teaching Interpersonal and Community Living Skills*
Handicapped adolescents and adults. This book provides a guide for devising objectives and instructional activities to develop community living skills among handicapped adolescents and adults. Emphasis is placed on skills relating to work, consumerism, citizenship, transportation, family living, learning, and recreation. (Pro-Ed)

*Leisure Programs for Handicapped Persons*
Moderately/Severely Handicapped. Curriculum useful for developing instructional programs for the leisure-time activities of handicapped adults and children. Contents include: (a) Normalization, (b) Leisure skills assessment, (c) Leisure instruction, (d) Adapting leisure skills, (e) Curriculum design and format, (f) Hobbies, (g) Sports, (h) Games, (i) Object manipulation, and (j) Program implementation. (Pro-Ed)

## Books—Pupil

*Handling Your Ups and Downs*
Primary. A children's book about emotions. (Word Books)

*Learning to Care: Classroom Activities for*
*Social and Affective Development*
Elementary. Instructional activities designed to help children (a) recognize and label various emotions, (b) assume and experience another's viewpoint, and (c) empathize with the experiences of others. (Scott, Foresman and Company)

*Human Development Program "Magic Circle" Story*
*and Activities Booklets*
Elementary. Cartoons are used to depict the procedures of Magic Circle, including introduction, pupil participation, listening skill development, and review of main concepts. Set of 10 books. (Human Development Training Institute)

*Homer and the Homely Hound Dog*
Elementary. The book uses a dog character to convey how irrational thoughts can lead to negative feelings and self-defeating behavior. Thirty-three pages and illustrated. (Institute for Rational Living, Inc.)

*Nice Nifty Innovations for Creative Expression*
Elementary to junior high. Book contains ideas, activities, games, and learning center for enhancing self-concept and more positive interpersonal relationships. Includes individual, small group, and class activities. (Love Publishing Company)

*Coping with Series* (Revised)
Secondary. Twenty-three books dealing with serious ethical and personal problems and everyday problems of school, home, and friendship. Attention is given to many different kinds of relationships. Titles include "Easing the Scene," "To Like and Be Liked," "You Always Communicate Something," "Can You Talk with Someone Else?" Includes manual. (American Guidance Service)

## AUDIO-VISUAL

## Filmstrips and Cassettes

*Getting Along in School*
   Preschool to primary. Filmstrips give children examples of good behavior and work habits to help them do better in classes and with relationships with other children. Titles include: "Being on Time," "Doing Things for Yourself," "Taking Care of Things," "Working with Others," "How Quiet Helps," and "Listening and Following Instructions." (Nasco Learning Fun)

*Kindle V: I Can Tell*
   Early childhood D-3. Explores world of nonverbal communication and how it can help us understand ourselves and others better. Filmstrips include: "Talking Hands," "What Faces Say," "Rainbows and Raindrops," and "Twist 'n' Turn." Unit includes five color filmstrips, records or cassettes, teaching guide, and storage box. (Scholastic Instructional Materials)

*Who Are You?*
   K to 3. Filmstrip series that explores relationships between children and their families, teachers, and friends. Titles include: "Who Am I Anyway?," "How Your Parents See You," "How Your Brothers and Sisters See You," "How Your Friends See You," "How Grownups See You," and "Who I Really Am!" Set of six filmstrips and three cassettes (Troll Associates)

*Kindle III: Getting Along*
   K to 3. Five filmstrips introduce children to the concept of relationships and why they are important to us. Titles include: "It's Mine," "Sticks 'n' Stones," "Will You Be My Friend?," "Smiles Don't Just Happen," and "I Don't Care Anyhow." Unit includes five color filmstrips, records or cassettes, teaching guide, and storage box. (Scholastic Instructional Materials)

*Winnie the Witch: Stories About Values*
   Primary. Animated people teach about honesty, responsibility, diligence, and forgiveness in fantasy settings. Encourages children to relate their own feelings and experiences. Set of four color filmstrips, four cassettes, and guide. (Society for Visual Education)

*Kindle IV: Mixing In*
   K to 3. Explores with children some of the individual problems we all have in learning to get along with others. Five filmstrips include: "Do I Have to Win?," "White Lies Don't Count," "All Alone," and "Who Me?" Unit includes five color filmstrips, records, or cassettes, teaching guide, and storage box. (Scholastic Instructional Materials)

*The Adventures of the Lollipop Dragon*

Primary. Full-color filmstrips illustrate a green dragon helping children become aware of the rights of others and learn that cooperation promotes happier living. Titles include, "How the Lollipop Dragon Got His Name," "Working Together," "Avoiding Litter," "Care of Property," "Taking Turns," and "Kindness to Animals." Six filmstrips, three cassettes, and guide. (Society of Visual Education)

*Developing Basic Values*

Primary to intermediate. Full-color filmstrips illustrate the need for moral and ethical values in everyday living. Titles include: "Respect for Property," "Consideration for Others," "Acceptance of Differences," and "Recognition of Responsibilities." Set of four filmstrips, two cassettes, and four guides. (Society for Visual Education)

*Feelings*

Primary to intermediate. Light-hearted stories help children understand and deal with feelings. Appropriate for children with learning problems. Each set consists of four color filmstrips with four cassettes.

Set 1: Feelings—"Outside/Inside," "When I Grow Up," "I am Many Different People," and "Stop Acting Like a Baby."

Set 2: Feelings—"That's Not Fair," "Everybody's Afraid of Something," "G-r-r-r-r," and "But I Don't Know How." (ATC Publishing Corp.)

*Winnie the Witch and the Frightened Ghost*

Primary to intermediate. Animated creatures teach children that it's dumb to be afraid of others just because they're different. Color filmstrip, cassette, and guide. (Society for Visual Education)

*Tales of Winnie the Witch*

Primary to intermediate. Animated creatures teach children the values of love, sharing, being neighborly and unselfish, looking at both sides of a story, and the Golden Rule. Program consists of six color filmstrips, six cassettes, and guide. (Society for Visual Education)

*Winning and Losing*

Grades 2 to 5. Filmstrip series helps children put competition into perspective. Reasons for competing in school and at play are presented, and good sportsmanship is emphasized. Titles include: "Why We Compete," "Any Number Can Play," "Winners and Losers," and "It's Only a Game." Set of four filmstrips and four cassettes. (Troll Associates)

*Understanding Your Fears*

Elementary. Filmstrips introduce the emotions of anger, fear, sadness, and happiness. Children learn ways of expressing these emotions and are encouraged to discuss their feelings. (Opportunities for Learning, Inc.)

*Responsible Decision Making*

Elementary. Presents experiences in responsible decision making and reinforces social skills, self-concept, communication skills, and problem-solving techniques. Based on Dreikur's guides. Complete program includes six filmstrips, six cassettes, and teacher's guide. Separate titles are: "Returning Other People's Things," "Listening to Directions," "Overcoming Shyness," "Earning Friends," "Keeping Promises," and "Helping Yourself and Others." Individual filmstrip/cassette. (Gamco Industries, Inc.)

*Making Friends*

Grades 4 to 6. Captioned filmstrips explore desirable personality and behavior traits. Designed as a unit in personal guidance with review frames and checklists for students to rate themselves. Titles include: "How Do You Rate at Home?", "How Do You Rate at School?", and "How Do You Rate with Your Friends?" Set of three filmstrips (captioned). (BFA Educational Media)

*Get in Touch With Your Emotions*

Grades 3 to 6. Color filmstrips help students to become more aware of their emotions. Manual contains scripts and discussion questions. Titles include: "It's Natural to be Angry or Afraid," "You Can Show Love and Affection," "Adjusting to Unhappiness," "The Brighter Side of Life." Set of four filmstrips, two cassettes, and manual. (Kimbo Educational Activities)

*Values: Making Choices*

Grades 4 to 6. Filmstrip series presents open-ended stories about jealousy, loyalty, trust, and privacy, group conformity vs. individual ideas, and the issue of "what price winning." Titles include: "The Tree House," "The Field Trip," "The Championship Game," and "The Class Project." Set of four filmstrips and four cassettes. (BFA Educational Media)

*Learning To Be Together*

Grades 9 to 12. Filmstrip series helps students examine behavior and attitudes that hinder communication between people and find alternative ways to handle feelings and attitudes. Titles include: "Keeping People Apart," "People are People," "Putting People in Boxes," and "Love." Set of four filmstrips and four cassettes. (BFA Educational Media)

*Healthy Feelings*

Filmstrip series about four teenagers helps students learn that certain feelings can cause other feelings, that feeling can be related to physical health, and that a behavior change can affect the way they feel. Titles include: "Feelings: Ours and Others," "Feelings Are Made," "Feelings: What We Do," and "Feeling Good." Set of four sound filmstrips and four cassettes. (BFA Educational Media)

*Understanding and Accepting Yourself*

Ungraded. Four color filmstrips with four cassettes and teacher guide. Titles include: "Health and Behavior," "Feelings and Behavior," "Experience and Behavior," "Controlling Your Behavior." (Learning Tree Filmstrips)

## Records and Cassettes

*Ideas, Thoughts, and Feelings*

Preschool to primary. Emphasis in album is on discovery, problem solving, and independent thinking. Activities can be done in small groups, or with partners. Some titles are: "Everybody Has Feelings," "I Like Me," "Making Friends," "I Don't Like Me," and "Things I'm Thankful For." (Lyons)

*Songs About My Feelings*

Preschool to primary. Children relate to their moods and feelings through participation songs and activities. Deals with human relations concepts such as how we feel about ourselves and others. Includes guide. (Lyons)

*Feelin' Free*

Preschool to primary. Record encourages young children to use their minds and bodies to express themselves, not only to move but to verbalize feelings. Teacher's guide contains activities, suggestions, and lyrics for each song. (Lyons)

*The Learning Party*

Primary. Musical album helps the young child understand growing, senses, family, and relating to others. Includes guide. (Constructive Playthings)

*Everybody Cries Sometimes*

Elementary. Album that helps create an atmosphere of understanding and respect for each other. Includes songs: "Everybody Says," "Lonely Blues," "Scary Things," and "Is There Room In the Boat?" (Educational Activities, Inc.)

*Relaxation—The Key To Life*
Elementary. Goldsmith, Rachelle C. and Barry Goldsmith. Recorded on Kimbo L.P. 9080. Manual. (Kimbo Educational Activities, 1973)

*Peace, Harmony, Awareness*
All ages. Audio program that teaches relaxation, self-confidence and control, and helps improve relationships. Can be used with individuals, groups, and children with special needs. Consists of a manual, six audio cassettes, and seven 8" × 10" color photographs. (Teaching Resources Corporation)

*Socialization Skills—Adaptive Behavior*
Handicapped children. Sixteen songs on record or cassette presenting concepts involving sharing, emotional awareness, social skills, manners, and listening. (Kimbo Educational)

*Peace, Harmony, Awareness*
All ages. Audio program that teaches relaxation, self-confidence and control, and helps improve relationships. Can be used with individuals, groups, and children with special needs. Consists of a manual, six audio cassettes, and seven 8" × 10" color photographs. (Teaching Resources Corporation)

# Films

*Values: Understanding Others*
Elementary. Film that discusses how people are different and encourages children to ask themselves, "How would I feel if I were he?" $8\frac{1}{4}$ minutes and color. (BFA Educational Media)

*Learning Values with Fat Albert*
Elementary. Set of 16 animated films with the live presence of Bill Cosby as host. Films address real-life problems typically experienced by young people and means for problem solving. Subject matter of these films includes: animal care/protection, misjudgment, individuality, drugs, doctors/hospitals, nutrition, honesty, alcoholism, smoking, new people/places, shoplifting, death/dying, deafness, and friendship. (McGraw-Hill)

*Feelings: Don't Stay Mad*
Elementary. Film about the universality of anger, necessity of expressing it, but in a way that doesn't hurt others. Film is in color, $14\frac{3}{4}$ minutes. (BFA Educational Media)

*Feelings: What Are You Afraid Of?*
Elementary. Film about fears: universality of fears, expressing fears, and getting help with fears. Film encourages viewers to talk about their own personal fears. $12\frac{1}{2}$ minutes, color. (BFA Educational Media)

*Getting Angry*
Elementary. Film about boy who takes his new birthday present to school and it is broken on the playground. A chain reaction of anger follows in which many children are involved. Encourages class discussion. 10 minutes, color. (BFA Educational Media)

*Values: Cooperation*
Elementary. Film that shows three friends helping each other and having fun in the process of cooperating. Color and 11 minutes. (BFA Educational Media)

*The New Kid*
Elementary. Film about making friends in a new neighborhood. Color, 11 minutes. (BFA Educational Media)

*Values: Playing Fair*
Elementary. Film shows examples of playing fair and not playing fair. Children are shown from preschool to junior high age learning to take turns and becoming part of a team. 10 minutes. (BFA Educational Media)

*Delicious Inventions from Willy Wonka and the Chocolate Factory*
Elementary. Five children tour Wonka's wonderful factory and receive a sweet lesson in manners. 15 minute full color film. (Films Incorporated)

*School Problems: Getting Along With Others*
Elementary. Film about five typical school problems that need decision making. At end of each sequence viewers are asked to discuss the problem and suggest possible solutions. Film is $10\frac{1}{2}$ minutes and in color. (BFA Educational Media)

*Positive Interactions for Success with Children*
Elementary. Series of five 17-minute color videotapes available in $\frac{3}{4}''$, VHS, or Beta. Designed to accompany written program *Getting Along with Others*. Includes step-by-step outline of major program components, including setting expectations for social behavior and using specific teaching strategies. (Social Effectiveness Training)

*Worry: I'm In Big Trouble Now*
Intermediate to Junior High. Billy, who is in charge of his little brother, loses him while exploring a barn with a friend. Provokes discussion on responsibility, guilt, fear, and worry. Color, 12 minutes, videocassette. (Guidance Associates)

*The Transformation of Mabel Wells*
Intermediate to Junior High-Secondary. A cranky old woman returns from the hospital to find get-well cards and gifts from many people. Provokes discussion of loneliness, helping, and friendship. Color, 12 minutes. Cine Golden Eagle Award. (Guidance Associates)

*Loneliness: The Empty Tree House*
Intermediate to Junior High. John's best friend moves. Another boy initiates a friendship but leaves when a group asks them to go sledding. John hesitates to go. 10 minutes. (Guidance Associates)

*Jealousy: I Won't Be Your Friend*
Intermediate to Junior High. Tony sees his best friend spending more and more time with a new boy. Provokes discussion on demands we make on friends and how we can prepare for changes in a relationship. 13 minutes. (Guidance Associates)

*Who Did What To Whom?*
Secondary. Film for improving human relations. Introduces principles of human interaction to almost any group. Principles covered are positive and negative reinforcement, punishment, and extinction. Film shows 40 short scenes that occur every day at home, in school, and around the office. Discussion time is provided after every scene. Film is $16\frac{1}{2}$ minutes in length. Sufficient for a full 2-hour session. Also includes a leader's guide. (Research Press)

## Pictorial Materials

*Social Development Picture Packet*
4- to 9-year-olds. Full color pictures stimulate social and language development. Each set includes 12 pictures, and teacher's resource sheet. (Constructive Playthings)

*Moods and Emotions*
K to 3. Sixteen dramatic photographs ($12\frac{1}{4}'' \times 17''$) and 40-page teacher's manual help children deal with emotions. (Lyons)

*Understanding Our Feelings*
Elementary. Twenty-eight picture photographs of children and adults expressing a wide variety of positive and negative feelings. Stimulates discussion of feelings. (Constructive Playthings)

*Nonverbal Communication*
Secondary. Transparencies, with the use of pictorial aids, show importance of nonverbal communication and awareness of unsuspected messages. Covers grooming, mannerisms, gestures, audio, tactile, and visual clues, and double messages. Includes 25 transparencies and teacher guide. (Lansford Publishing Co., Inc.)

## DRAMATIC PLAY MATERIALS

*The Magic of Puppetry*
Primary. Set of four puppets: a mother, a father, a boy, and a girl, with a 142-page manual providing instruction on staging puppet plays and making puppets. Designed to facilitate communication and social skills in young children. (American Guidance Service)

*Family Face Puppets*
Elementary. Set of six 12″ hardboard masks. Included are mother, father, sister, brother, grandmother, and grandfather. Children can role play their feelings with these props. (Constructive Playthings)

*People Puppets*
Elementary. Set of eight cotton puppets, includes father, mother, boy, girl, policeman, farmer, and fireman. (Constructive Playthings)

## GAMES/GAME CONSTRUCTION

*Creative Games for Learning: Games for*
*Parents and Teachers to Make*
Ages 3 to 8 years. 50 games to make that promote social, motoric, cognitive, and academic learning. Includes objective for each game, drawing of game, materials needed, steps for construction, and rules for playing. Spiralbound, 160 pp. (The Council for Exceptional Children)

*Human Relations Games*
Secondary. Includes transparencies and games dealing with the following concepts: self-awareness, self-esteem, semantics, nonverbal communication, decision making, problem solving, cooperation and competition, etc. Set

consists of: 21 transparencies, game manual, class worksheets, and supplements. (Lansford Publishing Co., Inc.)

*Roll-a-Role*

Ages 8 to adult. A communications game based on role playing. A pair of players roll the character cubes and have three minutes to act out a situation or subject. Set consists of plastic character cubes, a talk topic deck of cards, where-it-happens chart, and a timer. For large or small groups. (Opportunities for Learning, Inc.)

*Wipe-Off Game Boards*

Elementary. Set of four boards. Each is sturdy 14″ × 22″ plastic coated board and wipes clean. Use together with game pieces to create games for individualization and small group learning. (Constructive Playthings)

*Game Maker Set*

Elementary. Includes items for making your own games: wipe-off spinner, 40 cards and game field, 15 game pieces, 4 dice, crayons, and idea book. Packed in storage carton. Helpful for individualizing for special needs. (Constructive Playthings)

*Talking-Feeling-Doing Game*

Elementary. A board game primarily for use in counseling or therapy with children, which also has some potential for social skills training. (Creative Therapeutics)

*Animal Town Game Company*

All Ages. A resource of cooperative and noncompetitive board games. The games are intended to foster cooperation, social skills, and social well being. (Animal Town Game Co.)

*Stacking the Deck*

Mildly to Moderately Mentally Retarded Adolescents/Adults. A social skills game designed to teach skills related to general social skills, social/vocational skills and social/sexual skills. Game consists of a deck of 48 cards that contain social situations to which the players are to react. The format is a table game that involves successive turns and progressive movement around the game board. (Research Press)

*Socialization Games for Mentally Retarded Adolescents and Adults*

Handicapped adolescents and adults. Contents include a description of use of socialization games, organizational and environmental requirements, uses with groups, and specific games. (Charles C Thomas)

# Appendix B
# Listing of Publishers

Advanced Learning Concepts
211 W. Wisconsin Avenue
Milwaukee, Wisconsin 53203

American Guidance Service
Publisher's Building
Circle Pines, Minnesota 55014

Animal Town Game Co.
P.O. Box 2002
Santa Barbara, California 93120

Argus Communications
7440 Natchez Avenue
Niles, Illinois 60658

ATC Publishing Corp.
J.S. Latta, Inc.
P.O. Box 1276
Huntington, West Virginia 25715

BFA Educational Media
2211 Michigan Avenue
P.O. Box 1795
Santa Monica, California 90406

Constructive Playthings
1040 East 85th Street
Kansas City, Missouri 64131

The Council for Exceptional Children
1920 Association Drive
Reston, Virginia 22901

Creative Therapeutics
155 County Road
Cresskill, New Jersey 07626

DLM Teaching Resources
One DLM Park
Allen, Texas 75002

Developmental Learning Materials
7740 Natchez Avenue
Niles, Illinois 60658

EBSCO Curriculum Materials
Division EBSCO Industries, Inc.
Box 11521
Birmingham, Alabama 35202

Educational Activities, Inc.
P.O. Box 392
Freeport, New York 11520

Films Incorporated
733 Green Bay Road
Wilmette, Illinois 60091

Gamco Industries, Inc.
P.O. Box 1862 K
Big Spring, Texas 79720

Guidance Associates
Communications Park
Box 3000
Mount Kisco, New York 10549

Human Development Training
Institute
4455 Twain Avenue, Suite H
San Diego, California 92120

Human Science Press
72 Fifth Avenue
New York, New York 10011

Institute for Rational Living
45 East 65th Street
New York, New York 10021

J. Weston Walch, Publisher
Portland, Maine 04104

Kimbo Educational Activities
P.O. Box 477
Long Branch, New Jersey 07740

Kino Publications
P.O. Box 43584
Tucson, Arizona 85733

Lansford Publishing Company
P.O. Box 8711
San Jose, California 95155

Learning Tree Filmstrips
P.O. Box 4116
Englewood, Colorado 80155

Love Publishing Company
1777 South Bellaire St.
Denver, Colorado 80222

Lyons
5030 Riverview Avenue
Elkhart, Indiana 46514

McGraw-Hill
Cedar Hollow & Matthews Hill Rd.
Paoli, Pennsylvania 19301

Nasco Learning Fun
901 Janesville Avenue
Fort Atkinson, Wisconsin 53538

Opportunities for Learning, Inc.
8950 Lurline Avenue
Department 9AB
Chatsworth, California 91311

Pro-Ed
5341 Industrial Oaks Blvd.
Austin, Texas 78735

Prentice-Hall
Englewood Cliffs, New Jersey 07632

Research Press
Box 31773
Champaign, Illlinois 61821

Scholastic Instructional Materials
904 Sylvan Avenue
Englewood Cliffs, New Jersey 07632

Scott Foresman and Company
1900 East Lake Avenue
Glenview, Illinois 60025

Social Effectiveness Training
P.O. Box 6664
Reno, Nevada 89513-6664

Society for Visual Education
1345 Diversey Parkway
Chicago, Illinois 60614

Teaching Resources Corp.
100 Boylston Street
Boston, Massachusetts 02116

Troll Associates
320 Route 17
Mahwah, New Jersey 07430

Walker Educational Book Corp.
720 Fifth Avenue
New York, New York 10019

Word Books
Word Incorporated
P.O. Box 1790
Waco, Texas 76703

# Appendix C
# Social Skills List*

## ENVIRONMENTAL BEHAVIORS (EB)

Care for the Environment (CE)
    To dispose of trash in the proper container.
    To drink properly from water fountain.
    To clean up after breaking or spilling something.
    To use classroom equipment and materials correctly.
    To use playground equipment safely.
Dealing with Emergency (DE)
    To follow rules for emergencies.
    To identify accident or emergency situations that should be reported to the teacher.
    To report accident or other emergency to the teacher.
Lunchroom Behavior (LR)
    To use eating utensils properly.
    To handle and eat only one's own food.
    To dispose of unwanted food properly.
Movement Around Environment (MO)
    To walk through the hall quietly at a reasonable pace.
    To enter classroom and take seat without disturbing objects and other people.
    To form and walk in a line.
    To follow safety rules in crossing streets.

## INTERPERSONAL BEHAVIORS (IP)

Accepting Authority (AA)
    To comply with request of adult in position of authority.
    To comply with request of peer in position of authority.

---

*Taken from: Stephens, T. M. (1978) *Social skills in the classroom*. Columbus, OH: Cedars Press.

To know and follow classroom rules.

To follow classroom rules in the absence of the teacher.

To question rules that may be unjust.

Coping with Conflict (CC)

To respond to teasing or name-calling by ignoring, changing the subject, or using some other constructive means.

To respond to physical assault by leaving the situation, calling for help, or using some other constructive means.

To walk away from peer when angry to avoid hitting.

To refuse the request of another politely.

To express anger with nonaggressive words rather than physical action or aggressive words.

To handle constructively criticism or punishment perceived as undeserved.

Gaining Attention (GA)

To gain teacher's attention in class by raising hand.

To wait quietly for recognition before speaking out in class.

To use please and thank-you when making requests of others.

To approach teacher and ask appropriately for help, explanation, instructions, etc.

To gain attention from peers in appropriate ways.

To ask a peer for help.

Greeting Others (GR)

To look others in the eye when greeting them

To state one's name when asked.

To smile when encountering a friend or acquaintance.

To greet adults and peers by name.

To respond to an introduction by shaking hands and saying how-do-you-do.

To introduce oneself to another person.

To introduce two people to each other.

Helping Others (HP)

To help teacher when asked.

To help peer when asked.

To give simple directions to a peer.

To offer help to teacher.

To offer help to a classmate.

To come to defense of peer in trouble.

To express sympathy to peer about problems or difficulties.

Making Conversation (MC)

To pay attention in a conversation to the person speaking.

To talk to others in a tone of voice appropriate to the situation.

To wait for pauses in a conversation before speaking.

To make relevant remarks in a conversation with peers.

To make relevant remarks in a conversation with adults.

To ignore interruptions of others in a conversation.

To initiate conversation with peers in an informal situation.

Organized Play (OP)

To follow rules when playing a game.

To wait for one's turn when playing a game.

To display effort to the best of one's ability in a competitive game.

To accept defeat and congratulate the winner in a competitive game.

Positive Attitude toward Others (PA)

To make positive statements about qualities and accomplishments of others.

To compliment another person.

To display tolerance for persons with characteristics different from one's own.

Playing Informally (PL)

To ask another student to play on the playground.

To ask to be included in a playground activity in progress.

To share toys and equipment in a play situation.

To give in to reasonable wishes of the group in a play situation.

To suggest an activity for the group on the playground.

Property: Own and Others' (PR)

To distinguish one's own property from the property of others.

To lend possessions to others when asked.

To use and return others' property without damaging it.

To ask permission to use another's property.

## SELF-RELATED BEHAVIORS (SR)

Accepting Consequences (AC)

To report to the teacher when one has spilled or broken something.

To make apology when actions have injured or infringed on another.

To accept deserved consequences of wrongdoing.

Ethical Behavior (EB)

To distinguish truth from untruth.

To answer truthfully when asked about possible wrongdoing.

To identify consequences of behavior involving wrongdoing.

To avoid doing something wrong when encouraged by a peer.

Expressing Feelings (EF)

To describe one's own feelings or moods verbally.

To recognize and label moods of others.

Positive Attitude toward Self (PA)

To say thank you when complimented or praised.

To be willing to have one's work displayed.

To make positive statements when asked about oneself.

To undertake a new task with a positive attitude.

Responsible Behavior (RB)

To be regular in school attendance.

To arrive at school on time.

To hang up one's clothes in required place.

To keep one's desk in order.

To take care of one's own possessions.

To carry messages for the teacher.

To bring required materials to school.

Self-Care (SC)

To use toilet facilities properly.

To put on clothing without assistance.

To keep face and hands clean.

## TASK-RELATED BEHAVIOR (TR)

Asking and Answering Questions (AQ)

To answer or attempt to answer a question when called on by teacher.

To acknowledge when one does not know the answer to a question.

To volunteer an answer to teacher's question.

To ask a question appropriate to the information needed.

Attending Behavior (AT)

To look at the teacher when a lesson is being presented.

To watch an audio-visual presentation quietly.

To listen to someone speaking to the class.

Classroom Discussion (CD)

To use tone of voice in classroom discussion appropriate to the situation.

To make relevant remarks in a classroom discussion.

To participate in a classroom discussion initiated by teacher.

To bring things to class that are relevant to classroom discussion.

To express opinion in classroom discussion even when contrary to opinions of others.

To provide reasons for opinions expressed in group discussion.

Completing Tasks (CT)

To complete assigned academic work.

To complete assigned academic work within the required time.

To continue working on a difficult task until it is completed.

To complete and return homework assignments.

Following Directions (FD)

To follow teacher's verbal directions.

To follow written directions.

To follow directions in taking a test.

Group Activities (GA)

To share materials with others in a work situation.

To work cooperatively on a task with a partner.

To carry out plans or decisions formulated by the group.

To accept ideas presented in a group task situation that are different from one's own.

To initiate and help carry out a group activity.

Independent Work (IW)

To attempt to solve a problem with school work before asking for help.

To find productive use of time while waiting for teacher assistance.

To find acceptable ways of using free time when work is completed.

On-Task Behavior (OT)

To sit straight at desk when required by teacher.

To do a seat-work assignment quietly.

To work steadily for the required length of time.

To ignore distractions from peers when doing a seatwork assignment.

To discuss academic material with peers when appropriate.

To change from one activity to another when required by the teacher.

Performing before Others (PF)

To participate in a role playing activity.

To read aloud in a small group.

To read aloud before a large group of the entire class.

To make a report before a small group.

To make a report before a large group or the entire class.

Quality of Work (QW)

To turn in neat papers.

To accept correction of school work.

To make use of teacher's corrections to improve work.

To go back over work to check for errors.

# Author Index

# Subject Index

373

# About the Editors and Contributors

**Gwendolyn Cartledge** (PhD, The Ohio State University) is an associate professor at Cleveland State University in the College of Education, where her primary responsibility is training teachers to work with children with special needs. She has been a classroom teacher and supervisor of programs for learning disabled and emotionally disturbed children. Professional interests center on developing academic and social skills in handicapped learners.

**JoAnne F. Milburn** (MSW, U.C.L.A.; PhD, The Ohio State University) is director of the Starr Commonwealth/Hannah Neil Center for Children in Columbus, Ohio, a multiservice children's mental health program. She has worked with children in several settings, has served on the faculty of the College of Social Work, and holds an adjunct appointment on the Faculty for Human Services Education at the Ohio State University.

*     *     *     *     *

**Mary Ann S. Bash** (MA, University of Northern Colorado) is an Instructional Consultant for elementary Chapter I reading/writing instruction in Denver Public Schools. She was a classroom teacher and reading resource teacher before writing the Think Aloud curriculum under Title IV-C funding for innovative educational programs. She has been training teachers and parents to use the Think Aloud problem-solving approach since 1975. Most recently she has focused on teaching reading and writing as problem-solving activities.

**Bonnie W. Camp** (PhD, MD, FAAP, is a Professor of Pediatrics and Psychiatry at the University of Colorado Medical School. She received her BA from Mississippi State College for Women, her PhD from Indiana University, and her MD from the University of Colorado School of Medicine. She also completed specialty training in pediatrics at the University of Colorado Medical Center. The work described in this volume was done during the time she was a recipient of a Research Career Development Award from the National Institute of Mental Health.

**N. Jane Gershaw** (PhD, Syracuse University) is Chief of the Syracuse VA Mental Hygiene Clinic and holds academic rank as Adjunct Assistant Professor of Psychology at Syracuse University and Clinical Assistant Professor of Psychology at the SUNY Upstate Medical Center. She has been involved in research and clinical application of behavioral techniques in group psychotherapy.

**Arnold P. Goldstein** (PhD, Pennsylvania State University) is Professor of Special Education at Syracuse University. His major research interest is the teaching of prosocial behavior to antisocial, aggressive populations.

**Paul Klein** (MS, State University of New York at Cortland) is a consulting teacher on special assignment with the Syracuse School District for programs for severely emotionally disturbed children in resource classrooms. He has directed alternative school programs for adolescents and preadolescents for the Syracuse School District, and has served as a consultant in behavior management techniques for other school districts within the central New York area.

**Sherri Oden** (PhD, University of Illinois) is Research Associate in the Department of Health Behavior and Health Education at the School of Public Health, University of Michigan, Ann Arbor, where she currently directs a research project on the self-management of health behaviors in older adults. Her primary research interests include children's social skills, peer-relationship development, and interventions for children's mental health.

**Mara Sapon-Shevin** (EdD, University of Rochester) is Associate Professor of Elementary Education and Special Education in the Center for Teaching and Learning at the University of North Dakota. Her major research interests are in the areas of mainstreaming, social skills development, cooperative learning activities, and the ethical and political implications of special education.

**Stuart J. Schleien** (PhD, University of Maryland) is Assistant Professor of Therapeutic Recreation and Special Education at the University of Minnesota-Minneapolis. His major research interests are in the areas of leisure skills development and the integration of persons with severe handicaps into recreation programs.

**Robert P. Sprafkin** (PhD, Ohio State University) is Chief of the Syracuse VA Day Treatment Center, as well as Adjunct Associate Professor of Psychology at Syracuse University and Clinical Associate Professor of Psychology at the SUNY Upstate Medical Center. He has been involved in the development of psychoeducational training programs for diverse groups.

**Paul Wehman** (PhD, University of Wisconsin–Madison) is Professor of Special Education at Virginia Commonwealth University in Richmond, Virginia. His current research interests are employment of persons with severe disabilities.

# Pergamon General Psychology Series

Editors: Arnold P. Goldstein, Syracuse University
Leonard Krasner, SUNY at Stony Brook